EMDR
CASEBOOK

Advance Praise for *EMDR Casebook*

"This is a well written, highly interesting text that shows how EMDR can be utilized and integrated within a variety of therapeutic frameworks. Experienced cllincians provide excellent case presentations that detail their thinking, strategies, and choice points and thereby highlight how EMDR can be utilized in complex cases. *EMDR Casebook* will be very helpful for both the novice and experienced EMDR clinician."

—Roger M. Solomon, Ph.D., Senior Faculty, EMDR Institute
and Director, Critical Incident Recovery Resources

"This book is a *must have* for every EMDR clinician. The rich, detailed case studies convey the many ways that EMDR can be integrated into clinical practice, illustrating skillfully how practitioners from diverse theoretical orientations apply EMDR to help a wide range of clients. This second edition has all the strengths of the first, and has several new cases that expand the types of clinical problems addressed. This book will be invaluable in helping clinicians broaden their understanding about how to use EMDR effectively in real world practice settings. In particular, it demonstrates how EMDR is utilized within a comprehensive approach to treatment and adapted to meet the needs of complex clients. In addition, readers are exposed to diverse approaches to cognitive interweaves and unblocking."

—Nancy J. Smyth, Ph.D., CSW, CASAC,
University at Buffalo School of Social Work

A Norton Professional Book

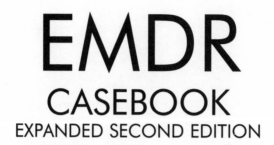

EMDR
CASEBOOK
EXPANDED SECOND EDITION

EDITED BY

PHILIP MANFIELD, PH.D.

W. W. Norton & Company
New York • London

Production Manager: Leeann Graham
Manufacturing by Haddon Craftsmen, Inc.

Library of Congress Cataloging-in-Publication Data

EMDR casebook / edited by Philip Manfield.—Expanded, 2nd ed.
    p.   cm.
First ed. published under the title: Extending EMDR
Includes bibliographical references and index.
"A Norton professional book."
ISBN 0-393-70416-5 (pbk.)
1. Eye movement densensitization and reprocessing—Case studies.   I. Manfield, Philip.
II. Extending EMDR.

RC489.E98E98 2003
616.89'14—dc21   2003046454

W. W. Norton & Company, Inc., 500 Fifth Avenue, New York, N.Y. 10110
www.wwnorton. com

W. W. Norton & Company Ltd., Castle House, 75/76 Wells St., London W1T 3QT

1 3 5 7 9 0 8 6 4 2

CONTENTS

FOREWORD

EVERY IMPORTANT INNOVATION in psychotherapy has built upon or benefited from its predecessors, and EMDR is no exception. However, because EMDR (or EMD, as it was initially called) was inaugurated in 1987 by the accidental discovery of the effects of eye movements on cognitive and emotional process (see also Antrobus, Antrobus, & Singer, 1964; Kuiken, Bears, Miall, & Smith, 2001–2002; MacCulloch & Feldman, 1996; van den Hout, Muris, Salemink, & Kindt, 2001), many people mistakenly believe EMDR to represent a very narrow methodology, isolated from more traditional psychotherapeutic procedures and guiding principles. On the contrary, in the decade following its inception, EMDR has evolved into a methodology that incorporates aspects of many of the major, accepted psychotherapeutic orientations so as to form a focused approach for the treatment of a wide range of pathologies. For that reason, luminaries of diverse orientations have explicitly described how EMDR dovetails with, complements, and extends the outcomes of their chosen paradigm and practices (Shapiro, 2002).

EMDR has been evaluated as an effective treatment for posttraumatic stress disorder in the practice guidelines of a variety of organizations (e.g., Belich, Kotler, Kutx, & Shaley, 2002; Chemtob, Tolin, van der Kolk, & Pitman, 2002). Preliminary research also has indicated its potential in other clinical applications. One of the many strengths of Philip Manfield's excellent edited collection is that it provides a multifaceted look at EMDR clinical practice. *EMDR Casebook* takes the reader far beyond the applications of EMDR to simple posttraumatic stress disorder and, by means of vivid case descriptions, explores the implications of the information processing model by which EMDR practice is guided. Manfield and his colleagues also show how the use of its procedures dovetails with and is enhanced by the knowledge and skill of the experienced clinician, regardless of his or her theoretical background and specialization. *EMDR Casebook* will not only serve as a fascinating introduction for therapists of various orientations, but will also provide a valuable roadmap for experienced EMDR clinicians.

The Adaptive Information Processing model (AIP) (see Shapiro, 2001, 2002; Shapiro & Forrest, 1997) was advanced as a possible explanation of EMDR treatment effects and subsequently led to the incorporation of a number of its primary tenets into standard EMDR clinical practice. A number of these tenets are particularly relevant to this volume. Of particular importance is the claim that dysfunctional behaviors and nonadaptive characteristics are the result of earlier experiences which have been stored in the brain as state-dependent memories. That is, what the client originally saw, heard, felt, and so on is stored fundamentally in the way that they were originally experienced. These memories form the basis of the client's current self-esteem, self-concept, self-efficacy, and relationship dynamics. Within the framework of AIP, it was posited that, with appropriate targeting and processing, even personality disorders could be modified. A second important tenet of the AIP model is that clinicians could facilitate profound therapeutic change in less time than had been traditionally assumed to be necessary. Moreover, it was found that rapid change could be achieved regardless of the amount of time that had elapsed since the debilitating event.

The clinicians contributing to this volume beautifully illustrate both of these tenets of AIP in their detailed and thought-provoking case studies. Whether the total EMDR treatment time is as brief as three sessions, or as long as three years, the clinician's judicious applications are consistently guided by client feedback and indicators of change. The clinical observations and case evaluations found in the pages of the *EMDR Casebook* point the way for systematic and controlled research in the future.

The use of EMDR for information processing—splendidly represented in the volume—should be conceptualized as a *catalyst* for learning. It is almost universally assumed by psychotherapists (regardless of orientation) that all nonorganic psychological dysfunctions are based in large part on earlier life experiences. With proper EMDR treatment, not only do emotional disturbances and other affective and somatic symptoms decline but the *meaning* of the earlier life experiences change for the client. Further, by means of carefully orchestrated therapeutic instruction, the client spontaneously acquires new self-concepts and patterns of behaviors. For that reason a three-pronged protocol is typically used in EMDR practice: (1) reprocessing the past experiences that laid the groundwork for the dysfunctions, (2) processing the present situations that cause disturbance, and (3) incorporating skills and behaviors necessary for future action. In the course of EMDR treatment, the client's negative images, beliefs, and affects become more diffuse and less valid, while positive images, beliefs, and affects become enhanced and more subjectively valid. Throughout this volume we see this protocol translated into actual clinical practice as clients are liberated from the bonds of the past and come alive into a new world of possibility.

In the first chapter, Dr. Manfield does an excellent job of preparing the reader for what is to come by defining the terms and parameters of EMDR treatment in the context of a straightforward clinical case. He has also done an extraordinary job in bringing together clinicians from different orientations—e.g., psychodynamic, behavioral, cognitive—in order to explore various complex applications of EMDR. The subsequent chapters illustrate the importance of stabilization and procedural fidelity when working with a fragmented client with attachment difficulties. Readers will also be shown the use of implementing the EMDR standard protocols so as to help identify targets, stimulate the information processing system, and incorporate necessary resources that permit both present processing and future optimal adaptation for a wide range of psychological disturbances and diagnoses.

Particularly admirable is the detailed manner in which some of the authors describe their rationale for incorporating diverse theoretical orientations into their treatment planning and direct EMDR interventions. It is through such perceptive and intelligent innovation that the client is best served *and* the EMDR methodology undergoes responsible evolution. In fact, the case described in Chapter 14, "Lifting the Burden of Shame," first published in 1998, became the springboard for subsequent clinical investigations that led to the development of more substantial means to affect stabilization for complex clients. These clinical developments have subsequently become part of standard EMDR practice (see Korn & Leeds, 2002; Shapiro, 2001, 2002). It is hoped that all the clinical applications in this volume will be further investigated. It is only through the judicious combination of practice and scientific investigation that we can define the best clinical practices.

Whether we choose to view the client's presenting complaint through the eyes of a psychodynamic, behavioral, cognitive, or systems therapist, or if we consider the complaint in terms of a personality or other disorder as defined by the *Diagnostic and Statistical Manual*, what we find in each chapter is a debilitated client who is able to change as the result of focused and sensitive therapeutic treatment. The clear descriptions of the client's healing process found in this book can be interpreted in the vocabulary of any of the major orientations, just as the characteristics of successful treatment effects are evident to the eyes of any practicing clinician. The authors of the chapters are to be congratulated for painstakingly showing not only the success of various interventions, but also the failures of other interventions. This makes for a volume that is instructive as we seek to define the very process and parameters of change.

EMDR has long been defined (Shapiro, 1994, 2001, 2002) as an integrative, client-centered approach, in which clinicians are encouraged to synthesize and incorporate into their treatments the relevant aspects of any or all of the well-known therapeutic modalities. Although from the client's perspective the goal of treatment is often merely the relief from debilitating symptoms, for the practicing clinician who is well-versed in EMDR the ultimate aim is generally to enhance the client's ability to love both self and others. Thus, the goal of treatment should not be merely to banish each client's overt suffering, but to help engender a new joy in living.

At the fifteen-year mark since its inception EMDR is still evolving. EMDR practitioners are striving to refine its ability to catalyze the internal healing process resident in all of us to positively impact symptomology observed throughout the clinical spectrum. This volume opens the door and allows us to view the practices of a diverse group of seasoned EMDR clinicians. *EMDR Casebook* allows readers to consider the implications of an integrated, focused therapeutic approach to the treatment of a wide range of often resistant pathologies. It also extends an open invitation to readers to further expand the EMDR knowledge-base in terms of both innovative theoretical and practical applications.

Francine Shapiro, Ph.D.

References

Antrobus, J. S., Antrobus, J. S., & Singer, J. L. (1964). Eye movements accompanying daydreaming, visual imagery, and though suppression. *Journal of Abnormal and Social Psychology, 69*, 244–252.

Belich, A., Kotler, M., Kutx, E., & Shaley, A. (2002). *A position paper of the [Israeli] National Council for Mental Health: Guidelines for the assessment and professional intervention with terror victims in the hospital and in the community.*

Chemtob, C. M., Tolin, D. F., van der Kolk, B. A., & Pitman, R. K. (2000). Eye movement desensitization and reprocessing. In E. B. Foa, T. M. Keane, & M. J. Friedman (Eds.), *Effective treatments for PTSD: Practice guidelines from the International Society for Traumatic Stress Studies* (pp. 139–155, 333–335). New York: Guilford Press.

Korn, D. L. & Leeds, A. (2002). Preliminary evidence of efficacy for EMDR resource development and installation in the stabilization phase of treatment of complex posttraumatic stress disorder. *Journal of Clinical Psychology, 58*, 1465–1487.

Kuiken, D., Bears, M., Miall, D., & Smith, L. (2001–2002). Eye movement desensitization reprocessing facilitates attentional orienting. *Imagination, Cognition, and Personality, 21*(1), 3–20.

MacCulloch, M. J. & Feldman, M. P. (1996). Eye movement desensitization treatment utilizes the positive visceral elements of the investigatory reflex to inhibit the memories of post traumatic stress disorder: A theoretical analysis. *British Journal of Psychiatry, 169,* 571–579.

Shapiro, F. (1994). EMDR: In the eye of a paradigm shift. *Behavior Therapist, 17,* 153–158.

Shapiro, F. (2001). *Eye movement desensitization and reprocessing: Basic principles, protocols, and procedures (2nd edition).* New York: Guilford Press.

Shapiro, F. & Forrest, M. S. (1997) *EMDR.* New York: Basic Books.

Shapiro, F. (2002). *EMDR as an integrative psychotherapy approach: Experts of diverse orientations explore the paradigm prism.* Washington, D.C.: American Psychological Association Press.

van den Hout, M., Muris, P., Salemink, E., & Kindt, M. (2001). Autobiographical memories become less vivid and emotional after eye movements. *British Journal of Clinical Psychology, 40,* 121–130.

ACKNOWLEDGMENTS

I'D LIKE TO THANK Steve Johnson for his good counsel when I was formulating the format for this book and for accurately warning me that it would be a much bigger project than I expected.

I'd like to thank David Manfield, Mindy Frank, Duncan Bennett, Joan Lovett, Andrew Leeds, and all others who generously read sections of the book and offered suggestions for improvement. I'd also like to thank Anne Fox for her editorial help and Uri Bergmann for his help with the neurobiology section of the introduction. My thanks especially to Karin Kleiner and Isabelle Pronovost, who carefully reviewed the new chapters for *EMDR Casebook* and made invaluable suggestions.

I am indebted to all of the contributors for the creativity they put into their writing and for their cheerful acceptance of the many revisions I asked of them. Special thanks to Jim Knipe and Liz Snyker both of whom came through under time pressure, as well as to my brother, David, who has supported me and consulted with me about this project from the beginning.

My thanks to my publisher, Norton Professional Books, and in particular to Susan Barrows Munro, the former director. From the outset, Ms. Munro recognized the value of this project, has given it her full support, and was a pleasure to work with. Thanks also to Margaret Ryan, the copyeditor for this book, for her outstanding work. Not only was she able to greatly improve the readability of the book, but, with her impressive knowledge of psychology, she was able to identify sections in which the content was lacking and, in some cases, inaccurate. More recently, my thanks to Deborah Malmud, the current director of Norton Professional Books, for conceiving of *EMDR Casebook* as an update to *Extending EMDR* and for patiently supporting this project through its completion and to Michael McGandy, who not only copyedited the additions to the book, but who reviewed and improved the entire edition.

xiv   EMDR Casebook

I am grateful to my secretary, Margaret Kilday, for her thoughtfulness, her thoroughness, and her continuing support for more than a decade. Meg has played a key role in almost every stage of this project, including translating my idiosyncratic shorthand into readable text.

My deep appreciation is extended to my wife, Janet. An EMDR-trained therapist herself, Janet has provided both professional and personal support throughout this project. She has read every chapter as it was submitted and offered invaluable feedback and suggestions. Of perhaps greater importance, Janet and my son, Mark, have been sources of great emotional support and satisfaction; together they have helped me to keep a proper perspective so this project and my other work did not eclipse other important aspects of life.

I'd like to thank Francine Shapiro not only for the fine foreword that she wrote, but for her support of this entire project from beginning to end. Her suggestions for structuring the book at the outset were extremely helpful and her continued involvement, including reading every chapter and making suggestions for clarity and accuracy, added substantially to the overall quality of the final product. Finally, I would like to express my particular appreciation to Dr. Shapiro of her extraordinary openness in sharing EMDR as well as for encouraging other clinicians to experiment with EMDR and contribute their creativity.

CONTRIBUTORS

Gina Colelli, C.S.W., an EMDRIA Approved Consultant and EMDR-HAP (Humanitarian Assistance Program) Facilitator, is the recent New York City Coordinator of the Disaster Mental Health Recovery Network, a program of EMDR-HAP. Gina specializes in EMDR consultation, affect disorders, and adults abused as children. She presents in-depth refresher and advanced clinical workshops in EMDR. She has a private practice in Manhattan, New York.

Lewis Engel, Ph.D., has been a psychologist for over twenty-five years in private practice in San Francisco. He is a senior member of the San Francisco Psychotherapy Research Group. He is the author (with Tom Ferguson, M.D.) of *Imaginary Crimes* (Houghton Mifflin, 1990), currently published by Pocket Books as *Hidden Guilt* (1991). Since completing his training in EMDR in 2000 Lewis has been very interested in integrating EMDR into some of his analytical work and has given a grand rounds presentation on this subject.

David Grand, L.C.S.W., is a facilitator and practitioner of EMDR. He wrote an article on resistance that was published in 1993 and regularly presents at the International EMDR Conference. David is a past president of the Nassau County Chapter of the New York State Society for Clinical Social Work, is currently chairperson of the Humanitarian Assistance Program (HAP) of the EMDR International Association, and is the coordinator of the Northern Ireland EMDR training being sponsored by HAP.

Jim Knipe, Ph.D., has been a psychologist in Colorado Springs since 1980. During that time, he helped establish a crisis center as well as an outpatient program of treatment services for chronically mentally ill individuals. He has specialized in providing therapy to adults with developmental disabilities. Jim has also served as President of the El Paso County Psychological Society. Following Level I and Level II trainings in 1992, he became an EMDR Facilitator in 1994. During the past three years, he has provided EMDR group consultation/supervision to other therapists and has been a research therapist in EMDR outcome studies by Wilson, Becker, and Tinker (1995) and Scheck, Gillette, and Shaffer (in press). Jim has given presentations on EMDR to mental health professionals in Colorado Springs and in Istanbul, Turkey. He has a special interest in the application of EMDR to relationship dysfunction and to personality disorders.

Andrew M. Leeds, Ph.D., became an authorized EMDR senior trainer in 1995 and has since served as a facilitator at over 60 EMDR Level I and Level II trainings, has taught a specialty presentation on "Case Formulation: Strategies and Criteria for Selection of Negative and Positive Cognitions" at some 20 Level II EMDR trainings, and has been an invited presenter at three of the four annual EMDR International Conferences (1995, 1994, 1993). Andrew is chair of the EMDR Professional Support Committee and is the moderator and co-listowner for the EMDR Institute Discussion List, an on-going electronic forum on the Internet in which EMDR trained clinicians participate from around the world.

Joan Lovett, M.D., is a behavioral pediatrician who practices in the San Francisco East Bay area and works with adults as well as children. Joan has been a facilitator for EMDR for three years and has presented at the past two annual International EMDR Conferences.

David Manfield, Ph.D., is a psychologist practicing in Portland, Oregon. He was trained in EMDR in 1991, is a facilitator of EMDR, and consults and supervises other clinicians in using EMDR with challenging cases. David delivered a paper on EMDR at the 2002 Annual Conference of the Oregon Psychological Association.

Philip Manfield, Ph.D., has been in private practice as a psychotherapist in the San Francisco East Bay area for over twenty years. He was first trained in EMDR in 1991 and has been an EMDR facilitator since 1992. Philip has trained clinicians in EMDR in the United States, Canada, Europe, and the Middle East. He has taught at JFK Graduate School of Professional Psychology (Orinda, CA) and University of California, Extension (Berkeley, CA). Philip has also written and contributed to numerous books including: *Split Self/Split Object, Understanding and Treating Borderline Narcissistic and Schizoid Disorders* (Jason Aronson, 1992; a second edition with new sections about using EMDR with personality disorders is forthcoming from I-Universe), and "The Application of EMDR to Personality

Disorders" in *Handbook of Personality Disorders* (Wiley & Sons, 2003; the chapter is coauthored with Dr. Francine Shapiro, the creator and developer of EMDR).

Laurel Parnell, Ph.D., is a clinical psychologist with sixteen years experience specializing in the treatment of trauma-related problems. She has worked as a facilitator for the EMDR Institute. Laurel was one of the first to adapt EMDR training to a graduate school setting by teaching EMDR at the California Institute of Integral Studies in the psychology doctoral program; she subsequently shared her curriculum and teaching recommendations with other clinicians at the 1996 International EMDR Conference. Laurel has presented papers on EMDR and the treatment of sexual abuse survivors at both the 1994 American Psychological Association Meeting and the 1995 International EMDR Conference. At the 1996 International EMDR Conference she presented on the use of imagery with EMDR. She is a guest presenter at the EMDR Institute's Level II trainings on using EMDR with sexual abuse survivors and also conducts intensive one-day seminars on this subject sponsored by the EMDR Institute. She is the author of the popular book, *Transforming Trauma: EMDR the Revolutionary New Therapy for Freeing the Mind, Clearing the Body, and Opening the Heart* (W.W. Norton, 1997).

Elizabeth Snyker, L.C.S.W., has been a psychotherapist since 1980. For eight years she trained with Dr. Habib Davenloo in Intensive Short-Term Dynamic Psychotherapy. Elizabeth has written several papers that have been published in the *International Journal of Intensive Sort-Term Dynamic Psychotherapy*. She was trained in EMDR in 1991 and has facilitated at EMDR trainings, both domestically and internationally, since 1992. In addition to ongoing EMDR consultation, Elizabeth has made numerous presentations about EMDR.

Silke Vogelmann-Sine, Ph.D., is a practitioner and facilitator of EMDR. She has presented widely including at each of the International EMDR Conferences during the period of 1998–2002 and has written numerous journal articles about EMDR including one coauthored with Dr. Francine Shapiro in the *Journal of Psychoactive Drugs* in 1994.

EMDR
CASEBOOK

INTRODUCTION

MY FIRST INFORMATION about eye movement desensitization and re-processing (EMDR) came in 1990 when I read Francine Shapiro's ground-breaking study (1989) in which she reported impressive results using a new method that involved eye movements to treat a group of people who had experienced severe single-incident traumas. Since Shapiro's first published paper (1989), EMDR has had an ever-increasing impact on the practice of psychotherapy. Over 25,000 clinicians are now trained in EMDR. According to the EMDR Institute, the number of therapists being trained through the Institute has grown each year, with 4,000 trained last year in the United States alone. Trainings are now being conducted worldwide, including Europe, Asia, the Middle East, and South and Central America.

During the first few years after I was trained in EMDR, many of my colleagues remained skeptical. Often, when I would talk to them about the excellent results I was achieving using EMDR, they would respond, "Where's the research?" The views that the claims of efficacy for EMDR were not supported by research were reinforced when the widely read *Harvard Mental Health News Letter* published an article (Herbert, 1995) in late 1995 about EMDR that ignored much of the published research and all of the powerful research in press at that time. The following month the highly respected *Journal of Consulting and Clinical Psychology* published the now well-known Wilson, Becker, and Tinker study (1995) of EMDR in which 80 victims of trauma were given three sessions each of EMDR in a carefully designed controlled study with astounding results; this study finally put most of the skeptics' objections to rest. Two years later, the *Journal of Consulting and Clinical Psychology* published the 15-month follow-up to the Wilson study (Wilson, Becker, & Tinker, 1997), establishing that 84% of the subjects from the original study still, after 15 months, no longer met the criteria for PTSD.

3

With the publication of over a dozen controlled studies capped by the Wilson follow-up study, it is clear that EMDR is a powerful tool for treatment of the residual psychological effects of acute single-incident trauma. This "strange" treatment, involving alternate stimulation of the right and left hemispheres of the brain through visual, auditory, or kinesthetic cues, produces a rapid salutary effect. Perhaps now it is time to ask in what other areas EMDR can be helpful? In particular, how effective is EMDR in cases involving ongoing childhood trauma? In discussions among EMDR practitioners and at EMDR conferences many clinicians have reported excellent results using EMDR with a wide range of clients.

This book contains fourteen case reports intended to accomplish the following:

- Encourage the use of EMDR for a broader range of cases

Since EMDR was first introduced in 1989, it has been continuously refined. Shapiro has encouraged other clinicians to experiment with the method, and to contribute new ideas and protocols, which she has often incorporated into the EMDR trainings. This book is part of that process. While in most cases it is still too early to publish protocols for new applications of EMDR, we believe that clinical examples of the successful use of EMDR with difficult cases will help EMDR-trained practitioners identify additional situations in which EMDR might be effective by providing models for approaching these relatively complex cases. James Knipe points out in his chapter that there are *anecdotes* and there is *evidence*, but there is no such thing as *anecdotal evidence*. In this book we do not intend to propose protocols or prove the effectiveness of EMDR for particular types of cases. Instead, we present individual cases in which EMDR has been used effectively in bringing about a complete adaptive resolution of a condition or in helping a client make progress.

- Provide dramatic illustrations of the power of EMDR in treating trauma

With the publication of *EMDR Casebook*, I have added three new chapters to those included in the original *Extending EMDR*. Unlike most of the other cases in the book, these cases are all trauma focused, and illustrate the power of EMDR when other approaches were ineffective. One of these cases resulted from the World Trade Center disaster of September 11, 2001. In the aftermath of that disaster, many of the rescue workers needed help in accepting their losses and processing extremely distressful experiences. Most were disappointed with the effectiveness of initial treatment they received. Gina

Colelli coordinated a volunteer effort by EMDR therapists to help the victims of this disaster. In her chapter she writes about one of the fire fighters
she treated. I have contributed a chapter describing a four-hour treatment
of an almost life-long snake phobia that had been unsuccessfully treated
using graduated exposure, as well as another chapter considering the rapid
treatment of a veteran who had suffered for thirty years from the aftermath
of his experience fighting in Vietnam.

  • Help newly trained EMDR clinicians make the transition to clinical
    practice

The practicum experience in the EMDR trainings generally involves trainees using EMDR to treat old memories, traumas, anxieties, phobias, and
limiting beliefs arising from a set of discrete initial experiences. In this setting the trainees serve as clients for each other. Most cases in a typical
psychotherapy practice, however, are more complex and difficult to work
with; generally, clients are lower functioning than EMDR trainees and have
more complex problems that often do not have single, discrete identifiable
source memories. For most trainees, moving from the training experience to
their actual clinical settings is difficult, and some trainees report that they
are unable to make the transition to using EMDR with their clients. The
case examples in this book describe in detail how EMDR was used in clinical
settings; they can serve as practical instructional models for applying EMDR
and as sources of encouragement and inspiration as well.

  • Demystify EMDR

After the publication of the first study by Wilson and colleagues (1995),
one of my colleagues with a psychodynamic orientation read the study and
declared, "I don't care how good the research is, no one is going to convince
me that finger wagging is therapy." EMDR is not "finger wagging" and it is
not hand waving; it is a method that can be integrated into a variety of
psychotherapeutic approaches. The cases in this book illustrate how EMDR
can be utilized to enhance an ongoing treatment. The reader will recognize
that the results obtained through EMDR make therapeutic sense; often they
resemble those produced by more traditional psychotherapies, except they are
achieved more rapidly with EMDR.

Initially, one of the most difficult aspects of EMDR for me to appreciate,
as I imagine it will be for most traditional psychotherapists, is the role of
cognitions, beliefs clients hold about themselves. In EMDR work, shifts in
clients' cognitions usually remain stable over time and can be quite significant. In psychodynamic work insights are seen as the cornerstone of change

and healing. Though these insights seem quite significant when they are first discovered, they are often forgotten by clients or become less meaningful to them, ultimately leading to little or no behavioral change or symptomatic relief. The cognitions that become the focus of EMDR, however, are not usually discovered as insights. They are self-statements that the client normally already *knows* to be true but *feels* to be untrue (such as, "I am loveable" or "I can take care of myself"), especially when considered in the context of the disturbing memory or other disturbing material that is the current focus of treatment. Part of the EMDR standard protocol is for the therapist to check frequently the integrity and durability of the EMDR work that has been done to date; this includes measuring the felt validity of these self-statements as reported by the client on the Validity of Cognition Scale (VOC). Remarkably, cognitions that have become completely true in a felt sense normally remain that way. For this reason, when a shift occurs in a significant cognition during an EMDR session, the clinician regards it as an indication of solid progress. Clinicians reading this book should keep in mind the importance of these cognitive shifts when they occur on a gut level; they usually represent lasting adaptive change.

What Is the Effect of Eye Movements?

Although there are theories, this question has yet to be definitively answered. When colleagues and friends ask me what effect the EMDR eye movements have, I often offer them a micro-experience of the eye-movement effect. First, I ask them to think of a mildly disturbing memory. Once they have done this, I ask them to follow my fingers with their eyes through twenty eye movements (passing my hand back and forth across their field of vision). Then I ask them to recall the memory again and ask if anything has changed. Consistently, people experience a dimming or distancing of the memory. They describe it as feeling less intense, less vivid, or more remote. Common phrases are, "Now it feels like it's just something that happened" or "I feel more like an observer now." These are the same effects that my clients consistently report. In the context of Dr. Shapiro's Accelerated Information Processing Model, one can think of this effect as reflecting the connecting up of the isolated painful memory to the larger informational system of the mind.

Clinicians using other models might describe the client as operating out of a child ego-state when recalling an early traumatic memory; others might describe the memory as triggering splitting, in which the client is accessing a distorted view of self and object with associated disturbing affect. Whatever the language used to describe it, most clinicians would agree that these memories must somehow be linked up to a more mature reality-based adult perspective in order to be metabolized. Indeed, it appears that a significant salutary role played by therapists is to act as a tether to a healthy adult perspective when the client begins to dissociate into the memory of a formative childhood experience. One theory explaining the observed accelerating effect produced by EM's in processing of these memories (Shapiro, 2001; van der Kolk, 2002; Wachtel, 2002) is that the client is being asked to perform a task in present time while recalling the past, and this dual awareness causes a rapid oscillation of attention and awareness between the present and past perspectives, allowing for the swift integration of the two. (Manfield & Shapiro, 2003)

In the context of neurobiology, the eye movements apparently stimulate the movement of information through the corpus collosum (van der Kolk, 1997) from the right hemisphere of the brain to the left. I think of the dimming effect as arising from the processing of the memory, converting a fixed literal image stored in the right hemisphere into a more flexible symbolic one stored in the left. During normal processing, literal images are evaluated for meaning, placed in a narrative, and stripped of extraneous information. The symbolic image that results contains only the details that are essential for the memory to make sense. During a traumatic experience this processing is impaired. EMDR stimulates the processing of raw or incompletely processed memories.

A more precise explanation of why EMDR is effective in resolving trauma was offered recently by Bessel van der Kolk (1997) in discussing the recent research of Martin Teicher and his associates (1997). Teicher and his colleagues analyzed brain functioning in subjects with and without histories of childhood sexual abuse as they recalled a memory of their worst childhood experience and a memory of their best one. When asked to recall the painful event, the group with histories of abuse activated only the right hemisphere of their brains to the exclusion of the left. The left hemisphere is responsible for many of the functions necessary for psychotherapy, language and the ability to use it to gain distance from the source of distress, the ability to orient in time, and the ability to translate experience into meaning. Because the left hemisphere becomes inactive when a traumatic memory is recalled, it is understandable, that traditional verbal psychotherapies have been relatively ineffective in treating this type of client. EMDR provides a non-verbal method that apparently stimulates interhemispheric activity, making it possible for clients with histories of severe childhood trauma to recall these painful memories and continue to adaptively process them. Not only does EMDR stimulate interhemispheric communication in brains with abnormal brain lateralization caused by a history of trauma, but van der Kolk and his associates (van der Kolk, 1997) demonstrated that increased bilateral hemispheric activity is sustained after EMDR treatment has been completed. The exact mechanism by which the eye movements or hand taps stimulate interhemispheric communication is unknown, however Bergmann offers a possible answer in two papers "Speculations on the Neurobiology of EMDR" (1998) and "Further Thoughts on the Neurobiology of EMDR" (2000).

Personality Disorders and Complex PTSD

Neurobiological research also lays a foundation for understanding why EMDR might be effective in treating more complex disorders, especially those in which there is a history of ongoing childhood trauma. Resnick and colleagues (1995) found that adults who experienced ongoing traumatic abuse as children are likely to have low blood levels of cortisol, a chemical released in the brain to help people calm themselves after a flight-fight response. The implication is that these people will have difficulty with self-regulation and self-soothing, two central characteristics of personality disorders (Manfield, 1992). Poorly functioning clients with histories of abuse often meet the diagnostic criterion for borderline (BPD) or other personality disorders; these diagnoses can obscure the importance of the abuse as a source of the client's dysfunction. These clients would sometimes more accurately be described as suffering from *complex PTSD*, (Herman, 1992a, 1992b) a disorder resulting from childhood physical abuse and its aftermath which does not appear in the DSM IV (APA, 1994).

Complex PTSD

The proportion of personality disordered clients who have in fact been physically or sexually abused is high. Reports by Stone (1981) and Bryer and associates (1987) have suggested that over 75% of borderline clients have been sexually abused as children. Herman (1992a, 1992b) challenged the practice of diagnosing personality disorders in patients with a history of severe trauma, suggesting that they should be diagnosed as *complex PTSD* to take into account the effect on personality and future interpersonal relationships of repeated trauma.

A recent neurobiological study of trauma by Teicher and his colleagues (1997) appeared to support the usefulness of the complex PTSD diagnosis. One of his findings is that childhood sexual abuse and childhood neglect each correlates highly with abnormal physical maturation of the brain, resulting in particular in a significantly smaller corpus collosum, the part of the brain whose purpose is interhemispheric communication. Referencing Joseph (1988) and Muller (1992), Teicher and colleagues concluded, "Muller theorized that borderline personality disorder may be the result of deficient hemispheric integration. . . . Deficient right and left hemisphere integration could result in the misperception of affect and foster a situation in which the right and left cerebral cortex may act in an uncooperative manner, giving rise to intrapsychic conflict and splitting" (1997, p. 171). Because EMDR seems to stimulate the activity of the corpus collosum (van der Kolk, 1997), this finding suggests that EMDR may be an effective treatment tool for clients with a childhood history of sexual abuse or neglect.

It is interesting to note also that, while the correlation just discussed involved childhood neglect, there was no correlation in Teicher's results between abnormal corpus collosum maturation and psychological abuse. It would, then, seem to be useful to distinguish between personality disorders on the basis of early history. Those cases involving childhood neglect will probably respond better to EMDR than those involving solely psychological abuse. My own clinical experience, as well as that of many of my colleagues, supports this conclusion.

EMDR Casebook

The three chapters most recently included in *EMDR Casebook* that were not in *Extending EMDR* illustrate the type of case for which EMDR is best suited. In each there is a small collection of specific traumatic events that are responsible for the condition being treated. Several chapters focus on traumas that are over thirty years old; others focus on relatively recent events.

Extending EMDR

It is relatively easy to conduct outcome research on the use of EMDR with single incident or several incident traumas. Because of the increased complexity and length of time involved, however, it is far more difficult to research it's effectiveness with more complex cases, for instance those arising from a series of repressed traumatic memories or those involving ongoing childhood trauma or abuse. Given the absence of controlled outcome studies, this book explores individual cases in which the use of EMDR was successfully expanded beyond its standard applications. Many of these cases have in common that the clients have extreme parental neglect, physical, sexual or psychological abuse in their histories. The challenge faced by the treating clinician was to identify memories of neglect or abuse and formulate them into effective EMDR targets that the client could process without becoming overwhelmed. In most cases clients were prepared in innovative ways before EMDR processing of target material could begin.

Many of the cases described in this book fit the complex PTSD diagnosis. Complex PTSD is well suited to EMDR treatment because traumatic memories are usually clearly identifiable and vivid, making them excellent EMDR targets. It is often difficult to treat, however, because the client may lack the emotional resources necessary to address painful target memories and reach an adaptive resolution. Many of these clients have no memory of ever feeling loved; many have no model in their mind of a loving and nurturing adult. For many clients, the messages of blame or shame have been so pervasive through childhood that the resulting maladaptive self-statements are extremely difficult to challenge. Although EMDR targets may be easily identified for clients with complex PTSD, they often do not respond to the standard EMDR treatment method. Each of the contributors to this book discussing a case of this type has placed a strong emphasis on client preparation as a way to stabilize the client and address the client's dearth of resources. The methods of preparation vary, and not all involve EMDR, but in each case the result has been excellent.

On the other hand, Chapter 13, on treating narcissistic vulnerability, addresses a type of case in which the childhood experience involves psychological abuse without childhood neglect or physical or sexual abuse. While this client demonstrates improvement over time, progress is slow and the role of EMDR in the overall treatment is not as great as in the cases of complex PTSD. Narcissism is extremely challenging to treat; the historical source material appears to be diffuse and the clients defenses formidable. Whereas in most cases, when a suitable EMDR target is clearly defined and developed, the client tends to work as an ally with the therapists in exploring the various chains of associations connected to the target, these clients often steer away from emotionally charged material, into irrelevant or distracting associations. These clients require vigilance, patience, empathy, and creativity on the part of the therapist, for whom EMDR can be a resource but will be ancillary to more traditional treatment methods.

About the Contributors

The contributors to this book were already experienced and capable clinicians before being introduced to EMDR. All have trained extensively in the use of EMDR, and all but one have been involved significantly in training others in the use of EMDR. In their chapters they discuss their backgrounds, the process they went through in incorporating EMDR into their treatment approaches, and the way they adapted EMDR for use with their particular patient populations. In many of the cases discussed in this book, the impact of EMDR is less dramatic or rapid than in the single-incident PTSD cases for which it is optimally suited. Although many of these cases followed a similar course, as they would have if treated in a more traditional way, it is apparent that EMDR accelerated the treatment. Because there are no research-validated EMDR protocols for the types of cases we are presenting, the approach of each contributor is, in some respects, singular and offers new possibilities to those seeking creative ways to expand the effectiveness of their clinical work.

Conventions Used Throughout This Book

We have adopted several conventions to maximize consistency among chapters. Although some of the authors customarily use surnames to describe their clients when writing about them, for consistency all authors in this book will refer to their clients by first name. Similarly we refer throughout this book to *clients* rather than *patients*, a term that some of the authors prefer. Because it is awkward to make frequent reference to *his or her, he or she*, we have attempted to balance the use of male and female gender references by using the following system: When a person representative of a particular client population is referred to in general, he or she are referenced by the same gender as the client being discussed in the chapter. When therapists are referred to in general, they are referenced by the same gender as the author of that particular chapter.

In the transcripts that appear throughout this book, the ►◄►◄►◄ sign indicates a set of reprocessing stimuli that may take the form of alternating eye movements or alternating auditory or kinesthetic stimuli. Visual, auditory, and kinesthetic cueing are all referred to as eye movements (EM). In some transcripts this sign will be followed by a number indicating the number of EM in the set. Unless otherwise indicated, it can be assumed that the client was directed by the therapist to focus on whatever material had just come up, and that at the end of the set of eye movements, the therapist asked the client a question like, "What came up?" or "What are you noticing now?" to elicit information about the client's experience during the set of EM.

Each contributing author for this book has altered identifying details of the presented case so as to protect the privacy of the client. We have, at times, changed names, professions, genders, family constellations, and specific life events.

Order of Chapters

To follow the cases presented in this book, a rudimentary familiarity with the basic EMDR protocol and terminology is necessary. EMDR is normally incorporated into a treatment procedure that includes eight phases of treatment. These are summarized in text boxes in the first chapter. Readers who want a more in-depth examination of the EMDR protocols are referred to Shapiro's text (1995).

To illustrate the spontaneous curative process as it occurs with EMDR, the first chapter also describes aspects of the treatment of an uncomplicated case, including partial transcripts of sessions to provide precision and clarity. The client in the sample case is the type of client who responds most readily to EMDR: He is highly motivated and maintains intellectual and emotional continuity throughout his nine-session treatment process; he independently identifies traumatic memories that continue to impact his life negatively; he is able to recall these memories with appropriate affect; and he is able to maintain his attention on the memories while he explores them further, deepens his memory, and expands his understanding of them. Typically, he spontaneously demonstrates an empathic parental attitude towards himself as he reprocesses painful childhood events. He develops a new perspective on what happened, and the event ceases to have a negative impact on him. This client began treatment with a variety of complaints, including depression. In the course of the treatment he identified nearly a dozen traumatic life events, processed their memories, and terminated symptom-free.

EMDR Casebook is divided into two parts: those cases in which it was possible to target a relatively small number of distinct traumatic experiences, and those in which the clients' symptoms have resulted from ongoing childhood trauma or neglect for which they are unable to identify representative discrete traumatic events.

The cases in which clear targets were available required the therapists to identify those targets and work with a variety of resistances in order to resolve them. These clients could generally address their maladaptive defenses directly. Typically, their therapists relied on extensive cognitive interweave, structuring, support and sometimes direct nurturing to make it possible for these clients to tolerate and utilize EMDR to process their targeted traumas.

Where there were no distinct memories to target, the therapists needed to create innovative interventions. Their clients tended to be unable to address their maladaptive defenses directly without fragmenting or closing off. These cases required far more treatment time than those for which there were a limited number of discrete traumatic memories to target and process. Therapists working with these clients needed to find a way to strengthen their ability to maintain internal cohesion and increase their sense of safety so that they could relinquish defenses without the threat of becoming overwhelmed and fragmented. Several of the therapists attempted to address directly the deficits that prevented their clients from recalling their past experiences, organizing them, and gaining access to specific memories and affect.

Central questions addressed in each chapter include:

- How can I provide my client with the resources that will enable her to process the material that is at the source of her dysfunction?
- How can I make it unnecessary for her to avoid or defend against this material?
- How can I provide tools that are presently unavailable, if necessary?

For some of the cases the therapist provides support and guidance; for others, cognitive interweaves help the client integrate the material that is surfacing. For still others the therapist prepares the client by reparenting or helping her develop a foundation of positive resources that can be available to facilitate an adaptive integration of traumatic material.

The quantity and quality of internal and external resources with which the client comes into treatment determine how extensively the therapist must first enhance the client's preparedness for treatment. For the clinicians whose work is described here, the client's developing relationship with the therapist is of great importance, yet the traditional approach of relying on the therapeutic alliance as the primary source of necessary safety and resources requires a period of treatment that seems unnecessarily long. Each of the contributing authors has found a singular solution to the problems his or her client presented which I believe to be creative and instructive. It is my hope that these singular solutions may offer helpful possibilities to other clinicians who face similar difficulties and that may eventually lead to research designed to determine if these clinical innovations merit wide spread use.

References

American Psychiatric Association (1994). *Diagnostic and statistical manual of mental disorders*, Fourth Edition. Washington, DC: American Psychiatric Association

Bergmann, U. (1998). Speculations on the neurobiology of EMDR. *Traumatologye*, 4(1): Article 2. Available at http://www.fsu.edu/~trauma/art1v4il.html

Bergmann, U. (2000). Further thoughts on the neurobiology of EMDR: the role of the cerebellum in accelerated information processing. *Traumatology*, 6(3), 175–200.

Bryer, J. B., Nelson, B. A., Miller, J. B., & Krol, P. A. (1987). Childhood sexual and physical abuse as factors in adult psychiatric illness. *American Journal of Psychiatry*, 144, 1426–1430.

Herbert, J. (1995). What is EMDR? *The Harvard Mental Health Letter*, 12(2), 8.

Herman, J. L. (1992a). Complex PTSD: A syndrome in survivors of prolonged and repeated trauma. *Journal of Traumatic Stress*, 5, 377–391.

Herman, J. L. (1992b). *Trauma and recovery*. New York: Basic Books.

Joseph, R. (1988). The right cerebral hemisphere; Emotion, music, visual-spacial skills, body image, dreams, and awareness. *Journal of Clinical Psychology*, 44, 630–673.

Linehan, M. M. (1993). *Cognitive-behavioral treatment of borderline personality disorders*. New York: Guilford Press.

Manfield, P. (1992). *Split self/split object: Understanding and treating borderline, narcissistic and schizoid disorders*. Northvale, NJ: Jason Aronson Publishers.

Manfield, P., & Shapiro, F. (in press). "The application of EMDR to Personality Disorders." In J. Magnavita (Ed.), *Handbook of personality disorders*, New York: Wiley.

Masterson, J. F. (1976). *Psychotherapy of the borderline adult—A developmental approach*. New York: Brunner/Mazel.

Masterson, J. F. (1981). *The narcissistic and borderline disorders—An integrated developmental approach*. New York: Brunner/Mazel.

Muller, R. J. (1992). Is there a neural basis for borderline splitting? *Comprehensive Psychiatry*, 33, 92–104.

Rauch, S., van der Kolk, B., Fisler, R., Alpert, N., Orr, S., Savage, C., Fischman, A., Jenike, M., & Pitman, R. (1996). A symptom provocation study of posttraumatic stress disorder using positron emission tomography and script-drive imagery. *Archives of General Psychiatry*, 53, 380–387.

Resnick, H., Yehuda, R., Pittman, R. K., & Foy, D. W. (1995). Effect of previous trauma on acute plasma cortisol level following rape. *American Journal of Psychiatry*, 152, 1675–1677.

Shapiro, F. (1989). Eye movement desensitization: A new treatment for posttraumatic stress disorder. *Journal of Behavior Therapy and Experimental Psychiatry*, 20, 211–217.

Shapiro, F. (1995). *Eye movement desensitization and reprocessing*. New York: Guilford Press.

Shapiro, F. (2001). *Eye movement desensitization and reprocessing: Basic principles, protocols, and procedures* (2nd ed.). New York: Guilford Press.

Stone, M. H. (1981). Psychiatrically ill relatives of borderline patients: A family study. *Psychiatric Quarterly, 58,* 71–83.

Teicher, M., Ito, Y., Glod, C., Anderson, S., Dumont, N., & Ackerman, E. (1997). Preliminary evidence for abnormal cortical development in physically and sexually abused children, using EEG coherence and MRI. *New York Academy of Sciences, 821,* 160–175.

van der Kolk, B. (1996). The body keeps score: Approaches to the psychobiology of posttraumatic stress disorder. In B. van der Kolk, A. McFarlane, A., L. Weisaeth (Eds.), *Traumatic stress* (pp. 214–241). New York: Guilford Press.

van der Kolk, B. (1997, July). *Current understanding of the psychology of trauma.* Paper presented at the 1997 EMDRIA Conference, San Francisco, California.

van der Kolk, B. (2002). Beyond the talking cure: Somatic experience and subcortical imprints in the treatment of trauma. In F. Shapiro (Ed.), *EMDR as an integrative psychotherapy approach: Experts of diverse orientations explore the paradigm prism* (pp. 57–83). Washington, DC: American Psychological Association Press.

van der Kolk, B., McFarlane, A., & Weisaeth, L. (Eds.) (1996). *Traumatic stress.* New York: Guilford Press.

Wachtel, P. L. (2002). EMDR and psychoanalysis. In F. Shapiro (Ed.), *EMDR as an integrative psychotherapy approach: Experts of diverse orientations explore the paradigm prism* (pp. 123–150). Washington, DC: American Psychological Association Press.

Wilson, S., Becker, L., & Tinker, R. (1995). Eye movement desensitization and reprocessing (EMDR) treatment for psychologically traumatized individuals. *Journal of Consulting and Clinical Psychology, 63,* 928–937.

Wilson, S., Becker, L., & Tinker, R. (1997). Fifteen-month follow-up of eye movement desensitization and reprocessing (EMDR) treatment for posttraumatic stress disorder and psychological trauma. *Journal of Consulting and Clinical Psychology, 65,* 1047–1056.

PART I

TARGETING DISCRETE TRAUMATIC MEMORIES

1

EMDR TERMS AND PROCEDURES
Resolution of Uncomplicated Depression

Philip Manfield

THIS CHAPTER PRESENTS an example of a relatively uncomplicated EMDR treatment, which can provide a basis for understanding the more complex aspects of cases in the chapters that follow. Basic EMDR protocol as well as EMDR terminology are outlined in boxes set apart from the case description. A full description of the EMDR procedure can be found in Shapiro's book, *Eye Movement Desensitization and Reprocessing: Basic Principles, Protocols, and Procedures* (1995).

Therapist's Background

I have a combined object relations and self-psychological orientation. I am interested in the client's view of herself and others, and how these are reflected in her character issues. From this perspective, I always view the meaning of the client's therapeutic work in terms of its relationship to both the presenting problem and his developmental process.

My original training encompassed many therapeutic approaches, including Reichian, Gestalt, and family therapy. My more recent training in analytically oriented therapy had caused me to set aside these approaches. However, as I used EMDR, I discovered that all these approaches, including the analytic perspective, blended well with it. "George's" case illustrates how these diverse approaches can come together when using EMDR. Although EMDR attempts to use the client's own spontaneously generated associations to direct further therapeutic exploration, the therapist still plays a relatively active role, making EMDR essentially incompatible with nondirective approaches to treatment. This has caused me to change my fundamental stance and adopt a more active role with the clients I work with using EMDR.

Client's History and Background

George, a slender, well-dressed man in his early forties, introduced himself in the first session as someone whom people "don't seem to trust." It troubled him that he was perceived to be a secretive person, although he acknowledged a tendency to withhold information for no reason, and sometimes simply to lie, even though nothing was to be gained from the lies. He said, "I don't know why I do it. Maybe having information that they don't gives me a feeling of being one up, a certain sense of power. But all this creates a sense of things not being quite right with me."

In addition, he said that he was in the process of a divorce he did not want. This was his second marriage. His first wife had left him for another man, and he had felt deeply betrayed. It had taken him 12 years to build enough trust in a woman to marry again, and now his present wife was seeking a divorce. He acknowledged that the relationship had become "empty and desolate," but said he loved his wife and two young children and wanted very much to keep his family together. He wanted his wife to join him in seeking professional help for the relationship, but she viewed him as irreparably overly controlling and wanted the divorce. He felt helpless, impotent, and depressed in the divorce process.

First Session

As recommended in the basic EMDR protocol, I devoted the first session of treatment to taking a history, identifying potential EMDR *targets* and establishing a *safe place* (see Box 1). George's childhood narrative revealed a moderate amount of instability. Although his family had remained intact, his father switched jobs often, forcing the family to move from state to state. He characterized his parents' relationship as one of distance and deception; his mother had affairs she attempted to conceal from her husband and children, but from an early age George was aware of them. His father lost his temper with his mother on a daily basis and, on rare occasions, would "slap her once or twice" when she "provoked the hell out of him." As George put

---

Box 1: Phases I & II: Client History and Preparation

Phase I: In the first session the patient's history and an overall treatment plan are discussed. During this process the therapist identifies and clarifies potential TARGETS for EMDR. *Target* refers to a disturbing issue, event, feeling, or memory for use as an initial focus for EMDR. Maladaptive beliefs are also identified.

Phase II: Before beginning EMDR for the first time, it is recommended that the client identify a SAFE PLACE, an image or memory that elicits comfortable feelings and a positive sense of self. This safe place can be used later to bring closure to an incomplete session or to help a client tolerate a particularly upsetting session.

---

it, "I always feared they might get a divorce. That's what really scared me. I thought then that if a divorce happened, something unnameable, unspeakable, would happen to me. Just thinking about it brought up a feeling of terror."

He read voraciously as a child and had an active fantasy life. "I became very involved with the characters I'd read about," George said. "The world of books became more palatable than the world I lived in." His tendency to lie and his extremely active fantasy life as a child made him feel distant and separate from other people, although he described himself as having many friends in his adult life. During his twenties he had experimented with alcohol and a variety of drugs but was now a "clean liver." He had seen a variety of therapists since he was in his late teens, including a child psychiatrist, a psychoanalyst, a gestalt therapist, an eclectic therapist, a neuro-linguistic programming (NLP) practitioner, and a hypnotist. At those times his primary complaints were depression, sexual concerns, and a negative self-image.

Second Session

I introduced EMDR in the second session. The first issue George raised as a target for EMDR was his excessive need to be in control. I told him I thought this would be a relatively difficult target since he was unable to identify an early source memory. The focus George chose for his first EMDR target was his childhood experience of knowing that his mother was having affairs, a secret he had had to keep from his father.

We followed the standard EMDR protocol for targeting this memory (detailed in Box 2).

After a fair amount of exploration, he chose the negative cognition (NC) "I can't trust adults." He was not able to identify a particular image, and

---

Box 2: Phase III: Assessment

In developing a target for EMDR, prior to beginning the eye movements, a snapshot image is identified that represents the target and the disturbance associated with it. Using that image as a way to help the client focus on the target, a NEGATIVE COGNITION (NC) is identified—a negative statement about the self that feels especially true when the client focuses on the target image. A POSITIVE COGNITION (PC) is also identified—a positive self-statement that is preferable to the negative cognition. The positive and negative cognitions tend to be opposites. Normally, the positive cognition does not *feel* entirely true when the client focuses on the target image, but the client *believes* it to be true. The level to which the client feels the positive cognition to be true while focusing on the target image is reported on a Validity of Cognition Scale (VOC) developed by Shapiro (1995), where a scale of *one* means the positive cognition feels entirely untrue and a *seven* means the positive cognition feels entirely true. The client is then asked to identify the disturbing emotions related to the target image. One would expect that the irrational (emotional) aspect of the target memory reflects the disparity between the level of validity that is *felt* concerning this cognition and the level at which it is rationally held to be true. In general, we find that as the level of disturbance associated with the target drops, the level of validity that is felt with respect to the positive self-statement increases. The client measures the level of disturbance subjectively, using the Subjective Units of Disturbance Scale (SUDS) developed by Wolpe (1991), where *zero* represents no disturbance and *ten* represents the most the client can imagine. The therapist asks the client to identify where he feels the disturbance physically in his body.

he could not easily identify the positive cognition (PC), so we postponed determining the positive cognition until more processing had occurred. The affect associated with this memory was "slight sadness," and he was not able to identify any body sensation connected to this feeling. The Subjective Units of Distress Scale (SUDS) level was 4.

Ideally, to begin an EMDR session it is best to first identify a disturbing image and the accompanying feelings associated with the target. The therapist asks the client where he experiences the disturbing feelings as a physical sensation in his body. These together with the negative cognition facilitate the client's accessing of the target. EMDR processing is certainly possible when one or more of these elements is not available to the client, but in some cases the processing can be more difficult. For instance, clients who have difficulty accessing disturbing affects related to targets tend to be more difficult to work with. Similarly, clients whose targets are primarily feelings and maladaptive beliefs without discrete disturbing images are some of the more complex people to treat with EMDR. Personality disorders tend to fall into this category.

Box 3 describes the EMDR desensitization phase in which the eye-movement work occurs.

In George's first EMDR session, his associations appeared to be fairly spontaneous. He noticed a variety of body sensations and had several images come to mind that made no sense to him. My experience is that people who have spontaneous associations that do not make sense at first in the context of the target but eventually prove to be meaningful tend to respond very well to EMDR. After six sets of eye movements, George recalled walking in on his mother when she was with a strange man—not a new memory for him. He became extremely drowsy during the next set of eye movements and almost fell asleep in front of me. Describing the experience, he said, "My body is doing things to interfere, to keep whatever is there out of consciousness." I asked him what he thought he would be feeling if he were not feeling drowsy, and he said he would probably feel hopeless—he had pondered this particular memory in therapy so many times that he "didn't expect to find anything." During the next set of eye movements, however, he felt his sadness "growing and intensifying." After another set of eye movements, he said, "The sadness is definitely increasing. I'm feeling a disorientation in time, like my experience in this room is diminishing and my experience in that place is becoming stronger."

He was uncomfortable with what he was experiencing as a loss of control. Since he had already tried to distance himself from this memory by becoming sleepy, I suggested the analogy of the train ride (described in Box 4) to

---

Box 3: Phase IV: Desensitization

The therapist asks the patient to focus simultaneously on the image, the negative cognition, and the disturbing emotion or body sensation. Then the therapist usually asks the client to follow a moving object with his eyes; the object moves alternately from side to side so that the client's eyes also move back and forth. (Alternate sensory approaches include the use of earphones with a tone that alternates between the two earpieces, or tapping the client's hands alternately.) After a number of eye movements (referred to as a *set*) or a set of eye movements (SEM), the client is asked to report *briefly* on what has come up: This may be a thought, a feeling, a physical sensation, an image, a memory, or a change in any one of the above. In the initial instructions to the client, the therapist encourages the client to feel free to say there is nothing new to report. Typically, after the client reports, the therapist asks him or her to focus on whatever has just come up, and begins a new set of eye movements (EMs). Under certain conditions, however, the therapist directs the client to focus on the original target memory or on some other image, thought, feeling, fantasy, physical sensation, or memory. From time to time the therapist may query the client about his current level of distress (SUDS). The desensitization phase ends when the SUDS has reached 0 or 1.

---

help make the experience more tolerable for him. He preferred to think of himself as looking through an "ordinary window."

During the next several sets of eye movements, George's memory became broader and clearer and then faded. He again became somewhat removed from the therapy process, this time through what he described as a slight hallucination and a feeling of disorientation. In the next set he was able to regain his focus on the memory, and he again felt the sadness deepening, accompanied by several associated body sensations. Over the next ten sets of eye movements he continued in this pattern of beginning to distance himself from the memory and then going deeper into it, each time with more affect. Eventually, the affect turned from sadness to "panic and agitation." I did not ask him to rate the level of his disturbance because it was apparent that it had become increasingly intense. The following is a transcript of the

---

Box 4: The Train Ride and Gas Pedal Analogies

Several analogies are suggested by Shapiro (1995) for presentation to clients who are experiencing strong, painful affects during EMDR processing. One analogy is that of the client's disturbing memories or "old stuff" being likened to the scenery one might view through the window of a fast-moving train; the scenery is seen, and then it passes and is gone. The therapist reminds the client of this analogy by saying, "You're not in the scenery; you're just passing by it on the train," or "It's just old stuff passing by." Another analogy is that of driving a car through a dark tunnel. The client is reminded that if the tunnel is dark and frightening, it is far less upsetting to push one's gas pedal to the floor and move through the tunnel as quickly as possible than to take one's foot off the pedal and languish in the tunnel. This analogy is used when very painful affect emerges and the client's reflex is to stop the eye movements or try not to think about the source of the disturbing feelings.

---

remaining portion of the session. In this transcript the sign ►◄►◄►◄ is followed by a parenthetical number indicating a set of that number of eye movements. Unless otherwise indicated, it can be assumed that I suggested to George that he focus on whatever material had just come up.

George: ►◄►◄►◄ (25) I sat up and felt more alert for a bit and then began again to sink into a stupor, trying to stay with the lights. [*I was using a* light bar, *a device with a three-foot row of small lights that oscillate from one end to the other, for the client to follow with his eyes.*] I had a feeling of concern. Something about the misfortune of it all. ►◄►◄►◄ (30) It was hard to make my eyes focus on the lights. It takes a real effort, especially when they stop. Physically, I feel lighter. There is a little heaviness in my chest. ►◄►◄►◄ (27) More. [*He wanted to continue the eye movements.*] ►◄►◄►◄ (39) Some image—a family setting.

PM: A reverie?

George: No. Like the Bill Cosby show when the whole family is in the kitchen. Like that. ►◄►◄►◄ (26) Physically, nothing. No thoughts. I feel more energetic, alert. The beginning of a panic or agitated anxiety feeling.

►◄►◄►◄ (25) I was feeling more alert, and then I had some sort of sponta-neous recollection which I don't recall now. This is the first time ever in therapy that the therapist took a lot of notes like you do. The feeling in my chest is more generalized. There is also something across my eyes, head, and in my throat. ►◄►◄►◄ (25) There is something more playful coming up. Maybe just kind of the energy that goes with humor and joking. I am finding the lights amusing and interesting.

PM: What else are you noticing?

George: Things are changing. There is a sweetness to it. It's not something that's heavy and tragic or sad. There is a bittersweet quality to it.

With more difficult clients it could easily be unclear here whether they are avoiding the panicky, agitated feeling that is beginning to emerge or metabolizing the feeling through the eye movements, so that the affect is now truly lighter and more playful as a result. Although George had begun to feel distant from the treatment process on many occasions, he had not demonstrated an active tendency to avoid or distract himself from uncomfortable areas of exploration. I felt confident that his lighter affect was not avoidance.

George: ►◄►◄►◄ (23) I found myself more alert, more in the exterior. Not burdened. More interested in other things in the room.

PM: Now focus back on the memory of discovering your mother with the man. What stands out about that memory now?

Since the channel of the memory network associated with the current node appeared to have been cleared, I suggested that he focus again on the target and find out what aspect of it was now salient. If the channel were not cleared but the client were instead avoiding the panic and agitated feeling that had come up, this would become apparent by his response to the next few sets of eye movements. (See Box 5.)

George: The day felt warmer than it usually does. I can see them on the floor. Hmmm. As I said that, I got some kind of sensation right here in my left shoulder. ►◄►◄►◄ (25) The tones in that room seem warmer and brighter than usual. More colorfully lit. The image seems closer. ►◄►◄►◄ (28) The feeling in my chest has dropped into my abdomen. It seems warmer. The pressure in my head is more dissipated.

George seems willing to focus again on the target, and the resulting associations appear to be spontaneous and fresh. In general, the associations that George reports after sets of eye movements are rich, incorporating visual changes and many body sensations that emerge, change, and disappear. The variety and spontaneous nature of his responses, and especially the way the body sensations emerge and resolve, are also typical of a client for whom the EMDR work will be straightforward and usually successful.

Box 5: Return to Target

Shapiro (1995) suggested the analogy of a cluster of neurons in the brain, which she calls a "neural network," representing the target memory and its associations. At the center of the cluster or network is the target or NODE, and branching from it are a number of CHANNELS through which flow thoughts, feelings, body sensations, images, and memories associated to the target. A target usually has more than one channel connected with it. If the channel of associations the client has been following during EMDR processing appears to be clear, as might be indicated by the absence of disturbing affect, the basic EMDR protocol suggests focusing on the target again and finding out if there is any other aspect of it that continues to be disturbing. If so, this new source of disturbance then identifies the next channel to be explored.

PM: You got that image of seeing them on the floor and your eyes became moist, and then you seemed to move on. Is that because you were finished with that image or because it was uncomfortable to focus on?

This is a question I often ask to check my work with a client. I could see the affect come up, but he hadn't reported it. I wanted to know if he were aware of the affect and, if so, if he were consciously directing himself away from it. In the case of George, I did not think he would be avoiding the affect, so the main function of the question was to find out if the feeling had registered and been metabolized. If not, this question is usually helpful in calling it to the client's attention.

George: I moved on because the memory changed afterward. I had won something and was exuberant. They began shifting and adjusting their clothing. I turned and went upstairs and . . . ▶◀▶◀▶◀ [*He talks as he is moving his eyes.*] I feel a lot of disappointment. The excited, elated mood is suddenly collapsing, sinking into disappointment and confusion. Not knowing how to deal with it. [*He is recalling the memory from the child perspective.*] Realizing that makes me sad again [*the adult ego state*]. I feel very sad for that little boy.

This is the spontaneous response that often happens in an uncomplicated EMDR session when the client is recalling a painful memory and shifts from the child perspective of the memory to an adult perspective, feeling and expressing empathy for the child in the memory. When this shift does not occur spontaneously, the therapist must often intervene more ac-

tively to help the client reach an adaptive resolution. Typically, the therapist asks a question that will stimulate the client to access some needed information, or the therapist provides that information directly, or suggests that the client think about an existing resource that was not being considered. This relatively active intervention, termed "cognitive interweave" by Shapiro, is described further in Box 6. My next question in this transcript is normally unnecessary once the client has made this shift into empathy, but time was running out on the session, and I made this intervention to bring the session to a successful close.

PM: What do you want to say to that little boy?

George: I feel that it's such a shame that this great misfortune had to happen and leave marks that would last a lifetime. I want to tell him, "I'm so sorry that had to happen to you, that it would leave an insurmountable barrier that would change your life in almost every way. I think it's been the source of every sad experience you've ever had." [*Eye movements stop.*] That feeling of a kind and compassionate adult seeing the suffering that had been given to this child to bear all his life. Every bit of his happiness snatched away. I feel compassion and tenderness and love for him [*sobbing*].

Again, George spontaneously offers the child the nurturing adult perspective that was not available to him at the time the event took place. This shift in perspective usually occurs spontaneously in uncomplicated EMDR sessions. With more difficult clients the therapist sometimes supplies this shift in perspective for the client in order to help resolve the memory.

George: ►◄►◄►◄ (57) [*sobbing*] Just those tender feelings for that small child. ►◄►◄►◄ (53) [*sobbing*] I was just feeling as thought felt that sadness and that pain and then right before you stopped the lights, my mind came into the present and I saw my wife and had some words with her—of understanding. I was just thinking about the idea that, for everybody, there is some original wound. I feel a little reflective [*as an adult*].

PM: When you think about the memory you started with today, how disturbing does it feel now on a scale of 0 to 10?

George: Three [*laughs*]. "What fools these mortals be"—from *Midsummer Night's Dream*. Everybody does the best they can with the limited information they have. If my mother had known I'd come bursting into the room, or if she had taken better precautions against that possibility—people don't realize the far-reaching consequences of their actions.

PM: Does the positive statement "I can trust people when they are well intentioned" still fit? [*This is the positive cognition he had eventually chosen.*]

George: Yes. And I do.

Box 6: Cognitive Interweave

The term COGNITIVE INTERWEAVE was coined by Shapiro (1995) to refer to the process of offering the client information or other resources that the client has not linked into the processing of the target image. Usually these resources are already available to the client and would eventually be used spontaneously, but the cognitive interweave hastens the process. This intervention is used when the client seems to be stuck on the same series of content, cognition, and affect (referred to as LOOPING) and has not progressed during several sets of eye movements, or when time is running short in the session and the therapist wants to help the client resolve the target in the time that is left, or when there is information the client does not have that would be useful.

For example, cognitive interweave was first used with adults who had been sexually abused as children. Shapiro noticed three elements that seemed to be necessary for the abuse memories to be resolved. The adult client needs to feel safe from the childhood abuser; the self-blame that often accompanies these experiences needs to be challenged and put into appropriate perspective; and the client needs to feel empowered by realizing that, as an adult, she is no longer a victim but instead has choices. Shapiro found that if one or more of these elements did not spontaneously arise and become resolved, the EMDR processing would stall or loop. She found that productive processing could be catalyzed by asking the client to consider the missing element. For instance, she might ask, "Who was to blame for what happened to you?" or "If that happened to your daughter, whose fault would it be?" In this way the client is encouraged to bring into play the adult perspective that was not available to the child at the time the incident occurred so that the memory can be adaptively metabolized.

PM: Good, think of that while you recall the image of discovering your mother with that man.

In the EMDR standard protocol this process is referred to as installation *(described in Box 7). Time was running out on this session. The SUDS level on this target had not yet reached 1 or 0, as it should before installation is performed. However, the perceived validity of the positive cognition had gone fully to true, and there was significant resolution in the target disturbance. I concluded that an installation of the positive cognition would be a beneficial way of ending the session. During this process there often is a further lowering of the SUDS level or an increase on the Validity of Cognition Scale (VOC).*

George: ►◄►◄►◄ (26) I was just reminded of people in my life who are well-intentioned and the warmth I can feel about that. And I was thinking that it's nice to just be able to recognize those that aren't, without making a big deal out of that. [*Time had run out, and the session was ended.*]

In the following session the client reported that the memory was still sad for him, but it was "a comfortable sort of sadness." He was sad to reflect on how much of his life had been influenced by that event, giving numerous examples, including his "distorted view of women in general," and the particular choice he had made in marrying the woman he was now in the process of divorcing. When I asked George about the SUDS level for this target in a later session, he reported that it was completely down and that the mem-

---

Box 7: Phases V & VI: Installation and Body Scan

Phase V: The INSTALLATION process is normally done only after the SUDS has reached 0 or 1 and the VOC has reached 6 or 7. The therapist asks the client to hold in mind simultaneously the positive cognition and whatever is left of the original target image during several more brief sets of eye movements. The installation process tends to reinforce the positive cognition, solidifying it in the client's mind. A VOC of 6 or 6.5 often becomes higher. The client usually also experiences a feeling of well-being and a sense of accomplishment.

Phase VI: If a target appears to be completely desensitized, the client is asked to scan his body for any remaining disturbing sensations. If a disturbing sensation is located in the BODY SCAN, it becomes the focus of a few sets of eye movements to see if there is more material related to the original target.

ory felt as if it were a story about something that had happened to someone else.

Third Session

After discussing the impact of the previous session (*reevaluation*), the client went on to discuss additional aspects of his childhood. I asked him to recall a "top-ten list" of his most disturbing memories (Shapiro, 1995). He was able to recall only four of them, which he described. During the week between sessions, he was able to think of three more. Four of the seven were moderately severe, with SUDS levels of 5 or 6, and the other three were more severe, with the most severe, a molest experience that occurred when he was a teenager, rated at 8.

Fourth Session

During this session, which was scheduled for an hour and a half, two of these moderately disturbing memories were processed using EMDR, with the SUDS level of the first memory diminishing to 0, and the second reducing substantially. The transcript that follows represents the processing of the second target in that session. It illustrates how, even in a relatively uncomplicated EMDR treatment, there is often more than one facet or channel of the problem, and each channel needs to be processed separately and completely. The targeted memory was of George trying to participate in an elementary school class joke-telling session. He ended up feeling humiliated in front of the class. The first channel related to a feeling that he had made a fool of himself and felt worthless. The second channel was deeper; it had to do with a feeling that the world is a disappointing and threatening place where danger from authorities lurks. Although the SUDS was reduced, not enough time remained to process the second channel completely, so the EMDR was closed down with a cognitive interweave and completed in the following session.

George: I'm sitting there in class listening to the other kids telling jokes. It seems easy enough, and I want to do it, too. It looks like fun, and more and more I'm feeling the impulse to create something like that. So I try to do something, to tell a joke, and it doesn't go anywhere. I just end up losing my focus, and the joke comes out sounding meandering and senseless. The teacher tells me to sit down, and then she criticizes me. I don't remember exactly what she said. I know I felt humiliated, unfairly criticized and attacked. I also felt like I had let myself down. I had put myself at risk to become a target, and I had paid the price.

[*The image he selected was that of the teacher criticizing him, and the negative self-statement was "I can't protect myself".*]

This is a split I've seen a lot in myself. I have the impulse to do something, and the part of me that is supposed to take care of me and let me know if something isn't safe, doesn't. I end up in an awkward, embarrassing situation, which a person with more adequate controls wouldn't do in the first place. I get in over my head often, and then I have to sink or swim.

I think a more accurate statement would be, "When I'm impulsive, I can't or don't protect myself." I think to myself, "It's OK to try, even if you do fail," but then I get carried away, feeling invincible, as if other people understand and make allowances or simply appreciate a little outrageousness.

In formulating his positive self-statement (PC), he first came up with "I belong." But this felt entirely untrue to him, and it also didn't relate directly to his negative cognition. I suggested he select a statement he preferred over the negative cognition that felt at least somewhat true. He settled on, "I can learn when to go forward—when it's safe and appropriate."

George: When my teacher said those hurtful, attacking things, I felt like crawling under a table. I felt humiliated, the outsider, that I didn't measure up, an embarrassment, the object of ridicule and deserving of it. I felt my energy collapsing and felt like going to sleep. My head was fogging up, my breathing became labored, I felt listless, my words less distinct. [*He reported a SUDS of 7 and a VOC of 2. He located physical tension in his forehead, eyes, neck, and shoulders. Desensitization was begun.*] ►◄►◄►◄ (30) The feelings seem a little more intense. The level of disturbance feels now like an 8." ►◄►◄►◄ (26) I thought, "No, wait a minute." It's a voice I hear in my head. ►◄►◄►◄ (24) What's the big deal? My voice sounds more energized. The tension in my eyes is evaporating. ►◄►◄►◄ (29) I'm laughing about it, hearing, What's the big deal? It was a funny off-moment. But that's not all of who I am. My value and self-worth shouldn't be judged on some stupid, impulsive activity. I have a lot more to me. I'm saying to myself, You are more than that.

The client's preceding comments represent a shift in perspective from the child who had the experience to the adult recalling it. For many clients, this shift may be a way to avoid the uncomfortable feelings the child experienced. If, however, the childhood experience has been fully recalled, this shift usually indicates that the eye movements have triggered an integra-

tion of the painful memory with the adult resources. To determine what the shift represented, I asked him: "When you say to yourself, 'You are more than that,' is that something that feels true in your gut or is it something that your head is telling you is true?" His response, however, did not clarify the nature of the shift until he had experienced another set of eye movements.

George: Well, it's an adult voice that's saying it. ▶◀▶◀▶◀ (26) An adult version of myself enjoying myself. Some person watching my four-year-old daughter and enjoying how full of herself she is. There is a knowingness. ▶◀▶◀▶◀ (26) It's a more compassionate, understanding voice. Like when a puppy pees on the floor—it's just something that happens. You can find enjoyment in it because that's a puppy's nature.

These last comments made it clear that the child paradigm of the original incident was now expanded to include the client's adult resources. This spontaneous shifting of perspective occurs commonly in almost all types of therapy and is central to the healing process. With uncomplicated EMDR clients, this kind of shift can occur in nearly every session. With the shift in perspective usually comes compassion for the child who experienced the event, a sense of self-appreciation or love where there may have been guilt or shame, a change in cognition or self-perception related to the event, and relief from the disturbing emotional component of the memory. My next question was an attempt to verify the extent of the shift. I could also have simply asked him directly to go back to target.

PM: What about the teacher?

George: She was a fool. She never gave me the help I needed. The targets of her criticism never got attended to. Her response in situations was just to get angry or sometimes punish the behavior that didn't meet her criteria or standards. She didn't have the understanding that she was dealing with children who needed to be helped and supported. [*Here, again, is the adult perspective.*] ▶◀▶◀▶◀ (26) I heard that voice saying to the child, Don't let her get you down. The voice is supportive, kind, and protective of that small child. Then I noticed that the physical sensation in my body was vanishing. I feel more engaged by the room. ▶◀▶◀▶◀ (26) There's another voice that's energized—whiny, crying, complaining: "Why does the world have to be such a hurtful and disappointing place." Sad, whiny [*Here he shifts back to the child perspective and spontaneously begins processing another channel related to the original target.*] ▶◀▶◀▶◀ (26) I hold an opinion about the world that weighs me down and gives me a negative-force thing. I think this is the real legacy of that experience—the belief that the world is a sad and disappointing place where it's not OK to take chances, and where people in authority can inflict pain.

Spontaneous is the key word for an uncomplicated EMDR case. Here, George again shifts into the adult perspective, spontaneously elaborating on the negative cognition and then identifying a positive cognition that is more appropriate.

George: ►◄►◄►◄ (26) I felt a surge of energy in my body, but then I retreated. I hear myself saying, "The world is many things. It's also a place with many wonderful and beautiful things. Trying things can be rewarding." ►◄►◄►◄ (28) I'm feeling more alert, but not that crisp, energized feeling.

PM: Go back to the image you started with and tell me what stands out about it now. [*I'm testing to see if there is yet another channel that needs to be processed.*]

George: It's hard to bring it in. It keeps slipping away. I see the desk I sat at, the floor, the walkway past the teacher's desk. I just had an odd, disorienting feeling, almost like I was dozing off for a moment, and the room had an unreal quality to it. It makes me feel edgy and fidgety. My eyes don't have that sharp focus that they did. ►◄►◄►◄ (26) I feel a funny transitioning feeling, like I'm between something and something.

Normally, I would have a client focus on this new feeling because it does appear to represent another disturbing facet of the target memory. Instead, I asked George to go back to the original target. I don't remember why. Perhaps he looked groggy, and I was hoping to help him become more connected to processing the target material.

PM: Focus again on the original image.

George: I see the guy who went ahead of me standing on a chair in front of the room. There's overhead lighting. ►◄►◄►◄ (26) I'm going through the experience. This time, when I'm confronted with the decision, I feel more solid; my vision clears up. I feel strong somehow.

PM: So this is the moment before you made the decision to stand up and tell a joke.

George: Yes. ►◄►◄►◄ (26) I'm thinking, "I want to do that; I want that attention." ►◄►◄►◄ (27) I'm thinking, "Why can't I have that attention?" Attention seems to be very important suddenly. ►◄►◄►◄ (26) There's something about feeling neglected. My mind goes back to my family life. I think I was feeling neglected in my family somehow. [*During this set of eye movements and the beginning of the next, he appeared to become groggy.*] ►◄►◄►◄ (26) I was thinking that that broke apart somehow, and then I noticed that my vision was clearing and the tension in the front of my head was relaxing.

I interpreted George's use of the phrase "broke apart" as describing the moment when an emotionally charged memory or image loses its charge. The congruence between George's thoughts and physical sensations makes it easy to evaluate his progress. EMDR can be somewhat more complex when the client tends to report positive-sounding shifts in attitude that are not accompanied by a corresponding reduction in disturbing physical sensations.

George: ►◄►◄►◄ (26) I'm more in touch with the room.

PM: Now go back and recall the image you started with today of the teacher criticizing you. What stands out now about that image?

George: Things seem to still want to—there is something there. I can feel it in my vision [*meaning the quality of his vision*]. ►◄►◄►◄ (13) I feel as though someone is pushing against my chest somehow.

PM: Think of the boy telling the joke. How would you, the adult, have helped him if you were there? [*This intervention is an example of a cognitive interweave, which I introduced at this point in an attempt to bring the session to a successful close.*]

George: I get a sweet feeling. I wake up immediately [*referring, I assume, to the groggy sensation he mentioned and the "feeling" of his vision*]. We're enjoying life together.

PM: Does the positive statement "I can learn when it's safe and appropriate to go forward" still fit for you now after the processing you've just done?

George: What I'm telling the child is, "Sometimes, even if you think you know you are wrong, you do the best you can. There aren't any guarantees. But we'll do a better job of it in the future." ►◄►◄►◄ (24) And it's OK.

Fifth Session

The next session began with a discussion of the outcome of the previous session and the week that followed. The first target was still completely devoid of disturbing affect; however, the disturbance level of the second was only partially reduced. George reported a SUDS of 3 or 4. This memory was again targeted, and the SUDS level dropped immediately after a few sets of eye movements, until George reported that the image he had started with was "shredding." He said that the part of the recollection in which he had not taken care of himself was "disintegrating," that he felt comfortable now with the memory as well as the positive cognition he had drawn from the last session: "There are no guarantees. You do the best you can."

Indicating that he wanted to work on another target, he proceeded to identify three targets. The first, the divorce mediation he was going through with his wife, related to the previous target, he realized, in that it was an unfortunate situation and one in which he needed to take care of himself.

The second and third were from his original list of disturbing memories. Both responded quickly to EMDR, with the SUDS dropping to zero and the body scan clean. The VOC in each case went to 7. George was amused by how rapidly these memories were resolving. He said, "I feel like Buck Rogers here with the disintegrating ray. I aim it at a memory, and then *poof*, it's gone."

The next target George addressed was the memory of being repeatedly chosen last for baseball teams. This type of memory comes up frequently as an EMDR target with clients, and it was also one of my own painful memories. I've wondered to myself, "Everybody can't have been chosen last all the time. Somebody must have been chosen next-to-last—what ever happened to them?" George's negative cognition was "There's something wrong with me," and the positive cognition was, "I'm capable." The VOC was reported as 1 and the SUDS as 9. Normally, with a VOC of 1, I would work with the client to find a positive cognition with a slightly higher validity rating, but considering the ease with which George's previous EMDR targets seemed to resolve, I decided to stay with the positive cognition he had chosen. This target took slightly longer to process than the previous two, but it did resolve completely. Shortly into the process, George became sleepy, but this passed after four sets of eye movements, and he reported that his vision was becoming clearer and that it was easier for him to follow with his eyes. The original image became less stable with succeeding sets of

---

Box 8: Phases VII & VIII: Closure and Reevaluation

Phase VII: When a target has been thoroughly processed in a session and it is completely desensitized, the therapist brings CLOSURE to the session by debriefing the client and encouraging him to keep a log of whatever he notices that might be useful to target in the future. If the target has not been completely desensitized, the therapist can use various techniques to help the client leave the session feeling comfortable and with an appreciation of what has been accomplished.

Phase VIII: Even if the target appears to be completely desensitized, the therapist begins the following session with a REEVALUATION of the results of the previous session to see if they have held.

eye movements, until it was hard for George to retrieve. In this case, unlike the other EMDR work he'd done, George did not take a parental view of the memory, but the picture became harder and harder to hold, and the level of disturbance dropped off completely. The VOC ended up between 6 and 7, and the body scan was clear.

Sixth Session

In the next session George began by talking about his divorce, which had been bothering him most of the week. He had a desire to give up; the mediation process seemed futile, and he felt downcast, dismayed, and as if he had no resources. These feelings were permeating the rest of his life. He reported physical sensations but could not find an image that captured this target, so those sensations were targeted with EMDR. During the processing he reported several images and a feeling of aliveness and expansiveness. Eventually, the disturbance level fell to 0 and his body felt relaxed. The following week he described this session as "very successful." Referring to his depression, he reported that his mood had improved noticeably and that other people had commented on the change.

Seventh Session

In this next session the divorce process was again uppermost in George's mind. The target he chose for EMDR was the feeling he got when he talked to his wife on the telephone. He pictured himself sitting in his living room, talking with her on the phone. His palms would perspire as well as his armpits. He would feel "like a child," defensive and angry. The negative cognition about himself was "I'm inadequate; I don't measure up; I'm not good enough." The positive cognition chosen was "I'm a mature, responsible adult." The VOC started at 2 and the SUDS at 8. This EMDR session resembled the previous ones in that the SUDS dropped rapidly to "0 or 1," but an unfinished feeling still remained. Scanning his body, he identified a sense of anxiety in his eyes and at the top of his head. As he focused on the anxiety, he identified a "feeling of dread" and reported a new image, which intensified until it reached a SUDS level of 8. Eventually, he reported "pleasurable sensations." The SUDS had come down to "1 or 2" and related to "a little corner of the picture." Finally, the image "collapsed" and the SUDS dropped to 0; there was no more body tension.

To me, the fact that the divorce was continuing to disturb him did not indicate that the results of the EMDR work were not holding. Divorce is a very complex experience, with many upsetting aspects, including conflict, loss, hurt, and often betrayal. Confirming the progress he was making, George began the following session by saying, "The two times I talked to her this week she got pretty acrimonious, but I felt solid and was firm. I didn't get drawn in. As a result of this process, things seem noticeably improved in my life. A lot of small things seem different, but they are very noticeable. I feel easier, happier, more comfortable, more accepting of myself, not subject to extreme mood swings."

The ability to accept and give validity to feelings, body sensations, images, and associations that are at first unclear or do not make sense can lead to powerful and healing discoveries, as George's progress demonstrates. Clients who have difficulty accepting an image or sensation they don't understand tend to have more difficulty fully using EMDR and represent a challenge to the EMDR practitioner.

Eighth Session

In the next session, George decided to address the molestation, the only remaining target from the original list. The work was again illustrative of phenomena that often occur spontaneously in uncomplicated EMDR sessions. George described the circumstances of the molest and what took place, and this was processed with EMDR. The negative self-statement was "I'm unworthy, I'm shameful." The positive cognition was "I deserve respect" and "I was a victim." The VOC was 2 and the SUDS was "9 or 10."

Some of the memory was unclear, so I suggested that he begin by processing the aspects of the memory that he could clearly recall. Each disturbing image that came up was processed until the disturbance associated with it disappeared. Finally, towards the end of the session, he reported that an image of an open area was coming up again. He had reported it coming up several times during the session and had not understood its significance. Now, after another series of eye movements, he realized that the open area was the parking lot that was outside the window where the molestation had taken place. The image had retained a strong level of disturbance, because he had focused on it during the molest as a way to avoid experiencing the shame he associated with what was taking place. Until the processing described in the following excerpt, however, he had been unaware of exactly what the image was or why it was disturbing to him.

George: ►◄►◄►◄ (50) That image won't stabilize. The parking lot seems to be coming up again. ►◄►◄►◄ (50) I realized why it keeps coming up. I was looking at the parking lot through the window in the bathroom while it was happening. I was looking out the window, disassociating myself ►◄►◄►◄ (50) It collapsed. I'm marvelling at how complex these memories are. I found myself wishing my wife Jackie could take advantage of this technique. Then I imagined her arguing against it. I'm also having a sense of pleasure and slight euphoria and feeling good in my stomach. I'm noticing a relaxed feeling in my head, my eyes, and the back of my neck.

[*At this point the body scan was clean and the VOC was high, so the full memory and the positive cognition were installed.*] ►◄►◄►◄ (20) When I went back and tried to retrieve the memory, it exploded into a big circle with a cross through it. I couldn't retrieve the memory. I am worthwhile. I am feeling touched deep inside myself. There are certain kinds of feelings that are reminiscent of how I felt at the age—young and innocent and naive. And there is an appreciation for that. [*George returned the following week and said he thought he had accomplished what he had wanted to and did not feel a need for further treatment.*]

Conclusions

EMDR is a means of helping clients identify and focus on sources of disturbing affect, maladaptive world views, and negative self-perceptions, desensitizing these and processing them in an accelerated way until an adaptive resolution is achieved. George's case is considerably less complex than the cases described in subsequent chapters. He had good recall of most of his childhood. His issues usually related to a single painful memory or a few painful memories, not to a prolonged childhood period of suffering, abuse, or deprivation. George had easy access to healthy parental feelings and would spontaneously feel compassion for himself as a child in the disturbing memories that he recalled. He had access to his feelings and was comfortable with them. He was also comfortable with the physical sensations that would spontaneously arise during EMDR, and he was comfortable experiencing sensations and images without knowing what they meant. For the most part, issues were resolved during the first session in which they were targeted, and sometimes more than one issue could be completely treated in a single 90-minute session.

In the treatment described, George's depression completely lifted, he was able to deal more comfortably and effectively with the unpleasant divorce process, and he was relieved of the lingering effects of his most upsetting memories. I contacted him two years after he had terminated treatment to find out how he felt about my writing about his therapy; he was happy to hear that I was interested in writing about his work, and he confirmed that the results achieved during these nine sessions had endured.

References

Shapiro, F. (1995). *Eye movement desensitization and reprocessing: Basic principles, protocols, and procedures*. New York: Guilford Press.
Wolpe, J. (1991). *The practice of behavior therapy* (4th Ed.). New York: Pergamon Press.

2

POSTPARTUM DEPRESSION
Helping a New Mother Bond

Laurel Parnell

KAREN WAS A YOUNG MOTHER who came to see me in desperate shape, suffering from acute postpartum depression, unable to bond with, or to take care of, her new baby. This case demonstrates how a therapist can skillfully integrate EMDR with dreams, imagery, and inner child work in intensive brief therapy.

Therapist's Background

I have had a wide range of training and experience in working with adults, adolescents, and children in both long- and short-term psychotherapy. My psychotherapeutic orientation includes a pragmatic developmental psycho-dynamic perspective incorporating ego and self psychology, and a Jungian orientation that takes into consideration the unconscious symbols of the archetypal level. I have worked with dreams, imagery, and active imagina-tion for many years and have been trained in hypnotherapy and relaxation techniques. I also have 24 years of experience with various meditation prac-tices, including Vipassana meditation as taught by Joseph Goldstein and Jack Kornfield (Goldstein, 1976; Parnell, 1996). As a result of my training in EMDR I have become more sensitive to clients' beliefs and somatic experi-ences, including their emotions, energy changes, and physical sensations.

Although I had only recently been trained in EMDR when I began seeing Karen, the client discussed in this chapter, I felt comfortable and adept at using the method right away.

Client's History and Background

In her mid-thirties, Karen was a pretty, petite, keenly intelligent woman with long brown hair. Karen grew up in an intact middle-class family in Southern California, the third of four children. She described her family as basically happy. Her parents had a good marriage and provided well for their children. She always did well in school, graduating with honors from a top Ivy League university.

High strung and perfectionistic, she had a very active mind. Karen received her MBA in the mid 1980s and then worked as a business executive in four different positions, all of which were highly visible, highly stressful, and highly remunerative. She did exceedingly well in all of her jobs but experienced the more personal aspects of her life as wanting. She dated very little, and usually men who did not treat her well. Three years ago she met her husband, whom she described as bringing happiness and a sense of stability to her chaotic personal life.

High-powered jobs were very alluring to her, as she had a strong need to be recognized as being smarter, faster, and better than everybody else. She described a tendency to "run when backed into a corner" or when she found herself in a situation she did not like. She would frequently change jobs, apartments, cities. She enjoyed living with a lot of change.

In our first session she told me that she had always been "slightly neurotic" and given to "irrational panic attacks." She said that her nervous system seemed quite delicate, causing her to shake at very little provocation. She had a deep-seated, uncontrollable fear of death, and could not stand to hear the topic discussed or watch violent movies. She feared her own death extraordinarily. She tended to be hypochondriacal and suffered from panic attacks triggered by imagined life-threatening illnesses. Since meeting her husband, these fear-inducing fantasies had significantly diminished. She attributed this to her husband's intolerance of them and her feeling more secure with him.

She had seen psychotherapists three times in her past, all for short periods of time. The first time was as a child. She was taken at the insistence of her mother who was having difficulty dealing with her behavior. The other times were voluntary when, as a young adult, she had chosen to work on life issues and her intermittent bouts with anxiety. In both of these cases she did not connect with the therapist and left after only a few visits.

Pregnancy and Birth

Karen reported that she had been delighted to become pregnant. She had thought she would be a good mother. She was old enough to fully understand the emotional and financial commitment required, and felt sure that she had found the right father. She had also decided that she did not want to work full-time after having the baby; she wanted to be with her baby while it grew up.

Karen described her pregnancy as uneventful. Her weight gain was gradual and she had morning sickness in the second and third months. She did, however, experience a great deal of stress during her pregnancy. In her fourth month she was fired from her executive position, a situation that came as a great surprise. With legal assistance, she fought the discharge and was subsequently reinstated during her seventh month. Her beloved grandmother also became quite ill during this time. Karen spent as much time as she could taking care of her and found it extremely upsetting to watch her grandmother slipping away. She was very concerned about the effect of all this stress on her baby.

The baby arrived a week early. Her labor was relatively easy and she felt a loving bond to her baby girl while in the hospital. However, everything changed when Karen came home from the hospital with her baby. She described what happened.

> I was in a panic when I first came home from the hospital . . . actually, the panic probably started when I found out I was pregnant. I had really pushed myself to see that everything for the baby was perfect: her nursery, her clothes, her diapers. I was completely overwhelmed by the reality of her—first, that she was a person and not the object of my fantasies, and second, that she was so dependent. I felt that one slip of my hand could kill her. I also felt that as I was nursing her . . . like a perfect mother should . . . I was solely responsible for her. I felt like Atlas with this tiny, little world wearing me down. Also my grandmother, whom I was very close to, had a stroke and died over a few weeks' period.
>
> Then I started getting these scary pictures in my mind. Sometime during the first few weeks of my daughter's life, an occasional picture would

flash into my mind, usually when I was nursing her: I would see her little hand with the fingers cut off. Or, while pushing her stroller over a bridge, I would see myself throwing her into the water. Or I would see myself putting her into the oven or the fireplace. Or, when taking a bath with her, I would become afraid that I would drown her. Each time, I was overwhelmed by her inability to help herself. These pictures scared me to death. I thought it was hormonal, or some such thing. I never believed I would actually hurt her, but I couldn't explain the pictures. I attributed my anxiety about the baby to my anxiety about my dying grandmother.

During this time Karen was home on her own a lot. They had recently moved to a new house in a city on the east coast where she had few family or friends. She looked for part-time work and acknowledged feeling isolated but not un-happy. She said she always felt eager for her husband to come home.

About three weeks before she came to see me, a series of disturbing events took place: Her husband went out of town for a week, she developed a whole host of physical symptoms that made her believe that she was starting to menstruate again, and she started fearing that she might hurt her baby somehow. The fear of hurting her baby was a "nameless fear" that completely panicked her. Her obstetrician recommended that she go back to work. The doctor also said that some nursing mothers develop postmenopausal symp-toms and that perhaps she should give up nursing. Her doctor also referred her to a psychiatrist to talk to about her fears.

Karen went to see the psychiatrist, who offered her antidepressants which she refused, telling herself that her situation was not so desperate. She did give up nursing. In her four sessions with the psychiatrist they discussed the fact that she had a lot of fears about life that manifested themselves as scary thoughts. The psychiatrist recommended that she learn how to feel her fears.

Her symptoms of anxiety and depression continued to worsen, as did the frightening images of hurting her baby. She "felt fine" a diminishing amount of time. Black moods would settle over her, making her feel that life was not worth living. She became frightened that she would hurt herself or that she would lose her mind and be institutionalized. Thoughts like "I'll never be with my family again . . . I'll never love my daughter again . . . I'll never be safe from a mental breakdown again" would run through her mind, further feeding the anxiety and depression. The panic continued to worsen, at times completely overtaking her. Finally, at the advice of her doctors she decided to come to California, where her sisters and mother were living, to take advantage of their offer to help.

Postpartum Depression

Karen's description of her symptoms are typical of the 10% of women who develop postpartum depression (Beck, 1992, 1993; DeAngelis, 1997; Stowe & Nemeroff, 1995; Ugarriza, 1995). In contrast to the more common "baby blues," the deep depression and feelings of anger that characterize postpartum depression usually begin to surface one to two months after the birth. Feelings of sadness, doubt, guilt, helplessness, or hopelessness increase with each week and can disrupt a woman's normal functioning to the point where she is not able to care for herself or her baby. Extreme concern and worry about the baby, as well as the opposite—lack of interest in or feelings about the baby—interfere with the woman's ability to love and bond with her baby. Anxiety and panic attacks are common symptoms, as are fears of harming her baby and/or herself. Women seldom act out these feelings, but they are very frightening for them nevertheless.

It is not known why some women develop postpartum depression and others do not. One important contributing factor is biology: The hormonal and physical changes women experience after birth can affect a woman's mood and behavior for days or weeks. Environmental factors such as stress and lack of family support, along with the woman's psychological make-up, can also contribute to the creation of postpartum depression. Because no two women have the same biological/psychological make-up or life experience, the factors that cause it are unique for each woman.

Overview of Treatment

Prior to the birth of her baby, Karen had led a highly functioning life, holding down a challenging job and involved in a happy marriage. She tended to be slightly neurotic and used obsessive-compulsive and intellectualization defenses. Much of her behavior was driven by anxiety. However, by the time she came to see me, her functioning had nearly completely broken down; she was unable to care for herself or her baby, and she was desperate to get help.

When I began to see her, she had left her home on the East Coast to live temporarily with her eldest sister in Northern California, who could offer her comfort and support. She had given over the care of her baby daughter to this sister because she didn't trust herself with her baby and couldn't tolerate the feelings of anxiety just being around her evoked. Karen's goals in therapy were to reduce her symptoms enough so that she could bond with her daughter and be able to take care of her and then to reunite with her husband back home.

I thought Karen was a good candidate for EMDR for many reasons. First of all she was highly motivated to get better, and she had the time and financial resources to see me several times a week, if she needed to. Because she wasn't working and her one priority was to get better, she had the flexibility to adapt to my schedule. This made it possible for me to see her as frequently as she needed. She did not appear to have a character disorder, as evidenced by her history of stable relationships with friends and family members and her ability to connect with me rapidly (despite her difficulty with former therapists) and trust me enough to openly reveal her pain and suffering. This meant that we could begin the EMDR processing without needing weeks or months to establish a working relationship. I have found that clients with borderline or narcissistic characters require much more time to develop the feeling of safety before beginning the EMDR processing and that transference issues often need to be addressed before they can begin to process material with the eye movements.

Safety was another important concern in considering using EMDR with Karen. I felt comfortable working intensively with her, seeing her several hours a week, uncovering painful core material, because I knew that she and her baby were being completely taken care of at home by her sisters. I knew that she and her baby were safe. This is a very important consideration when working with mothers and very vulnerable babies. If the mother is unable to fully function after the session, the baby could be at risk of harm. Some sessions ended with Karen still feeling upset, but she knew that she could call me and that she would see me in the next day or so.

My goals in the first few sessions were to get to know her, assess her emotional strengths and weaknesses, look for possible targets for EMDR processing, as well as create an empathic bond between us. I knew that she needed to be able to trust me and the process we were about to undertake in order to get better. I talked with her about her current problems and took a comprehensive history. The early sessions were focused on gathering information, offering compassionate support, and seeing how she responded to different interventions. I had no previous experience with postpartum depression and learned quite a bit about it from Karen, who was actively researching it. Her problems appeared to stem from a combination of physical/hormonal changes precipitated by the birth of her baby and preexisting emotional/psychological issues which the birth triggered. I also led her in some relaxation exercises and did some guided imagery and inner child work with her (Taylor, 1991). EMDR was one of many tools I utilized. Clearly adjunctive therapeutic supports were also needed; she again investigated the possibility of medication and participated in a support group for women with postpartum depression.

Karen's sessions were typically very intense and emotional. Most of our work focused on her early childhood. Throughout our work I had the impression that I was working with both a two-and-a-half-year-old and a highly intelligent adult observer. Oftentimes she would come into my office and curl up on the couch with a blanket. She was completely vulnerable and regressed. Yet, even through the most emotionally wrenching sessions, she maintained a kind of witness awareness that found the whole experience fascinating. She was able to be in her experience and watch it at the same time. She was curious, inquisitive, and insightful, constantly trying to make sense out of what was happening to her.

Karen and I very quickly established a close empathic bond. She was able to share her most troubling thoughts and feelings with me and to openly express her emotions. I believe that her ability to trust me greatly accelerated the healing process. My office became like a home or sanctuary to her where she felt safe to be herself totally, to drop all pretensions and superficiality. Feeling so lost and desperate, she was able to give up control and to let go.

First Session

During our first session Karen was extremely agitated and nervous. She said that she felt so tense that she could physically feel the tension. She resembled a terrified little girl, helpless and out of control. In this intensely agitated state, she was unable to provide me with more than a meager history. I would need to wait to do EMDR or any other uncovering work with her until she was adequately contained.

She was taking tranquilizers prescribed by a psychiatrist, giving her temporary relief from the anxiety. Some mornings she woke up feeling fine, but then the anxiety would come. Other mornings she would wake up shaking and knew the anxiety was already there. She was convinced that her hormones were at the base of her problem and intended to pursue that as far as she could. She appeared too fragile to begin EMDR processing.

After the first session I wrote in my notes that Karen was overidentified with a false self and had very little contact with her true self. She was a very controlled and anxious woman, used to channeling her anxiety into work.

However, all of her frenzied activity had come to a stop when she had the baby. It seemed to me that she was still full of nervous energy, but now without work as an outlet for it, she found her mind creating fearful thoughts. Her fears and anxieties seemed to have something to do with being so out of touch with herself. She needed to connect to her true self, her body and her life. We planned to meet two to three times a week.

Second Session (Two Days Later)

Casually dressed in jeans and a sweatshirt with her hair pulled back in a braid, Karen immediately plopped down on the couch and spoke to me with a familiarity which belied the brevity of our relationship. I learned more about Karen's history and background this session. Her scary thoughts were continuing. She was terrified of knives and scissors, afraid that she would pick one up and stab her baby with it. These fearful thoughts seemed oddly disconnected from how she was feeling in a particular moment. For instance, she could be feeling happy and relaxed and then, seeing a knife on the kitchen counter, thoughts of stabbing her baby would pop into her mind, scaring her. I taught her to disidentify with the thoughts by making the mental note *thinking, thinking* when they appeared, allowing them to disappear. This advice was based on the instructions used in Vipassana meditation (Goldstein, 1976). In learning to witness one's thoughts without judgment by using the technique of noting them, the thoughts lose their emotional charge, dissipating into phantoms that lack any substance. The thoughts of hurting her baby were only thoughts; it was her focus on them that scared her and caused her anxiety.

I also taught Karen how to do systematic relaxation exercises in this session. Prior to beginning any EMDR processing, I decided that Karen needed to learn how to relax to help her control her anxiety. She experienced her anxiety as being out of control. Teaching clients self-control techniques is an important adjunct to EMDR. It also helps them to cope between sessions if new, emotionally-laden material arises. During the relaxation exercise Karen experienced difficulties with intrusive thoughts. I asked her what would happen to her if she relaxed. Karen replied, "I won't exist if I'm quiet." Karen was so afraid of not existing that she obsessed about staying in control.

She told me that she was looking for a support group for women with postpartum depression. I thought that was a good idea, for it would give her information and comfort through this highly distressing time.

Third Session (Four Days Later)

Karen arrived for this session looking tired and unrested. She began to notice that she was very self-critical: "A part of me doesn't want me to be
happy." Karen noted that whenever she would begin to feel good, part of
herself would try to scare her or put her down. Compared to her first two
sessions, Karen was reasonably composed in this session. At this point, I
would have considered beginning to use EMDR with her if I'd known her
better, but given her scattered presentation in the first two sessions, I did
not feel I had elicited a full history.

Karen gave me some information about her early childhood that she felt
might be relevant to what she was experiencing. She told me that up until
she was three years old, her older sister used to share a bedroom with her.
She felt comforted and safe with her sister in the room. Then, when her baby
sister was six months old, she was put in her room and her older sister left.
She remembered her mother telling her to "take care of your little sister."
Karen believed that she was supposed to *literally* take care of this helpless
baby—which she, as a three-year-old, was incapable of doing. This feeling of
responsibility was terrifying and overwhelming to her. She also remarked that
her baby daughter looked just like her baby sister decades ago.

As she was telling me this story, she noted that she felt pain in her chest.
The story she was telling about herself as a child, left with what she perceived to be enormous responsibility for the care of her baby sister, was
triggering this sensation in her. She was feeling the fear of her child self left
in the bedroom with her baby sister and no one to take care of *her*. Using
this pain as a starting place, I guided her into doing "inner child work"
(Whitfield, 1987). I decided to use guided imagery because I wanted to
explore her inner experience in a controlled manner. I didn't feel confident
yet that her resources were adequate to begin EMDR processing. Oftentimes
EMDR opens a Pandora's box of affect-laden psychological material. Using
guided imagery, I believed we could briefly explore her three-year-old child
self's experience slowly and systematically. I wanted to build in a sense of
safety, control, and nurturance that she could call on in future sessions. I
also wanted to have a clearer sense of her inner strengths and weaknesses,
which I could assess through this inner work, and then bring her back to
her adult functioning self safely by the end of the session.

I instructed Karen to close her eyes and imagine that there was a protective circle around her. As she did this, she told me that she felt herself to
be three years old and could see her baby sister in front of her. As she got
in touch with her frightened three-year-old self she began to cry, telling me

that she was afraid and couldn't take care of her little sister. The imagery, thoughts, and feelings she conveyed were very real to her. She vividly described her experience while she kept her eyes closed.

Next we began to dialogue back and forth. Karen's three-year-old self told me that her mother yelled at her a lot and that her father was away and distant. She felt unloved. "I want my daddy to hold me," she sobbed. The little girl then said that she hated the baby and wanted her to go away. The baby was so cute and she felt ugly. She felt herself to be a devil. She saw herself in a red devil costume. "I hate my sister, so I must be bad," she said. "My mother is like God and she told me I was bad," she sobbed. "I just want my mommy to hold me." She felt abandoned by her mother, and although her father still loved her, he was far away.

She was struggling with long buried feelings of being bad, which she located in her chest and throat. I asked her to visualize the three-year-old Karen in front of her and to relate to her, this time with the adult self talking to the child self.

"She's so little!" she exclaimed. She was so surprised to see how little this three-year-old was and instantly felt compassion for her. "The little girl has a broken leg and no one is there to help her. She has her arms out, yearning for someone to come and pick her up and hold her." She imagined the adult Karen holding and comforting her and telling her that she loved her and that she would take care of her. She rocked and soothed her, telling her that she wasn't a bad little girl. Karen reported that the child felt comforted and the feeling in her chest eased. "This is how I want to hold my baby. I never want her to be unhappy." Karen was feeling very connected to her three-year-old child self.

It seemed to me that having a baby triggered Karen's early feelings of being overwhelmed and unable to care for her helpless baby sister. In her very regressed state, she again felt incapable of taking care of a baby. Part of her didn't realize that she was an adult who possessed the resources to care for a baby.

I suggested that, now that she had access to this nurturing adult part of herself, she take tender loving care of her child self during the week. I also told her to pay attention to her dreams.

Fourth Session (Three Days Later)

Reporting that she had felt a bit better the last few days, Karen looked more rested and relaxed. She expressed a need to reevaluate her life and began by talking about the feeling of badness. She said that her mother scolded her a lot as a child, which made her feel like a "bad girl." Always yearning for her mother's love and approval but never getting it had left her with a feeling of pain and emptiness.

Karen then recounted another story from her childhood related to the feeling of being bad. She told me that she "ran away" when she was two! Her mother chased after her and fell and broke her ankle. Karen felt *very bad*. She had hurt her mother. This little girl who was mad at her mother had caused her real bodily harm. This must have made her feel very powerful too powerful for a two-year-old. As she spoke, her voice was high and soft like a little girl's.

Near the end of the session Karen recalled that she had been very small as a child and that her mother carried her all the time. She was slow to walk and talk. Her mother pulled away from her when her sister was born, which was very upsetting to Karen. She had tantrums until she was six years old. She said she had always been feisty and testy with people.

During this session she was more relaxed, tearful at times but more contained, more her real self: "I don't want to pretend to be all right when I don't feel good."

In these past two sessions we had focused on her child self who believed she was bad because of the anger she felt at her mother for rejecting her and replacing her with a new baby. She also believed she was bad because she hated her little sister for being born. These memories would provide good targets for EMDR processing.

Fifth Session (Four Days Later)

Karen began the session by telling me that she felt like she was falling apart. She looked terrible. Her hair was a mess, as if she had just gotten out of bed, and she was wearing old wrinkled clothes. She was full of feelings of despair and anxiety. On the positive side, she said that she was feeling closer to her baby and able to comfort her, and the scary thoughts about harming her had decreased. She said she now considered her feelings of not liking to get up to feed her in the middle of the night to be normal. But now she was having fearful thoughts of killing *herself*. Through her tears she told me she was afraid she was falling apart completely and would be institutionalized. I learned that other factors were compounding the postpartum depression: Her husband had a new job and they were having financial problems.

The anxiety and worry were overwhelming her and she didn't know what to do.

I decided to use EMDR this session because I thought it might help to reduce her anxiety. Karen seemed ready to begin EMDR because she was more stable and, by this time, we had established a strong empathic bond. I also knew she would be taken care of following the session.

We did an abbreviated EMDR set-up using her current anxious feelings as a target. I did not take a Subjective Units of Distress (SUDs) or Validity of Cognition (VOC) reading because Karen was in a regressed child state in which asking for numeric ratings on a scale would have taken her out of her immediate experience and would have felt like an empathic break. My intention in using EMDR was for anxiety reduction and exploration. Because Karen was so focused mentally on her obsessive fears, I also wanted to help her focus more on her body.

I asked her where she felt the anxiety in her body. She said that she felt a tightness in her chest and solar plexus. I told her to "focus on that" as she moved her eyes back and forth, "just letting whatever happens happen, without censoring it." After the first set of eye movements she reported seeing beautiful images of the tension turning into a mountain range. Her anxiety decreased and she reported happy images of a clown. But her anxiety increased again with the next set of eye movements, as the scary thought of cutting the feeling out with a knife came into her mind. With the next set of eye movements she again felt more peaceful but began to cry, "Will I ever get better?" She felt overwhelmed with sadness and just wanted to curl up into a ball and cry. She stopped doing the eye movements and laid down on the couch. I covered her with a blanket. She was like a little rag doll, limp from feeling so hopeless and helpless. She obviously did not want to continue with the eye movements. What she really wanted was comforting and to feel better. My sense was that she wanted Mommy to make her feel safe. I sat next to her on the couch and rubbed her back, saying comforting things to her. She cried and cried until she felt some relief.

Since 1991 when I conducted this session, the EMDR method has evolved and been refined. At that time it was not unusual to use EMDR to reduce anxiety by targeting the physical sensations. Over time, it has become clear that using EMDR in an initial session to focus on a physical sensation is too unpredictable and can lead to overwhelmingly intense reactions, as this case illustrates. Initially, the EMDR target should be more contained, including a specific image or memory, cognition, and body sensation. After I have worked with a client using EMDR and can anticipate how she will respond,

I will sometimes target a physical sensation like anxiety directly; I have found that the eye movements can often help dissolve the anxiety that is experienced in the body.

We ended the session with her feeling safe for now, less overwhelmed, but still very depressed. I told her that she could call me if she needed to and we made an appointment to meet in two days.

Sixth Session (Two Days Later)

Karen came in feeling very depressed and tearful, looking like she hadn't slept in the last two days. Despair and hopelessness were overwhelming her. "Will I ever get better? Will these terrible feelings ever go away?" she sobbed. Karen felt she was becoming lost in the despair of never being normal again and was losing all perspective. These feelings of complete and total despair would just come upon her out of nowhere, reducing her to uncontrollable crying. In hindsight, I wondered if her reaction was partly a result of the incomplete EMDR session we had done two days previous, during which she felt so overwhelmed.

Despite all of the difficult feelings she was living with, Karen was determined to do everything she could think of to get better. She had found a support group for women with postpartum depression that she liked. The women in the group all shared similar experiences to hers, which gave her new hope.

She was also continuing to ask for help from her sisters, whom she said were very supportive of her. They held her and talked to her in times of great distress. She felt their comforting and support was of immeasurable value in her healing.

Karen's mother, however, was not so emotionally or physically available to her. Her mother wanted to go to Europe on vacation for two weeks and wasn't going to change her plans on Karen's account. Karen was very upset about the prospect of her mother's leaving during this most difficult time and didn't want her to be out of reach.

Karen appeared too fragmented and distraught for EMDR, so I decided to help her relax by doing a guided relaxation exercise, leading her systematically through her body. I then guided her down a stairway in her mind, becoming increasingly relaxed with each step. At the bottom of the stairway I suggested that she go to an imaginary safe place. In her safe place Karen found some relief from her suffering and anxiety.

Seventh Session (The Next Day)

Karen arrived for this session again feeling very sad and depressed. She had awakened at 1:30 in the morning with an adrenaline rush and couldn't get back to sleep. She was losing weight and felt terrible. "I'm in hell," she said. She reported not wanting to take care of her baby because of feeling so terrible; her sisters were taking care of the baby now. It really looked like she was getting progressively worse and I was very concerned about her. I decided not to do EMDR processing this session, because Karen was much too distraught. She mostly needed to feel nurtured and cared for.

Karen lay down on the couch and covered herself up in the blanket and cried. Her mother had left for Europe. She felt abandoned and terrible: "I want my mommy!"

As she lay on the couch, she tried to bring up images of her mother comforting her but instead got images of scolding and punishment. She said her mother never told her she loved her until she was in college. Karen had heard her roommate tell her mother that she loved her—something new for Karen. She imitated her roommate and told her mother that she loved her, and her mother responded in kind. She said that she felt some comfort from her mother on the phone but that in person she felt nervous around her. It was my sense that this lack of nurturing from her mother made it hard for her to nurture herself or her daughter.

Eighth Session (A Few Days Later)

Karen reported that she had felt less anxious and depressed the last few days. Appearing calmer and more composed, she said she wanted to work on the feeling of being bad that we had talked about in the previous sessions. Karen appeared ready for EMDR processing in this session. She could focus and was not emotionally distraught. This EMDR session was full of insights for Karen with shifts on a physical and emotional level that greatly accelerated her progress. Karen's feeling that she was a "bad girl" was a core belief, which created a pervasive sense of low self-esteem against which she continually defended. It was as if this belief resided in the back of her mind, influencing everything in her life, from the kind of jobs she performed to the kinds of relationships she had with people.

We did a double EMDR session focused on Karen's persistent feeling of being bad. I asked Karen to close her eyes and bring her attention to this feeling, noticing where it was located in her body and then to trace it back in time. This is a method I frequently use with clients to help them come up with early memories that are connected to the negative cognition and body sensation. Clients can usually discover early memories that are effectively connected to the current problem. In this case Karen came up with a memory of disobeying her mother as a very little girl. The memory was of climbing a bookshelf in the den in her family home after her mother had repeatedly told her not to do so. When she was near the top, the bookshelf toppled over on her. The negative belief she had about herself associated with that memory was "I'm a bad girl." The positive cognition she came up with was "I was a little girl who disobeyed her mother and got hurt." The belief that she was bad for disobeying her mother was very strong. I then instructed her to bring up the picture of the bookshelf falling on her, the feelings in her body associated with that, and the thoughts "I'm a bad girl," and to follow my fingers as I passed them in front of her eyes. The following is a transcript of what occurred.

Karen: ►◄►◄►◄ [*speaking in a soft, little-girl voice*] I remember my mother telling me not to climb up on the bookshelf. I feel bad. ►◄►◄►◄ I remember my baby sister. I love her and hate her. I can see my mother holding her and rocking her. She is giving all of her love and attention to her. I thought I'd climb the bookshelf to be naughty and get Mommy's attention. It is the only time she pays attention to me. ►◄►◄►◄ [*Her voice sounds a bit older now, stronger.*] I remember feeling bad all my life. In high school the boys liked me because I was bad. I used all kinds of drugs and slept around a lot. In fourth grade a friend of mine shoplifted and so did I. I feel bad.

LP: Where do you feel that in your body? [*She has been giving me images and cognitions. I want to see what is happening in her body if anything has changed at all.*]

Karen: In my chest, and in my stomach, and my throat feels tight. [*The feeling is still quite strong so I want to keep her focused on the sensations. This is a client who tends to stay up in her head.*]

LP: Go with the feeling of badness.

Karen: ►◄►◄►◄ I see pictures of death. Old people. Mommy said that old people die.

LP: What are you feeling in your body? [*Again, I bring it back to her body.*]

Karen: Fear. ►◄►◄►◄ I'm realizing that all my frantic activity, in my mind and in my life, is a *defense* against feeling bad. [*This insight arises spontaneously for her. She is connecting different channels together.*] ►◄►◄►◄ It is a pitiful feeling. I felt so bad all my life. [*She is seeing how the bad feeling has pervaded her life.*] ►◄►◄►◄ I am feeling comforting feelings. I see my father's mouth. I see two bears—a big bear and a little bear. I saw this picture as a little girl. [*Her positive internal resources are surfacing.*]

Karen continued to process pictures of the big bear, which changed from comforting to scary. Her associations seemed to be going in a non-productive direction, and her level of distress was increasing again without any indication of having progressed. It seemed possible that looping was occurring or that she had gone off on some tangential associative channels. A general guideline I use when I am not sure where the client is in the processing is to ask her to return to the target and then follow with the question: "What comes up for you now when you bring up the original picture?" This gives me a reading on what changes, if any, have occurred with the original picture, helps to refocus the processing, and lets me know where to go next.

As Karen brought up the image of the bookshelf falling on her, she reported: "I feel scared. I don't feel like a bad girl anymore. I feel terrified! The fear is *way* bigger than the bad girl. The bad girl is a defense against the fear." She is clearly having an important insight: Having reprocessed the layer of feeling bad, she is now experiencing the next layer, which is the fear she felt as a little girl. I encouraged her to "go with the fear . . . really let yourself feel it."

As Karen focused on the fear and continued to move her eyes, she seemed to be processing a lot of material. In the next few sets she described how she had always been easily startled and had a "high-strung" nervous system. She also said that, as a child, she'd always had fears at night. With the next set of eye movements she entered into a lovely fantasy of pretty little fairies coming to comfort the little girl, and she reported feeling less afraid.

After the completion of these several sets, I asked her to return to the original picture with the bookshelf falling on her and to tell me what she experienced. She seemed to have processed a lot of material and I wanted to see if the original picture had changed.

Karen: The bad girl is *gone!* I no longer feel her to be bad. The fear is less, but it is still there.

LP: When you look at that picture of yourself as a little girl, what do you believe about yourself now? [*Although the affective charge is not totally gone from the incident, the feeling of badness has shifted. I want to check to see if her belief about herself has changed.*]

Karen: I believe that I was a little girl who disobeyed my mother and a frightening thing happened to me. ►◄►◄►◄ *I was adventurous!* That's why I ran away. I felt the world was there for me to explore. I *wasn't* bad. [*Her self belief has significantly shifted.*]

LP: I want you to think of that now, "I was adventurous."

This is the positive cognition, slightly different from the one she started with, but the more accurate one. This is the new and more valid way of viewing herself that replaces the old belief of being a bad girl. I asked her to think of it again and to do some more sets of eye movements to install it.

Karen: ►◄►◄►◄ I feel much better—more relaxed and calm.

I ended the session by suggesting that she keep a journal and write down any thoughts, feelings, memories, or dreams that might come up. A lot of processing had been done in this session, but the fear channel had not been cleared completely. I knew that there was more to do there. Nevertheless, in this session Karen had accomplished a great deal. She had spent her whole life avoiding her worst fears, and now, with the help of EMDR, she was learning to face them directly and experience them fully, emerging from the experience feeling much better. By gently directing her to pay attention to her body, I was helping her learn that she could safely experience her feelings and that they would pass *through* her. The integration of the emotion/sensation component was an important antidote to her usual defenses of intellectualization and obsessive thinking. She was also changing her self-image from bad girl to adventurous spirit. With this session she began to gain confidence in the process and to look forward to further EMDR work.

Ninth Session (One Week Later)

Karen came into this session looking calm and rested. Her hair was pulled back in a barrette and she seemed much more self-contained. This session marked a turning point in Karen's recovery, which I attributed to the power of the prior EMDR session. She was beginning to get better. She reported that the feeling of being bad was gone. "I was always afraid when I saw a policeman, feeling that he was going to arrest me for something I had done wrong. I saw a policeman yesterday and the feeling was gone. I haven't done anything wrong." She was feeling so much better that she planned to move back home with her daughter in one week. That was amazing considering that only ten days ago she had felt desperate and out of control, overwhelmed by scary thoughts and feelings. She told me that her postpartum depression group was very impressed with the progress she had made. The group leader, who herself had suffered greatly from her own postpartum depression and had subsequently led many of these groups, called me to find out more about EMDR. She told me that she had never seen such a rapid recovery in anyone from such a severe postpartum depression.

Karen still had some fear and anxiety; our work was not yet complete. We planned to focus on those feelings more the next session when we did EMDR.

We spent much of this session talking about her grandmother's death. She had been very close to her grandmother and had been intensively involved in her care as she was dying. Karen had spent all of her free time, when not working long hours at the office, taking care of her. This all ceased abruptly when her daughter was born. It was like a car going 200 miles per hour suddenly coming to a halt, with the engine still running. The outside activity had ceased abruptly, but the internal processing had not. She was still emotionally revved up, never able to relax. Karen felt tremendous grief and sadness about her grandmother's death, which had occurred just a few weeks after the birth of her baby, and missed her terribly. She cried throughout the session as she told me about this loss. She had been so consumed with the care of her newborn that she had had no time to grieve.

Curling up into a little ball on my couch with the blanket around her, she cried and cried, finally letting out her grief.

Tenth Session (Four Days Later)

Karen began this session eager to use EMDR. She was fully engaged in the process of uncovering, discovering, and reprocessing her past and was feeling better each day.

During this session we focused on some of her irrational fears. This was a two-hour session, giving us enough time to complete the processing. With eyes closed, I asked her to explore some of the scary thoughts and beliefs that seemed connected to her underlying fear. She focused inwardly and contacted the feeling, saying, "Something that I can't control is going to get me at night and torture me." She described a fear of being tortured, of being a random victim of some crazed killer. She also talked about a fear of becoming fatally ill and succumbing to an untimely death.

I asked her to trace this feeling back in time and tell me if any memories related to it came to mind. With her eyes closed she said that when she was eight or nine years old, she remembered being so frightened at night that she could not comfort herself. She remembered being afraid of the Zodiac killer who was randomly killing people. These killings distressed her very much, upsetting the sense of order in her life. She said that she felt these feelings in the area of her chest. In going more deeply into the feelings, she said that she felt panic and terror. The belief connected with this feeling was "I deserve punishment. I'm such a bad girl, this should happen to me."

Children can be traumatized in a number of ways other than through direct experience. Because their imaginations are so active, events that they read about or hear about may become real to them in their own fantasy lives, creating lifelong fears and irrational beliefs. Into the neuro-network goes images, body sensations, and beliefs of something that didn't actually happen to them but which they imagined with such intensity that it seems as if it did. These images can later be processed with EMDR, just like any other memory or dream. Karen had heard about the Zodiac killer as a little girl and had created a nightmarish fantasy in her mind of what he would do to her. Because of her feelings of being bad, she had imagined that she would be a target of the killer—an image that had haunted her childhood.

To begin the EMDR processing, we used as the target the image of the Zodiac killer coming into her bedroom when she was eight years old. She focused on that image, felt the tension in her chest area, and repeated to herself the negative cognition "I deserve punishment."

Karen: ►◄►◄►◄ I remember when I was a very little girl picking up a knife and threatening to hurt myself. I was trying to hurt myself to show my mother. I was feeling angry at my mother.

LP: Go with the anger at your mother.

Karen: ►◄►◄►◄ I deserve to be scared [*her self-punishing belief*]. ►◄►◄►◄ I don't deserve to be scared and there's nothing to be afraid of [*a new insight*]. I am comforting the little girl. [*Her adult self spontaneously came forward to comfort her child self. Perhaps the inner child work we had done in a previous session had helped facilitate this process.*] ►◄►◄►◄ [*This was a very long set of eye movements, during which I could tell Karen was experiencing a lot of feeling. She showed accelerated shallow breathing, her eyes were wide, and she seemed to be processing feelings of panic and anxiety.*] I went through many changes. All kinds of things happened. I had an early recurrent dream. Someone has tied me up and is in the next room. I try to call out on the phone, but I can't get through to get help.

LP: What are you feeling now?

Karen: Isolated . . . frustrated . . . I can't communicate. [*We went through several more sets. Near the end of the session I asked her to go back to the original picture of the Zodiac killer climbing through her window and tell me what she experienced.*] She [the little girl] is sleeping and the man is climbing up her wall. She isn't afraid. [*Her SUDs appeared to be quite low.*]

LP: What do you believe about yourself now in that picture?

Karen: There are things to be afraid of, but I don't have to be afraid of them [*calmly and matter-of-factly*].

We did another set of eye movements to install that positive cognition. She took a deep breath at the end of the set of eye movements and reported feeling calm and peaceful. Her face was relaxed and she sat with her hands gently cradled in her lap. With a confident smile on her face she told me that she realized her fear was internal and under her control. This was a major shift for Karen. In this session she had reprocessed a great deal of old fear and had developed a new belief about herself. She didn't have to live in fear of the unknown.

Eleventh Session (Two Days Later)

Karen came into this session feeling much better. Her hair was brushed and she looked like she was well rested. With each EMDR session there had been a marked relief from her disturbing symptoms. She was feeling very enthusiastic about the work we were doing and very hopeful for recovery. So much had changed and shifted in her. I was amazed. She was much more relaxed and comfortable with herself. She reported that she felt much less anxiety and fear after our last session. She was feeling good about herself and her depression was lifting. Instead of the very limited range of affect with which she had begun therapy, she reported a rich array of feelings, including joy and love for her baby. She was spending more time with her daughter now and really enjoying her. She also reported a new-found spirituality and an increased appreciation for life. It was such a remarkable change. She was sparkling and full of energy.

She told me about a dream she had in which she has left her husband and has come West with her baby. He is angry and has her arrested. She goes with the police. They stop and listen to a group of psychologists talk, and she is saying, "I have this problem, I'm innocent." But no one will listen to her. She said the feelings associated with the dream were fear, anger, and guilt.

Using the dream as the target for the EMDR, I asked her to bring up the dream image, the feelings of fear, anger, and guilt, and the negative belief about herself "I am guilty" as she followed my fingers with her eyes. What came up for her first was tremendous rage—she saw herself with a horrible face. With the next set of eye movements she entered into a very rich and detailed fantasy world in a primordial jungle setting. In this imagery a primitive mother is caring for her crying baby and brings her to safety. This was a very long inner journey, very moving and meaningful to Karen. She was totally involved and immersed in the story. Through this waking dream she was beginning to see that she could care for her crying baby, she *could* trust her own primitive instincts to do so. The baby's helplessness was not to be feared. In contact with her own mothering instincts—rather than a head full of obsessive worries she would know just what to do.

This EMDR session was full of dream-like imagery that was symbolic and very meaningful to her. She had a wide range of associations, from the jungle scene with the mother taking care of her baby, to pictures of her mother feeling guilty about something, to feelings of anxiety, fear, and apprehension, and back to a place of peacefulness. She was very absorbed in the processing, and it seemed to be flowing in a productive direction. Feelings of depression dissolved into an image of a beautiful landscape, and she again felt restored. At one point she saw a labyrinthine image that represented to her just how hard things had been for her in life. We both felt this to be a deep and powerful session. So much inner work was transpiring, to which I was mostly a witness and a facilitator. I could tell from her face and all of the changing emotions that she was processing very deep material.

At the end of the session I asked her to return again to the dream image with which we had started. She reported that the image had diminished and the feeling of guilt was gone. She said: "Authorities make mistakes. Mothers can make mistakes." We installed that cognition with another set of eye movements. The anxiety was not completely cleared from her system, though, and she reported a small lump in her throat when I asked her what she felt in her body. Nevertheless, she said she felt much better, calmer and more peaceful.

Twelfth Session (The Next Day)

This final EMDR session took both Karen and me over our "edges" into totally unknown territory, as thoughts and feelings that were forbidden and considered dangerous came forth. For much of the two hours I felt like we were on a death-defying roller coaster ride, holding on for dear life through tremendous ups and downs, all the while trusting that we would arrive safely at the end.

As a result of the successes in our previous sessions, Karen trusted me and had come to trust herself and her own innate capacity for healing. She had felt a lot of relief after our last session, and she was preparing to return home with her baby to her husband. She felt very good about the work that we had done. This session completed the healing Karen had come to do with me.

In this session she wanted to work on her fear and anxiety associated with sharp objects. Although the intensity had diminished, she still had fearful thoughts about hurting her baby with sharp objects. Because of this fear, she avoided being around knives and scissors. She was also hypersensitive to possible dangerous conditions, especially those that could harm her baby.

The target image we selected for the EMDR was of her holding a pair of scissors the day before. The emotion was intense fear. Her negative cognition was "Scissors are dangerous and I could kill someone." The belief she wanted to have was "I can use sharp objects without fear." Starting with the image, the fear, and the negative cognition, we began the eye movements.

Karen: ►◄►◄►◄ I am feeling afraid of stabbing myself. A memory has come up. I am enraged at my mother as a little girl. I am getting a knife from the drawer. The image has changed. I am stabbing myself. I am cutting my neck. My head falls back . . . I put the head back on. [*She is in the child's state; her memories and fantasies are all of the little girl. Her voice is high-pitched and soft, like a little girl's*].

LP: Stay with the fear and the image of putting the head back on.

Karen: ►◄►◄►◄ I am afraid of death.

LP: Let yourself die.

This is going over an edge for her. I am asking her to think about and imagine something that she has been terrified of all her life. I believed that openly exploring this material would help her to release the fear. During a long set of eye movements, Karen had an intense abreaction. Her face contorted with fear, she writhed on the couch, tears flowed from her eyes, and then she was silent.

Karen: [*speaking in a soft, full, awe-inspired voice*] I see myself dead and peaceful. It is a deeply peaceful feeling. I have never allowed myself to go into this. I have always feared death. As a child I rejected the Judeo-Christian religion with its heaven and hell because I didn't believe the story of Adam and Eve.

We stopped the eye movement work for a while, because she wanted to talk about the deep realization she had just had. With a sweet, peaceful smile on her face, she told me that she had spent her entire adult life working compulsively, keeping her mind occupied so that she would not have to face the question of her own mortality—which terrified her. She saw that the compulsive activity took her away from her deepest self. Having faced death, seen herself dead, she no longer feared it.

Now that she knew that death was not to be feared, she said that she wanted to slow down, enjoy her baby, work fewer hours, and begin to develop a spiritual life. She was deeply moved and felt a shift take place in her way of viewing herself and the world. She felt this to be a very profound insight, one that would change the way in which she lived her life.

She thought again about her fear of being killed. The image of the man climbing through her window came up. We did a set of eye movements. Then she said, "I don't have to be afraid. When death comes, it comes." Next she reported an image of a Monte Python picture.

Karen: ►◄►◄►◄ Fear of my baby being hurt. I am afraid of stabbing my baby.

LP: Imagine stabbing your baby.

Karen: I can't do that.

LP: It's OK. This is only in your imagination. Just go with it.

I am taking her over another edge into a forbidden, taboo area. This is the fear that was plaguing her from the beginning of our work together—the fear that she would act on the irrational, terrifying thoughts. I was asking her to think about and imagine the most forbidden act—killing her own child in a brutal, bloody way. I trusted the process, knowing that going through those images and feelings was essential for her to heal. We were going into totally unknown territory. I had no idea what would come up for her.

Karen: ►◄►◄►◄

This was a long set of eye movements and intense emotional release. Karen cried, hyperventilated, looked extremely upset. I kept her moving through it for several minutes with the eye movements. I had no idea what she was experiencing, but I was transfixed by her intensity and remained connected to her as she went through the process of releasing this old fear Suddenly she started to laugh, opened her eyes, and told me calmly and clearly what she had experienced.

Karen: I got a picture of myself killing my baby. I was stabbing her over and over again. She's a crazy woman. The baby laughs at her. She is full of holes . . . but she keeps smiling and laughing. *I can't kill my baby.*

She realizes the truth of the statement she has just made. She cannot kill her baby. Her fear has been that she could kill her baby, but she really could not. Her unconscious has given her a clear message about her capacity for committing such an egregious act. She feels totally relieved. The anxiety and tension she has been carrying just disappear.

Karen: ►◄►◄►◄ I saw pictures of all of the ways she [*the crazy woman*] could kill the baby. ►◄►◄►◄ I feel relaxed. The two selves, the crazy one and my usual self, are calm. The crazy woman dissolved. ►◄►◄►◄ I see a protective light around me, the baby, and my husband. The light is love. The crazy woman is outside of the light. I still feel apprehensive about the crazy woman.

LP: Go with the feeling of fearing the crazy woman.

Karen: ►◄►◄►◄ She turned into me as a little girl having tantrums. She is wild and out of control but not dangerous.

Karen realizes that this dangerous, crazy part of her self is none other than the little girl who is furious at her mother for having a baby and abandoning her . . . the same little girl who ran away, disobeyed her mother by climbing on the bookshelf, grabbed knives and scissors to get attention, and had wild tantrums . . . the same little girl who both loved and hated her little sister.

LP: Go with that understanding.

Karen: ►◄►◄►◄ I had images of the bad girl and the good girl selves. The good girl calms the bad girl. She feels better and they merge into one.

The split self-images of good versus bad that have always been experienced as separate are now recognized as parts of the same person. The bad girl is no longer disowned. The two parts become one integrated whole person who is both good and bad, loving and angry.

LP: Go back to the original picture of you holding a pair of scissors yesterday and tell me what comes up for you now.

Karen: The picture has very little feeling to it now. It seems like a movie. I feel distant from it. [*It seems that her SUDs is very low now.*]

LP: How true does the statement "I can use sharp objects without fear" feel to you now, as you bring up the image of holding the scissors?

Karen: It feels almost totally true, but I still feel some anxiety. I feel more time is needed for it to be totally true. You can't expect all of my anxiety to be gone after I've had it for a lifetime.

We did another set of eye movements combining the positive cognition with the image. She reported feeling calm and peaceful after that set. Her body was free of tension. It felt to her as if she had dropped a tremendous load of psychological and emotional baggage. Karen felt very good about all of the insights and releases and said she was ready to go on with her life. She was excited and hopeful for the future. She felt a deep connection to herself and to her baby girl. She recognized that more work on her fears and anxieties remained to be done but that she had accomplished a great deal.

Summary

Karen was a previously high-functioning woman with obsessive-compulsive tendencies who, after the birth of her baby, began to suffer from psychotic-like thoughts, deep depression, and overwhelming anxiety—all symptoms typical of postpartum depression. We worked intensively over four weeks, meeting several hours a week. The first sessions focused on history-taking, assessment, stabilization, anxiety reduction, and the development of a trusting working relationship. I used relaxation exercises and inner child work in the initial sessions to help ease her distress and for assessment purposes. Our initial EMDR session was also used primarily for anxiety reduction, for which it was not very effective, probably because the target was not well enough developed. Subsequent EMDR sessions were more focused due to developed targets that included disturbing images, emotions, body sensations, and negative cognitions. Karen's symptoms rapidly began to diminish following EMDR sessions, culminating in a significant improvement in functioning.

During the course of our work together Karen had several realizations that contributed to her rapid recovery. She realized that the real problem was that her childhood self wanted to kill her baby sister, not that her adult self wanted to kill her daughter. She understood then that her unconscious mind was merging the past and present. EMDR helped her to distinguish what was in the past (her anger at her baby sister and at her mother for having the baby) and what was in the present (her birth of a baby daughter).

She also realized that the crazy woman, of whom she was so afraid, was none other than her angry child self. Like Dorothy pulling the curtain on the threatening Wizard of Oz, Karen's ability to see the crazy woman for who she really was immediately depotentiated the image. She was then able to have compassion for the angry little girl who felt rejected and abandoned by her mother. The EMDR facilitated an integration of the previously split-off self constructs of good girl and bad girl. She realized that both good and bad were parts of the same person.

Karen came to understand that the feeling of badness she had lived with originated with her anger at her mother and baby sister. She saw that this feeling was in the distant past and that the little girl was hurt and angry, but not bad. The feeling of badness was cleared out of her system with the EMDR processing.

Karen also faced her fear of death with the EMDR. She'd had a scary experience when she was little: A bookshelf had toppled on her as she climbed on it, disobeying her mother. As Karen faced her fear of death, she was able to clear the emotional charge from the memory and found that her fear dissolved.

Lastly, she realized that she would not really hurt her baby daughter. The thoughts scared her, but she finally realized she would not act on them.

It is apparent that Karen's acute disturbance in the present was being triggered by unconscious material from the past. When we experience a traumatic event (like Karen's experience of having her helpless baby sister put in her room when she was three and told to take care of her), the event becomes locked into the body-mind *in the way it was experienced at the time*. Internal or external reminders of the event trigger the past experience, bringing it into consciousness in the original form. Karen's baby looked like her baby sister and was equally helpless, triggering the old memories of being the resentful and overwhelmed three-year-old with too much perceived responsibility.

In all likelihood the change in hormones after the birth of her baby also made her feel more childlike and vulnerable, further activating the child state. I also believe the hormonal changes she experienced served to amplify her preexisting psychological issues from childhood, thus leading to the terribly disturbing symptoms of postpartum depression. Many of these early psychological issues were related to the birth of her baby sister, which became triggered with the birth of her own baby. EMDR combined with inner child work helped Karen to reprocess and integrate these early experiences and to make sense out of what was happening to her.

The nurturing and comforting Karen received from me were also important to her recovery. I felt deep empathy for how unseen and ignored she felt by her mother, whom she had experienced as rejecting her as a young child and throughout her life, and who had once again abandoned her by leaving for Europe during Karen's time of crisis. She needed me to be there to care for her and empathize with her, as a good mother would. I believe that the EMDR therapy itself can be experienced by the client as a kind of empathic mirroring. If the therapist can mirror the client and be present with the client's unfolding process without interfering or controlling it, the client is likely to experience the therapy as healing.

Karen made a remarkable recovery. In four weeks' time she had significantly reduced her depression and anxiety; she no longer felt totally overwhelmed; she was sleeping and eating better; her level of self-care had greatly improved (she was now neatly groomed and dressed), and she was feeling optimistic about her future. The disturbing thoughts and fears of killing herself and her baby had significantly decreased. When thoughts did arise, she could recognize them as just thoughts-nothing to worry about. She was now able to feel deep love for her baby daughter, to bond with her and care for her. She felt ready to be with her husband and create the kind of family life she desired.

Karen knew that she had undergone a transformation that required time to integrate. She did not want to go back to her old compulsive way of living, filling every bit of her life with thoughts and activity. She wanted to slow down, enjoy her daughter, and explore the deeper questions about life and her reason for living. She wanted to explore her spirituality.

She promised to call me and let me know if she needed any further help, and I gave her the name of an EMDR-trained therapist in her city.

When she called me later that week, she told me that she continued to feel good and planned to fly out the next day to reunite with her husband. She felt her life had changed, but she also knew there was more to do. She continued to believe that hormonal changes brought about by the birth were contributing to her moodiness and anxiety. She felt very excited and satisfied with the work we had done.

Epilogue

Five years after our last session I called Karen to see how she was doing and to ask for her permission to write about her sessions with me. She told me that she had benefited a great deal from our EMDR sessions and my nurturing of her. Our work helped her to develop a new perspective on herself and the scary thoughts, which in turn allowed her to bond with her baby. Despite these positive changes, however, she continued to be plagued by the disturbing thoughts that seemed to be caused by a chemical imbalance brought about by the change in hormones after the birth of her baby. She sought help from a psychiatrist who prescribed medication for obsessive compulsive disorder. The medication was quite helpful to her and she used it prophylactically before giving birth to her next two children. With the combination of the medication and solid emotional support from family, friends, and her therapist the postpartum depression did not return with the births of her other children.

References

Beck, C. T. (1992). The lived experience of postpartum depression: A phenomenological study. *Nurse Research, 41*(3), 166–170.

Beck, C. T. (1993). Teetering on the edge: A substantive theory of postpartum depression. *Nurse Research, 42*(1), 42–48.

DeAngelis, T. (1997). There's new hope for women with postpartum blues. *APA Monitor, 28*(9), 22–23.

Goldstein, J. (1976). *The experience of insight.* Boulder, CO: Shambhala.

Parnell, L. (1996). Eye movement desensitization and reprocessing (EMDR) and spiritual unfolding. *The Journal of Transpersonal Psychology, 28*(2), 129–153.

Parnell, L. (1997). *Transforming trauma: EMDR.* New York: Norton.

Shapiro, F. (1995). *Eye movement desensitization and reprocessing: Basic principles, protocols, and procedures.* New York: Guilford Press.

Stowe, Z. N., & Nemeroff, C.B. (1995). Women at risk for postpartum-onset major depression. *American Journal of Obstetric Gynecology, 173*(2), 639–645.

Taylor, C. L. (1991). *The inner child workbook.* Los Angeles: Jeremy P. Tarcher, Inc.

Ugarriza, D. N. (1995). A descriptive study of postpartum depression. *Perspectives on Psychiatric Care, 31*(3), 25–29.

Whitfield, C. L. (1987). *Healing the child within.* Pompano Beach, FL: Health Communications, Inc.

3

EMERGING FROM THE COFFIN
Treatment of a Masochistic Personality Disorder

David Grand

MY ORIGINAL CLINICAL TRAINING, which was at a traditional psychoanalytic institute, instilled in me a classical analytic orientation (drive/
conflict) with a leaning towards developmental theory (ego psychology and
object relations). Feeling restricted by the detached, inactive analytic treatment stance I was assuming, I gradually evolved a more active, relaxed, human style in session. Maintaining a historical, developmental, and dynamic
perspective, I also incorporated interpersonal, cognitive, and systems orientations into my clinical approach.

Shortly after a colleague told me about his experimentation with EMDR,
I attended Level I training, where my powerful abreactive experience as client in the initial practicum convinced me of the power of the method. After
the training I tried EMDR with three clients of different diagnoses and backgrounds, who uniformly responded with rapid reprocessing that culminated
in a fading image and sense that the target was in the past and no longer of
much importance. Having never observed this commonality of response
from disparate clients, I could not help but believe that the clients had somehow consulted with each other and conspired to present themselves in an
identical manner!

With ongoing experience with EMDR, I began to anticipate this rapid
reprocessing effect. I also noticed some striking parallels with the analytic
approach: the significance of early childhood memories and the focus on
unconscious processes, insight, abreaction, catharsis, symbolism, and free
association. During EMDR the client is instructed to observe and report, if

69

they choose, any thoughts, feelings, bodily sensations, or memories that occur during each set of eye movements. However, in direct contrast with the analytic orientation, any immediate discussion of these associations is discouraged to avoid interference with the ongoing processing. Historically, in analytic therapy, free association has been used to plumb symbolic meanings expressed through dreams, screen memories, and parapraxes (e.g., slips of the tongue, mislaying of objects). I began asking clients if they would like to try processing these phenomena with EMDR and quickly found this to be a more reliable and efficient method of helping them understand the workings of their unconscious processes. I also observed that EMDR dramatically sped up the associative process, almost like putting a tape into fast forward. I refer to this as "accelerated associating."

I, as well as my clients, experienced the material elicited during EMDR processing as accurate and true, and I was startled by how inaccurate I had been in my prior assumptions. Accordingly, I found that using EMDR in hundreds of sessions clearly enhanced my analytic listening and sharpened my diagnostic skills in non-EMDR clinical work. Presently, I use varying degrees of EMDR with most of my clients.

Client's History and Background

Dan was a 48-year-old married man who, despite ten years of psychoanalytic treatment, awakened every morning with the image of lying dead in a coffin. This dovetailed with his experience of daily life as devoid of meaning and pleasure. Despite his apparent relentless suffering and preoccupation with death, Dan reported never having been actively suicidal. In fact, his life appeared to be oddly homeostatic. He sought out therapy at the urging of his wife, who was exasperated by his pervasive negativity.

The first year of his two-year treatment entailed weekly single sessions of an insight-oriented and supportive nature. Sporadic EMDR targeting was incorporated but usually not followed up because of his passive resistance. Early in the second year of therapy, Dan agreed to weekly double sessions of EMDR in the attempt to break through the treatment impasse. This paradigm shift initiated incremental change through direct processing of targeted core material. It took three months to fully reprocess the first protocol, with two and a half months needed to complete the second designated memory. Subsequent EMDR processing gradually accelerated, leading to a successful completion of Dan's therapy.

This case illustrates the successful use of longer-term EMDR characterized by the multiple sessions and many months to fully reprocess individual protocols. Treatment was completed, with Dan free of coffin fantasies and capable of experiencing hope, joy, and purpose for the first time in his life. His positive response, over time, indicates that individuals with characterological defenses can process, albeit incrementally, difficult material and ultimately reach a level of full resolution. Since my success with Dan, I have replicated this startling outcome with numerous clients in periods ranging from nine to 18 months. This was inconceivable for me in my pre-EMDR days when many years of treatment yielded far more limited results.

Dan had grown up in a chaotic family where he was exposed regularly to poor sexual boundaries and volatile parental arguments, which occasionally erupted into physical confrontations. His sister, three years his senior, engaged him in mutual masturbation from ages five through ten. Dan was also overstimulated by his mother's casual nudity and repeated exposure to the primal scene. These memories, as well as the intrusive sexual behavior of his sister, had been dissociated and were revealed through EMDR processing. He observed his father as "a broken man" who would trudge home after work from his self-described "daily torture." Dan's "escape from the madness" occurred every Saturday, when he would spend the entire day at the movies. This activity further embellished his active fantasy life, in which he would imagine himself possessing the power and control of a military hero, a star athlete, or a great lover, thereby attempting to counterbalance his pervasive inner experience of sadness, frustration, and impotence.

Dan had a small network of friends whom he described as "social outcasts like myself." Despite his high intellectual aptitude, he functioned at an average level and described his profile in school as "basically invisible." He struggled with high levels of self-consciousness and social inhibition. During early adolescence Dan became an avid reader, spending hours in his room lost in his books. By his mid-teens he was writing poetry and short stories, which heralded the emergence of healthy aspects of himself. Writing also served as a means of sublimating his emotions as well as a context for a new social network with other creatively oriented adolescents. In high school he excelled in English and formed positive identifications with a number of teachers. He also began to consider entering the field of teaching. Casting a pall over these healthy pursuits, however, were developing morbid fantasies that eventually coalesced into his awakening images of lying in a coffin.

Dan reported receiving no support or recognition for his accomplishments at home, where "life was crazier than ever." While attending a local college, Dan pursued a degree in education. Although he began to date, had his first girlfriend, and accomplished reasonable achievement in his studies, he became more entrenched in depressive feelings and beliefs. Despite above-adequate functioning, he experienced a constant undercurrent of emotional pain, obsessions, and self-denigrating fantasies. This pattern of suffering internally while maintaining external stability became Dan's oddly stable way of conducting his life.

After working as a teacher for five years, he became engaged to and married another teacher. Two years later she decided to switch careers, entering medical school. After ten years in education Dan followed his wife's example and returned to school to become a physician's assistant. Ultimately, they entered practice together, with Dan acting as administrator as well as a medical support staff. He described being comfortable in this subordinate position and apparent gender role reversal. They never actively considered parenthood, apparently not by design but by default.

Eight years ago, Dan's father died and his mother moved to Florida and remarried. Dan subsequently acted out years of accumulated resentment by rejecting his mother, refusing to see or call her, even ripping up the checks she sent for his birthday. He also maintained no contact with his sister after their father's death.

Diagnostic Assessment

The diagnostic assessment of Dan should be reviewed before addressing the case material. The key question to be considered is the validity of "masochistic personality disorder" as the designation in this case. The *DSM-IV* (1994) defines a personality disorder as "an enduring pattern of inner experience and behavior that deviates markedly from the expectations of the individual's culture, is pervasive and inflexible, has an onset in adolescence or early adulthood, is stable over time, and leads to stress and impairment" (p. 629). Although the category of "masochistic personality disorder" is not included in the current *DSM-IV*, it would appear to be subsumed under the Cluster C grouping, which includes avoidant, dependent and obsessive-compulsive personality disorders (p. 630).

For the purposes of this discussion, I use the terms *personality disorder* and *character disorder* interchangeably. These conditions are usually asymptomatic and infiltrate the entire personality (Moore & Fine, 1990). Whereas individuals with neurotic symptoms suffer internally, those with character pathology tend to induce discomfort in those around them. Successful treatment usually requires many years and involves endless complications and powerful resistances. Reich (1976) coined the term "character armor" to describe the impenetrable, externalized defensive barrier encountered when treating these individuals. Kernberg categorized the "depressive-masochistic personality structure" (1975, p. 16) as a high-level character type manifesting reaction formations. This is in contrast to the less developed structures of borderline personalities in whom splitting is the predominant defense mechanism. He suggests that the masochist's traits of intense guilt and self-punishment may derive from overstimulation during childhood sexual development.

Treatment

As noted above, the initial year of Dan's therapy entailed weekly sessions of a supportive and insight-oriented nature, with EMDR employed only occasionally and undermined by Dan's reluctance. At times he would "filibuster" follow-up sessions set aside for EMDR work with a ceaseless reporting of the week's events. Occasionally, he would refuse to engage in EMDR, which I respected as his need and right to maintain control of the treatment modality. Attempts to point out or interpret these patterns were unsuccessful. In retrospect, this first phase of treatment may be viewed as preparatory for the focused EMDR targeting undertaken in the second phase. During that phase, four major protocols comprised the bulk of his processing work.

Dan began by choosing to address his relationship with his father and selected as his target a memory from age seven. Perhaps as a result of extensive prior treatment, Dan had little difficulty choosing an appropriate target. However, this is not always the case for rigidly defended clients. Frequently, the inexperienced EMDR therapist is confounded by the client's dearth of memories carrying any affective charge. At times, he cannot identify any meaningful recollections, and generating resonant cognitions may also appear to be futile. Perseverance, flexibility, creativity, and confidence in the process are required to avoid a seemingly inevitable treatment impasse. Reviewing background history can suggest reasonable avenues for exploration, to which the client may have assigned little significance. Often the optimal entry point may be an external stressor experienced by the client in the present, even if accompanied by only one or two components of the protocol. The clinician may be faced with a structure of hundreds of doors, searching for the one that is unlocked. If one is lucky, the tenth knob turned will yield entry. Nevertheless, the determined therapist must be prepared to probe every last portal in order to locate the entry point. In my experience it is the rare individual who cannot be ultimately guided into some form of processing.

Fortunately, this was not the case with Dan. His initial protocol was determined easily as follows:

> *Target Image:* At age seven, Dan was struggling to assemble an electric motor, while his father hung over his shoulder saying, "You'll never get it. You can't do anything right."
> *Negative Cognition:* "I am worthless and deserve to be punished."
> *Positive Cognition:* "I am good enough."
> *Validity of Cognition (VOC)*[1]: 1.
> *Emotions:* depression, guilt, and frustration.[2]
> *Subjective Units of Disturbance Scale (SUDS)*[3]: 10.
> *Body Sensations:* Tightening in the chest and stomach.

In the first session eye movements were elicited by finger waving, with sets averaging between 20 and 30 repetitions (back and forth). Processing yielded the following dialogue.

Dan: ►◄►◄►◄ (20) I see him standing over me, and I'm feeling, *he's right.* I'll never get it. I'm a failure. I'm worthless. ►◄►◄►◄ (20) I keep on trying, but I just can't get it right. I feel frustrated and disgusted. ►◄►◄►◄ (25) I hear my father's voice echoing over and over, saying I'm no good, I can't do anything right, I'll never amount to anything. I feel hopeless and worthless. [*To this point the processing appeared to be looping. However, circuitous processing of material is to be expected with rigid individuals.*] ►◄►◄►◄ (25) The scene jumps to the living room with my father coming through the door groaning, "I'm back from my daily torture." I see him drag across the room, plop down and sag into his chair. He's staring straight ahead in a daze, and he looks rumpled. [*The process is beginning to move.*] ►◄►◄►◄ (30) Now I see my mother come into the room. She goes over and starts talking to my father about something. He just stares ahead blankly, and she just keeps on talking. The room looks dark and dreary. ►◄►◄►◄ (30) Now we are at the dining-room table. My sister is there. She and my mother are babbling on and on, and no one is listening. My father is eating dinner with all the joy of a prison inmate. The picture looks like a replay of any or every family meal.
DG: How are you feeling now?

---

[1] A scale rating the validity of the P.C. from 1 as totally false to 7 as totally true.
[2] Elicited when pairing the image and the negative cognition.
[3] A scale rating the level of distress from 0 as neutral to 10 as maximum.

Dan: Dead.

Despite this response, I had observed increased facial flushing, pupil dilation, accelerated respiration, as well as a tic-like twitching of Dan's hands and feet. Emotionally constricted individuals often manifest what I have labeled internal abreacting *in contrast to the more characteristic outward affective outbursts. These subtle phenomena usually presage deepening movement that may be easily overlooked. Dan's self-described deadness appeared to be a profound sense of hopelessness and despair, not the apparent absence of affect.*

Dan: ►◄►◄►◄ (30) I see myself in the coffin. I'm neither sad nor happy. I'm just there, lying there in the coffin, staring straight up with no expression on my face. ►◄►◄►◄ (30) I'm still in the coffin. There is a pillow under my head and a blanket over me. I hear some music in the background, but I can't make it out. ►◄►◄►◄ (30) Now I'm lying in my bed [*the coffin has metamorphosed*] with my head on the same pillow, covered with the blanket. I can still hear the music. It sounds classical with violins, but I can't make it out. ►◄►◄►◄ (30) The music sounds like Mozart. Why the hell would I be hearing that? [*Repressed material appears to be emerging.*]

DG: Go with the music and that question.

Dan: ►◄►◄►◄ (30) I'm on my bed, and I hear the Mozart playing while my parents are arguing. My mother is screaming at my father, and every once in a while he bellows back. [*pause*] My parents liked classical music, especially Mozart. They used to have it on the Victrola all the time when I was young. They also used to argue all the time. Some combo—Mozart and screaming. I must be to blame. I am worthless. I deserve to be punished. ►◄►◄►◄ (30) I'm back in the coffin. I'm feeling hopeless and worthless. Just lying there, feeling hopeless. [*His associations suggest that the coffin represents not only self-punishment but also serves as an escape.*] ►◄►◄►◄ (30) I am lying in the coffin, not moving. I don't know if I can't move, don't deserve to move, or don't want to move.

During the next few sets, Dan continues to fixate on these images and cognitions. I bring him back to the target, both to assess his progress and to attempt to reignite his processing.

DG: If you go back to the target image, what does it look like now?

Dan: It looks pretty much the same, except the focus looks slightly sharper.

It is essential to be aware that the original image changes in look and feel as a result of processing. As a rule, the therapist should encourage the client to return to the most recent image, not to the beginning image. To do otherwise is to confound the processing, which has accomplished the goal of moving the client ahead.

DG: If you put this image together with the belief, "I am worthless and deserve to be punished," what emotions do you feel?

Dan: Guilt, frustration, and sadness.

DG: If you rated these feelings from 10, which is the worst you can imagine, to 0, which is neutral, what number would you give to them now?

Dan: 9 or 10.

DG: And where do you feel them in your body now?

Dan: In my stomach. I'm tied up inside.

As evidenced by shifts in imagery, memory, affect, and body sensation, considerable process-ing had taken place, but with the barest movement of the distress level and the self-punitive ideation. As the end of the session (90 minutes) was approaching, I employed a closing exercise and then devoted the remaining ten minutes to debriefing.

At the beginning of the following session, we reviewed the events and the low-level processing Dan had observed during the course of the previous week. When discussing how to proceed with the EMDR, he was confused and needed direction.

Dan: Where should I start today?

DG: Let's go back to the target we worked with last week.

Dan: But that's not really where I'm at now. There is something else I would like to work with.

DG: It may be difficult to understand, but when you do not finish a protocol the previous week, it is important to return to it until it has been worked through. In all likelihood, you will probably go back to where you finished or jump ahead to where you need to be anyway.

Although EMDR is a highly client-centered process, the therapist must understand when to assert himself when issues of technical importance arise. In this case, the continued return to the target protocol until it was fully reprocessed (SUDS of 0 and VOC of 7) was essential in order for the treatment to provide maximum effect. The clinician who allows the target to wander from session to session without fully reprocessing the original protocol may facilitate significant client movement, but many problem areas, especially core issues, may remain unresolved. This is especially the case when working with individuals who protect themselves with seemingly impenetrable personality defenses.

After six weeks of processing the first protocol, Dan's SUDS level had dropped to 5. Following week two, I had incorporated the use of the mechanical light bar, which allowed for a higher number of eye movements (from 100 to 300) per set, as well as relieving the strain on the muscles of my shoulder and elbow. During the course of session six, I introduced a modification of technique I refer to as body processing, *aimed at softening the character armor (Reich, 1976). The following interchange illustrates this approach.*

DG: If you bring up the target image now, what does it look like?

Dan: It's harder to make it out. It seems further away [*evidence that movement has occurred*].

DG: When you put that image together with "I am good enough," how true does that statement seem to you now on a scale of 1 to 7, where 1 is totally false and 7 is totally true?

Dan: About a 4.

DG: And if you put that image together with the statement "I am worthless and deserve to be punished," what emotions come to you now?

Dan: Anger, confusion, frustration, guilt. [*The nature of the affect is changing.*]

DG: If you rate these emotions on a scale of 0 to 10, where 0 is neutral and 10 is the worst you can feel, what number would you give to it now?

Dan: 5.

DG: And where do you feel that 5 in your body now?

Dan: In my head [*a new location*].

DG: Take the image, the statement "I am worthless and deserve to be punished," and the emotions and feeling in your head, and follow the lights.

Dan: ►◄►◄►◄ (30) The feeling rose to the top of my head.

DG: Using your imagination, if there were an object either in or on your head creating that sensation, what would it be? [*As Dan was generating physical sensations, I decided to provide an augmentation by using imagery to further define his body experience.*]

Dan: A weight.

DG: What kind of weight?

Dan: You know, a metal plate like they use in a gym.

DG: Describe the size, shape, color, and temperature of the object.

Dan: Well, it's about three feet in diameter, it weighs 50 pounds, and it is black and cold.

DG: I want you to start with the sensation and image and see where it goes from there.

Dan: ►◄►◄►◄ (100) I turned around and told my father to leave me alone. I felt angry but afraid of his retaliation.

DG: What body sensations are you getting now?

Dan: The feeling on my head has eased. [*The retargeting has revealed a shift in the sensation and imagery.*]

DG: Describe the object now.

Dan: The plate is about one foot in diameter, ten pounds, gray and cool in temperature.

DG: Continue with the body sensations and imagery.

Dan: ►◄►◄►◄ (200) My father is backing away, and I am getting larger and he is getting smaller. I'm feeling less fear and guilt.

DG: What are you getting in your body now?

Dan: My head feels much less pressure. The plate is about two inches in diameter, a lighter gray, weighs about a pound, and is room temperature.

DG: Continue with the sensations in your head and the image.

Dan: ►◄►◄►◄ (200) Now I am the same size as my father, and I am looking at him face to face. He seems intimidated. This feels really strange.

DG: Body sensations?

Dan: Now I have a quarter on my head ►◄►◄►◄ (200) I flipped the quarter off my head. It feels clear now. I was even larger than my father, but instead of intimidating him like he did to me, I just walked away. I feel calmer and more in control. [*Repeatedly returning to body sensations and imagery appeared to focus and accelerate Dan's processing. He completed the session with a SUDS level of 4 and a VOC of 5.*]

For the subsequent four weeks, movement proceeded at the same gradual pace until Dan reached a SUDS of 1. Careful examination yielded that Dan was terrified of what would occur if he reached 0, because it represented a total surrender of control and entering into unknown territory. He also feared the hammer blow of his own self-punishment, which historically followed on the heels of allowing himself any successful goal attainment. Two more weeks of 90-minute sessions were necessary to complete the reprocessing. Ascending this final rung on the ladder was far more crucial and challenging than any preceding step, because it represented accepting the success he had previously denied himself. The following is an excerpt from the last session of the first protocol.

DG: What does the image look like now?

Dan: It looks far off in the distance, almost at the horizon.

DG: If you put the image together with the belief "I am worthless and deserve to be punished," what do you get now?

Dan: It's simply not true.

DG: Are you feeling any distress at all?

Dan: I'd like to say 0, but I'm afraid. It still feels like a risk for me. I'm afraid of being punished.

DG: Why don't you go with that?

Dan: OK. ►◄►◄►◄ (100) I saw myself with my hands extended over a cliff, holding onto another image of myself hanging from the cliff. I feel in danger. [*Is this regression or moving towards a final resolution?*] ►◄►◄►◄ (150) I pulled my other self up to safety, and I comforted myself. Then we embraced each other. I'm beginning to feel safe now [*confirmation of the positive*]. ►◄►◄►◄ (150) [*smiling*] As we were embracing, we blended into one being. Then we walked away from the cliff to safety [*a graphic symbol of healthy integration*]. ►◄►◄►◄ (200) I went back and told my father that I can forgive him now for putting me down. He smiled and embraced me. [*The internalizations are now reprocessing.*]

DG: What do you get when you bring up the target image now?

Dan: The horizon at sunset. A peaceful feeling.

DG: If you put the image together with the belief "I am worthless and deserve to be punished," what do you get now?

Dan: [*smiling broadly*] It's a 0. I can take the risk now. I am clear. ►◄►◄►◄ (100) Things stayed the same.

DG: What number would you now give to rate the statement "I am good enough," with 1 being totally false and 7 being totally true?

Dan: [*without hesitation*] 7. ►◄►◄►◄ (30) [*Fewer repetitions are usually necessary to install the positive cognition.*] I'm there. A 7 is a 7 is a 7!

One might have expected the profound breakthrough of Dan's first successfully completed protocol to have generalized in significant ways to other areas of his internal life. Despite the shift, however, he was still awakening with coffin images, although they were slightly less intense. The limited effect was also evidenced by the equally high level of disturbance elicited by the subsequent targets addressed. In my clinical experience, this restricted ability to transfer major shifts from one mental sphere to another is characteristic of individuals with a matrix of rigidly self-protective personality defenses. (This need to tightly defend the self appears to be in response to countless, early micro-traumas, as illustrated by Dan.) However, a positive result from the initial reprocessing was observed in the enhanced speed and quality of processing in the EMDR work that followed. The second protocol focused on issues with Dan's mother.

Target Image: I am about age six or seven, and my mother is walking through the living room with no clothes on. I am secretly staring at her, and I feel aroused and mortified.

Negative Cognition: "I am dirty and deserve to be punished."

Positive Cognition: "I am normal."

VOC: 1.

Emotions: Arousal, disgust, anxiety, guilt, humiliation, and anger.

SUDS: 10

Body Sensations: Heat in the genital area and a nauseous feeling in the chest and throat.

DG: Hold together the image, the belief "I am dirty and deserve to be punished," your emotions, and the body sensations, and follow the light.

Dan: ►◄►◄►◄ (50) She walked across the room and into the bedroom. I watched her all the way, aroused but feeling guilty and dirty. ►◄►◄►◄ (50) I lost the picture, but I feel a sickening fear in my gut. ►◄►◄►◄ (100) I have the feeling that I'm in the bedroom with my mother, and I feel aroused, afraid, and terribly guilty. Did this really happen, or am I making it up?

DG: Process the image, your feelings, and that question.

Dan: ►◄►◄►◄ (100) I think I'm three or four now. I see myself in bed with my mother. She has no clothes on, and I have an erection. This is very weird. What's going on?

DG: The best way to find out is to keep on processing; continue on.

Dan: ►◄►◄►◄ (50) Although my mother isn't touching my penis, she is cuddling me, and I think she is enjoying my being aroused. I feel excited, but I'm also ashamed and afraid. Could this have really happened?

DG: All we can know for certain now is that you are getting these images. You'll ultimately make your own determination about it. Keep going.

Dan: ►◄►◄►◄ (200) I now remember being terrified that my father would walk in. I also felt aroused and very confused. ►◄►◄►◄ (200) It's over, and I wasn't caught. I feel very relieved but also guilty and angry. How could she have done this to me? ►◄►◄►◄ (200) I feel like it's over, and yet it's not over. I keep on playing this scene over and over.

DG: What are you feeling in your body now?

Dan: I can't really identify anything.

Dan's reported absence of physical sensations precluded the use of body processing to break through this apparent blocking. I accordingly incorporated an alternative technique—

repeated returns to the target—which I have also found effective in surmounting points of resistance.

DG: If you bring up the target image, what does it look and feel like to you now?

Dan: It looks the same, but it feels slightly less intense.

DG: Process the image and feelings.

Dan: ►◄►◄►◄ (50) The picture looks a bit further away and feels slightly less frightening and confusing. ►◄►◄►◄ (100) [*silence*]

DG: When you bring up the image now, what does it look and feel like?

Dan: My mother is walking out of the room. I see her from the back.

DG: And how does it feel to you now?

Dan: A little less threatening, but I still feel guilt and shame.

DG: Go ahead with the picture and those feelings.

Dan: ►◄►◄►◄ (100) A little more distant. [*With 15 minutes left in the session, I decided to move the processing to a close. I checked the SUDS and VOC ratings to assess movement.*]

DG: If you put the image together with the statement "I am dirty and deserve to be punished," what level of distress do you get now?

Dan: About a 9.

DG: If you put the image together with the statement "I am normal," how true does it seem to you now?

Dan: About a 1 or 2.

The repeated return to the target appeared to succeed in catalyzing further movement when the blocking arose. However, despite the active processing in this double session, as with the first protocol, a dramatic shift in the rating scales did not occur. This incremental pattern continued as sessions proceeded. After five sessions devoted to the second protocol, the SUDS had dropped to 4 and the VOC had risen to 4. Dan started the sixth session by presenting this dream from the preceding night.

Dan: I want to tell you about this disturbing dream I had last night. It really freaked me out. I'm still buzzing from it. I was walking down the street when I heard noises that sounded like somebody was being beaten coming from a house. I pushed through the bushes and looked into a side window and witnessed a woman hitting a man with a blackjack. She knocked him down and kept on striking him while he lay motionless on the ground. I was completely immobilized while witnessing this, feeling both horrified and fascinated. My excitement only sickened me more. My eyes were glued to the scene, and I kept watching and watching.

Prior to learning EMDR, I would have responded by using psychoanalytic dream interpretation, directing Dan to free associate to different aspects and symbols in his dream. This would be followed by a collaborative analysis of his associations and insights, leading to a hypothetical understanding of the material in the context of what had been transpiring in his treatment. However, I have found EMDR to be a far more accurate and reliable tool in deciphering the coded communication of dream symbolism. This is illustrated in the following interchange.

DG: Can you process this dream as a whole, or do you need to target parts of it?

Dan: I can target it as a whole ►◄►◄►◄ (100) [*shocked*] I'm remembering seeing my parents having sex. I heard grunting noises coming from my parents' bedroom. The door was half open, so I looked in. My mother was on top of my father, and she was moving furiously while he lay motionless. It looked like a mugging. I was horrified, but I didn't turn away. I just stood there watching. I felt dirty and worthless. ►◄►◄►◄ (100) This happened more than once, but I don't know how many times I saw it. At times, I've had a haunting sense of this image, but I never remembered this event before.

DG: How old do you think you were?

Dan: Five or six. ►◄►◄►◄ (200) [*with astonishment*] I realized that the image of my lying passively in a coffin is just like the way my father was lying there motionless underneath my mother ►◄►◄►◄ (200) I saw my father lying next to me in the coffin. We were both dead . . . punished but at peace. [*pause*] The coffin is both a punishment and an escape for me. My father and I are escaping our torture. ►◄►◄►◄ (150) I am back alone in the coffin, put out of my misery.

DG: Who put you out of your misery?

Dan: [*pause*] Me. I guess I'm both the executed and the executioner.

DG: Does that mean the power to resolve it lies within yourself?

Dan: It must. If I put myself in the coffin, then I suppose I can take myself out of it.

A cognitive interweave is typically used to facilitate movement when a client is stuck. However, my intervention here is an example of a dynamic interweave aimed at accelerating or focusing unimpeded processing. In analytic treatment an interpretation is properly timed when it elicits preconscious material about to break through to consciousness. The same criterion applies to effective application of a dynamic interweave. In the above interchange, my listening perspective suggested to me that Dan was close to grasping emotionally that his struggles were between different aspects of himself. The realization that his primary conflicts were internal led to his recognition that these crippling issues could possibly be resolved within himself—in fact, only within himself.

This sixth session of the second protocol addressing Dan's mother's poor sexual boundaries started with his dream. The protocol had not been incorporated into this session to this point. I have found that, in these instances, returning directly to the target for a few sets of eye movements can weave together the content of the session into the ongoing information processing. The session finished as follows.

DG: If you go back to the target now, what do you get?

Dan: I feel less connected to the image of my mother.

DG: If you combine that image with the statement "I am dirty and deserve to be punished," what emotions do you get now?

Dan: I still feel like I'm bad, only not as much. I do feel angry about what both my parents exposed me to. I didn't need that.

DG: What level of distress does that bring to you now?

Dan: It feels like a 3.

DG: Where do you feel it in your body?

Dan: A mild tightness in my chest.

DG: Go with the image, the belief that "I am dirty and deserve to be punished," your emotions, and the tightness in your chest.

Dan: ►◄►◄►◄ (100) My mind jumped around. First, I saw my mother walking across the room. Then I saw myself in bed with my mother. Then I saw my parents in bed. Then I saw myself in the coffin with my father. Then I was in the coffin alone. ►◄►◄►◄ (100) My mind is clearer. I feel more relaxed.

By the ninth session of this second protocol, the SUDS level had dropped to 1, with the VOC rating at 6. Again, Dan feared the letting go entailed in taking the final step of completion. By the end of the session, he assessed his distress as "almost 0." Following are excerpts from the tenth and final session in the second protocol.

DG: If you go back to the target image, what does it look like now?

Dan: The image of my mother looks almost blanched out.

DG: If you put this image together with the belief "I am dirty and deserve to be punished," what emotions do you feel now?

Dan: Very slight discomfort.

DG: If you rated the discomfort from 10 being the worst, to 0 being neutral, what number would you give to it now?

Dan: A shade over 0.

DG: What makes it that shade over, instead of a clear 0?

Dan: It's probably a 0, but I don't want to admit it.

DG: Why is that?

Dan: It's a risk . . . like climbing out of the coffin. I'm not happy there any-more, but it still represents safety. Although it's changed, I still wake up with the coffin image. I haven't given it up yet.

DG: Do you feel any sensation in your body now?

Dan: A mild flutter in my stomach.

DG: Hold together what's left of the image, the belief "I am dirty and de-serve to be punished," any emotions you still have, and the stomach flutter.

Dan: ►◄►◄►◄ (50) I saw my adult self saying to my mother, "Why don't you cover yourself up? I don't need to see that." She went into her room and got a robe. I feel like I've taken control of the situation. The flutter is gone from my stomach. ►◄►◄►◄ (100) Now I'm talking to mother and my father. I'm telling them I don't want them to expose me to sex or fighting anymore. Enough of the craziness. I tell them not to take away the Mozart, though, since I gained an appreciation of music that way.

The imagery produced during these last two sets exemplifies movement into pictorial represen-tations of positive cognitions. This spontaneous phenomenon, usually manifested via thought or emotion, is a pure form of reprocessing that should be encouraged whenever it emerges.

Dan: ►◄►◄►◄ (100) I'm ready to say 0 now.

DG: How does that feel to you?

Dan: Good. I can take control of my life now.

DG: Does the positive belief "I am normal" still fit for you now?

Dan: I like "I am good" better.

DG: If you put "I am good" together with whatever remains of the image, how true does it seem to you now?

Dan: [*immediately*] 7.

DG: Go with that.

Dan: I don't really need to.

DG: Humor me.

Dan: [*smiling*] OK. ►◄►◄►◄ (30) Like I always say, a 7 is a 7 is a 7!

Despite the resolution of these two major protocols, Dan continued to experience discomfort around the issue of betrayal. He described how he remained obsessed with an incident in which his wife, before their engagement, had a sexual liaison with a professor while studying in a summer program out of state. The third protocol was set up as follows.

Target Image: I see Ellen in bed with this guy Ted. He is giving her more satisfaction than I ever could. She has forgotten me.

Negative Cognition: "I am worthless and deserve to be betrayed."

Positive Cognition: "I am worthy of loyalty."

VOC: 2.

Emotions: Anger, anxiety, humiliation, guilt.

SUDS: 10.

Body Sensations: A tight feeling in the chest and stomach.

DG: Hold together the image, the belief "I am worthless and deserve to be betrayed," your emotions, the feeling in your chest and stomach, and proceed.

Dan: ►◄►◄►◄ (50) I'm looking through a door at Ellen in bed with Ted. I feel small, betrayed, and left out.

What follows is an example of the dynamic interweave in the form of Socratic questioning. This is an effective technique that can deepen and accelerate the resolution of conflict or trauma when properly applied. It is ideally activated by a well-timed, leading inquiry that will likely be responded to in the affirmative. The positive retort can then be immediately installed with great effectiveness. For example, an attuned reading of facial cues or body language might generate the question, "Are you angry?" Thus the client is guided into introspection, leading to a spontaneous reply—usually an emphatic yes. In this open-ended procedure, the client's neurophysiological system is stimulated to produce internally accurate material, as opposed to the unreliable responses elicited when suggestions are given by the therapist. I sensed here that the timing was right to introduce a mildly directive question that would likely lead to a predictably desired reply.

DG: Does that remind you of anything?

Dan: You mean, watching my parents? ►◄►◄►◄ (100) I just realized that I felt betrayed by my parents, not just because they exposed me to their sex but because they left me out as well! ►◄►◄►◄ (100) I'm in the room with Ellen and Ted, and they invite me into the bed. Reluctantly I get in. I don't feel so excluded, but I am confused. I'm afraid to be there, but I'm also afraid of getting thrown out. ►◄►◄►◄ (200) We get into this discussion, Woody Allen-like, of which two of us can stay and which one should leave. Ted and I even discuss having Ellen leave. We decide to all stay together for now, and I remain confused. ►◄►◄►◄ (200) I now find myself in a small dark room. I can barely make out anything but a slight reflection on the wall. I feel sick to my stomach.

DG: Hold that feeling and go ahead.

Dan: ►◄►◄►◄ (100) There is somebody else in the room. It looks like a girl. I feel very nervous and my stomach is turning over. ►◄►◄►◄ (100)

It's my sister. We are in the bathroom. I feel afraid. I also feel ashamed. She's doing something to me. What's happening ►◄►◄►◄ (100) My sister is rubbing my penis, and she's rubbing my hand on her vagina. Is this real, or am I making this up? ►◄►◄►◄ (100) [with uncharacteristic tears in his eyes] It did happen. I must have completely blocked it out. I think this happened when I was six or seven. My sister is three years older than I. [pause] No wonder I'm so screwed up. ►◄►◄►◄ (100) I feel afraid and ashamed, but I also feel stimulated. ►◄►◄►◄ (100) I feel like I'm worthless—like a rag doll to be used like a plaything and then thrown away. ►◄►◄►◄ (100) I'm starting to feel angry. How could she do this to me? I'm her brother. No wonder I'm so screwed up. [I have repeatedly observed that redirecting anger outward signals a turning point for the trauma victim, who has heretofore felt worthless and responsible for the abuse.] ►◄►◄►◄ (50) I see myself grabbing my hand away from my sister and pushing her hand off of me. I get up and run out of the bathroom. ►◄►◄►◄ (100) I can take control of my body. I can take control of my life. [Dan is spontaneously generating positive cognitions.]

DG: [nearing the end of the session] If you go back to the target, what does it look like and feel like to you now?

Dan: Ellen is now in bed by herself. Ted is gone. Things look and feel less charged now.

DG: If you put this picture together with the statement "I am worthless and deserve to be betrayed," what level of distress comes to you now on a scale of 0 to 10?

Dan: 4, 5. I still have a lot of mixed feelings. I feel confused, afraid, ashamed, angry.

This was the first EMDR session in which Dan's distress level showed a significant diminution (from 10 to 4, 5), suggesting that his rigid character protection was softening and a network of more adaptive defenses was forming. The emergence of the memories of his sister's intrusive sexual behavior, although overwhelming, were not shattering to him. The memory retrieval and the opportunity to process these profound events also appear to have contributed to the substantial drop in disturbance. Only two additional sessions were required to fully reprocess this protocol, in contrast to the months needed to complete the first two. The final target was developed as follows.

DG: What would you like to address now?

Dan: Despite all the changes, I'm still waking up with the coffin image, even though it feels far less gripping. Is it possible that if we worked with it, I might finally let it go?

DG: What do you think?

Dan: It's possible.

DG: The only way to know is to try it and see what happens. What does the image look like when you bring it up now?

Dan: I see myself lying in a coffin made of polished wood with metal handles. The coffin is on the floor of my bedroom. There is a blank expression on my face. I am alive, but I know I'm in a coffin, which is for the dead.

DG: What negative belief goes best with the picture?

Dan: I can't live life.

DG: What would you like to believe about yourself?

Dan: I can live life and enjoy it.

DG: If you combine the image with the statement "I can live life and enjoy it," how true does this feel to you now, where 1 is totally false and 7 is totally true?

Dan: About a 3.

DG: If you put the image together with the belief "I can't live life," what emotions do you feel now?

Dan: Sadness and frustration.

DG: If you rated how distressing the sadness and frustration feel to you now, with 10 being the worst possible and 0 being neutral, what number would you give it?

Dan: It feels like a 6.

DG: Where do you feel it in your body now?

Dan: I feel a heaviness throughout my body.

DG: Hold together the coffin image, the belief "I can't live life," your emotions, the heaviness in your body, and follow the light.

Dan: ►◄►◄►◄ (50) This is weird. There are helium balloons attached all around the coffin, and it is gently floating up into the air. [*The shift from somatic heaviness to images of lightness suggests reprocessing is quickly beginning.*] ►◄►◄►◄ (50) The coffin is hanging in the air, and it slowly starts to rock back and forth. (100) The rocking is making me feel nauseous. [*The shift from imagery to body sensations often foreshadows significant processing activity.*]

DG: Where do you feel it in your body? ►◄►◄►◄ (100) Now I'm feeling the nausea in my chest [*moving upward*].

DG: Using your imagination, if there were an object in or on your chest, what would it be?

Dan: Hundreds of feathers swirling in my chest. ►◄►◄►◄ (150) I feel the feathers up in my throat [*moving higher*].

This fluctuation in location and form of body sensations during processing is often a diagnostic indicator of anxiety or panic conditions. However, the emergence of anxiety in Dan at this juncture in treatment is a reflection of the ego-syntonic character pathology becoming ego-dystonic. It is this experience of discomfort that can spur real growth and change in the individual. The movement upward also suggests the expelling of feelings or beliefs that have been trapped inside.

Dan: ►◄►◄►◄ (150) The feathers are swirling in my head, and there are less of them than before. [*The shift here is not only up from the chest but to fewer feathers.*] ►◄►◄►◄ (200) The feathers are floating out of my mouth and into the air. [*The body processing is moving towards resolution.*] ►◄►◄►◄ (200) All the feathers are out. [*The process is completed.*]

DG: What are you getting in your body now?

Dan: My body feels clear.

DG: If you go back to the target, what does it look like now?

Dan: The coffin is back on the floor, and I'm sitting up in it [*further confirmation of significant movement in the processing*]. ►◄►◄►◄ (50) I have one leg out of the coffin. I can't believe it, but I feel pretty calm. ►◄►◄►◄ (50) I'm sitting on the edge of the coffin with both feet on the ground. I feel a bit apprehensive about getting up. ►◄►◄►◄ (50) I'm standing up now, looking down at the coffin. I feel wobbly, but it's good to be out. ►◄►◄►◄ (50) I'm standing up more confidently now.

DG: [*nearing the end of the session*] If you put this image together with the statement "I can't face life," what number, from 10 being the worst to 0 being none, rates the distress you feel now?

Dan: 1. There is that little corner of me that's still hanging on.

DG: If you put together the image with the statement "I can face and enjoy life," how true does it feel to you now, from 1 being totally false to 7 being totally true?

Dan: I would give it a 6—not quite all the way there.

In the previous session Dan demonstrated accelerated processing, confirmed by the significant movement on the rating scales, while addressing core issues. This progress suggested the development of greater "elasticity" in his previously inflexible ego mechanisms. His profound accomplishment in emerging from the coffin was reflected by meaningful changes in his daily life: his relentless state of suffering dissipated as he began to allow himself simple enjoyments. He became more assertive in relationships and treated himself to gifts, such as vintage movie posters and desirable theater tickets. He also renewed his hobby of gourmet cooking. The session that follows reflects Dan's final resolution of his personality disorder.

Dan: I'm afraid to jinx myself, but for three straight mornings I've awakened with no coffin images. I also had three great days. ►◄►◄►◄ (50) I saw myself at a riverbank, pushing the coffin into the river [*further confirmation of his letting go*]. ►◄►◄►◄ (50) The coffin slowly floated away in the river. I saw it drift farther and farther off, until it was completely out of sight. I felt a strange sense of sadness, like I was saying goodbye to an old friend [*reflecting an appropriate sense of mourning for a departed aspect of the self*]. ►◄►◄►◄ (100) [*with tears in his eyes*] After the coffin slipped out of sight, it slowly returned. It changed into a basket carrying a baby, like Moses in the bulrushes. The basket drifted over to me, and I realized the baby was myself [*clear imagery of a spiritual rebirth*]. ►◄►◄►◄ (100) [*Dan's crying reflects his newly developed ability to abreact outwardly.*] I picked up the baby, held it, and said, "I will take care of you now." I walked away from the riverbank holding the baby to my chest.

DG: [*long pause*] If you bring up the coffin image now, what do you see? [*I am probing to determine if the reprocessing has been completed.*]

Dan: That image is gone. I now see myself looking in the mirror. My reflection speaks to me and says, "I love you." [*This is a powerful confirmation of reprocessing.*]

DG: If you put this image together with the belief "I can't live life," what number would you give to it now?

Dan: [*crying while smiling*] 0 . . . definitely 0! [*Another shift is reflected by Dan speaking for the first time during the 100 repetitions.*] The reflection in the mirror is my friend. I'm a different person now. I don't have to be afraid. I can face the person in the mirror. I can take an active role in shaping my destiny. I can love myself. I can shape circumstances in the world to give myself reasons to love myself. [*This is another example of spontaneously generating positive cognitions, which is the highest form of reprocessing.*]

DG: I suppose it is superfluous to ask you to give a number to your statement "I can live life"?

Dan: A 7 is a 7 is a 7!

Before finishing, I briefly reassessed all previously completed protocols that had remained fully reprocessed. I have found this to be a valuable practice before considering termination of treatment. Any targets with SUDS levels that have climbed above 0 or VOCs that have dropped below 7 should be reprocessed to a point of full resolution. Only when all previous issues have remained fully reworked are discussions of finishing therapy in order.

However, EMDR clinicians should not assume that the (longer-term) client's emotional integration, symptom elimination, and an improved level of functioning are sufficient criteria to immediately end sessions. The essential aspect in treatment is the relationship itself. This healing environment exists apart from the defined objectives and goals of the process. The timing of the severing of this human bond should be handled with sensitivity and attunement and mutually negotiated. The corrective experience of determining the conclusion of therapy is both required and deserved by people who have suffered the total loss of choice and control entailed in their histories of severe trauma. Even those seen in brief therapy may form a significant attachment, resulting from their profound treatment experience, which may need to be addressed with one or two additional concluding sessions.

Dan chose to finish after three more sessions, two for verbal debriefing, saving the final meeting for a celebration of our success. He discussed how he had decided to reconnect with his mother. He realized that she was a vulnerable old woman no longer capable of invading his boundaries. Dan visited his father's grave and described his catharsis in verbalizing sentiments of forgiveness and loss. He was then able to recognize the positive qualities and experiences he had internalized from both of his parents.

Dan took charge of the details for the "graduation session." He arranged a spread of kosher delicatessen on my desk: corned beef, pastrami, pickles, and fresh rye bread. I decided not to tell my host that I don't eat meat and indulged in the thick sandwich. To me, the way Dan asserted and expressed himself in a very personal manner in taking control of this concluding session was both a sign and an experience of his having resolved his passivity and masochism. He emotionally expressed his appreciation for my helping him to come alive. I expressed my mixed feelings regarding his termination feeling thrilled by his accomplishments but sad in saying goodbye to an "old friend."

Discussion of Diagnosis and Specific Treatment Technique

As noted in the beginning of this chapter, Dan fulfilled most of the diagnostic criteria for the diagnosis of masochistic personality disorder. He held the longstanding belief that he deserved to suffer, and he carried a pervasive sense of worthlessness. His internal experience was both stable and ego-syntonic, and the good/bad splitting tendencies of borderline pathology were relatively absent in his thinking processes and object relations. Dan's "character armor" and his investment in self-defeat had negated the effect of prior treatment attempts.

Herman presented the viewpoint that individuals suffering the aftereffects of repeated trauma are often mislabeled as having personality disorders. They may be labeled as "'dependent,' 'masochistic,' or 'self-defeating'" (1992, p. 117). She posited that treatment will be effective only if directed at healing the corrosive effects of the traumatic events on the victim's self-perception and self-esteem. Shapiro corroborated this viewpoint, observing that "global diagnoses, such as personality disorder, often serve to chain the client to an immovable object" (1995, p. 52). She recommended avoiding the trap of diagnostic labeling by attending to the earlier experiences that can be located on a continuum of trauma. Dan's condition can also be seen as trauma-based, since he was sexually stimulated as a young child by his sister and was exposed to relentless family chaos, verbal abuse, and porous sexual and personal parental boundaries.

EMDR can serve as a powerful, accurate diagnostic tool. For example, when movement is blocked or when glacially incremental reduction in the SUDS distress rating occurs, despite active processing in session, it often signifies that an underlying personality or dissociative disorder is present. Both types of disorders arise from exposure to repeated early trauma, which forces the development of pervasive, primitive defenses. The diagnostic differential between characterological and dissociative tendencies usually appears with continued application of EMDR. In time, either the hardened, stable personality defenses of a characterological disorder or the manifestations of flashback or alter phenomena will tend to emerge.

Accomplishing significant movement with individuals impaired by personality disorders is extremely difficult with any clinical approach. The question of the effectiveness of EMDR with this population remains controversial. Many experienced EMDR practitioners report difficulty in accomplishing any meaningful growth with clients possessing rigid, ego-syntonic, maladaptive character features. By contrast, I find that EMDR is demonstrably the most effective clinical tool in altering character structure, as illustrated in this chapter examining Dan's successful therapy. I have repeatedly facilitated this outcome with people suffering from either personality or dissociative conditions. However, modifications of technique and longer terms of treatment are regularly required to address the special needs of these populations. Additionally, no meaningful work can proceed unless rapport and sufficient trust have been established—and such connections cannot be rushed.

The novice EMDR therapist is frequently able to observe startlingly powerful and rapid results from the simple application of the protocol combined with eye movements or other modes of bilateral stimulation. In contrast, the advanced practitioner is challenged by experiencing EMDR as an increasingly technical procedure. As illustrated above, Dan's successful treatment outcome required negotiating a variety of modifications in technique. These included pursuing a complete 0 on the SUDS and repeated returns to target. Additional technical variations discussed in this chapter included the dynamic interweave, dream processing, organizing by retargeting at session's end, and reassessing previously completed targets.

Shapiro (1995) stressed the importance of pursuing the designated target and its derived protocol until complete desensitization and reprocessing has been accomplished, as indicated by attaining a 0 level on the SUDS and a VOC rating of 7. Often this occurs rapidly, and the protocol is completed in one to two extended sessions. However, with clients possessing systemic character pathology, even with the application of EMDR's accelerated information processing, change may be so gradual that it can appear almost imperceptible. As demonstrated with Dan, it is crucial to persevere with one protocol to a point of completion. Uniformly, this population has experienced repeated early traumas; accurate EMDR targeting of these events eventually results in a softening of the rigid defense structure and in increased relatedness, both within the self and with others. However, significant progress in the SUDS and the VOC levels may require many weeks and, at times, months of treatment. Unfortunately, many therapists accustomed to the lightning-quick shifts frequently seen with EMDR erroneously assume the procedure is ineffective and abandon it prematurely.

I have found that high counts of eye sweeps (100 to 200 or more) are needed to facilitate movement of concretized material and deeply distorted beliefs. Processing for the profoundly defended often does not commence until more than 100 repetitions. Limiting the number of saccades from 25 to 50 can contribute to clinicians' misperception of treatment failure. Therapists' intensifying arm fatigue can also preclude their discovering the value of increased stimulation. The alternate use of hand tapping or light or sound machines helps to minimize this restriction.

Bodily sensations are invaluable focal points for processing. The centrality of the somatic experience in EMDR is highlighted by its inclusion in the four-stage assessment. The clear body scan is additionally the fundamental criterion used to verify the completion of a treatment protocol. Physical reactions are often activated by attending to a traumatic memory; they may also be a component of the sensory experience of the target trauma itself (i.e., an accident or an attack) or elicited by the resonance of the negative cognition.

EMDR is traditionally initiated by the induction of eye movements while simultaneously holding in one's awareness the image, the negative cognition,

the associated affect, and the tactile sensations. However, effective processing can be elicited by targeting the soma when the image and cognition are
absent. There are rationales for deliberately targeting the physical response
despite the availability of images, cognitions, and affective material. This
technical modification can bypass blockages to processing or reduce agitation for clients who respond with problematic levels of flooding, regression,
or dissociation. Additional useful approaches include the symbolic imaging of
physical perceptions, repeated returns to body target, and reprocessing of "traveling" and metamorphosing sensations. Particularly effective is the application of body processing to the treatment of somatically charged conditions,
such as hypochondriasis, panic disorders, chronic fatigue, pain, and other
somatic-based conditions (i.e., TMJ, muscle spasms, headaches, irritable
bowel syndrome, and asthma).

Shapiro stated that a protocol is completed when the client's SUDS level
has been desensitized to a 0 or a 1. She also states that "stopping the sets
prematurely may leave important unexplored areas or unwarranted levels of
disturbance" (1995, p. 157). Dan's treatment illustrates the profound experiential difference between a 1 and a 0 on the SUDS, especially in the extended treatments where each drop of a numerical notch represents the
bridging of a wide chasm. For Dan, this final step in every protocol posed
the greatest challenge and was essential for full resolution. Accordingly, the
significance of the differential between 0 and I should be carefully assessed
on a case specific basis before moving ahead to the next phase of treatment.

Another feature of this case was the use of repeated returns to target,
which can facilitate overcoming impasses or accelerate lagging movement.
Following each set of eye movements, the usual opportunity is provided for
reflection. The client is then instructed to return to the image and negative
cognition, even if processing has resumed. Varied numbers of repetitions are
employed after each application. Four to six of these returns to target often
serve as a change of pace that effectively reactivates a meaningful flow of
associations.

Follow-Up

On the one-year anniversary date of his conclusion of therapy, Dan telephoned me. He reported that, in addition to maintaining his gains in
treatment, he had continued to experience ongoing low-level processing
throughout the subsequent 12 months. Dan described how his self-esteem

and sense of integration had continued to grow, as did his ability to relate to others, especially his wife, with maturity, trust, and confidence.

These follow-up results are consistent with those of other clients with whom I have used this EMDR-based treatment of personality and dissociative conditions.

References

American Psychiatric Association. (1994). *Diagnostic and statistical manual of mental disorders* (4th ed.). Washington, D.C.: Author.

Herman, J. (1992). *Trauma and recovery*. New York: Basic Books.

Kernberg, O. (1975). *Borderline conditions and pathological narcissism*. New York: Jason Aronson.

Moore, B., & Fine, B. (1990). *Psychoanalytic terms and concepts*. New Haven, CT: Yale University Press.

Reich, W. (1976). *Character analysis*. New York: Farrar, Straus, & Giroux.

Shapiro, F. (1995). *Eye movement desensitization and reprocessing: Basic principles, protocols, and procedure*. New York: Guilford Press

4

THE INVISIBLE VOLCANO

Overcoming Denial of Rage

Elizabeth Snyker

THE CASE IN THIS CHAPTER integrates EMDR (Shapiro, 1995) and interpretive short-term dynamic therapy (Davanloo, 1980; Malan, 1976; Sifneos, 1972), as contrasted with cognitive, interpersonal, or existential short-term therapies. I became interested in Davanloo's (1980) technique of intensive short-term dynamic psychotherapy (ISTDP) after attending a workshop in 1981. Short-term dynamic therapy, which is rooted in psychoanalytic theory, emphasizes brevity, focus, therapist activity, and patient selection. The goal is to effect change in the personality or character structure of the person, not simply alleviate symptoms. The treatment is dynamic in that it emphasizes a single focal issue that serves as a link to core conflicts arising from early life experiences. The transference relationship is used to examine and reexperience important past relationships that account for current difficulties. In addition to dealing with issues of transference and complexity of the case (single versus multi-foci), handling resistance (conscious and unconscious) aimed at avoiding painful affects must be addressed.

Resistance is of two types: (1) resistance from *repression* against what is painful and unacceptable; and (2) resistance from the *superego*, which stems from the patient's unconscious guilt and need for punishment and whose consequences are repetitive self-sabotaging, self-destructive behaviors. Freud, in his paper, "Analysis Terminable and Interminable" (1937/1958), concluded that his techniques were powerless against the resistance that came from a punitive superego. In the late 1970s, Davanloo (1980) was able to evolve a methodology, which, unlike Freud's passive, free-associative, classical technique, engaged the therapist in actively and firmly clarifying, challenging, and confronting the patient's defenses against closeness and intimacy with others and connection with the self. Further explanation of his complex and subtle methodology is beyond the scope of this chapter. Davanloo's eight-phase central dynamic sequence is two-fold. First, the patient's aggressive and most painful affects are brought to the surface and experienced. Second, the "unlocking of the unconscious" results in the spontaneous emergence of material related to the focal issues of the therapy, such as loss, early childhood traumas, oedipal issues, and sibling rivalry.

Davanloo's results were far-reaching. Patients experienced feelings of empowerment that enabled them to implement positive, growth-enhancing behavioral changes. In essence, a liberated ego emerged able to competently manage the demands of id and superego, external reality and significant others. The changes obtained through the use of ISTDP are similar to what we see with EMDR. When the self is freed from the limitations placed on it by the impact of unresolved trauma, both major and minor, living becomes a richer and more joyful experience.

All of Davanloo's work was videotaped, and it was required that we also videotape our work. This made it easier to understand theoretical concepts such as unlocking the unconscious, transference, and mechanisms of defense. As with training videotapes of EMDR, learning the technique is an easier and richer experience when other parts of the process, such as the results of different interventions or the consequences of "technical errors," are easier to identify and correct. I began my training in EMDR in 1992 and became a facilitator the following year. I found EMDR to be very compatible with my psychodynamic orientation. As one client, who had experienced both techniques, summarized it, "Short-term therapy is like a battering ram to get the walls of the defenses down, but EMDR strings all the things together, like beads on a rosary, so they all make sense."

Combining a psychodynamic method with EMDR involves introducing transference issues to the EMDR session. I have found EMDR particularly useful in this regard. I shift the focus of the session temporarily and I become the EMDR target along with whatever negative cognitions and feelings may be linked. After several sets of eye movements the client's focus usually shifts from me to the source material I represent.

Emotions may be thought of as split-second plans to handle life's conflicts (Goleman, 1995). All emotions have survival value and give life direction. Guilt keeps us moral; love keeps us bonded, disgust keeps us from taking in what is toxic; fear alerts and preserves us from danger; shame from repeating mistakes. Anna Freud (1937/1966), in *The Ego and the Mechanism of Defense*, stressed that of all the emotions, anger is considered to be the most danger-ous and the one most commonly defended against.

Psychodynamic theory emphasizes emotions and their defenses. There are two main defensive styles: hysterical and obsessive. *Affect* is composed of sensations and the significance one attaches to them; it has both somatic and mental components. Clients with a hysterical defensive style display what appears to be a lot of feeling, but it is *pseudofeeling* because they are discon-nected from its meaning. In contrast, clients with the obsessive-compulsive defensive style are cut off from the sensations related to their affect. They are able to think about and understand their affect but not to feel it. A third defensive style is a combination of hysterical and obsessive-compulsive.

One reason ISTDP is effective is that it keeps the client focused on the here and now, forcing her to think about both the body sensations and the meaning of her experience. According to van der Kolk (1997), people with childhood histories of excessive trauma use only the right hemisphere of their brains when recalling these painful memories. This makes it difficult, if not impossible, to think about and make logical sense of what has hap-pened; they are unable to gain distance from their traumatic memory by converting it into language and placing it in the past. Van der Kolk con-cluded that the most effective psychotherapy for these clients is one that focuses them on the here and now and trains them to use left hemispheric processes. He posits that EMDR stimulates interhemispheric communica-tion. (See Manfield's Introduction [this volume] for more information about neurobiological research on the effects of childhood trauma.)

In Shapiro's development of EMDR, emotions, physical sensations, posi-tive and negative cognitions about the self, and memories of the traumatic or disturbing events are all central. The client is asked to name the felt emotion, give it a subjective unit of rating, and give regular feedback on what is happening to the emotional component as the reprocessing takes place. The importance of the clinician's sensitivity to the amount of emo-tional distress the client is undergoing is repeatedly stressed. In order to avoid retraumatization, protocol instructions emphasize heeding a client's request to stop when the processing becomes too intense. This provision strengthens the client's sense of self-control. Shapiro concluded that "Approximately 40% of the time the alignment of the standard components (image, cognition, body sensation) together with the eye movements will allow full processing to take place. In the remainder of the cases alternative procedural strategies are necessary for therapeutic effectiveness" (1995, p. 7). This chapter offers a case example of an alternative procedural strategy for those clients who do not experience full processing with this alignment.

Overview of the Hysterical Personality

In psychodynamic terms the client in my case example would be viewed as using a hysterical pattern of defense. This style of coping is characterized by repression (forgetting) of ideational content but not of affect. Perceptions tend to be global, selective, and lacking in detail, impressionistic rather than objective. Main symptoms of hysterical personalities include conversion reactions and somatic complaints (such as headaches, gastrointestinal disturbances, breathing difficulties, repeated choking, coughing, clearing of the throat, muscle tension resulting in aches and pains), dissociative episodes, and anxiety attacks. Typically, cognitive avoidance of events that activate strong emotions is demonstrated. Characteristic statements of the hysteric include "I don't know," "I don't remember," "I don't want to think about that," "I can't see myself doing that," "I couldn't imagine those kinds of thoughts," "It never occurred to me." Unlike the obsessive defensive style in which aggression/guilt themes predominate, sexual guilt is the more dominant motif in the hysteric, as there is confusion between affectional-nurturance and sexual–genital need. Interpersonal relationships tend to be attention-seeking and impulsive, with repetitive behaviors characterized by themes of victim/aggressor, child/parent, and rescue/rape types of interactions. The hysteric wants to be taken care of like a child but responds like a woman. The therapeutic goal is to help her think about that which she does not want to know.

Client's History and Background

During the initial evaluation, Joanne, a 53-year-old divorced mother of three adult children, reported being depressed over the loss of her job a year ago. She had done office work for 15 years and was fired for repeated tardiness. Joanne stated that for five years she had driven two hours one way to get to work and would often get stuck in city traffic. Unable to find other employment, she moved back home with her overly protective ("she treats me like a baby") 80-year-old mother. Joanne described her deceased father as having been verbally and physically abusive. Considerably older than her mother, he had been married twice and was emphatic about not wanting children. Nevertheless, they had Joanne and her two younger brothers. The client described herself as having been "painfully shy as a child."

Joanne married a man who was both physically and emotionally abusive. After ten years of marriage and three children, Joanne decided she could no longer tolerate the abuse and left him. Taking her children, she moved out-of-state and, with the help of friends, found a job despite the fact that she had never worked. Her husband refused to assist the family financially and eventually divorced her. When her relatives (brother, sister-in-law, and mother) realized that Joanne was unable to adequately support herself and the children, who were being neglected, they removed the children against her will. "My parents took my kids. I blocked it out."

Her family returned the children to their father, who in turn split them up and sent them to live with his brother and sister. Additionally, he blocked Joanne's attempts to visit the children, and she never regained custody. She abused alcohol and attempted suicide during this time in her life.

Joanne exhibited many symptoms of posttraumatic stress disorder in response to the loss of her children. She scored 49 on the Horowitz Impact of Events Scale (Horowitz, Wilmer, & Alvarez, 1979), indicating a more than clinically significant reaction for people who had experienced a traumatic event. She scored "severe" on the Beck Anxiety Inventory and "borderline moderate-severe" on the Beck Inventory of Depression. When asked to estimate the severity of her problems (depression, unemployment), she rated herself in the "mildly upsetting" range.

Joanne was referred to me for EMDR by a close friend. We began using EMDR at the second session. She wanted to target her health concerns, reporting problems with her thyroid, recurrent headaches, and a fear of dying. The positive cognition installed regarding her health concerns was "I can take care of it." She followed through on this issue by getting a complete physical exam and was told she was in good health.

Joanne was 15 minutes late for the third session. She reported feeling better, attributing the improvement to Prozac, which she had begun taking a week earlier. Concerns during this session centered on her relationship with her mother, whom she described as "smothering—she treats me like a baby." Additional assertions included, "She took over my kids. . . . I want her to stop. . . . I don't have a personality. . . . I can't cope." Repeatedly, Joanne asked "Why would she do that?" after describing a negative interaction with her mother. The positive cognition installed was that her mother was not going to change, but "I can change." Joanne reported feeling "better," but her affect remained very blunted. The next session was canceled due to illness ("My stomach is upset"). She spent the week alone because her mother had gone to visit friends.

At our fourth session Joanne continued to look depressed, though she was still saying that she "felt better." Whatever pleasure she experienced with her mother's absence was barely noticeable. She was apologetic about the cancellation of the previous session. She then reported talking to Raymond, her youngest brother, about their father, and how neither one of them had cried when he had died. She described being puzzled by her own lack of reaction.

Treatment

It was during this session that I decided to modify the standard EMDR approach in favor of a more active and interpretive role on my part. This decision was prompted by a number of observations:

- the lack of emotional reactivity to both past and present events that should have had some affect connected to them;
- the lack of attention to the significance or meaning of these events;
- the tendency to somatization (i.e., development of a headache) whenever there was an indication that she might have been feeling angry.

The more standardized EMDR protocol requires the clinician to stay in the observing mode in relation to the client's processing of her experiences. The type of session I intended to do with this client required a more active level of involvement. Combining EMDR and a very modified version of ISTDP, I hoped to facilitate a more complete processing of the affective component than I have found possible with standard EMDR and cognitive interweaves. It may take several sessions before the client becomes fully comfortable with the experience of her emotions, especially anger and the aggressive thinking this particular emotion generates. My primary focus in this session was on helping Joanne (1) identify the defenses that keep her cut off from her thoughts and emotionally numb; (2) identify the unacceptable thoughts and feelings behind the defenses; (3) educate her about the conversion of feelings into somatic symptoms; and (4) help her become aware of the sense of relief that accompanies the expression of intense feelings, such as rage, in thought and fantasy.

Transcript of Fourth Session

Joanne: My father was not brutal, but he was very critical. He could say things that would frustrate me so much, I'd tell him I hated him. He didn't respond, except to say I was a terrible person. I would come home and my mother would tell me, "Go see your father. Go hug him." I always had to go to him; I had to be the one to give. It was always my fault if anything went wrong. I don't hate him now. I just wonder how he could do that. He was home, he didn't drink, but he didn't participate in our activities. I would come to the dinner table and not talk.

These opening statements capture the distant relationship between father and daughter. Even as an adult, Joanne's mother would tell her how to relate to her father ("go hug him") and she would do it but then feel resentful towards both. In her first statements we can begin to identify resistance in the form of denial (he is not brutal; she does not hate him). In her last statement she comments on how she feels (she doesn't understand how he could behave the way he did). This is not a statement of feeling but rather a description of what she is thinking. The comments are delivered unemotionally, with a sense of la belle indifference.

LS: What would happen if you talked?

Joanne: Be sent to my room from the table. Children were to be seen and not heard. As a teen I once hugged him and he shoved me away. From that moment on, I stayed away.

Joanne then talked about her father's death in 1970 and about attending his memorial service. She described herself as feeling "numb" at the funeral. Twenty years later, however, she was "very surprised" that, while attending the funeral of a friend's father, she became emotional and tearful.

Joanne: I started to cry. I couldn't understand why. [*Her inability to connect the significance of the event and her affect is a state-dependent phenomenon that suggested I would have to re-target this particular event repeatedly until her feelings began to emerge.*] I have a problem talking to men. The men I got involved with were like my father. I can't relate to men. I don't know what to say. And if I do become involved, they get abusive. I wish Dad were here so I could talk to him. Why did he treat me the way he did? I felt he hated me or disliked me.

LS: What are your feelings towards your father, given that he didn't establish a relationship with you?

Joanne: I resent the part of him that treated me so badly—his criticism and indifference. I admired him as a person. He wasn't crude. He was sensitive. Sometimes he would see a sad movie and I know he would get sad and cry. [*Joanne began her response by identifying the feeling of resentment. The natural step is to direct her towards an actual experience of it.*]

LS: How resentful do you feel?

Joanne: It's pretty big. I lost out on a relationship with him.

LS: Where do you experience your resentment?

Joanne: It hurts me.

LS: Where do you feel the hurt?

Joanne: In my heart.

Note the discrepancy in these statements. She is talking about resentment but describes feeling hurt. She seems in touch with the effect of his actions on her but not with her feelings towards him for acting critically and indifferently. For now hurt and resentment are just words, as she is numb and isolated from her emotions. Nonverbal indicators of affect are lacking.

Setting up of a target for EMDR follows next. Because her opening statement is a denial that her father was brutal, I hoped for the emergence of a target related to this issue rather than his death or her reaction to her friend's father's death.

LS: How does your father come into your mind?

Joanne: Dad was always yelling and being critical.

LS: What was your belief about yourself when he yelled?

Joanne: There's something wrong with me.

LS: How would you have preferred to feel about yourself?

Joanne: I would like to feel I was worthy of his love without being yelled or screamed at.

LS: What's the feeling?

Joanne: Frustration.

LS: Where do you feel it?

Joanne: In my heart.

LS: Rate it for me.

Joanne: 9.

LS: What does the feeling feel like?

Joanne: A sense of loss. I'm angry at myself. I must have done something wrong to cause him to be verbally abusive, to be physical with me.

Anger is displaced against the self with the comment "I must have done something wrong." Although she does not verbalize it, Joanne is operating from an underlying dysfunctional belief about herself that "I am defective." She has been denying that her father was physically abusive of her, and doesn't realize that this is inconsistent with what she says now and what she told me at the initial interview.

LS: Is there a specific memory of your dad being critical?

Joanne: On a beach party. I did something wrong. He said I was always causing problems and that I had a terrible disposition. He even said that he hated me. It was devastating to me. He really hates me.

LS: Stay with that, the beach party, "I must have done something wrong," and the frustration.

[*The spontaneous memory that emerged for the EMDR target related to a moment when she experienced her father as verbally brutal.*]

Joanne: ►◄►◄►◄ I felt despicable.

LS: Clear your mind.

Joanne: I kept thinking over and over, "Why did he do that?" He'd say this in front of others. He was humiliating to me. To this day, I can't stand to have anyone do this in public. I cringe when they do that. [*Being humiliated is a recurrent theme.*] ►◄►◄►◄ On different occasions, I got so angry I lost control.

LS: What do you mean, you lost control? [*She is sitting very still and stiffly in the chair. This statement reflects her tendency to be global and lacking in detail.*]

Joanne: I told the person off. But in the back of my mind there was my father doing that to me again. [*She rubs the back of her neck.*] I get tense in the back of my neck. It's so rude. I think if I say something, I should take them aside. You don't humiliate them in public. I hate that. I'm thinking that's another way to deal with anger. ►◄►◄►◄

LS: [*Note that as she begins to talk about her anger, there is an immediate conversion reaction to a somatic symptom.*] How is the back of your neck now?

Joanne: All right. Just a little tense.

LS: Feel it. [*With EMDR the physical sensation can be targeted and reduced.*]

Joanne: ►◄►◄►◄ If that situation came up, I'd like to tell the person, "Let's discuss this in another time and place. Let's discuss it in private." ►◄►◄►◄ [*The return to the original target here is dictated by her positive desire to handle this differently.*]

LS: Go back to the original target, the beach party.

Joanne: ►◄►◄►◄ I was thinking about being so angry and frustrated. [*Note that she is thinking about being angry, not feeling it. She is still not emotionally in the experience.*]

LS: Stay with that.

Joanne: ►◄►◄►◄ But he'd yell at me if I said anything. I had all those emotions inside, but I couldn't do anything with them. ►◄►◄►◄ I'm trying to figure out what is wrong with me. I wanted him to stop, to treat me differently. I just kept thinking, "Something is wrong with me."

She has begun to loop with her references to something being wrong with her. Another dysfunctional belief is "I can't yell at my father. I'm defective." I considered using a possible cognitive interweave here to take her back in time to when she decided there was something wrong with her. I also considered using the Socratic method to challenge her thinking process. However, both of these approaches might lengthen the session, given the number of negative thoughts depressed people think on a daily basis. My choice instead is to facilitate an affective experience of the negative cognition.

LS: You're in your head. How did you feel towards him when he was critical?

Joanne: ►◄►◄►◄ I hated him for it. I was angry. Horrible feeling. I didn't want to feel that. I wanted to make him stop. I wanted to yell, "Why are you doing this?" I wanted to hurt him with words.

She again mentions feeling hatred and anger. In order for her to know that the experience of these emotions is unpleasant, she would have had to experience them in a split second and then defend against them by denial. Another underlying dysfunctional belief seems to be, "It is not all right for me to be angry with my father." The defense is passivity. She avoids taking any action that would amount to an expression of her aggressive feelings.

LS: What would you have liked to have said to him?

Joanne: ►◄►◄►◄ "You're horrible. You're humiliating me and being mean. I can't stand how you treat me." I wanted to tell him that some girls don't have parents who treat them like that. He had hurt me.

The comments are made with no emotional force behind them. There is no expression of what she feels. When the idea of telling someone off is coupled with the feeling, the client typically experiences a sense of relief. For her there is no relief. Telling her father off at this stage is premature. Instead she experiences an increase in tension. I considered the intervention of asking her what she would have liked to have said to him a technical error on my part. She is not ready to experience her true feeling at this point. The increased tension she feels may be related to hidden anger towards me for pushing her to do something she actively avoids: confronting her feelings. Her tendency is to please others but at her own expense.

LS: What are you feeling now in your body?

Joanne: ►◄►◄►◄ Tense in the neck. My head is starting to hurt.

LS: Do you ever get aggressive thoughts?

Confronted with her anger and being unable to express it verbally, she begins to displace it into her body. Asking her about aggressive thoughts is an attempt to help her begin to connect thoughts and sensations, as it is the simultaneous awareness of both thought and bodily sensations that results in the cognitive experience of affect.

Joanne: ►◄►◄►◄ No, not really. I don't have those types of thoughts. I don't want to be violent. [*Here we see the defense of denial in the service of keeping her thoughts and body sensations isolated.*]

LS: What do you mean, "No, not really"?

Joanne: ►◄►◄►◄ I don't want to hurt anyone physically because I know how that feels.

LS: In the moment that you feel hatred in your body, what's going on in your head?

Joanne: ►◄►◄►◄ What came up was just to tell him.

LS: What do you imagine his reaction would be if you hurt him verbally?

Joanne: ►◄►◄►◄ It would hurt him, but he wouldn't communicate it. I know he was sensitive. At different movies he would cry.

LS: Do you think that would have stopped him from being critical?

Joanne: ►◄►◄►◄ No, because I don't think he really liked me.

Multiple negative beliefs seem to be operating: "I am unlovable." "It is not OK to feel my feelings." "It is not OK for me to want to hurt another" (although this is the behavior her father modeled for her repeatedly). The attempt here is to help her connect her thoughts and feelings and get beyond the denial.

LS: Are you trying to convince yourself that you'd never be violent?

Joanne: ►◄►◄►◄ I never saw violence till I was married. My exhusband used to hit me, bang my head against the wall. He reminded me of my father. Called me filthy names. Checked the ashtrays to make sure I had not been visited by another man.

Note the denial and contradiction again. She describes her exhusband as physically abusive and similar to her father. She seems unaware of the significance of what she is communicating. This is an example of a cognitive distortion. It is very unlikely that anyone today could live 18 years without witnessing violence.

LS: How did you feel towards your ex-husband?

Joanne: ►◄►◄►◄ I fought back. I hated him.

LS: What's the difference between the hatred you felt towards your father and your ex?

Joanne: ►◄►◄►◄ I was trying to protect myself. My father would humiliate me but was never physically abusive. My husband was hateful. [*Another implied dysfunctional belief here seems to be, "I don't have the right to protect myself from an abusive father." She is still not remembering that she told me during the initial interview he was physically abusive.*] ►◄►◄►◄ I saw myself in the kitchen. I was preparing a piece of meat. I took a knife and I was stabbing the meat. I was in that moment stabbing my husband.

For the first time she begins to access aggressive thoughts and feelings: the meat represents her husband. This could easily become an EMDR target. Since there have been multiple episodes of domestic violence, however, it is better to wait and target them at a later time. The focus at present is on her father being verbally abusive and her feelings towards him for treating her in that manner.

LS: In that moment you had a thought of killing your husband.
Joanne: [*Her upper body turns away from me and she shudders. The long-term goal is to help her accept unacceptable thoughts and tolerate uncomfortable feelings.*]
LS: Can you stay with the fantasy?
Joanne: I can't stand violence. I see blood and I see something else. I feel sick. [*She clutches her stomach and covers her mouth.*]

As details about the significance of her fantasy emerge, there is an increase of anxiety, which she feels in her gut. For this type of reaction to be taking place, one can imagine she most likely fantasized stabbing him to death and is physically sickened by the sight. It is not uncommon for people to feel disgust and want to throw up after a killing. Notice that she is reacting to the thought or fantasy of killing her husband, not the actual deed.

Joanne: That's not an acceptable thought. It is not right to think that way.
LS: What kind of thought?
Joanne: ►◄►◄►◄ I'd defend myself, but I did not want to kill. Once he tried to choke me. I got loose. I started to choke him. He started to turn red. I can't do this. Why throw myself away for someone like this?

Note the pattern:

1. *An event triggers rage. Connection of thought and feeling begins to lead to a self-defensive action;*
2. *She begins to recognize the significance of her action when he starts to turn red (she will strangle him to death if she does not stop);*
3. *Immediate resistance to the experience of rage and desire to attack, even in self-defense, with denial and recognition of the act as self-sabotaging.*

Lost on her is the significance of this event: Why is she letting herself be used and abused by staying with such a dangerous person? Her pattern of repeatedly censoring her thoughts and feelings makes this possible. If she begins to feel her anger and rage at her husband, she would also have to acknowledge its presence towards significant others, like her father.

LS: You closed your eyes.

Closing the eyes is a way to avoid seeing herself as violent; it is a form of magical thinking that "if I don't see it, it didn't happen." Bringing her attention to the eyes mobilizes the emergence of more unconscious material. Her use of denial begins to break down.

Joanne: It's horrible for me to think of those things. I hate it. I've been beaten on before.

LS: What happened?

Joanne: ►◄►◄►◄ A guy took a belt. Hit me with the wrong end of it. I had cuts on my back. A boyfriend I had years later after I left my husband.

LS: How did you feel towards him?

Joanne: ►◄►◄►◄ Scared. I was seeing myself . . . trying to reason with him. I got away from him.

LS: How long after the beating before you were able to get away?

Joanne: ►◄►◄►◄ An hour . . . [*hesitates*] . . . he did something to me [*falls silent*].

LS: Stay with what else he did.

Joanne: ►◄►◄►◄ He sodomized me. I had to think of things to say . . . had to say I cared for him. I knew him for only a few months before I was able to get out. I don't want to think about this. I try to block it out.

LS: What are the long-term consequences for you of not wanting to think, of blocking?

This intervention is intended to alert her to the fact that there is a price she pays for not thinking and not feeling. The question also serves as a cognitive interweave because she tends to be impulsive—a short-term planner—rather than thinking of long-term consequences.

Joanne: ►◄►◄►◄ I have to see it in my mind. I have to remember . . . [*smiles*].

LS: You smile.

The smile is resistance, another form of tactical defense. Smiles throw us off-track by deceiving us into thinking things are OK. Saying "I have to see it in my mind, I have to remember" sounds like the right thing to say. But in this moment, I wonder what is funny about being beaten and sodomized?

Joanne: I got to the point that I hated myself. All I ever got was abuse.

The impulse is quickly turned against the self. It doesn't make a difference if we unconsciously find someone to abuse us (i.e., marry an abusive partner) or we abuse ourselves by engaging in self-sabotaging behaviors, such as reckless driving, using drugs, and engaging in unprotected sex. The consequence is the same: suffering and pain. Missing is the motivation for what drives such self-destructiveness. A core dysfunctional belief would be, "There must be something wrong with me. I deserve abuse." This is a rationalization, an introjected form of verbal abuse similar to what her father communicated to her when he was verbally abusive.

LS: Who was the first person to ever abuse you?

Joanne: ▶◀▶◀▶◀ Verbally, my father. Physically, my ex-husband. There's something about me that causes others to abuse me verbally and physically. [*Here we see resistance in the form of the rationalization and dysfunctional belief of "I deserve abuse. There's something wrong with me."*]

LS: When is the first time you realized this?

Joanne: ▶◀▶◀▶◀ At the beach party. I was 14 or 15. My father always said humiliating things to me.

LS: If someone today told you you were hateful, what then? [*This is a cognitive interweave introducing the adult perspective, but she is unable to make use of it.*]

Joanne: ▶◀▶◀▶◀ I just get this horrible feeling. I don't like it.

LS: What's the feeling like?

Joanne: ▶◀▶◀▶◀ I get tense in my neck and shoulders, like a band around my head. [*She rubs the back of her neck.*]

LS: Is it there now?

Joanne: Yes, a little tightness.

LS: Rate it.

Joanne: 9. [*She greatly minimizes her physical sensations.*]

LS: So the tenseness is there when you think of your dad at the beach. What's the meaning of the tightness?

Joanne: I was angry he had said it. I was embarrassed, humiliated. He was always picking on me but not my brother.

LS: We know you censored the violent part of yourself in that moment. What would you have become aware of if you had not censored it?

Joanne: ▶◀▶◀▶◀ I would have thought I was crazy because only crazy people think like that. [*She verbalizes another negative feeling, anger, but she is vague. The goal is to help her become specific.*] ▶◀▶◀▶◀ I don't remember thinking of wanting to be physical with my father. The only time I wanted to be physical was with my husband. He was abusive and I wanted to make him stop.

LS: So how did you imagine stopping him?

Joanne: Slap him.

LS: How hard?

Having clients describe their actions in concrete detail in the moment helps to put them into the original experience and closer to the possibility of feeling their feelings. It also slows down the emergence of additional resistance, makes it easier for more unconscious material to emerge, and forces the client to try to better understand the meaning of what is happening.

Joanne: ►◄►◄►◄ I just thought of something. Our last fight. He drank. We were at his sister's house. He started to pull my hair. Jumped on my back. I thought, "If he hits me again, I'll kill him." I had a skillet. My children were there. I thought "I'm not going to kill you."

Here we see the return of a familiar pattern:

1. *The triggering event is immediately followed by the emergence of the impulse to strike out;*
2. *Defenses against the feeling of murderous rage include passivity, denial, and rationalization (cannot act because children are present);*
3. *The pattern is concluded with a censoring of the aggressive impulse;*
4. *Problem-solving is short-term ("if he hits me, I'll kill him");*
5. *There is a continuing inability to reflect on the meaning and long-term consequences for herself and her children of living with continual abuse.*

Seligman's (1975) theory of learned helplessness offers one type of explanation. The psychoanalytic position would be that the penalty for feeling murderous rage is unconscious guilt and punishment by the punitive superego in the form of self-sabotaging behaviors.

LS: Can you picture yourself hitting him [her ex-husband] with the skillet? I know this is an unpleasant thought, but can you stay with it?

Joanne: ►◄►◄►◄ I guess I did want to hit him. I wanted to be violent. I would have felt good but also sorry. [*She more honestly acknowledges her ambivalence-aggression and regret, as well as the sense of relief that comes with discharge of the impulse.*]

LS: Can we just stay with the part of you that felt good?

Joanne: ►◄►◄►◄ I probably felt good and wanted to get back for the other times.

Use of the word probably *qualifies the experience; the effect is to commit herself only partially. Since resistance is still present, I propose staying with the "good feeling"—i.e., the relief from striking out—because this is the more unacceptable feeling in the moment.*

LS: How is your head?

Joanne: There's a little tension left.

LS: How often would you have hit him?

Joanne: ►◄►◄►◄ Several times. [*Looking very uncomfortable, she squirms in her chair, averting her eyes.*]

LS: In thought and fantasy only. Not that you would ever do this in real life.

Use of the specifying phrase in thought and fantasy only *is extremely important. Many people experience internal confusion when they mistakenly believe that if they think or imagine themselves being aggressive, they will reflexively act out of their aggressive impulses. The thought is not the deed. People with a history of impulsive, aggressive behavior are not suitable for a therapy that confronts their defenses because they lack the very defenses that inhibit aggressive behavior. If you confront, they'll attack!*

Joanne: ►◄►◄►◄ Yes, I wanted to hurt him [*closing her eyes and smiling*].

LS: Again you close your eyes and smile and hide the part of you that wanted to be violent. We're not here to judge your behavior but, rather, to understand your thoughts and feelings. So if you hit him repeatedly . . . again, you close your eyes. [*She opens them.*]

Joanne: ►◄►◄►◄ I don't want to see blood or his big wound. It makes me sick.

LS: But the reality is that, if you take a skillet and hit someone on the head, you'll see more than blood.

Joanne: ►◄►◄►◄ My stomach is upset. [*Here we see a displacement of her feeling into a somatic symptom, indicating anxiety at the idea, not the actual deed, of striking out.*]

LS: How are you feeling towards me right now?

Joanne: ►◄►◄►◄ Good.

I test to find out what her transference feelings towards me are. Good *is not a feeling and only indicates something in the positive range. She is still out of touch, only this time with a positive affect. The significance of this is her continuing inability to experience the mix of positive and negative feelings. Her thinking remains dichotomous: A or B, not A and B.*

LS: If you felt angry with me, would you tell me?

Joanne: [*She smiles and looks away.*]

LS: We know a part of you wants to censor angry thoughts. Why would such thoughts about me be an exception?

Joanne: ►◄►◄►◄ I don't like him. He was terrible, he was abusive. I tried everything.

LS: As violent as you felt, you censored it. So what happened to that violent part?

Joanne: ►◄►◄►◄ I block it out now. [*She changes the subject in order to avoid dealing with her feelings in the transference. I deliberately choose not to pursue any transference issues at this time.*]

LS: You protected him.

Joanne: ►◄►◄►◄ Not the right thing to do.

LS: You are not violent towards him, yet you stay in a situation in which violence is perpetrated against you. How do you explain this to yourself?

Joanne: ►◄►◄►◄ I stayed because I had four kids and my mother told me to stay with him. He didn't let me work. How could I take care of the kids? I took it as long as I could.

Multiple defenses emerge. She rationalizes staying for the children but lacks awareness of the impact on them. She is unaware that she had the choice of remaining passive, childlike, and helpless—doing what the parent says—or acting as a responsible adult. These statements also reveal her identification with a passive mother who did not model assertive behavior or act adequately to protect her.

LS: Years later, you do the same thing. [*I'm referring to the repetition compulsion of bonding with another abusive male, the man who hits her with the belt.*]

Joanne: ►◄►◄►◄ I felt I should be treated that way. [*The defense is one of thinking with her feelings, a cognitive distortion, and points to the strength of her core negative belief, "There must be something wrong with me. I am defective."*]

LS: How long have you been censoring your aggressive thoughts?

Joanne: ►◄►◄►◄ I don't remember.

LS: You protected him. What happened to your murderous rage? Because if you let go of it, you'd crack his skull with the skillet.

Joanne: ►◄►◄►◄ Something snapped in my head. [*Her defense is to split her awareness.*]

LS: That's how you protected him. There are two parts of you. The good side won out. What happened to the violent part of you?

Joanne: ►◄►◄►◄ I buried it.

LS: Where?

Joanne: ►◄►◄►◄ I don't want to think about it.

LS: If you take a moment now to think about it, what comes up?

Joanne: ►◄►◄►◄ I feel tense in the back of my head. [*She begins to somaticize again.*]

LS: So when you feel tension, is that the violent side of you that you are feeling?

Joanne: ►◄►◄►◄ Could be.

LS: What came up?

Joanne: ►◄►◄►◄ Maybe it is still there.

LS: So not to think about it will . . .

Joanne: ►◄►◄►◄ I want to get rid of it—it's horrible.

LS: Is this wishful thinking or reality?

Joanne: ►◄►◄►◄ Everybody gets angry, but they don't act on it. I felt like a murderer.

LS: In your thoughts. But in reality you didn't murder anyone.

Joanne: ►◄►◄►◄ I guess in your mind you feel like you could murder. I can see, in my mind, hitting him.

LS: But you can't see yourself killing him.

Joanne: ►◄►◄►◄ I'm good at blocking and censoring.

LS: What would happen if you killed him in your mind?

Joanne: ►◄►◄►◄ He'd be mad at me. I can't kill him.

LS: Who says?

Joanne: ►◄►◄►◄ The courts.

LS: This is in your head. You protected him. What are the consequences of blocking and censoring?

Joanne: ►◄►◄►◄ It can make you sick. I was getting a lot of headaches. [*She connects her denial of her feelings and her somatic symptoms.*]

LS: Or is the headache the way you block?

Joanne: ►◄►◄►◄ Yes.

LS: How would you prefer to think about yourself when you get violent thoughts?

Joanne: ►◄►◄►◄ I can deal with them and realize they're just thoughts. It's normal to have those kinds of thoughts.

LS: So when you say there is something wrong with you . . .

Joanne: ►◄►◄►◄ I'm human. I'm entitled to feel angry [*smiling.*]

LS: You smile.

Joanne: ►◄►◄►◄ It's silly. I'm too hard on myself. I don't let go. I had it done to me.

Note that the smile is more appropriate this time. Because emotions are part of being human, it is silly, serves no purpose, to be hard on herself. The major cognitive error this client made is that of equating the thought of murder with the deed. This error needed to be challenged as soon as possible.

LS: Target the beach.

Joanne: ►◄►◄►◄ [*She smiles.*]

LS: What came up?

Joanne: ►◄►◄►◄ I was thinking, maybe I wanted to smack my father once for treating me that way. But I don't feel angry with him anymore. I feel sad.

LS: What's your belief now when you think about that beach party?

Joanne: ►◄►◄►◄ I don't remember what I did. I deserve better.

LS: Hold those two things together, the beach party and "I deserve better."

Joanne: ►◄►◄►◄ I wanted his respect. That's what my parents wanted. I should get respect.

LS: Think of the beach and scan your body.

Joanne: ►◄►◄►◄ I feel better. I'd want to reason with him.

LS: How much did this bother you before and what is it now?

Joanne: It bothered me before at a 10; now it's 0.

At the next session a number of significant changes took place. Joanne reported behaving more assertively. Memories earlier than adolescence began to emerge. She remembered that her father was physically abusive with her younger brothers as well. She concluded that the things she remembered helped her to better understand why both she and her brother did not feel anything when their father died. She no longer thought of herself as "crazy" whenever she felt angry. Regarding our last session, she said, "I felt good and it was helpful. Prior to the session I thought that something was really wrong with me . . . maybe I was violent or mentally ill."

This session continued to focus on her father and the beach incident. By the end of the session she was feeling sad and tearful that she never got to know him very well. The more standard EMDR protocol of staying out of the client's process was followed. Of note is that she accessed her feelings much faster and with less resistance.

LS: You made a pair of fists. Did you notice?

Joanne: Yes.

LS: Does that part of you want to physically strike out?

Joanne: Yes.

LS: At whom?

Joanne: Demanding customers. [*She had been talking about her old job.*]

LS: Can you do that in your thoughts?
Joanne: ►◄►◄►◄ [silence]
LS: How do you feel?
Joanne: Relief.

Discussion

The case described is that of a self-punitive woman with a moderately severe degree of ego-syntonic character pathology. Her style of relating is to engage in masochistic, passive-aggressive behavior that invariably provokes others to attack her. On Davanloo's (1985) spectrum of neurosis, where the extreme left represents neurotic patients with a very low degree of resistance, and the extreme right represents patients with the most rigid and ego-syntonic characterological traits, she is in the middle range. The further to the right one moves on the spectrum, the greater the degree of isolation of affect from cognition.

Joanne became immediately anxious when asked about her feelings towards her father. And while she could use words such as *anger, resentment*, and *hatred* to describe her feelings, the reality was that these were just words; she was emotionally numb. As she became aware of her defenses, which were repeatedly pointed out to her, she was able to express increasingly aggressive material related to other men in her life—but not towards her father, whom she unconsciously protected from her own rage. It took her a full hour to finally acknowledge aggressive thoughts (wanting to slap) towards her father as well. Eventually, she was able to acknowledge deeper emotions. And while this was both disturbing and painful to her, she realized that the experience made her human, not mentally ill or violent. This is a moment of insight and new learning.

In ISTDP, feeling takes precedence over content, and resistance to feeling is gently and firmly confronted. With this type of client, the systematic challenging of her defenses against intimacy and closeness might take three to five hours. The introduction of EMDR with select patients and for restricted and predetermined psychodynamic focus hastens the dissolution of isolation between affect and thought (to approximately an hour, in this case). Further benefits are the emergence of multiple insights:

1. thought and fantasy can be used in the service of discharging intense emotions such as anger and rage;
2. one's worse fears, such as losing control and hurting another physically, do not materialize;

3. imaginary, aggressive, acting-out behavior while feeling the sensation of the emotion brings a feeling of relief and prevents conversion into symptoms (somatic complaints, depression, anxiety attacks, etc.); and
4. psychic energy is released for problem-solving, assertive behavior, and a more realistic, balanced, and compassionate appraisal of the significant figures from the past.

References

Davanloo, H. (1979). Techniques of short-term dynamic psychotherapy. *Psychiatric Clinics of North America, 2,* 11–22.

Davanloo, H. (Ed.). (1980). *Short-term dynamic psychotherapy, Vol. 1.* New York: Jason Aronson.

Davanloo, H. (1985). Short-term dynamic psychotherapy. In H. I. Kaplan & B. J. Saddock (Eds.), *Comprehensive textbook of psychiatry (4th ed.)* (pp. 1460–1467). Baltimore, MD: Williams & Wilkins.

Freud, A. (1966). *The ego and the mechanisms of defense (rev. ed.).* New York: International Universities Press. (Originally published 1937)

Freud, S. (1958). Analysis terminable and interminable. In J. Strachey (Trans. & Ed.), *The standard edition of the complete psychological works of Sigmund Freud,* (Vol. 23, pp. 209–253). New York: Norton. (Originally published 1937)

Goleman, D. (1995). *Emotional intelligence.* New York: Bantam Books.

Horowitz, M., Wilmer, N., & Alvarez, W. (1979). Impact of Events Scale: A measure of subjective stress. *Psychosomatic Medicine, 41*(3), 209–218.

Malan, D. H. (1976). *The frontier of brief psychotherapy.* New York: Plenum Medical Book.

Seligman, M. (1975). *Helplessness: On depression, development, and death.* San Francisco: W. H. Freeman.

Shapiro, F. (1995). *Eye movement desensitization and reprocessing: Basic principles, protocols, and procedures.* New York: Guilford Press.

Sifneos, P. E. (1972). *Short-term psychotherapy and emotional crisis.* Cambridge, MA: Harvard University Press.

van der Kolk, B. (1997, July). *Current understanding of the psychology of trauma.* Paper Presented at the EMDRIA Conference, San Francisco.

5

FILLING THE VOID
Resolution of a Major Depression

Philip Manfield

JANE WAS AN ATTRACTIVE 36-year-old single woman who had been severely depressed for six months following surgery for the removal of a large benign growth next to her stomach. The emptiness she felt after the removal of the tissue brought up a deep sense of loss and hopelessness about feeling whole again. Although her immediate complaint was the depression, it quickly became apparent that Jane was also continuing to encounter life-long difficulties in her relationships and career choices.

This case demonstrates the value of EMDR in rapidly resolving a major depression by processing a series of traumatic memories. The themes of loss, overwhelming helplessness, and inadequacy weave through each of these memories and tie them together. Major depression, Jane's primary diagnosis, is not one of the diagnoses typically thought of as responsive to EMDR. This case is particularly interesting because of the breadth of change Jane experienced as a result of processing these traumatic memories and the follow-up integrative work we did; the depression was relieved as well as a cluster of other issues that appeared to be more characterological.

Client's History and Background

Jane described herself as feeling "hopeless about [her] life." Her body felt "wooden" and without feeling. The problem requiring the surgery had arisen suddenly and had created chaos in her life. She believed that she could no longer count on anything in her life to be stable; she could not make future plans. Any reminder of the surgery was painful for her. A therapist friend of hers had referred her to me, suggesting that EMDR might be effective for her problem, and Jane specifically requested EMDR when she called for her first appointment.

Prior to treatment her unmourned losses had increased her sensitivity to separation and exaggerated her difficulty with establishing and maintaining a meaningful and committed love relationship. Because she was clinging to a partner who was not really available, her ability to function effectively in a relationship had appeared at first to be poorer than it actually was.

Throughout the description of this case I have included my thoughts about the process that led me to make particular clinical choices. Compliance or dependency indicators that arose in the treatment were addressed, so that the drawbacks of the relatively active role I played as the therapist during EMDR were avoided during the treatment of the acute symptoms. Subsequently, as the treatment progressed to termination, it became clear that there was also no negative longer-term impact from my relatively active role.

First Session

I devoted Jane's first appointment to history-taking and helping her select a "safe place," an environment she could think of when she wanted to feel calm and secure. She originally thought of a beach for her image of a safe place, but then a disturbing memory surfaced, which she reported. While walking on the beach several years ago, she had discovered a large land turtle marooned on its back at the edge of the ocean. She recognized that the turtle didn't belong at the ocean and was helpless to right itself. While she considered what to do, a wave came in and swept the turtle out to sea. As she described this memory, she said that she could imagine the turtle's screams for help. Toward the end of the session she identified a more suitable safe place.

Jane appeared to me to be reasonably high-functioning and had a supportive, intact family of origin. She had grown up in a small town, gotten good grades in school, and had lived in only two houses during her childhood and adolescence. These indications of a reasonably stable childhood suggested that her internal self and object representations were probably fairly stable and integrated; I did not expect severe complications from transference issues. Viewing the treatment as short-term, I decided to use EMDR in each session.

Second Session

Jane described her memory of the surgery as being more painful than she was ready to process so early in treatment. The upsetting image of the over-turned turtle on the beach had first come up when she was trying to find a safe space, and it had been surprisingly disturbing to her. On the Subjective Units of Disturbance Scale (SUDS; Wolpe, 1991) from 0 to 10, with 0 representing no disturbance and 10 representing the highest level of distur-bance, Jane rated this memory at 7. Since fear and a sense of helplessness were keeping her from exploring the surgery directly, I suggested focusing on the memory of the turtle as the target for EMDR because her belief that the turtle felt fearful and helpless was a prominent part of that memory. When a client comes for EMDR to work out feelings about an overwhelming memory, I often suggest beginning with a peripheral image or memory to familiarize her with the EMDR process and create in her the confidence that she can resolve the more strongly disturbing feelings.

Jane began with the image of the turtle upside down on the beach, the waves lapping at it. The theme that emerged during this session was the pain-fulness of loss of control, of feeling helpless. She had not taken action to help the turtle, and now it was too late. Jane felt guilty that her inaction had led to the turtle's unfortunate fate. She identified with the helpless-ness of the turtle and believed that, just as she had done nothing to protect the turtle, she had also not protected herself sufficiently with respect to the surgery. A minor reduction (from 7 to 6) occurred in the level of distur-bance associated with the memory of the turtle incident during the EMDR processing.

This session accomplished the objective of familiarizing Jane with the EMDR process; however, the reduction in disturbance level was small. I attributed the minor movement in SUDS to the close connection between the targeted peripheral issue and the main target of the surgery itself. My experience is that, if the target has been significantly disturbing to the client, even a small reduction in disturbance level can feel like an accomplishment.

Third Session

Jane began the next session by reporting that she felt "pretty good." She mentioned several more associations related to the material explored in the previous session that had come to mind during the week. When I checked if the SUDS reduction had held from the previous week, she reported that the level of distress related to the memory of the turtle was further reduced to a 4. The fact that she had had additional associations during the week indicated that she was continuing to process the material from the previous session, and I was not surprised that the SUDS level had dropped further. It also indicated that there would likely be continuity between sessions and that she would probably respond well to EMDR.

Now Jane reported feeling tense. She said, "I feel a huge gap in my life. I can't sense what to do next from moment to moment." She acknowledged that the previous session had been "real rough" and that "that was all I managed to do the entire day." She still did not feel ready to try to desensitize the surgery itself, saying that just the thought of doing so made her feel anxious. Keeping with the general therapeutic principle of working with the resistance, I suggested focusing on the anxiety as the target for EMDR, and she agreed. The image she associated with the anxiety was of herself "cringing, withdrawing." She located the anxiety physically in her throat and stomach and indicated a SUDS level of 8. The negative cognition she chose first was "I'm not safe." The positive cognition was "I can trust my body." On a Validity of Cognition (VOC) scale (Shapiro, 1995) from 1 (completely false) to 7 (completely true), she reported a validity of 2 for this cognition when simultaneously holding in her mind the image of herself cringing. She felt a disturbing sense of loss of control related to her body becoming sick and requiring surgery. The associations that followed revolved around her physical size—her painful awareness of how much she had "shrunk" because of the surgery. At the end of the session, Jane reported that the original target image seemed "livelier" and that she felt less like cringing when she imaged it. The SUDS was now gauged at 2. She decided that a more appropriate positive cognition was "I can learn from my body," and she gave this new positive cognition a VOC of 4.

With a SUDS level of 2, I would normally expect a VOC of 5 or more. In hindsight, I attribute this discrepancy to the possibility that the positive cognition was ill-chosen. A better one might have been "I can trust myself."

Jane's report of the picture seeming livelier was a positive shift, and there was notable movement in the SUDS level. Overall, I considered this to be a beneficial outcome for the session.

Fourth Session

At the beginning of this session, Jane said that she felt ready to deal directly with the trauma of the surgery. "I'm ready for anything," she announced. She identified feelings ranging from outrage to loss. She began with the image of getting out of the car with a friend in front of the hospital entrance and noted feelings of anxiety and anger. Her associations during the eye movements included the memory of being unintentionally pregnant and feeling "so angry, like aliens had invaded my body." This memory was metaphorically close to that of her surgery to remove a growth, especially since both the growth and the fetus were located in a similar place in her body, and both had been removed surgically.

In subsequent sets of eye movements she focused on her depression. She appeared frustrated, sad, and hopeless as she explained, "I can't make any plans. I don't feel like doing anything. I just . . . [she burst into intense sobbing]. There isn't any sense of a future. I used to have one, but now it's gone. I don't seem to be able to think about it. I just focus on each day, one at a time . . . I find it crippling." Although Jane had begun the session certain that she was "ready for anything," she clearly was not; the feelings coming up were overwhelming for her. I recognized her opening statement as part of a pattern in which, ignoring her feelings and the messages from her body, she allowed herself to be guided by her thoughts about how she should be responding. In this case her mind was saying she was ready for anything, but her gut was responding otherwise. Her feeling of having been betrayed by her body was consistent with this pattern. Toward the end of this session, I remarked to Jane that she had had an intense life-changing experience and it made sense that she should feel some disorientation about her direction as she reevaluated her priorities. I emphasized the importance of paying attention to her body and her feelings. I questioned whether it made sense to plow on with her day-to-day work without acknowledging the significance of the experience she had just been through, and I asked if she had considered taking a break from work, a vacation.

The directive nature of this intervention diverges greatly from my therapeutic style prior to learning EMDR. I viewed myself here, however, as participating in a short-term process. My purpose was to help Jane with her depression. After a session as emotionally cathartic as this one, I expected a greater shift in her view of herself than I saw. Wondering what seemed to be interfering with this shift, I concluded that, consistent with the pattern I described earlier, her depression was being fed by the expectation that she be able to resume her normal life after the surgery without hesitation. Introducing the notion of taking a vacation was one way of normalizing the idea that after a significant life experience like a major surgery, some kind of processing is necessary; one can't just ignore major surgery and move on as though it had never happened.

I then asked her to picture a vacation place where she could feel comfortable and relaxed. She imagined Peru, which she finds "incredibly exciting." At the end of the session, I challenged the client's belief that she no longer cared about anything by pointing out the intensity of her feeling about going to Peru. This was a cognitive intervention which, judging from the beginning of the next session, was apparently effective.

Fifth Session

Jane began the session by describing an experience from the past week when she felt something change in her. Unable to sleep one night, she had begun to imagine her future. She said, "I felt the color seep back in. I was charged up all the next day. I kept thinking about what I really want. I thought of different things, a lot of them dumb, in different areas of my life. I actually made a list. Then yesterday I dove into a bad mood." She associated the bad mood to things happening at work and her relationship with her boyfriend. Perhaps the security of knowing that she had an upcoming therapy session in which she would be able to work out the bad feelings also played a role. Her comments at the beginning of this session not only suggested to me that she was regaining a hopefulness about her future but also that she was willing to permit herself to experience dysphoria before and during sessions. Thus it was unlikely that my direct intervention in the previous session about the possibility of taking a vacation had fueled a fantasy in her that therapy would be a place to simply feel good.

Further evidence that this fantasy had not been activated came as Jane talked about wanting to say "goodbye" to the surgery and her preoccupation with it. She wondered if she were ready. She said, "I have the feeling that if I waited until I was ready, I'd never be ready." I asked if this belief that she would never be ready had been prominent in her earlier life. She said that in late adolescence she had tried to take charge of her life by leaving her parents' home and living in a house with a group of people somewhat older than she. In that house she had always felt as if she were the child, that she was comparatively inexperienced and not ready to be out in the world. She said she has felt that way ever since. I viewed the belief that she would never be ready to work through this trauma as a blocking belief and suggested using the negative cognition "I'll never be ready" as the target for EMDR.

The image she associated with this belief was of the house she had moved into when she left home. She pictured the house and the people with whom she had lived. She compared her experience of herself to that of "a child living with grown-ups"; she had felt unprepared to be living away from home. Upsetting memories came up, including one she chose not to describe to me. She commented about not being happy to find this "nest of stuff" again. The negative cognition was "I'm weak," and the positive cognition was "I was young then, and I've grown up" (VOC = 5; SUDS = 4). She talked about "feeling a little bit of tears starting." Though she appeared to be feeling emotions, no intense affect was emerging. She described being on the edge of a "nest of memories" and struggling over whether to "charge at them," even though they seemed overwhelming and she did not feel ready. She referenced the discussion she and I had had at the outset of the previous session about charging ahead when she did not feel ready.

What follows is a transcript of the next portion of that session. It begins with my suggestion that these memories might be more manageable if she placed her adult self in the memories and then watched them unfold. This is the first time that I had used this technique with Jane, which I will discuss later in this chapter. She followed my suggestion and reported feeling calmer.

PM: These memories are painful to reexperience. I think it would be less painful for you if you place your adult self in the memories and watch them unfold.

Jane: ►◄►◄►◄ (87) I feel calmer.

PM: Do you feel finished with those memories?

Jane: There are a lot of them. I think there are more.

PM: Stay with them.

Jane: ►◄►◄►◄ (90) The headache is still there, but it's interesting. What you suggested feels helpful. It doesn't feel like it could ever finish, but it could, couldn't it?

PM: Just watch the memories go by as if you were on the train looking out the window, like we talked about.

Jane: ►◄►◄►◄ (78) I felt almost as if I were guarding the young me. ►◄►◄►◄ (58) I was thinking about—I moved on a tiny bit from that time. I'm thinking about meeting the man whom I came to California to be with. Early last spring I sent him a book. He sent me a cloisonné pendant. It was a time that Frank and I were breaking up. In some weird way I got into a big block about it. It was too much for me to respond to somehow. ►◄►◄►◄ (40) I feel blocked in my chest. ►◄►◄►◄ (44) Shoes. [*She is covering her chest and abdomen with her arms and hands.*] ►◄►◄►◄ (52) I have a sense of myself being small and clingy. I see my mother's legs. I'm being shooed away from her for being small and clingy. I want to hold onto her legs, and she won't let me. (36) Can we keep doing this for as long as I need to? I don't mean today, of course.

PM: Are you asking me, "Are you going to cut this off?" You were recalling a memory in which your needs were not being responded to, and you became similarly concerned that your needs here would not be met.

Jane: ▶◀▶◀▶◀ (38) I have a very clear image of being small, three or something, and the space around me feels empty and dark and quiet. The sense of it is that I'm not going to get what I feel I need, but if I'm quiet and contained I might get a little of it. ▶◀▶◀▶◀ (41) The child seems awfully little to be so constrained.

For a client like Jane to recall painful childhood memories with appropriate affect, she must as an adult feel empathy for herself as the child in those memories. Jane's spontaneous comment that the child seemed awfully little to be so constrained indicated the beginning of that empathy, and the moistening of her eyes at that point confirmed this.

PM: What are you feeling now?

Jane: There is a feeling, but I don't know how to identify it.

In order to strengthen her empathy for the child, I again suggested placing her adult self in the image. As was the case previously, this direct intervention did not appear to produce passivity in her; on the contrary, it was followed with many spontaneous, meaningful associations.

PM: Picture your adult self with the three-year-old. Imagine your adult self giving the three-year-old what she needs.

Jane: ▶◀▶◀▶◀ (39) I picked her up, holding her close, laughing and being playful. It struck me that the empty space was like when we moved, and I took her out to show her the lawn of the new house, and—[*she breaks into sobs and is unable to talk*] ▶◀▶◀▶◀ (49) I immediately felt, "This is so trite. I'm not going to do this. I don't want to revisit my childhood memories." It felt like when I rejected the Primal Therapy stuff the people in that house were into. One of my roommates sort of blew his brains out with that stuff.

PM: What are you feeling now?

Jane: Sad, tears. There's something so rote and forced and manufactured about Primal Therapy. Like people are emoting on cue, almost like they're following a script.

PM: Are you concerned that these tears of yours might be melodramatic?

Jane: Yes.

PM: What do you think? Do you think they are?

Jane: No. They came so suddenly, but they weren't forced. They surprised me. ►◄►◄►◄ (25) The lawn seems like this bittersweet place. It's a wonderful lawn, but also pretty lonely.

PM: Is this unpleasant for you to recall?

Jane: It's a little abrasive but not completely unpleasant. I feel a lot of tension around the upper part of my body. Not that the actual things I'm thinking of are upsetting to recall, but the process is uncomfortable. Thinking of these things makes me feel that I can have the memories, and it will be all right.

In the sets of eye movements that followed, Jane continued to review memories and eventually moved into more current ones relating to attempts at breaking up with her boyfriend Frank. The session came to an end with an installation after the VOC on "I was young then and I've grown up" was checked and reported as 7. I regarded this as a very successful session, not only because the disturbing feeling disappeared and the VOC went to 7, but because the memory was a mixed one, both "wonderful" and "pretty lonely," indicating a relatively realistic integration of the memory.

Sixth Session

At the beginning of this session, Jane reported talking with her boyfriend Frank about the memories that had come up in the previous session. She had realized that the spontaneous image of her mother's shoes was a pun in that it also seemed to relate to her being "shooed" out. She was struck with how the association that "didn't seem to make any sense [had] turned out to be the richest." Then she described going to the hospital the prior week to see the tissue that had been removed from her in the surgery. She had previously declined to do this. Seeing the tissue had made her realize that the doctors had had no choice but to remove as much as they did. She accepted the way the surgery had been performed and described the day's experience as "one little piece closing the circle, and it was big." I viewed this decision to go back to the hospital and look at the tissue she had lost as a healthy sign, she was able to do something she had been avoiding because the feelings of loss were now tolerable to her. It confirmed my impression that the previous session had been effective.

For her present EMDR target she went back to the three-year-old child-hood memory of clinging to her mother's legs. The issue of having to con-tain herself came up, and she identified the negative cognition as "It's useless to ask for the things I love." The positive cognition was "I have a right to ask for what I need and want." The SUDS was reported as 12 (off the scale). The feelings were of sadness and desperation. She felt an intense headache and tension in her stomach, chest, and torso. Upon beginning the eye move-ments, her immediate association was to the spot in her backyard "where I buried one of my cats. The image was of furiously digging up the cat's coffin with my hands. That was the image."

After the next set of eye movements, she said, "It doesn't seem like I'll ever get through this sadness." After the next set, "I retreated from the sad-ness, slid away from it." Addressing her resistance, I suggested focusing on how hard the sadness was for her to experience. After a set of eye move-ments, she reported having difficulty focusing. I asked what she thought might happen if she were able to focus. After a set of eye movements, she reported, "The thought was that then I would let go." After another set of eye movements, her eyes were wet, and she said, "I don't want to let go. I don't want to let go of Blossom, my cat." As she began the next set of eye movements, Jane burst into tears, saying, "This sounds so nutty, but I realized that I'd been thinking about her some this weekend on a below-conscious level."

In the associations and comments that followed the eye movements, she described crying about and mourning the loss of this cat for five years. The specific image that came up was that of the cat trying to drink from her bowl and repeatedly being unable to because of an intestinal tumor. This event was extraordinarily painful to Jane at the time it had occurred and remained so now, as she recalled it. She sobbed intensely. She remembered calling the veterinarian and having the cat put to sleep and how difficult and painful that was to do. She felt angry about having to make that deci-sion. She felt guilty and helpless at being unable to do something for the cat. Finally, I pointed out the parallel between her feelings about the cat's sickness and those about her own surgery. She felt responsible in both cases for the suffering and believed there must have been something else she could have done to make the situation better. I summarized her comments with the sentence, "I don't have to accept this." This brought up more affect, and after a set of eye movements, she said, "It already happened. It's a done deal." Jane finally said, "I accept that she died and I had to have her put to sleep." I reflected, "The turtle's suffering, the cat's death, your sickness, the way the surgery was performed—these events are particularly painful for you because they are all things for which you feel responsibility but which were realistically out of your control." After a set of eye movements, she added with a chuckle, "Maybe for an animal, I can accept that if he wants to leave [die], it's not under my control."

As in many of the previous sessions, this one involved genuine catharsis, and I believe an important mourning process took place. However, it is apparent that, in spite of therapeutic movement in the session, she still believed she could have done, or should have done, something more in the situation. I commented to her that this belief seemed to be overarching. With respect to her surgery, she blamed herself for not having done enough to take care of herself; the helplessness she had felt was extremely painful. She felt those same feelings with the memories involving the turtle and her cat Blossom. The helplessness was also prominent in her reaction to her mother's rejection and her memory of her experience of living in the house with older roommates after she'd left home. She seemed relieved by my comment.

Seventh Session

Jane arrived at this session 25 minutes late, saying that she had misjudged the traffic. She began by describing how good it had felt when, at the end of the previous session, I had said, "These are all things that are out of your control." She said it had tied everything together in a way she hadn't considered before. Because little time remained in the session, we agreed to focus the EMDR on a small piece of the material that was coming up. The target selected was the positive cognition "I can accept that there are some things that are outside my control," with the idea that the eye movements would be used to find an appropriate target image (VOC = 4). What came up was something she felt was "too big for her to deal with" in the amount of time remaining: She described a sinking feeling in her abdomen and then an image of something icy, thick, slippery, and cold. She said, "When I picture this icy thing, I feel inadequate, like withdrawing. It's hard to put into words. It just seems so much bigger than I am—that there is no way for me to relate to it." Again, there was not much progress on the positive cognition.

I view this as an example of one of my most frequent errors in doing EMDR: not allowing enough time in a session to adequately treat the selected target. It had been selected as a small piece of the central issue but, in reality, was itself central and required far more time than was available.

Eighth Session

In the next session Jane began by saying she felt good and that she had three things to report. One had to do with a loss she'd experienced that week, which she felt she'd handled well. Another involved a new openness to recalling memories of her cat Blossom. She said, "I was going through photos this week, and I came across a photo of Blossom, and I could put it on my desk—and I've even been enjoying it. In the past I would have just turned my head away and shoved it back in the bag." In the previous session I was concerned about Jane's lateness and whether it reflected the beginning of a pattern of resistance, but I found this report to be quite believable and another indication of progress towards resolving her feelings of loss. She went on to say, "Before last week I wouldn't have thought of Blossom as a memory I was avoiding. I wonder what else is hidden like that. I thought I'd pay attention and see if I can catch myself pushing things away, but so far I haven't been able to."

The third item she wanted to report was that she wanted to focus on her relationship with Frank but felt some embarrassment in talking about it. "I noticed in my feelings for him a feeling very similar to the clinging feeling I was talking about in that memory several weeks ago of me as a small child—the memory that started with that surprising image of the pair of shoes and the legs and then the memory of holding onto them. Right now, Frank and I are taking a three-week break from each other. Sometimes there is an emotional thing I get into with Frank that everything is black if we're not together. There are other times when I'm much more OK about how things are working out. The black state has some of that clinging, helpless feeling wrapped up in it."

Although Jane appears to have a more intact observing ego and to tolerate considerably more independent expression than one would expect from a client with a personality disorder, it is interesting how precisely her description of these alternating states matches the borderline/dependent split as conceptualized by Masterson (1976). She describes the clinging, helpless feelings characteristic of the positive part of the borderline/dependent split as well as the negative state in which everything is black when she's without Frank. Then, several minutes later, in a comment that demonstrated a lack of splitting, she indicated some ability to blend these two states. She said, "It seems like there might be a sense of sadness around this exhilarating feeling. It's all beautiful and open, but there is also some sense of being alone, which is sad."

She decided to target the way her feeling about herself changes radically, depending on whether or not she is with Frank. Since this target is so close to the fundamental split just discussed, I did not expect deep change to occur as a result of one or even a few sessions. After ten minutes of EMDR processing, she said she now understood what Frank meant when he described one of his therapy sessions as not going anywhere. She described herself as being stuck "in this spot, wherever it is." In my experience it has rarely been productive to focus on splitting phenomena as a target for EMDR, unless the splitting has become clearly ego-dystonic, yielding affective hooks into disturbing thoughts, feelings, or memories. In Jane's case it had not.

In order to focus on her resistance—the place she described herself as being stuck—I asked her what age correlated to the thoughts and feelings she was noticing.

Jane: Three, that's the age I pinpointed before with the clinging image . . . I feel I'm losing huge chunks of my past. ▶◀▶◀▶◀ I'm wandering in these thoughts, driving along, loosely thinking about Blossom, my cat, and I then thought of how another cat I had when I was a small child died just after we moved to the house in Boise.

My question about her age also helped her to engage her memories in a more affective way. She began sobbing as she described the cat's death and her effort to control her feelings at the time so that her mother would not feel bad.

After considerable processing and affective discharge, she recalled the loss of still another cat. The feelings surrounding this loss were even more intense, mainly because, in this instance, her parents seemed to have no empathy, and she had no one to support her during the experience of the loss. At first the feelings brought up by this memory were overwhelming, and it was not until she placed herself in the position of an observer that she could recall the events. She described the feeling as "this incredibly alone feeling. No kid should have to go through this." This comment indicated feelings of empathy arising for the child she remembered being, which in my experience usually indicates a developing readiness for the client to go deeper into the memory and achieve some resolution of it. She referred to "an incredible well of feeling" that she was unable to access.

I asked what the young girl needed at that time and suggested that she put herself into the memory as an adult and attempt to give the little girl what she needed. Her ability to do this successfully—to give herself as an adult what she needed as a child—means to me that she is reasonably intact and can play the role of the nurturing adult, clients who are more deeply disturbed usually cannot do this without more preparation. During the next set of eye movements, she saw many images of this cat, as if "looking through a photo album." She enjoyed the images that arose, and the memory was no longer disturbing. Her image of the original target of being away from Frank had changed somewhat as she now brought it back to mind. She described it as having "loosened" a little. She chose a new positive cognition of "I can support myself," and as she imaged being apart from Frank, she reported this new cognition as feeling completely true (VOC = 7).

Ninth Session

The session began with her again reporting feeling "pretty good." She said, "Sunday or Monday I realized that I was not all tied up in knots about Frank. That's a big change for me. I've been with him two years. I'm going, 'Is this real?'" She reported a sense of movement in other parts of her life, including work, and said, "I have a lot more energy, and I look forward to messages on my answering machine now."

She wanted to know about the potential of EMDR, about whether these discoveries of huge pockets of emotional memory could go on indefinitely. After considerable discussion, she asked if this therapy could influence the way she was pursuing her career. In particular, she was aware that she sacrificed the opportunity to work on projects of her own in favor of playing a support role in working on other people's projects. As she talked about it, the picture emerged of a person whose central struggle was to escape from her well-worn role as a support person for people with whom she was unable to set adequate boundaries and by whom she always ended up feeling used. Escape from this role would mean moving into the unfamiliar position of supporting herself and her own creative and individuating efforts.

Her reticence in launching her own projects seemed to come from a need for an external authority to validate the value of her work. "The things I have been able to establish have been supportive kinds of things or connective kinds of things in which I'm working on someone else's project, but I harbor resentment about that always being my focus." Many clients place this kind of importance on obtaining the approval of an authority because they lack a felt sense of identity and need other people to define and validate themselves. Although not completely convinced, I believed that

Jane was able to generate a sense of self-worth internally and that her need for external validation related primarily to her professional contributions.

She continued, "This is an area I think I can talk about here. I have an intellectual awareness that this goes on, but I'm thinking, "You're not going to make me look at this, are you?" I pointed out that her last comment seemed to be an example of what she was talking about: The therapy was, in a sense, *her* project, but she was turning it over to me as if she were only playing a supporting role. My comment had been confrontative and possibly not entirely accurate, and she reported feeling tight and threatened after I'd made it. She then told a peripherally relevant story, but when questioned about it, she acknowledged that the function of the story was primarily protective, to help her manage the feelings coming up at the time she began telling it. She talked about her feelings regarding the separation from Frank and how different it felt for her to not be continually thinking about him. She ended the session saying, "I've been thinking that if this state were to hold, I might be really ready to be OK with not being with him if he can't decide to be in our relationship in a committed way. That would be better than being close and having him waffling."

In my view this session represented a transition point in the treatment process. *The depression—her original purpose for being in treatment—was resolved.* She'd asked if this work could go on indefinitely, which reflected her amazement at the many pockets of intense affect she had discovered with EMDR, but also may have reflected a questioning about what she was doing in therapy now that her depression had lifted. This latter subject was not explicitly discussed in this session. She gave repeated indications that she recognized she had deeper issues and was in a process of determining whether or not she would explore these therapeutically.

Tenth Session

This session was focused on yet another loss: a mentor who had been supportive of Jane and had died some years back. Recalling this loss brought up very intense affect. The thoughts of the mentor were stimulated by a ceremony that had been held in her memory the morning of the session. I wondered if her thoughts about losing her mentor didn't also relate to the treatment process and the potential for it to end shortly.

At the end of the session Jane noted that Friday would be the end of the three-week separation from Frank and that he wanted to get together Saturday night, but a good friend of hers was having a celebration that night, so she'd put off seeing Frank until Sunday evening. To her, this reflected an independent perspective with which she was pleased.

Eleventh Session

I asked Jane about how her first meeting with Frank had gone after the three-week separation, and she said, "Oh, I guess I didn't tell you yet; we decided to break up. Neither of us had changed our positions. He still didn't want to make a commitment, and I wasn't willing to continue on that basis. I'm surprised that I haven't been thinking about him that much." I asked, "Did you think about him a lot the last time you broke up?" and her response was, "You mean, was there a moment I *didn't* think about him?" She was pleased that this separation had not brought on her usual obsessional thinking.

In this session the focus chosen for EMDR was the feeling of not being worthy that came up for her around separations. The image was of "beating on or clinging to someone much larger than I." She associated to this the image of her mother's legs and the memory of wanting to cling to her mother's legs that had come up in an earlier session. Toward the end of the process, she brought up a situation at work involving a supervisor who was controlling and prevented projects from being worked on in an organized and efficient way. She felt frustrated and angry. Then a childhood fantasy came up, one that she said she did not feel comfortable sharing. During the next sets of eye movements, she displayed an increasingly intense terror response. The image that came up at the end of the session was of hitting her head. Time ran out in the session, and she said she thought she could hold this image until the next session.

Twelfth Session

Jane began her session saying, "I've been feeling wonderful." She explained that Frank and she would be seeing each other that afternoon because of a work situation that had arisen. She was looking forward to it; she had talked to Frank about it over the telephone and decided it was OK to do. They had agreed to go out together afterward for something to eat.

For this session she suggested targeting the "horrible place" from the last session. In my experience it generally isn't useful to try to pick up work on a deep affective state that was interrupted in a previous session by lack of

time, unless the client comes to the next session with that affect or associated body sensation accessible. There would have been no problem if the
original image had brought up the affect, but in this case Jane seemed to be
defending against this feeling by attempting to reconnect with Frank, despite
her resolve to hold out for a commitment from him. I should have focused
on the defense but, instead, went along with her suggestion.

After some time pursuing the material from the previous session, it became apparent that, despite some minimal affect, the material Jane was trying to access was not naturally emerging. Several interesting associations
arose amidst those more focused on the target issue; she mentioned wanting
validation from me and, later, some anger came up at me that did not make
sense to her. I suggested that the thought of seeing Frank that afternoon
had generated a sense of well-being she wasn't willing to spoil by accessing
disturbing thoughts and feelings. She said that she had felt a bit suspicious
during the week when she had gotten a "light in [her] eyes" for a man she
had known for some time. She said, "In the past that's a way I've created
distance," a way she's dealt with clingy feelings that have arisen during separations. She said that she had purposely not pursued this new romantic
interest.

Then she smiled and said that she was now feeling "real nervous." She
quipped, "Can't we go back to some safe childhood problem?" This remark
reminded me of her comment in the eighth session that I had confronted.
She said she had a desire to come into therapy with a sense of strength
because it's more comfortable; she'd been thinking about this recently and
decided that "maybe it's OK for there to be a time in the week for the more
unpleasant stuff to be there." She referred to something I had said several
weeks ago that had made her feel I was "sympathetic" and accepting of a
person like her. "I had a sense of acceptance, like maybe that part of me
could be accepted as well." I asked if her choice not to describe the childhood fantasy she referred to the last week had to do with her concern about
my acceptance. She said she had been deeply ashamed of this fantasy as a
child and realized from my question that she still was. Discussion continued
about the euphoric state she had manufactured for herself, which I finally
summarized as a state in which she wanted to maintain the view that all was
well with the world. I pointed out that, even though she could see that
nothing had changed in her relationship with Frank, she was avoiding the
unpleasant feelings that the separation was bringing up by saying to herself,
"Forget it, it feels good, so go with it." She responded, "Yes, that's exactly
right." In other words, she had resisted an impulse to cling earlier in the

week but was now caught up in clinging to Frank and her unrealistic, idealized fantasy of that relationship.

I viewed her ignoring her previous sober assessment of this relationship as another emergence of resistance. It seemed to represent a "rewarding unit" fantasy (Masterson, 1976) that is typical of the borderline/dependent character. In the rewarding unit, the positive part of the borderline/dependent split, the client clings to the object to maintain a sense of well-being and a feeling of being loved while avoiding feelings of abandonment that would arise from a separation or emotional distance. According to Masterson, these clients are extremely resistant to viewing their relationships realistically because every relationship has times of relative alienation or animosity. Such clients avoid experiences of partial rejection or abandonment even at great cost to themselves and their ability to function effectively (Manfield, 1992; Masterson, 1976). In my assessment, the appearance at this point in the treatment of avoidance and splitting to such a degree that they blocked therapeutic work was again a reflection of the shifting nature of the treatment towards Jane's deeper and more complex issues. The specter of separation from the therapist and from Frank combined to stimulate clinging.

The original major depression and feelings of loss were resolved. What remained were characterological issues that appeared to involve splitting and self-defeating behavior related to the anxiety produced by separation or autonomous or individuating acts. Addressing these issues would require more than the short-term treatment contract on which this therapy had been based to this point. It was now necessary to renegotiate that contract or begin to terminate the treatment.

Thirteenth Session

At the beginning of this session, Jane described how Frank and she had had dinner together and that he had said he wanted to commit himself to the relationship. She'd been ecstatic; however, several days later he called and began hedging. She again became clear that she wasn't interested in pursuing the relationship unless he could make more of a commitment. She had arrived at a balanced view of the relationship.

I told her that just as she was in a process of renegotiating her relationship contract with Frank, I thought that she and I needed to discuss our relationship contract as well. I indicated that, in my opinion, the original goals she had set for therapy had been met and that several deeper issues had come up, including her difficulty in taking independent action in her career and the emotional flip-flop that she does in relationships. I clarified that these were related to lifelong issues for her and were deeper than the ones we had been working on previously. She agreed. "What you are saying in terms of there being this shift about why I'm here makes sense to me. Especially in the last several weeks, I've had a feeling of life starting up again."

After some discussion of her relationship with Frank, I suggested that one reason a commitment from him was so important to her was that she saw this relationship as a way to make her life feel more meaningful, as a resolution of her anxiety about finding her own identity. She agreed and expanded further upon my comment. I said that I thought she might be making Frank her "project," that her attempt to find meaning through her relationship with Frank was similar to her career issue: She lacks a direction that is personally meaningful to her, so she works on someone else's project. This comment made her uncomfortable; the therapy hour was nearly over, and she wished aloud that the session would end. She also said she understood what I was saying and thought it was true. She decided that she would like to contract for six more weeks of treatment and then reevaluate. I said I thought that was reasonable, since the therapy process would be somewhat different and she did not know what the changes would be like for her.

Subsequent Treatment

In addition to those six sessions, there were six others for a total of 25. Jane's major depression was resolved by the tenth session and did not recur, as of this writing six months later. Although not fully resolved, her deeper issues showed clear evidence of progress. In my opinion, her willingness to set limits in her relationship with Frank showed a healthy move towards independence; it eventually resulted in a reshaping of that relationship with more appropriate balance and levels of commitment. The focus of sessions shifted to her difficulty in maintaining a realistic view of romantic relationships and continued to be punctuated by new memories of painful losses that had not been fully mourned or had left Jane feeling isolated and needy.

Another manifestation of her deeper issues had been her difficulty pursuing her own projects. She had noticed that she had shaped her career around men, whom she had ably supported in their work. However, she had consistently neglected to create opportunities to follow her own particular interests and directions. Towards the end of the treatment period, after processing this issue and using EMDR to explore a particular work environment in which she realized she was not being treated with appropriate respect, she set limits with her boss. Demonstrating a strong ability to separate and individuate, she stood her ground in the face of his refusal to acknowledge the legitimacy of her concerns. When he continued to fail to respond in a respectful way, she terminated that professional relationship and within weeks was offered a prestigious position as the director of another professional organization. She accepted the new position and has thrived in it. In addition, she has recently taken major steps to increase her exposure in the professional world and market herself in a way that allows her to play a central role, rather then relegating herself to the familiar position of a support person.

A Misleading Somatic Response

In session seven the image of "something icy" came up, which felt so big to Jane that there was no way to address it. Possibly related to this, in the eleventh session she had felt an intense terror, which she was unable to access in the following session. This terror resurfaced in several subsequent sessions; in response to it, her knee would jerk up spontaneously, as if to protect her from a blow, and she would hold the front of her neck. The meaning of this powerful sequence never became entirely clear. The connection to a possible molest was mentioned by Jane and explored; she could think of only one memory that seemed a vague possibility, but when she processed it further and discussed the circumstances of the memory with her mother, she became convinced that no molest had occurred. During additional processing of the surgery experience, the terror response arose again, and I decided to use EMDR to target the actual physical sensations associated with it. I found it productive to bring her back repeatedly to target (the physical sensation), bypassing associations that might have diffused her focus. The result was a marked reduction in the intensity of the physical sensations.

These feelings still came up later several times, though with minimal intensity. During two of these sessions, a fair amount of focus was given to these somatic responses, without much apparent therapeutic benefit. Approximately four sessions before termination, Jane raised the question of whether her somatic responses during these two EMDR sessions were really meaningful. She wondered if she was manufacturing them. Indeed, it had occurred to me that the somatic responses might constitute a familiar and relatively comfortable avenue of exploration for her as well as a means of satisfying a predisposition for drama and a high sensitivity to body sensations and movement. In fact, it seemed to me that the particular disturbance contributing to the SUDS level at the start of these EMDR processes was becoming obscured by the somatic associations that followed. I speculated to myself that in this way she might be avoiding more disturbing material.

This hypothesis was verified by several subsequent EMDR sessions in which I successfully used various techniques to help her maintain her focus. The first technique was to ask her periodically whether she thought the body sensations she was reporting were meaningful. If she thought they weren't, I suggested that she return to the original target. At times, I also directed her attention to the material that had been coming up before her focus became diffused. Eventually, I found it productive to redirect her repeatedly back to the original target and check what, if anything, was now disturbing about it. This redirection helped to prevent the diffusion of her focus by utilizing the original disturbance as the thread tying together all her associations. For instance, in one session, I suggested using as a target a loss that had been processed several times before and had reached a stable SUDS level of 2. By repeatedly focusing her attention back to the target and inquiring about what precisely was causing the level 2 disturbance, I found that she was able to identify an emotional block that had not been processed in previous sessions. As she focused on it, she realized that her sense of loss was so intense that she could not bear it. I suggested that she view the memory from the removed position of an outside observer. She did so, and she was able to process the loss completely (SUDS = 0). We were both surprised at the intensity of affect that emerged from what had stubbornly remained a target at level 2. I was reminded of the importance of pursuing targets repeatedly until they are fully resolved.

Discussion of Additional Treatment Techniques

This case is typical of many I have treated using EMDR. Although the targets, images, and memories come from the clients, I play an active role in helping them to select their targets and then in clarifying and intensifying their recall of them. As a general rule, the more fully clients connect with their initial targets, the more effective the EMDR that follows. As with many clients who have become depressed after a loss, the focus of most of the EMDR sessions with Jane was on processing previous losses. Among other things, EMDR appears to help the client tolerate recalling these memories with full affect so that they can be thoroughly processed.

At times, however, additional intervention seems appropriate in order to help the client complete a segment of work. One intervention used several times with Jane was the suggestion that she imagine the presence of her adult self (or another loving adult) at the time of the past painful event. In addition to its use with EMDR (Shapiro, 1995), this intervention has long been common in a variety of different therapeutic approaches. For example, it was described by Milton Erickson (1980; Erickson & Rossi, 1989) in his case descriptions of "The February Man," by Bob and Mary Goulding (Goulding & Goulding, 1979) in their redecision therapy, and is commonly used in "inner child" work (Bradshaw, 1990) and hypnotic therapies (Zeig, 1982). More recently, it has been described in Ecker and Hulley's *Depth-Oriented Brief Therapy* (1996). An application of this intervention was discussed in EMDR trainings in the context of utilizing "power symbols," and was elaborated by Wildwind in her presentation on depression at the first EMDR Advanced Clinical Applications Conference (1992). Wildwind discussed a technique she called "adoption," in which a variety of loving adults are either recalled or invented to serve as a new support group for the client. I have found this intervention especially helpful when the client is recalling an affect-laden memory from childhood but is either unable to access the affect or let go of the negative cognition she connects to the memory. In these situations I suggest that the client imagine a caring adult figure (parental or otherwise) intervening to help the young person in the memory.

This technique is so effective that I now develop a "loving person resource" with all clients before beginning to process disturbing memories. Particularly with clients for whom I suspect that images of loving figures are not readily available, I have found it important to identify these caring figures in advance so that they are easily accessed at the time they are needed. (I usually address this subject early in treatment, after identifying and working with the client's safe place.) It may be necessary to access fantasy figures or characters from television or feature films for a mental image. In the case of relatively healthy clients, the caring person may be the adult client herself inserted into the childhood memory to help the client-as-a-child; in these instances the client usually reports alternating between identifying with her child self—feeling the guilt, shame, horror, or fear—and identifying with herself as the capable, mature adult.

When I ask clients who are engaged in this scenario of the child being comforted by the fantasized adult to note when intense affect comes up, they usually report that they feel it when they are identifying with themselves *as the adult* rather than as the child. This answer is consistent with my understanding of what takes place. For the affect to be intensely felt, the client needs a container for it so that she will not be retraumatized—overwhelmed in the therapy by the intensity of her response and her inability to organize the experience internally, as she was in the original event. The necessary safety, structure, and support are provided by the caring adult inserted into the memory, so it is at the point of identification with this necessary resource that the affect can be permitted to come through, in turn allowing reprocessing of the memory.

Although this technique is used in relation to acute issues in the case presented here, I have also successfully used it to treat deep, lifelong issues. I think that this process increases the base of nurturing adult relationships (self objects) the client can draw upon, in addition to the therapist-client relationship, for a sense of safety and for help in organizing recalled experiences and the feelings these memories evoke.

I have found that any deliberate alteration of a traumatic image, if successful, is likely to lead towards an adaptive resolution. For example, images associated with PTSD are stored in a raw form that makes the "flashback" phenomenon possible: PTSD sufferers can experience the triggering of an old, disturbing memory as if it were happening in the present. Normally we cannot remember events in this vivid, as-if-it-were-happening-in-the-moment way. As nontraumatic sensory input is collected, it is processed by the limbic system, which determines what is relevant to retain in a symbolic representation (van der Kolk, 1996). For example, we remember the traffic light turning green, but we don't remember the details of the traffic light itself. Before an image can be deliberately altered, it must be converted into this symbolic rather than literal representation.

This "conversion" occurs spontaneously in the normal course of EMDR treatment. A Vietnam veteran I was working with (see Chapter 7) was processing the memory of a large jagged piece of shrapnel from an exploded rocket careening towards him. The memory was terrifying and he told me that the image was crystal clear and would, never change. During one of the sets of eye-movements, I could see the terror enter and leave his moving eyes as he focused on the image. At the end of that set he said, "This will sound crazy, but that piece of rocket changed into a huge marshmallow flying through the air." The image had been processed; it had changed from an eidetic image stored in the right hemisphere of the brain to a symbolic one stored in the left hemisphere (van der Kolk, 1996). I asked him to try to recall the image in its original form and he could not; from then on it was a fuzzy, symbolically constructed image. When something that normally occurs spontaneously during a successful treatment is not occurring, it is often helpful to suggest that the client make it happen. When I suggest that a client intentionally alter an eidetic image, it is sometimes processed, becomes symbolic, and loses its disturbing quality.

Evaluation of Outcome

I believe that the lifting of Jane's major depression represents a strong therapeutic result for a brief course of treatment. This treatment focused on the working through of painful and unmourned losses, the memories of which had been stimulated by her surgery. When I last saw her, she appeared to be demonstrating an increased ability to support her own self-actualizing needs. For example, she is setting appropriate limits in difficult situations, risking loss to maintain the integrity of her position in relationships, and apparently thriving on her successes and the increased responsibilities that have accompanied them. When I contacted her a year after she terminated treatment, she reaffirmed that her gains had remained stable. She continued to excel at her new job and enjoy it immensely. Her relationship with Frank was progressing well. She related some details of her life and then concluded, "I'm very happy."

In presenting this case, I am aware that the results produced in this brief period are not necessarily different from those that would be produced in another type of treatment—and, in fact, the clinical material that came up during the treatment was essentially what one would expect in other treatment approaches over a longer period of time. The effect of EMDR in this case was to shorten the length of treatment by rapidly bringing into focus the series of unresolved losses underlying the client's symptoms, and effectively resolving them. Once these losses were resolved, Jane was able to process other dysfunctional patterns of behavior that had resulted from her need to avoid loss.

References

Bradshaw, J. (1990). *Homecoming, reclaiming, and championing your inner child.* New York: Bantam Books.

Ecker, B., & Hulley, L. (1996). *Depth-oriented brief therapy.* San Francisco: Jossey-Bass.

Erickson, M. (1980). *The collected papers of Milton H. Erickson on hypnosis. Vol. IV. Innovative hypnotherapy.* (E. Rossi, Ed.). New York: Irvington.

Erickson, M., & E. Rossi. (1989). *The February man: Evolving consciousness and identity in hypnotherapy.* New York: Brunner/Mazel.

Goulding, R., & Goulding, M. (1979). *Changing lives through redecision therapy.* New York: Grove/Atlantic.

Guntrip, H. (1968). *Schizoid phenomena, object-relations and the self*. New York: Guilford Press.

Johnson, S. (1995). *Character styles*. New York: W. W. Norton.

Manfield, P. (1992). *Split self/split object: Understanding and treating borderline, narcissistic and schizoid disorders*. Northvale, NJ: Jason Aronson.

Masterson, J. E. (1976). *Psychotherapy of the borderline adult—A developmental approach*. New York: Brunner/Mazel.

Masterson, J. E. (1981). *The narcissistic and borderline disorders—An integrated developmental approach*. New York: Brunner/Mazel.

Shapiro, E. (1995). *Eye movement desensitization and reprocessing: Basic principles, protocols, and procedures*. New York: Guilford Press.

van der Kolk, B. (1996). The body keeps score: Approaches to the psychobiology of posttraumatic stress disorder. In B. van der Kolk, A. McFarlane, & L. Weisaeth (Eds.), *Traumatic stress* (pp. 214–241). New York: Guilford Press.

Wildwind, L. (1992, April). *Working with depression*. Paper presented at the Advanced Clinical Applications of EMDR Conference, Sunnyvale, CA.

Wolf, E. (1988). *Treating the self-elements of clinical self-psychology*. New York: Guilford Press.

Wolpe, J. (1991). *The practice of behavior therapy (4th ed.)*. New York: Pergamon Press.

Zeig, J. (Ed.). (1982). *Ericksonian approaches to hypnosis and psychotherapy*. New York: Brunner/Mazel.

6

IMAGINARY CRIMES
Resolving Survivor Guilt and Writer's Block

Lewis Engel

I AM A PSYCHOLOGIST in private practice in San Francisco. Approximately two-thirds of my practice involves long-term depth-oriented psychotherapy with individuals and couples. The balance is short-term work with individuals and couples on specific problems. For example, I often assist candidates having trouble completing dissertations or passing professional examinations. I have had training in Gestalt therapy and cognitive-behavioral therapy as well the primary approach that I now use, control mastery theory (CMT).

Control Mastery Theory

CMT is both psychodynamic and cognitive in approach. The theory assumes, as do theories underlying most psychodynamic therapies, that trauma from specific major incidents or problematic relationships with parents, or both, is the ultimate cause of psychological problems. Like most cognitive approaches, CMT holds that these traumatic experiences cause the client to have irrational beliefs. It is not the trauma but the resulting irrational beliefs that cause the client to suffer from maladaptive feelings and behaviors.

CMT is also clearly distinguishable from most cognitive and psychodynamic theories. Unlike most cognitive approaches, for example, CMT holds that many of these trauma-related maladaptive beliefs are unconscious and involve irrational guilt. Most cognitive approaches completely ignore or discount unconscious processes and give short shrift to guilt. Unlike many psychodynamic approaches, the CMT therapist does not strive to be neutral but to take a stance that will assist the client in overcoming her problems. This stance may be neutral, if that is what the therapist believes will help the client overcome her maladaptive beliefs, but it also may be active or even directive.

I took the EMDR training in 1995 and immediately began using it with both new and long-term clients. I think part of the reason I was able to begin using EMDR so readily is that it fits very well into both a dynamic and cognitive framework. From a dynamic point of view EMDR assumes, as does CMT, that problematic parenting or trauma of some kind is the root cause of clients' difficulties. From a cognitive point of view EMDR holds that clients' *beliefs* play a key role in their problems. In EMDR's terminology these are called *negative cognitions*. In addition, CMT is an approach in which the therapist endeavors to take the stance he feels will be most helpful to the client, rather than to achieve therapeutic neutrality. Because of this experience, the active stance required in EMDR was comfortable for me.

As I mentioned, one of the unique features of CMT is its emphasis on unconscious irrational guilt. One of the best examples of such guilt is survivor guilt—the irrational guilt felt by those left alive after the death of loved ones. The case I am presenting illustrates the importance of being sensitive to unconscious guilt as a cause of psychological problems. Because of my training in CMT, I am particularly aware of cognitions involving unconscious guilt, and I believe that my awareness of this theme has substantially improved my clinical effectiveness. In writing this chapter about a case illustrating unconscious guilt, I hope to encourage EMDR therapists to be sensitive to it.

My work with survivor guilt has required an adaptation of the standard EMDR protocol. A client who is not suffering from survivor guilt will express her negative cognitions in simple phrases, such as "I am worthless," "I am detestable," or "I am stupid." Negative cognitions of clients who suffer from some form of survivor guilt, however, are better expressed by more complex phrases, such as "If I am happy, it will hurt my mother," or "If I have a good life, it is unfair to my dead sister who has no life at all." Their positive cognitions can also be more complex. For example, "Even if it seems to upset my mother, I deserve to be happy," or "I deserve to have a good life even if my sister didn't get to have one."

Because of the CMT orientation of the work I do, and because most of my clients have read my book, *Hidden Guilt: How to Stop Punishing Yourself and Enjoy the Happiness You Deserve* (1990), I think they have been trained to formulate their cognitions in this more complex way, and I have found that these formulations work well with EMDR. I believe, however, that the components of these relatively complex cognitions would also be present in a different form if formulated using the standard EMDR protocol. For instance, the complex cognition "if I am happy, it will hurt my mother" might come up when the client recalls a memory of her mother being obviously displeased with her expression of pleasure or joy. In the standard EMDR protocol the cognition might be "I don't deserve to be happy." Although at first glance the two cognitions do not appear equivalent, the complexity of the guilt theme is present in the way the cognition is elicited from the client: "As you hold in your mind that image of your mother appearing displeased when you were telling her your exciting news, what thought comes to mind about yourself?" The negative cognition is inseparable from the image of the mother's displeasure, so that her displeasure at her daughter's excitement is an unspoken component of the client's cognition, "I don't deserve to be happy." Similarly, although this aspect of the original memory is not explicitly mentioned, its influence remains present through the installation phase, in which the client is instructed, "Now recall what remains of the original memory, and at the same time think of the phrase, 'I deserve to be happy.'"

In the case presented here, I utilized a combination of both simple and complex cognitions in EMDR processing, but the theme of unconscious guilt underpins the entire process. This case is ongoing but meetings are scheduled irregularly at the client's request. The client states that she would like to come regularly but cannot afford it. After the first EMDR session we no longer did 80-minute sessions. Again financial considerations dictated this, although the client did seem to work well in the 50-minute hour. The case report below covers the first eleven sessions.

Client's Presenting Problems

Michelle, an attractive 45-year-old divorced, creative writing professor consulted me after hearing that I had been of great help using EMDR with a colleague of hers. Her college didn't pay very well, and, having custody of her 11-year-old daughter, she had very little money, so the idea of treatment that would move quickly was particularly attractive to her. Her principal complaints were that she was moderately depressed; she was preoccupied with a relationship that had broken up two years earlier; and she was unable to write poems, short stories, and other creative work. On the positive side, Michelle reported that she was highly thought of as a teacher and administrator, and she had a close and satisfying relationship with her daughter. However, Michelle's primary identification was as a writer. Consequently, her inability to finish writing projects made her feel frustrated and ashamed.

First Session

In addition to providing the information above, Michelle gave more details of her preoccupation with her ex-boyfriend, Nick. By 10 A.M. on the days she was at home, Michelle would start to look out the window for the postman. When the postman arrived, Michelle would walk out to the mailbox with a sense of anticipation, hoping to find a letter from Nick. When there was no letter, she always felt terribly disappointed. Nick and she had lived together for 18 months but had now been apart for two years. She knew that it was highly unlikely that he would write her. Nevertheless, she had felt empty and anxious since their relationship ended. In spite of her knowledge that the relationship had been painful and destructive for both of them, she felt sure that if he invited her to, she would rush to his side.

For a year she had attended group therapy for clients suffering from depression, but had not found it helpful and had recently quit. Besides her depression, she had felt "close to the edge" at school and had gotten furious in a faculty meeting in a way that she thought might jeopardize her job. She also found herself extremely impatient with both her daughter and her cat.

She described her mother as bright and affectionate but also as depressed, whiny, and overly concerned with appearances. She felt her mother had never really developed herself or reached her potential. Her father was a small-town police chief whom she recalled as being critical, negative, distant, unaffectionate, and moralistic.

Ten years before she came into therapy, her younger sister (by two years) and only sibling had been murdered in a convenience store robbery, where she worked. The store had been robbed twice in the past and Michelle had strongly suggested to her sister that she find other work. She viewed her sister's death as a sort of suicide. Her sister had been less successful than Michelle, both socially and academically.

We talked about EMDR targets, and two came immediately to mind for her. The first was her obsessive preoccupation with the unlikely possibility of a letter in the mailbox, and the second were the angry eruptions. Since she had mentioned her sister's untimely death, I suggested we also focus on that. In my experience survivor guilt is a common cause of psychological problems, particularly when a sibling's death is a tragic one. I generally begin EMDR treatment by focusing on a few targets rather than making an inventory of all important incidents. I find that important earlier incidents usually emerge during the process of working on powerful incidents that are directly connected with the client's symptoms.

Michelle warned me that she had been in therapy several times in the past and "usually I find something lacking." This kind of statement from a client is often a signal that she will act out a drama of criticism and disappointment in the course of therapy. Often the client takes the role of a critical parent who cannot be satisfied. CMT holds that this is a way the client tries to overcome the irrational belief that she is not good enough. If the therapist can tolerate the criticism without feeling bad about himself, then the client can be helped to overcome the effects of the criticism she received (Weiss, 1993).

Second Session

We began the 80-minute session by identifying a memory that related to her former boyfriend. He had called her, sounding hysterical and insisting that she come right over to comfort him. She felt very torn because she had a class to teach and she had spent a lot of time preparing for it. Even though she didn't want to, she canceled the class at the last minute and comforted her boyfriend.

The negative cognitions were "I don't deserve love" and "I can't get what I want unless I'm perfect" (Subjective Units of Distress Scale [SUDS] = 7.5). The positive cognitions were "I deserve better" and "I can say no and feel OK" (Validity of Cognition Scale [VOC] = 2).

Michelle: ►◄►◄►◄ Please move your arm more slowly. You're going too fast. ►◄►◄►◄ My mind is blank. [*return to target*]

From time to time I tell the client, "I'd like you to recall the incident that you focused on at the beginning of our EMDR session and notice how it seems to you now." I have abbreviated this instruction throughout this chapter by the bracketed phrase, "return to target." Also notice that I allow the client to use multiple cognitions throughout this chapter. For example, "I don't deserve love" and "I can't get what I want unless I'm perfect" are really two separate negative cognitions. At the time I first worked with Michelle, I routinely allowed clients to have multiple negative and positive cognitions. Subsequently, however, I concluded that it was better to identify the most significant cognition and target only that one.

Michelle: I had to ask two people before I could find someone to take my class. It was so embarrassing. ►◄►◄►◄ The charge is off it now. I realize that I was terrified of Nick's anger. ►◄►◄►◄ The movement of the wand seems to be erasing the bad feelings. [*I use a wand instead of my hand because I have rotator cuff problems.*] [*return to target*] It's OK. [*She then reported that all the charge was off the target scene but that she still didn't feel fully confident of her positive cognitions (SUDS = 0, VOC = 5).*] ►◄►◄►◄ The pull of being a caretaker is very strong for me. Nick was a "basket case" at the beginning of our relationship. I had a vision of helping him become confident and happy. At first, I seemed to be able to fulfill that vision. But as time went on, it became increasingly difficult. His demands became more and more unreasonable and he seemed to get more and more desperate. The feeling of strength and satisfaction that I had initially experienced began to be replaced by a sense of powerlessness and being trapped. ►◄►◄►◄ I feel like things are shifting around in my head. My thoughts and feelings can get integrated and connected.

In EMDR sessions my clients commonly report this sense of integration. They feel as if warring parts of themselves are combining in ways that are both comforting and empowering. The insights achieved are not simply new concepts but constitute a powerful reordering of their psyches. Michelle had been in therapy before, and the thought that she had a tendency to be overly responsible was not new for her. In the past, however, this insight did not change the intensity of her need to rescue others. With EMDR she sensed that she would be less compelled to be the caretaker.

When we returned to the target at the end of the session, Michelle said, "I feel much better now, but I'm still a caretaker. I still have to get there" (SUDS = 2, VOC = 5). I considered this first session a very positive one. Michelle experienced a considerable drop in the intensity of her distress and had also become hopeful that "thoughts and feelings can be integrated." She gained some confidence that she would be able to master the obsessive thoughts and behaviors that had been plaguing her. In any client, but particularly those suffering from depression, establishing hope is a crucial first step.

Third Session

A week later Michelle came to her session looking much less depressed, and she was full of thoughts and feelings she was eager to share. She reported feeling better than she had in a very long time. This was especially striking to her because it was the middle of August, usually her worst month of the year. The intensification of her depression in August was due to the fact that another summer had gone by and she hadn't gotten any of her writing projects completed. Some of those projects dated back ten years. During the summer, she had no academic duties so she always hoped to get a great deal of writing done. But as the fall semester neared, she had to face her inability to complete creative work.

She also felt that she was "really beginning to let go of Nick." She had been aware all week of "a deep anger around feeling controlled." She wanted to work on this issue rather than do further work on her boyfriend. It is my practice to allow my clients to pursue whatever direction they choose, unless I think there is a strong reason not to. So unless I see evidence that the client is acting in a way that is counterproductive, I follow her lead.

By the time Michelle was finished sharing her new insights and feelings, we had only 20 minutes left. Because she'd had such a good result from the last EMDR, I agreed to spend the short time we had left doing EMDR, even though I knew we might not be able to finish.

Michelle produced a memory from her early twenties. She was freshly married and in graduate school. She recalled feeling controlled and claustrophobic. In a fit of anger she burned an almost-finished novel in the fireplace, ripping it to bits and then throwing the scraps in the fire.

The negative cognitions were "I'm stupid," "I can't do this," and "I'm out of control" (SUDS = 3). The positive cognitions were "I can learn to be in control by being adequate," and "I can roll with the punches" (VOC = 1).

In general, I have found it to be problematic to begin eye movements with a SUDS as low as 3. Without more affect to drive the process, there is sometimes very little movement. However, the incident was a powerful one and she was highly motivated to work on it. I concluded that we could move ahead with eye movements, even with the low SUDS.

In the first two sets she saw the scene as comical and even less upsetting. Yet when we returned to the target, she said, "It's almost like it could lead me to suicide." In three sets her SUDS went to 0 and her VOC went from 1 to 6. This sequence was confusing to me. I considered that her suicide comment referred to the self-destructive nature of turning her rage on her work, or to an identification with her sister's "suicide," but I wasn't sure. I am a bit at a loss to understand this EMDR sequence, but it did seem to detoxify the memory of destroying her novel. I asked her about the suicide comment. She stated that she had no intention of killing herself and felt better than she had in years.

My intuition had been that the work of this session was helpful, but I was somewhat confused-and very interested to see what would arise in the next session.

Fourth Session

Michelle began by telling me that she'd had a good week. This confirmed my thought that it had been fine to spend the short time that was available at the end of the previous session by doing eye movements. Her depression had continued to lift. However, she did notice she still had a compulsion to go the mailbox, although it was less intense. She was eager to use EMDR to work on that compulsion.

The target image was of going to the mailbox. She realized that she was always hoping to get a letter saying, "I love you, I want you back." Her negative cognitions were: "I'm needy and can't let go," and "I can't find anybody better" (SUDS = 4.5). Her positive cognitions were: "I deserve and can choose a relationship that's good for me," and "I can let go of Nick" (VOC = 2).

Michelle: ►◄►◄►◄ My heart is pounding. I feel terrified.

LE: Where do you feel terror?

Michelle: In my chest.

LE: Focus on the sensations in your chest.

Michelle: ►◄►◄►◄ The anxiety is being neutralized. It was a nice day before—it's still a nice day. ►◄►◄►◄ I have a lot to feel good about. My daughter is doing great and my classes are going well. ►◄►◄►◄ The bad feelings are getting more and more neutralized. [*return to target*] The focus is off Nick now and on to other people.

This is an interesting series in which the SUDS, which was moderate (4.5) to begin with, spiked upward (she felt terrified), and then rapidly subsided. This is an example of the way the EMDR can sometimes begin a rapid processing of strong feelings without an immediate accompanying insight. The result was that the image of Nick was less compelling and Michelle could move on to more productive images and thoughts.

The next ten sets were quite fascinating. Positive images and thoughts seemed to alternate with negative ones.

Michelle: ►◄►◄►◄ Last week I came this close to calling a man I am attracted to. His image is replacing the mailbox. ►◄►◄►◄ I'm OK and I can get a man interested in me. ►◄►◄►◄ I can hear defensiveness in my voice. I have to perform for these men. ►◄►◄►◄ I'm really getting to like my life. ►◄►◄►◄ I can maintain my own boundaries. ►◄►◄►◄ I am not sure I can maintain my boundaries. What if someone, especially a man, wants something? Something I don't want to give. [*return to target*] I feel like I'm becoming the ugly person my mom was.

I asked her to return to target to check whether this alternation between positive and negative was assisting her or getting her stuck. In the first group of sets, she began to think of a man whom she had almost invited on a date, followed by the thought that she was OK, that a man could be interested in her. Those positive thoughts alternated with the negative idea that she needed to perform for men. Then she came back to the positive thought that she had really been enjoying her life in the last few weeks. Next she shifted to the negative, fearful thought that she could not maintain reasonable boundaries in a relationship. She worried that men might want something from her that she didn't want to give.

Returning to target seemed to produce an important and potentially liberating insight: the thought that she was like her mother. Her clingy, dependent behavior was similar to her mother's behavior with her father, and sometimes with her. She was beginning to recognize that she was stuck in an identification with her mother. In the sets that follow, Michelle makes that insight explicit and senses the identification weakening through EMDR processing.

Michelle: ►◄►◄►◄ I'm like Mom, I can't be powerful. ►◄►◄►◄ I'm moving fast. I have to recognize these states of mind when I get into them. ►◄ ►◄►◄ I feel again like my thoughts and feelings are integrating. I don't like seeing these things about myself, but they are changing.

Since she seemed to be experiencing an important integration of her thoughts and feelings, I decided to return to target to check whether the processing was complete. Her response was "I see the mailbox. There will just be bills there. It will be much more mundane." Her VOC was 6, her SUDS, 0.

We installed this image along with the positive cognitions "I deserve and can choose a relationship that's good for me," and "I can let go of Nick." Michelle left the session feeling "much lighter and more optimistic."

The thought that she was acting like her mother was a particularly significant one. One of the important principles of CMT is that clients often get stuck in identifications with unhappy parents. They repeat negative aspects of these parents' lives out of a kind of irrational guilt that is a close cousin of survivor guilt, which I call "outdoing guilt." This is the guilt of those whose parents or siblings are unhappy or unsuccessful. It feels somehow wrong, unfair, and disloyal to be happy and successful if loved ones are not.

"If my mother is unfulfilled and hasn't developed her talents, what right have I to develop and fulfill myself?"

Very often this guilt is unconscious. Yet it drives people to repeat the behavior or attitudes of unhappy or unsuccessful parents or siblings. Repeating the parents' behavior or attitudes assuages the irrational guilt of being happy when they are not, being successful when they are not, or fulfilled when they are not. CMT holds that survivor guilt or outdoing guilt can be so potent that people may unconsciously choose to be unhappy or frustrated in their goals to avoid that guilt.

I considered this session a very successful one. Michelle was able to focus on her outdoing guilt towards her mother and her identification with her. As a result, she was able to recognize how that identification contributed to her obsessive feelings and behavior towards her boyfriend. In addition, she seemed to be able to emotionally integrate this knowledge in a way that decreased the grip of that guilt. During the EMDR she was less disturbed by thoughts of her boyfriend. I expected that she would be less bothered between sessions as well.

Fifth Session

This session took place after a two-week hiatus. Michelle used the beginning of the session to talk about the gains she had made. She again emphasized how August is always such an anxious time for her, because she must face that another summer has gone by without the accomplishment of any significant creative work. She was greatly struck by the fact that this August was so different. She was feeling good much of the time and was completing a number of stories and poems that had languished for many years. She was relieved to notice that she no longer felt disappointed when there was no letter from Nick in the mailbox.

She decided that she wanted to use the balance of our time in the next session to set up an EMDR that would focus on her inability to work creatively. The image she came up with was sitting on the couch, drinking bourbon, watching TV, and making notes for a novel or short story. She never used any of these notes and never worked on a novel or short story.

I made a mental note to assess her alcohol use at a later time.

Sixth Session

At the beginning of the hour Michelle told me that she had continued to feel unusually positive and optimistic. She was eager to get started with the target we had set up the week before sitting on the couch, drinking and making unproductive notes and plans.

Negative cognitions were: "I am superficial, a coward, phony, and a fake," "I don't have what it takes," and "I can't silence the [*inner*] critic."

Positive cognitions were: "I can put the work out and roll with the punches," and "I've got the right stuff."

Before getting started, I checked over the target image, the cognitions, and the SUDS and VOC to see if they had shifted. It is not uncommon for these measures to change over the course of the week. Sometimes material may even get worked through between sessions (without eye movements), once the issues have been clarified through the EMDR set-up process. In this case, little had changed and we began the eye movements (VOC = 5, SUDS = 7).

Michelle: ▶◀▶◀▶◀ I should turn the TV off and get involved in something more productive. ▶◀▶◀▶◀ I feel calmer. [*return to target*] The image of sitting in front of the TV is gone. I see myself teaching my class in a particularly creative way.

I suggested that she find a way to transfer the creativity that she shows in the classroom to her writing. I find it is often helpful to suggest to clients that they transfer attitudes and strategies from areas of their lives that are successful to those areas that feel less so.

Michelle: ▶◀▶◀▶◀ This is a good way to transfer the creativity to my own realm ▶◀▶◀▶◀ I feel calmer. [*return to target*] I'm just watching TV and relaxing. It's OK. But I do feel a little impatient. I feel energy in my hands and feet. [*I asked her to pay attention to the sensations in her hands and feet.*] ▶◀▶◀▶◀ I'm thinking about the first play I ever wrote and staged. It was fun, satisfying and exciting. ▶◀▶◀▶◀ I really am teaching an interesting variety of classes. But it is only teaching.

I suggested that the insertion of the word but *was a way of taking away her pleasure and satisfaction in her teaching work. She said she realized that she did that a lot. I suggested she try substituting the word* and *for* but. *I thought that she would do much better if she acknowledged the creativity she demonstrated in her teaching as a starting point for creative writing, rather than discounting it. Then I asked her to return to target to see what effect my suggestion had had.*

Michelle: [*return to target*] It is only teaching *and* it is worth doing. It reminds me that no matter what I did, I couldn't please my father. I have an image of him. He is not noticing me. He is looking past me. He is looking through me. ▶◀▶◀▶◀ I'm remembering an argument I had with my father over whether the Beatles were serious musicians. He insisted that they weren't, that their music had no value. I felt he couldn't appreciate anything that I valued. ►◄►◄►◄ There was a terrible vacuum in the house when I was growing up. My mom didn't want anybody to come over. ►◄►◄►◄ There was nothing to do, no place to go. My home is not like that. Kids from the neighborhood visit all the time. It's a place with lots of activity and comfort. [*return to target*] I get an image of my father in his attic study. He's ignoring me.

In this sequence she is thinking about how painful it was to grow up in a house with so much depression and so little validation and encouragement. Perhaps as a result of my encouragement, she is facing how discouraging her father was. She is also giving herself credit for establishing a vibrant and supportive environment for her daughter. I asked her to return to target at the end of this sequence because she seemed to be acknowledging how she was different from her parents. As a result, instead of the image she started with, a relevant image from her childhood came up, so we went with that.

Michelle: ►◄►◄►◄ I'm getting an image of my mother as a dead chicken. I feel sorry for her. I feel contempt and disgust—but I feel I have to protect her.

In this session so far, Michelle emphasizes the pain of rejection by her father and both worry and contempt for her mother. Her father's criticism and rejection is related to the feeling that her work isn't good enough. That feeling is an important impediment to her willingness to put her work out in the world where it could be judged and rejected.

There is also the implication that her worry about her mother may partially derive from feeling that her father neglected her mother. He would escape to his study and leave her mother alone with her anxieties. This supports the idea that her clingy and desperate behavior in relationships is the product of an unconscious identification with her mother.

Her feelings of contempt and disgust toward her mother predispose Michelle towards having the form of survivor guilt I discussed previously: outdoing guilt. A way to assuage her guilt over her disgust and contempt towards her mother is to be like her. If Michelle, too, is dependent, unhappy, and unfulfilled, then she has no legitimate right to feel contempt for her mother's dependence, unhappiness, and lack of fulfillment. She thereby protects herself from the guilt of outdoing her mother.

I asked her to return to target here in order to get a reading on her SUDS and VOC. Her VOC (5) was the same, but her SUDS (2) was down sharply.

Michelle: [*return to target*] The couch is a wonderful place to be. I can enjoy my time relaxing. ►◄►◄►◄ I don't have to assume that I will be dissatisfied. ►◄►◄►◄ I lose steam when I get to the middle of a project. ►◄►◄►◄

My sister, who was killed, comes up. ►◄►◄►◄ I never felt creatively blocked before my sister's death ►◄►◄►◄ I can't feel my full development because she never did. She could never get it out [*her writing*]. That's what I've done since she died [*been unable to write*]. She wanted to be me. She wanted to have my life, and now I'm having hers.

This is an example of the enormous potency of survivor guilt. In this group of sets Michelle realizes, for the first time, that her writer's block really dates from her sister's murder. Although she was laboring under the issues with her parents, it was not until the weight of her sister's death was added that she became chronically depressed and unable to finish writing projects.

Survivor guilt is the product of a primitive unconscious justice system. According to that justice system it was grossly unfair that Michelle's sister, Susan, was less popular, less successful in school, less approved of by their parents. In fact, poor Susan even wished she was Michelle and could live Michelle's life. Then when Susan was murdered, the whole situation became even more unjust. Michelle was being unfairly favored by being able to live out her life, while Susan's was tragically cut short. After Susan died, Michelle unconsciously proceeded to try to restore some fairness by living out her sister's life of frustration and unhappiness. If she couldn't give Susan a full, successful life like her own, she could at least make her own life less happy and successful. This was an act of loyal sacrifice to Susan—albeit a highly irrational one.

Trying to help her gain some relief, I then suggested she imagine a conversation with her sister while doing the eye movements. In this conversation she told her sister that she couldn't take care of her. Her sister responded that she was sorry she had been killed, that she hadn't meant to be killed. In the next set Michelle recalled some good times with her sister ("We had some very close times. There was a wonderful sweet side to her.") Michelle cried for several minutes. She began weeping while moving her eyes and then said that she wished to cry without doing eye movements.

She ended the session in touch with a lot of anger towards her parents. I didn't ask her for a final VOC and SUDS because it didn't seem appropriate, but I think the SUDS would have been high because she was so angry. I had already gone overtime, so I told her that if that was still up for her, we could deal with it next time. I offered her a copy of my book, which includes a focus on survivor guilt (Engel & Ferguson, 1990).

In spite of the fact that Michelle left our session upset, I considered that this session contained an important breakthrough. Making a clear connec-

tion between her creative block and survivor guilt towards her sister would
be invaluable to her in overcoming that block.

During the session I encouraged her to substitute *and* for *but* in order to
give herself credit for the things that were going well in her life. The CMT
therapist tries to ascertain what negative beliefs have been engendered in
the client by parental attitudes and behaviors. Then the therapist tries to
demonstrate attitudes that disprove or counterbalance those irrational, negative beliefs. It was my impression that her father was excessively critical,
emphasizing what was wrong or missing rather than what was right. I wanted
to make sure Michelle felt it was OK with me for her to feel good about
her accomplishments.

Another intervention was to suggest that Michelle transfer her successful
strategies as a teacher to her writing. This intervention carries the implication that I view her as successful. It also illustrated to her that I don't focus
only on what isn't going well, as her father did, but also on what is going
well. I am encouraging her to see herself as a successful person who only
needs to *extend* her success, rather than as a failure who needs to completely
transform herself. (This intervention has similarities to solution-oriented
therapies and other brief treatments.)

The third intervention was to offer Michelle a copy of my book. The
book is primarily about survivor and outdoing guilt. The act of giving it to
her contained the implicit message that I don't think she deserves to suffer
from this irrational torment. In fact, it implies that I believe she deserves to
be happy.

In this session we also get a clear picture of the powerful combination of
forces that hold Michelle's writer's block in place. The most powerful is
probably her survivor guilt toward her less favored and tragically murdered
sister. Her fear of not being good enough, which was rooted in her father's
criticalness and seeming lack of interest in her, is also an important impediment. Finally, her identification with her depressed and unfilled mother is
another compounding element. Since Michelle worked on all three aspects
of her writer's block in this session, I was hopeful that she would gain some
substantial relief in the coming week.

Seventh Session

At the beginning of this session Michelle expressed an insight about what
had been holding her back in her writing "She [her sister] never got the
chance to develop herself, and so I can't develop myself." Michelle also

reported, "I feel closer to the resolution of this problem than I ever have before."

Over the weekend Nick had called and spoken to her daughter, telling her that he was moving out of the area. The target image was Nick talking on the phone to her daughter and not asking for Michelle. Her negative cognitions focused on her obsession with him: "I can't let go. I can't control myself." Her positive cognitions focused on her outdoing guilt: "I can have a happy life, even if he doesn't."

It may be that part of Michelle's obsession with Nick—her inability to forget about him—is connected with the unconscious idea that remembering him will protect him. It is not uncommon for clients to harbor this kind of "magical thinking." Since we have already seen that Michelle saw herself as a caretaker, both in her family and her relationship with Nick, it well may be that to forget about him would seem like abandoning him.

The first four eye-movement sets consisted of depressing ideas with one positive image. Michelle continued the pattern of alternating between positive and negative images that ultimately culminated in a positive synthesis.

Michelle: ►◄►◄►◄ I'm not going to find anybody else. ►◄►◄►◄ I have an image of being old, sad, and lonely. ►◄►◄►◄ I have an image of being younger with a wide open future. ►◄►◄►◄ I'm having feelings of sadness, depression, and emptiness. [*I asked Michelle to return to target here because she was having a preponderance of negative images, and I wanted to be sure that processing was going on.*]

Michelle: The image of Nick calling seems less engaging now. It seems less vivid.

In the six sets below, the pattern of alternation continues and culminates in the image being even less upsetting. I had her return to target every three sets as a way of maintaining her focus and giving her a chance to rest from strong, negative feelings. However, I think it might well have worked fine to do more sets before returning to target.

Michelle: ►◄►◄►◄ I'm getting in touch with sexual feelings. One thing about the relationship with Nick was that we had terrific sex. ►◄►◄►◄ Actually, I've noticed that I'm getting interested in other men for the first time in a long time. There are two I'm attracted to. ►◄►◄►◄ I'm unattractive. [*return to target*] I can hardly bring up the image now. It's fading. ►◄►◄►◄ I feel so hurt. I cared so much for him. ►◄►◄►◄ The feeling of hurt is softening. ►◄►◄►◄ What are the good things I can save from the experience. [*return to target*] Part of the image is gone. The whole scene seems brighter.

After working to attenuate the feelings of hurt she had as a result of the loss of the relationship, Michelle returns to the model for her relationship with Nick: her relationship with her mother. The suffering she is going through may be partly an identification with her mother. She is sharing her mother's fate. This is a way of assuaging the outdoing guilt she feels towards her mother. By thinking and feeling this way, she is not better off than her mother, she is in the same boat. Therefore, she can feel less guilty towards her.

Michelle: ►◄►◄►◄ I'm getting an image of my mother. She was abandoned by Dad. ►◄►◄►◄ I see. My mother is Nick. ►◄►◄►◄ They both thought I was wonderful. ►◄►◄►◄ I wasn't allowed to have my own needs. ►◄►◄►◄ I just can't imagine being accepted, needs and all. ►◄►◄►◄ Wait. I can imagine it. I can see a man who is my friend and I am his. We know each other's strengths and weaknesses. We accept each other's needs. We help each other. ►◄►◄►◄ In the relationship with Nick, I was waiting and waiting to be able to express my needs. But he was always a basket case. I wasn't going to wait forever. ►◄►◄►◄ I had this image of myself as a knight in shining armor. [*return to target*] It's hardly upsetting at all now (SUDS = 1.5).

In this sequence of sets Michelle realizes that she had tried to rescue Nick, just as she had tried to rescue her mother. She recognizes the strong elements of maternal transference in her relationship with Nick and becomes aware of the gratifying aspect of the role of being the heroine-savior for both Mom and Nick. That role made her feel special, important, and powerful, but she also realizes that she had to give up her own needs for both nurturance and independence in relation to both her mother and her boyfriend.

In the set in which Michelle states "I wasn't going to wait forever," she alludes to the fact that it was she, not Nick, who initiated their breakup. Michelle realized that living with Nick was not a good situation for her daughter or herself and moved out of the house they were sharing. In most of her thinking she usually focused on herself as the jilted lover. This is a common pattern in clients who suffer from the idea that they are responsible for the happiness of others. Instead of being able to take credit for having the strength to end a bad relationship, Michelle acts like she has been abandoned. Being able to say "I wasn't going to wait forever" is a positive step for her. The series concludes with her feeling even more comfortable about letting go (SUDS = 1.5).

In the next series, Michelle examines her assumption that it is her fault if her mother or Nick are depressed and angry. If I had been treating Michelle without EMDR, I probably would have suggested that she was being irrationally responsible for things she couldn't control. But it is very gratifying to see her arrive spontaneously at interpretations I would usually make.

Michelle: ►◄►◄►◄ I'm remembering back to when things really began to go wrong. I began to feel lost. He was threatening suicide. I wasn't doing enough. ►◄►◄►◄ If somebody is depressed and angry, it is always somebody else's fault. With Nick I could never show my unhappiness. ►◄►◄►◄ In my family I was always in charge of being the positive influence. ►◄►◄►◄ I was the symbol of the fact that the family was doing OK. [*return to target*] I can see him calling and I hardly feel upset at all (VOC = 6, SUDS = 1).

In this final sequence Michelle is recalling that, even though she set aside her own needs, her "knight in shining armor" role wasn't working. Her boyfriend was more and more demanding, and she wasn't able to keep him happy. She also identified the role she felt she had to fill in her family: that of the "positive influence." In both situations the payoff of being the hero wasn't worth it. The price was too high. She had to give up her own needs for both nurturance and independence. And, finally, she couldn't pull it off anyway! Both her mother and Nick were depressed and anxious in spite of her best efforts.

Michelle finished the session by installing her positive cognition and noting to me that she had made substantial progress in her preoccupation with Nick. From that time to the date of this writing, her obsession with Nick never returned in a significant way.

In this session the negative cognitions were simple statements. However, the positive cognition "I can have a happy life, even if my sister didn't," is of the complex sort that is useful when there is powerful underlying guilt. I have not found that these complex cognitions cause problems for my clients and, in fact, usually work quite well.

Eighth Session

Michelle began the session saying that she felt "on the edge of a depression." She was feeling anxious about teaching her courses, had a strong impulse to give up, and had the thought that she shouldn't be any happier or more successful than she is now. We decided to spend the session working directly on her sister's murder, since survivor guilt was becoming a more and more obvious contributor to her problems.

Michelle told me that right after her sister's death, a mutual friend told her that her sister had admired and envied her. Her sister had wanted to be a writer and had even kept a secret scrapbook of Michelle's achievements.

The friend told her that Michelle's sister had said, "I hate my life, I want to be Michelle!"

The target image was that of her sister bleeding to death alone, behind the counter, from three hollow-point bullet wounds in her chest. Michelle had two negative cognitions: "There is a payback for being successful and having fun," and "I should have prevented this." The positive cognitions were "I deserve an expansive life, even though my sister didn't have one," and "I did the best I could." As in the last session, I did not try to work towards a simpler positive cognition. I believed the complexity of the statement "I deserve an expansive life, even though my sister didn't have one" was necessary to capture Michelle's dilemma. She *would* like to have an "expansive life," but her survivor guilt has made it seem unfair to do so.

Michelle: ►◄►◄►◄ She wanted to be me, so after she died, I became her. ►◄►◄►◄ I'm remembering smoking marijuana with my sister. We had some really good times together. ►◄►◄►◄ I can see a connection between my sister and my daughter. ►◄►◄►◄ When I became a mother, I was able to put a lot of the stuff with my sister behind me.

In this first group of sets Michelle begins with the belief that she is atoning for her sister's death by living out a depressed and unproductive life. Then she moves to memories of being close and nurturing to her sister. Those are followed by a recognition of how she nurtures her daughter (she is a loving and effective mother, and her daughter is a happy young girl). The implication is that she has tried to be a good sister and mother and should not punish herself. She is moving towards overcoming the survivor guilt that has handicapped her since her sister's death.

Michelle: ►◄►◄►◄ I'm remembering my mother's desperate worrying. She could never really enjoy anything. She was worried all the time. ►◄►◄►◄ This proves life is either dangerous or tragic. ►◄►◄►◄ I really withdrew in those years after my sister died. I made myself so small. ►◄►◄►◄ I see an image of my sister pointing a gun at herself. It is so sad.

These four sets point out how her sister's death combined with the experience of her mother's obsessive worrying prove that life is a grim business. It would be only appropriate to be worried and unhappy! It also points out that if she were happy and ambitious, she would be outdoing both her sister and her mother. Michelle has had a successful life in many ways. She would like to add recognition as a writer and a good relationship to the other good things in her life. These ambitions take her far beyond what either her mother or sister were able to achieve. She would also like to relax and enjoy her life, rather than spend her time chronically worrying, like her mother.

Michelle: ►◄►◄►◄ My sister got the worst of the family. I was the prize child. ►◄►◄►◄ I enjoyed being better than she. I liked being the star of the family. ►◄►◄►◄ She tried to follow in my footsteps. ►◄►◄►◄ I did help her as much as I could. [*return to target; at the end of the session the VOC was up to 5 and the SUDS was at 2.*]

In most families there is a natural competition between siblings for the parents' attention. In a family where there is a shortage of approval and affection, the children compete even more fiercely for the little that is available. The child who feels she has won this competition may also feel she has used up the love and attention that the others need to thrive. Therefore, the unhappiness of the other siblings becomes her responsibility. If the life of one or more of her siblings is tragic, as it was in this case, then that conscious or unconscious guilt can become overwhelming. Michelle has tried to assuage that guilt by living out a version of her dead sister's life: Her sister was a frustrated and unsuccessful writer, so she must be a frustrated and unsuccessful writer. Her sister was lonely and unhappy, so she must be lonely and unhappy.

There was more work to do, but I felt that the session had been extremely productive. Michelle was continuing to use the eye-movement work to face and work through the horror of her sister's murder. At the same time she was continuing to weaken the grip of the survivor and outdoing guilt that she suffered in relation to both her mother and sister.

Ninth Session

Michelle was feeling somewhat better. She spent the first 15 minutes describing how her daughter had given a wonderful performance as Anne in an adult community theater production of *Anne of Green Gables*. She had even gotten rave reviews in the local newspaper. Michelle was very proud of her daughter and had videotaped a number of her performances.

She also talked proudly, if a tad enviously, about a former student of hers who had just won a national literature prize. She went on to comment on the creative way she was teaching one of her classes and how excited her students were.

She then began to talk about the deeper sense she had gained of the impact of her sister's death on her daily life. She now openly acknowledged that she had adopted her sister's identity and role. Her sister had not been able to finish her writing, and she wasn't allowing herself to do that either.

I brought up the issue of her drinking, which we had not discussed before. She told me she had been having a couple of "doubles" every evening when she came home from work. It was the only way she could "turn off the critic in her head." Since beginning treatment, however, she had been drinking much less. We made an agreement that she would check in with me for a while to make sure she was able to hold to a moderate drinking pattern.

Over the course of the session, I had been struck by what a rich and potentially satisfying life she had fashioned for herself. She was a loving mother to a loving, adjusted daughter. She was successful and acknowledged in her teaching career. She even had a lovely place to live. I told her all this and added that her idea that she was living her sister's life was a lie. She actually had a wonderful life, but she wouldn't let herself enjoy it due to ongoing guilt in relation to her sister and mother.

I also suggested that part of her inability to enjoy those parts of her life that were going very well stemmed from the common belief that if she didn't worry and fret over the parts that weren't going well, she would not be motivated to do anything about them and they would never change. This belief may have been something she picked up from her mother, but it is also a widespread belief in our culture. I suggested that it was just as likely that she would do her creative work if she actually enjoyed the life she had *now*. It seemed that, at least for her, being unhappy and dissatisfied did not motivate her to write.

I made this suggestion because I had an intuition that she was beginning to feel free enough from outdoing guilt to allow herself more happiness. I also wanted to reinforce the implication that I felt she deserved to be happy and that it was OK to pay attention to the achievements and good fortune with which she was blessed. To the extent that there was a parental transference toward me, I wanted to be the kind of parent who celebrated her achievements and encouraged her to enjoy her life.

Although I had expected to do EMDR in this session, Michelle seemed to want to use the time to talk and consolidate the gains she had made. As the session progressed, it seemed to me to be a very good use of our time.

Tenth Session

Michelle started this session by commenting that she felt my suggestion to "look around—notice how great your life is" was a "breakthrough" for her. She was enjoying herself more consistently than she had in years. She had been trying not to put pressure on herself and felt much more relaxed. She also had been free from thoughts of Nick.

It is hard to know exactly why she was doing so much better. In the most recent EMDR session she had worked on the powerfully upsetting image of her sister's murder, and had worked through guilt over surviving her, competing successfully for attention, being more established professionally, and achieving greater fulfillment than her mother. She may have simply been complying with my suggestion that she had a "great life"—but I suspect that my comments, coupled with the EMDR work she did, had given her a kind of "permission" to enjoy herself. Her father was critical and her mother was worried and depressed. Neither of them was able to encourage her to enjoy herself. However, my comments made it clear that I thought she was doing well and I would not be worried or critical if she enjoyed herself. It may be that through a parental transference to me, she was able to allow herself to be happier without feeling guilty or disloyal.

Toward the end of the session, she opened up a new theme. She had been invited to give a talk to a professional association and was very anxious about that prospect. The underlying issues seemed to be fear of being judged and not being good enough. These were associated with her father's critical attitude. We agreed to use EMDR to work on these issues at our next meeting.

I took the emergence of these new themes to indicate that she had made real progress on her sense that she had done too well and thus injured her sister and mother. This allowed her to turn her attention to the contradictory problem that no matter what she did, she was not good enough to please her father. It also may be that my approval and encouragement made it safe to begin to look at her father's disapproving and discouraging attitudes.

In this session Michelle seemed more interested in talking than in EMDR. Again, I followed her lead and was pleased with the outcome. She seemed to use the time to consolidate previous gains and plan how to move forward.

Eleventh Session

Michelle began the session by commenting that she had been "putting aside time to write and had been writing really good stuff." She had not been checking the mailbox and felt like she was getting back to the way she felt prior to her relationship with Nick. In addition, she was beginning to notice that a number of men seemed to be attracted to her, and she was beginning to be attracted to them.

I considered Michelle's increasing ability to work a sign that her survivor guilt towards her sister was weakening. I also considered that her lack of obsessing about Nick and budding attraction to other men a sign that her guilt towards both Nick and her mother was abating. It was becoming safer to forget about Nick and her mother and leave them behind. The next obstacle that Michelle seemed to want to tackle was her sense that she wasn't good enough. It would become clear during this session that these feelings of inadequacy were connected with her father.

She recalled an incident in which she was on a panel giving a talk to a group of colleagues from other colleges and universities. She was more formally dressed than usual and she felt uncomfortable. When it was her turn to talk, she panicked and was unable to utter one word. It was a very humiliating experience for her. Her negative cognitions were: "I am phony, a fake, and I'm going to be exposed. I can't do it" (SUDS = 5). Her positive cognitions were "I can be myself and say what I really believe. I can be comfortable and confident" (VOC = 1).

Michelle: ►◄►◄►◄ I'm remembering this play I wrote and directed in my late teens. It was a great success and so much fun. ►◄►◄►◄ I can do fine in front of a class or faculty meeting. ►◄►◄►◄ Most of the faculty are more productive than I am. ►◄►◄►◄ My stuff is just as good, but I don't get it out there. ►◄►◄►◄ I need to stop therapy because I need the time to write.

I had established a pattern with Michelle of returning to target rather frequently. It seemed to work well so I stuck with it. It may be that it would have worked just as well to do many more sets between returns to target.

Michelle: [*return to target*] All I need to do is to put in two hours writing every morning.

In the above sequence Michelle once again illustrates her pattern of alternating positive and negative thoughts or images, leading to a positive outcome. She has two sets in which she recalls successful presentations (her play, classes, and faculty meetings). These are followed by a negative comparison with colleagues, who are "more productive than I am." Next she makes a positive comparison ("my stuff is just as good"). Finally, she has the negative thought that she will have to sacrifice her therapy, which she likes, in order to have time to write. The idea that she will have to give up something important in order to have something else important is probably connected to her survivor or outdoing guilt. She can't have it all, when her mother has so little and her sister hasn't even got a life. Ordinarily, I would probably interpret this to her, but in this case she seems to be processing it through the eye movements. At the end of this series, when asked to return to the image, she has the encouraging thought that she can simply put in two hours writing every morning and be able to be productive.

Michelle: ►◄►◄►◄ I'm feeling lots of positive energy in my stomach. ►◄►◄►◄ Those are just thoughts [*disparaging tone*]. ►◄►◄►◄ My friend Sven told me, "Don't teach, you will never have time for your writing. ►◄►◄►◄ You know, I'm trying to get back to my own sense of the world. ►◄►◄►◄ What is the nature of the beast that is fighting me? It is a carping, questioning critic. ►◄►◄►◄ It's my father.

Here we again see the alternating pattern between positive and negative thoughts and feelings, concluding with an important and potentially freeing insight. There is the pleasure of "positive energy in my stomach," followed by the discouraging idea that she can't both teach and write. Here, as in the last series of sets, we see the theme of not being able to have it all. Again, I don't make an interpretation, and the negative idea seems to get attenuated by the EMDR. Next she expresses a positive sense of getting back to her own view of the world, followed by the powerful realization that her internal critic is like her father.

Michelle: [*return to target*] I believe I can do it, but my gut feelings do not agree.

Before starting the next set, I suggested that she focus on her "gut feelings" while following my EMDR wand. This is one of the most useful aspects of EMDR. Very often, focusing on uncomfortable body sensations while moving one's eyes can cause the attenuation of those sensations. Since it is uncomfortable body sensations that often undermine our confidence, the rapid reduction of those sensations allows therapy to move more quickly. In this case, it allows Michelle's emotions to catch up with her level of insight. Of course, uncomfortable feelings may be important signals that danger still exists. EMDR does not seem to reduce discomfort if there is still some important external or internal danger to be processed.

After focusing on her "gut," Michelle felt much more relaxed and confident, even in the face of her financial difficulties.

Michelle: ►◄►◄►◄ I'm broke and I don't care. Things will be OK. ►◄►◄►◄ What I'm really trying to do is integrate my knowledge [*laughing and smiling*].

Michelle is experiencing the pleasure of the sense of congruence between her fresh insights and her emotions. This calls to mind the neurological model of brain functioning in which rational evaluation is stored in the dominant hemisphere and emotional evaluation is stored in the non-dominant. EMDR seems to help bring together those two sometimes disparate aspects (van der Kolk, 1997).

Michelle: [*return to target*] I'm picturing myself as my friend Anne [*a brash and successful author and lecturer*]. She really doesn't care what the audience thinks.

Although I have asked Michelle to return to target, instead she spontaneously develops an encouraging image for herself as someone who doesn't seem worried at all about the opinions of others. Michelle's friend Anne typifies this confident attitude. Next she imagines herself with that same confidence. This technique, which I sometimes suggest to clients, is a way of using imagery to overcome a difficult situation.

Michelle: ►◄►◄►◄ I'm picturing myself giving the speech. I'm just telling the truth. ►◄►◄►◄ Now there is no panic. I feel competent and confident. [*return to target*] I can do this, I really can (SUDS = 0, VOC = 6).

We installed the positive cognition "I can be myself and say what I really believe comfortably and confidently," while Michelle focused on the situation in which she had panicked. Then we moved to the upcoming talk she was dreading and were able to install the same cognition without further processing. She seemed happy and relieved.

In this session Michelle concentrated on feelings of inadequacy, which she associated with her father's criticalness and unavailability. This "legacy" seems to be a central obstacle to her being able to present her ideas or writing in a public forum. But we also can see that she continues to work on her survivor and outdoing guilt, suggested by the notion that to add something she wants to her life, she must give up something else important to her.

Summary

A 45-year-old female professor of creative writing complained of depression, obsessing about an ex-boyfriend, and a writing block. She is in ongoing but episodic treatment within the framework of a psychodynamic model, specifically control mastery theory (CMT), utilizing EMDR as an exploratory tool and treatment method. Issues of survivor guilt toward her murdered sister, identification with her anxious, unhappy mother, and compliance with her critical and rejecting father were addressed and at least partially worked through in the first 11 sessions (reported here). Her depression has lifted, she has been able to write freely for the first time in ten years, and has stopped obsessing about her ex-boyfriend. The therapist was able to combine CMT and EMDR to create a rapid but deep exploration and amelioration of the client's major, longstanding life problems.

The Benefits of EMDR

If I had not used EMDR, this case might well have proceeded in a similar fashion but I think there would have been important differences:

- I suspect that the case would have gone more slowly. It is my experience that EMDR often markedly increases the speed of working through difficult material.
- I suspect that progress would have been far less linear (more like, three steps forward followed by two steps back).
- Michelle may have had to suffer more as we opened up issues without being able to reduce the affect in relatively short order, particularly in regard to her sister's horrible murder.
- There may have been more direct transference reenactment. For example, I would have expected that Michelle would play out a drama involving being dissatisfied with me in the way she was dissatisfied with all her other therapists. This would have actually been a way of working on the irrational beliefs that came out of her relationship with her critical father and possibly also her chronically dissatisfied mother.

Final Note

After 17 sessions Michelle continues to be productive and free of significant depression. She has had three poems and two short stories accepted for publication. Although she was somewhat nervous, her talk went well and she was never at a loss for words. She thinks occasionally of Nick but does not obsess about him or long for him. She has been dating, which she had not done for two years. She is working on her tendency to fall for men who need to be taken care of, as well as her tendency to rush into the relationship and push for more than her partner is ready for. She plans to continue working in therapy, as finances permit, until these issues are resolved.

References

Engel, L., & Ferguson, T (1990). *Imaginary crimes: How we punish ourselves and how to stop.* Boston: Houghton-Mifflin Publishers. (Also published in 1991 as a paperback under the title, *Hidden guilt: How to stop punishing yourself and enjoy the happiness you deserve.* New York: Pocket Books.)

van der Kolk, B. (1997, July). *Current understanding of the psychology of trauma.* Paper presented at the EMDRIA Conference, San Francisco.

Weiss, J. (1993). *How psychotherapy works.* New York: Guilford Press

7

RECOVERY FROM
THE VIETNAM WAR
A Thirty-Second Cure

Philip Manfield

ALLEN, A VIETNAM VETERAN in his early fifties, made the following comments in 1996 at the beginning of his seventh EMDR session. Although his actual treatment required eight sessions, I whimsically refer to Allen's treatment as *the thirty-second EMDR cure.*

> I feel very good. My wife and I went on vacation this week and had a wonderful time. My relationships at home seems to be better with my wife and my daughter. There's more confidence on my behalf. I had the occasion to hike some trails and wasn't looking for booby traps or wondering what was behind the next corner or around the next bend in the trail. I went fishing for the first time in twenty five years. It sounds simple, but now I can relate to the relaxation of sitting and waiting for the fish to bite. I'm willing now to broaden my experiences to things that I've enjoyed in the past. My relationship with my wife is much better, and my relationship with my daughter seems to be thawing. I think my wife sees the progress. We are more intimate; we communicate better. I thoroughly enjoyed the vacation. We've started doing things that we've enjoyed together in the past. We signed up for a class in ballroom dancing, which we used to love to do together.

Background

When he first came to see me, Allen described himself as successful in most areas other than personal relationships. He had served as an officer in Vietnam, where he had led men into battle; he had felt responsible for the lives of those men as well as the lives of the soldiers he fought. Like most veterans of this war who were involved in active combat, after his tour of duty Allen had felt depressed and isolated upon returning to the United States. He had returned home to a world that he experienced quite differently than when he had left it. His mind had come to expect danger wherever he turned, and common everyday experiences that are entirely unremarkable to most people had become sources of disturbance—ranging from chronic anxiety to acute fear. A walk in the park, a bush moving with the breeze, the crack of a door slamming, the scratching of gravel shifting underfoot, the distant beat of the blades of a helicopter, any unexpected loud sound—these had all become encoded in Allen's brain as possible indications of life-threatening danger.

It had seemed that no one at home could possibly understand the experience Allen had just been through. Further, no one appreciated the intense adjustment that was required of him. His response was to withdraw emotionally and suppress his feelings. Allen had become emotionally unavailable to family and friends. When his relationship with his daughter, which had been extremely poor for many years, finally fell apart, Allen had decided to seek psychological help and telephoned me. He asked specifically if EMDR might be helpful for him. He had learned about EMDR from his brother-in-law's experience with an EMDR therapist.

Allen's first session was devoted to history taking. When he was eight, his ten year old sister had died suddenly of a disease. In describing his sister's death and the events leading up to it, he became quite teary, and I noted to myself that this would be a good target. Allen's parents had never recovered from their daughter's death. They became emotionally withdrawn and inaccessible to Allen. Since then he had never been able to feel close to his parents. His mother had died a year before he came to see me, and while he had become somewhat emotional at her funeral, he said that he had not felt that way since. Allen had no trouble identifying a variety of safe places and positive events. When I asked him to think of a nurturing, well-intentioned adult, he immediately thought of a now-deceased boss who had been a mentor to him in both business and life; he thought of this man quite fondly. He currently had no close friends, but wished he did.

He explained that he had processed his feelings about his experiences in Vietnam years ago with another therapist who had not done EMDR with him, and, when I asked him how disturbing these memories were for him now, Allen rated his current disturbance level with respect to these memories at a 1 or 2 on a scale of 0 to 10 (Subjective Units of Distress Scale [SUDS]). At the time he told me this, I accepted it but later learned that his rating of 2 only reflected the degree to which he had anesthetized himself to his feelings. In hindsight, I believe I should have pursued these memories a bit more to determine the specifics of them, and to evaluate for myself to what degree they had been resolved.

At the end of the session, I summarized how I understood Allen's problem. When his sister died, his parents had closed down emotionally and become distant—afraid to form close attachments and risk another loss. Allen, too, had learned to avoid close attachments, owing both to the loss of his sister and the subsequent emotional loss of his parents. He had married, but his wife had always been dissatisfied with his emotional availability. When his daughter was born, the specter of his 10-year-old sister suddenly dying became revitalized and he maintained emotional distance from his daughter. When Allen returned from Vietnam, he emotionally withdrew even further. Now, his goal in therapy was to reconnect to his emotional self and to his family.

Before writing this chapter, I reviewed the notes of my treatment of Allen and found aspects of the treatment that could have been better. It is a testimony to the robustness of the EMDR process that, despite these shortcomings, the treatment was exceptionally successful. Nevertheless, if I could go back and conduct it over again, I would make some different choices. In that respect, I hope this case will be instructive. In the remainder of this chapter, I intend to treat this case as if it were presented to me for consultation, and explain what I believe were the critical choice points, what the therapist (me) did that I think worked well, and where I would recommend different choices.

Session 2

Allen began the second session by asking to process the residual discomfort from his Vietnam experience, which, he had realized during the week subsequent to our history-taking session, was still somewhat more disturbing than he had realized. I could see from our discussion in the first session that he was extremely defensive about accessing these memories in an affective way, but I went along with this request. I agreed to begin with this target because

Allen requested it, and because I believed that the memories from Vietnam were discrete traumas that would be resolved easily with EMDR.

My therapeutic orientation at the time I began using EMDR had been analytic. In fact, I was just putting the finishing touches on my first book, *Split Self/Split Object* (1992), when I participated in my first EMDR training. For some years afterwards, I tried to find a way to integrate EMDR into my nondirective analytic style. I finally concluded that the two were inconsistent to the degree that, for EMDR to be maximally effective, the therapist needs to play an active role in the selection, sequencing, and development of targets. Perhaps, when I worked with Allen in 1996, I hadn't fully come to that conclusion. As a result I chose to follow his preference in the choice of a first target. In hindsight, I would probably have suggested first processing the loss of his sister, because that memory appeared to be most affectively accessible to him during history-taking and it chronologically preceded his Vietnam experience.

Allen: If I hear the propeller wash of a helicopter that will bring back memories.

PM: Can you give me an example of a memory it might bring back?

Allen: There are lots of them. I can see a dead Viet Cong soldier laying on the ground riddled with bullet holes.

PM: As you look at that image, how disturbing is it for you now on a scale of 0 to 10, where zero is "not disturbing at all" and 10 is "the most disturbing you can imagine"?

Although the evaluation of the level of disturbance (SUDS) is positioned later in the 8 phase EMDR protocol (see Chapter 1 of this volume), I often ask about SUDS levels for the various targets that come up during history taking and when I am determining the most appropriate target to select for processing in a particular session. I want a target that is genuinely disturbing but not overwhelming.

Allen: It's about a 2 or 3.

PM: What's the most disturbing aspect of that image?

Allen: I put the bullet holes in him. At one time I felt great guilt or remorse about that.

PM: How have you resolved it now?

Allen: Now I think, "It's just the inequalities of war; someone has to die."

This would have been the place to interrupt the targeting process and reassess whether this target was likely to be productive. Although, during history taking, Allen rated the SUDS on this memory a 5, it was apparent that he did not have access to affect as he talked about it now. Now, he said that, although he used to have feelings about this memory, he has since resolved it in a philosophical way, consistent with what appears to be his overall approach to disturbing material—he uses his intellect to insulate himself from associated dysphoric affect. Attempting to process a target around which a client is highly defended usually leads to a session that does not appear to be productive, even if it does have some preparatory value for the client. I see this as especially problematic when it is a first target in an EMDR treatment because I want my client's first EMDR experience to be a solid one, one that will give him confidence that he will be able to resolve his other issues with the help of EMDR. When a more emotionally-accessible target is available, as was the case here with Allen, I normally prefer it. Instead, with Allen, I went ahead and continued to attempt to develop this Viet Nam memory as a target. The negative cognition he arrived at was, "Life isn't fair."

PM: If we're successful today in influencing the way you think of this memory, what would you prefer to believe about it?

Allen: I'd like to believe that life is fair. I don't believe that. It just as easily could have been me lying there.

At this point, Allen's eyes became slightly glassy, indicating to me that he was accessing some emotion. Recognizing that the most difficult challenge in working with Allen would be to help him access his emotions, I decided to take advantage of this apparent affect. I did this instead of asking him for a better positive cognition, a Validity of Cognition Scale (VOC) or a SUDS rating, and risk losing the emotion.

PM: What are you feeling as you think of that memory?

Allen: Grief, remorse, guilt.

PM: Where do you feel it in your body?

Allen: In my gut. ►◄►◄►◄ 30 I think I've benefitted—learned from that experience in Vietnam. I developed survivorship skills. [*Allen appears to have retreated from his affect.*]

Allen: ►◄►◄►◄ (31) In my life, I've built on the survivorship skills I learned. The war was a two-edged sword. It's helped me know how to survive, but it's caused me to internalize a lot of feelings and emotions; I've withdrawn, become almost reclusive, ►◄►◄►◄ (35) a conviction on my part about the quality of life I'd like to enjoy. If I'm going to have that, I'm going to have to get beyond that repression.

PM: What are you feeling, now?

Allen: That I've made significant progress in putting behind me those Vietnam experiences.

This, of course is not a feeling. His response underscores the problem with this attempt at EMDR processing of a target to which he is not responding affectively.

PM: How disturbing is that memory now, when you bring it to mind?

Allen: Maybe it's a 1 or 2

PM: What stands out now as you think about it?

Allen: The youth of the Vietnamese soldier. ►◄►◄►◄ (37) Maybe just some memories about how physically difficult it was to endure the rigors of Vietnam ►◄►◄►◄ 31 I think I just feel that that's so much behind me now, that it seems almost like ancient history.

Allen maintains a lid on his emotions with respect to the Vietnam experience. At this point, he rates his disturbance level at 2. His responses to the EMDR processing are relatively intellectual, which will be the stumbling block to helping him resolve this Vietnam memories. Unless he recalls the experience at an emotional level, it can not be reprocessed. Recognizing this problem, I discussed with him the lack of emotional "juice" to this target and the desirability of starting with a more charged target. He responded by talking about being emotionally closed down after Vietnam and the effect his emotional distance has had on his family relationships.

Allen: It's too bad I wasn't able to let it go a long time ago. I just pretty much kept it all to myself.

PM: Why did you do that?

Allen: Most of us didn't talk about our experiences when we returned. What really upsets me now is what it's done to my family. I was just turned inward, and my relationships suffered. I think it may be too late now to have a connection to my daughter.

At this point, Allen asked to target his pain around the alienation between him and his daughter, which he rated as a SUDS of "5, 6, or 7." From the account of this session it is clear that letting the client determine the order of targets in an EMDR treatment is a mistake. Clients who have avoided focusing on their traumatic memories for many years are not going to immediately reverse that pattern now. Many clients have come to me for EMDR after years of analytically-oriented psychotherapy, sometimes many times per week; when I take a careful trauma history with these people, major traumas, including child abuse and near death experiences, often come to light that were never even touched upon in the previous treatment.

In EMDR treatment, there is often, as in Allen's case, a natural progression of targets that suggests itself. It is the therapist's job to guide the client to the appropriate target. Despite Allen's request to focus on his relationship difficulties with his daughter, I believe that the initial target in this treatment should have been Allen's loss of his sister. In the history, this was the one place where Allen became somewhat emotional. (This level of emotion is a good indication of a promising target, especially for a client who has difficulty accessing affect.) In addition, a clinician should always look for the earliest memory in a chain of related disturbing memories. If, as I did in this case, a therapist yields to the client's desire to focus on a relatively recent target, the therapist can do an *affect bridge* (Watkins, 1971) or *float back* technique (Shapiro, 2001; Young, Zangwill, Behary, 2002), which will usually shift the focus to the appropriate earlier memory. In the affect bridge, the therapist helps the client to identify and feel the affect related to the initial target and to locate associated body sensations. Then, the therapist asks the client to close his eyes and to allow his mind to float back in time and notice any earlier memories that he associates with this affect and body sensation.

Allen: There is no rapport. I feel emptiness and some remorse at not being a more effective father over the years.

PM: When you think of that is there an image that comes to mind?

Allen: An image of her, a beautiful young woman who I don't know. I don't know what she's feeling. I don't know her.

A therapist should not assume that the image the client gives is well elaborated in the client's mind and, therefore, one should not simply accept the image as it is given. Clients who are emotionally defended sometimes offer an image that is vague, intellectualized, or seems to fit the target logically but is not really a flash point; the image does not really capture the flavor of the disturbance. In Allen's case, I didn't know yet if the image he presented really captured his emotional response. To find out, I asked him for details about the image; I wanted to find out how emotionally real it was for him. Often I ask questions like, "What is she wearing?," "Where is she in the room?," or even, "What color are the walls?" I am looking for a real image, not a general idea; whether the client recalls the scene or makes it up, I want him to be able to see it.

PM: Can you describe what you see?

Allen: She's standing by herself.

PM: Where do you see her?

Allen: She's in our home, in the den.

PM: What is it about this image that makes it disturbing to think about now?

Allen: A young woman I don't know. I think of so many lost opportunities; I feel the need to build a relationship now. For years, I'd come home, say, "hello," and nothing more. I feel I'm more accessible now.

This image seemed to carry some poignancy, and I think it would have worked as a target; however, I wanted to find out if there was a more charged memory that represented a moment in time. My next question was akin to an affect bridge. It would have been better, however, if I'd put more emphasis on the feeling of loss as the point of the bridge by first focusing on a body sensation he associates with the loss.

PM: Do you have a specific memory that captures that feeling of loss?

Allen: Eight years ago, she was under significant stress and wouldn't go to school. I tried to make her do it and it caused a major rift between us; and I don't think it's ever been repaired since then.

PM: Is there a specific moment in time that comes to mind when you think of that memory, a worst moment?

Allen: Her looking at me and saying, "Dad, you've blown it." She was 11 then; I didn't have the sense to realize that times have changed and value systems need to adapt.

This was a more specific image of her that captures his pain. If I'd done another affect bridge at this point and suggested that he float way back into his past, he might have recalled the loss of his sister, which would have been a better target. My notes about this target do not indicate the cognitions or VOC, and it is possible that I skipped them in my attempt to start the processing before he again loses the affect to which he has connected.

PM: What are you feeling now, as you think of this image.

Allen: Sadness

PM: When you think of this image, how disturbing is it for you now on a scale of 0 to 10 where 0 is not disturbing at all and 10 is the most disturbing you can imagine?

Allen: Six. ►◄►◄►◄ (35) I can't go back in time and change that. My focus needs to be to start now to build a parent–adult relationship with her.

PM: What are you feeling as you say this?

Allen: I've attempted to do that unsuccessfully, ►◄►◄►◄ (30) I guess. I'd have to say, "It takes two to tango"

There continued to be a problem with the target. Allen had no real affect, and when I asked what he's feeling, he gave me a thought. At these times, it is sometimes helpful to ask the client to go back to the original target image or memory. This is what I did. If the image or target is still disturbing, what is the disturbance? What makes it disturbing? I try to help the client to identify specifically the most disturbing aspect of the target.

Allen: My inability to understand and relate. I now understand. ►◄►◄►◄ (30) I think I see it in perspective now. My childhood and Vietnam experiences prevented me from communicating. I never verbalized it before. ►◄►◄►◄ (40) Maybe I shouldn't feel sad and remorseful for something that may have been beyond my control. ►◄►◄►◄ (40) She doesn't recognize this and may not be able to. I'm just now recognizing that this relationship has to evolve over a long period of time. ►◄►◄►◄ (30) Building on that, I need to take a more patient approach, and just remind myself that this is a longer term relationship.

Although there is no overt affect displayed here, I did feel a poignancy to what Allen was saying and how he was saying it.

PM: You are viewing your relationship with her as a work in progress, rather than feeling like you've failed?

Allen: Yes. ►◄►◄►◄ (40) I may have destroyed it beyond repair, but I think there is still time to retrieve it. As I think about it, I am realizing that it is no more or no less than the relationship I had with my mother and father, ►◄►◄►◄ (45) especially how distant it was. I didn't communicate with my parents; they were responsible and took care of my needs, but they didn't connect to me on an emotional basis. Yet we survived. I can see how much we missed out on. My relationship with them was really no different than my relationship with my daughter. ►◄►◄►◄ (41) Just as I missed out on things I could have shared with my parents, pretty much the same is true for my relationship with my daughter. I couldn't do anything about it. So, my focus has to be on the here and now. ►◄►◄►◄ (40) Many things come into my mind. The focus needs to be on the future rather than the past. I really shouldn't have negative energy replaying what could have been.

PM: When you think of the time she told you you'd blown it, how disturbing is it for you now on a scale of 0 to 10?

Allen: Four. History is repeating itself. What my parents programmed in me became reality. I feel remorse that I didn't get enlightened earlier. ►◄►◄ ►◄ (42) The thing that comes into perspective now is time. There is still time. I should be guided by faith that my legacy with my daughter should be as it develops over the next 20 years rather than the past 20 years. ►◄ ►◄►◄ (28) There's got to be a relationship in the future.

PM: How disturbing is the memory for you now on a scale of 0 to 10?

Allen: As I think about it now, I'm not sure it was that much of a watershed event. I was just acting out the programming of my parents; it was automatic. I had never really looked at how their withdrawal effected me, and without my own awareness, sooner or later I was bound to do the same thing to my daughter. ►◄►◄►◄ (31) recognizing that my parents didn't do anything purposely to my life; they didn't mean any harm, and I didn't do anything purposely to my daughter's life. So, I shouldn't feel guilty. Somehow, this is hitting me in a new way, the recognition and understanding. It may be a bit of a breakthrough. ▶◀▶◀▶◀ (35) I'll be judged from today forward.

PM: How disturbing is the memory for you now?

Allen: 2 or 3.

This appears to be a surprisingly good result for a session in which the client kept the bulk of his affect closed off. The fact that there was no release of affect suggests that his low rating of SUDS may not be reliable. If the target had been the loss of his sister, I believe that there would have been more affect and it would have resolved in this session; however, it is possible that if we had chosen the loss of his sister, as soon as he focused in on it and began processing, he could have felt exposed, frightened by his own affect, and shut down emotionally.

Session 3

In the beginning of the next session, Allen's SUDS on his alienation from his daughter was back up to a "5, 6, or 7." My experience with unresolved targets has been that if one lets them accumulate, the client gradually feels worse and worse. Each unresolved target has, potentially, activated additional areas of anxiety or dysphoria; each can contribute, individually and collectively, to malaise. I chose to retarget the memory of his daughter telling him he had blown it. A better choice would have been to go back to the memory of his sister dying, with the understanding that resolving this earlier memory would have probably helped to resolve the memory involving his daughter.

The processing of his relationship with his daughter, however, was more successful this time. His target image was a family photo with people frowning instead of smiling. This image was more affectively alive for him than the one from the previous session. His negative cognition this time was "I'm a failure; there's no second chance." He reported a feeling of emptiness that he experienced in his gut, and in the processing he was able to track this visceral sensation. Although he did still intellectualize and lose the feeling more than once, he was able to regain a focus on it. My strategy in the EMDR processing was to bring him back to focusing on his feeling state after almost every set. The emptiness turned to tension in his gut, which then became sadness and remorse. Thoughts of the lack of connection with people in his childhood came up. His disturbance level went from "6 or 7" to "2 or 3." Toward the end of the session, I brought him back to target and asked again about his level of disturbance.

Allen: It's less. ►◄►◄►◄ (35) There are a lot of people and factors, and I made mistakes. It's all in the past now. I still feel the sadness, but it's less. ►◄►◄►◄ (31) My daughter is 17. She has a long life ahead of her. I've got time. I feel more complete. I'm putting the past in the past and focusing on the future.

At this point he still appeared to have some remaining affect; however, there was very little time left in the session and I decided to close it down. I decided to see if identifying and installing an appropriate positive cognition might help to bring the disturbance down further and close the session out. I wondered if his realizations about there still being time had something to do with processing the residual feelings from his sister's death, which was final and left him no time. Accordingly, I suggested, and he accepted, his statement, "I've got time," as the new positive cognition (VOC was "5 or 6"). I installed it with quite a few relatively short sets of eye movements. Some of Allen's comments were,

Allen: There is a relationship. We've lived in the same house for 19 years. I've been there for her, not properly focused or ideal, but i've been there. . . . It has been my intent to be there for her in the past and is my intent to be there in the future. [VOC was 6 or 7. He also suggested the PC, "I'm a well intentioned person."] I have to let my actions speak louder than words. [SUDS was 2] ►◄►◄►◄ Regardless of my perception, the key is in the future, because I can't change the past. That is where my energy needs to be focused. [SUDS was "1 or a half"] ►◄►◄►◄ Again that perception is real but during that exercise I realized that I am a caring individual although I'm not infallible. Being a caring individual doesn't carry with it perfection. ►◄►◄►◄ I thought about what I just said, and my thoughts were re-enforcing that that is true. We can't be perfect and even our best intentions don't always lead to success. [The SUDS was "0 or very low"] ►◄►◄►◄ . . . I'm beginning to see the possibility that there could be an image with the people smiling and my daughter with a husband, ►◄►◄►◄ and I see that image as consistent with a caring person.

The SUDS at this point was "not disturbing. We've shrunk it." Allen's response to the body scan, was, "I'm feeling very relaxed. I certainly don't have that feeling in my gut. I like the concept of the body scanning."

Session 4

Allen began the fourth session by saying that he felt good. When he thought of his daughter, however, he reported a disturbance level of 2. We did not start immediately with the same memory as was the EMDR target of the previous session, because his disturbance was somewhat different than it had been in the two previous sessions. Rather than being focused on his feelings of loss, he now seemed to be more focused on his fears and how they kept him from being emotionally available. I was not sure if this was a new target or a branch of the previous target that had not been processed, but the zero SUDS and clean body scan from that session led me to believe that this anxiety represented a new target.

Allen: I've been successful in my career and I'm proud of that, but it troubles me that I haven't been a successful father.

PM: Does that mean to you that feel you've failed?

Allen: Yes, I haven't given her what she needed growing up and I didn't provide her with a legacy for the future of a favorable father image. Even as a professional, I think my life could be richer, in addition to being successful. I guess you could say I want to be less of a businessman in both my professional and my personal life.

Allen talked about his conservative Midwestern upbringing and said he'd like to learn to be more spontaneous and take some risks, to not always need an agenda. My interpretation was that some of his need for control arose from the anxiety that was a residue from his wartime experiences. I reminded him that the premature death of his sister had created a feeling of uncertainty and fear of loss in his family; this also contributed to his need for control. He considered my comments, and talked about his need to bring closure to everything he did, to not leave anything half-done. Eventually, a memory came up for him of the Loma Prieta Earthquake, a very large quake that hit the San Francisco Bay area in 1990. He described diving under a table as the ground beneath him was shaking; his immediate association was to worse memories from Vietnam—of laying on the ground as white phosphorous or a hail of bullets was coming at him. He appeared to be shifting to the subject area of his fears and anxieties related largely to the war, and I suggested he tell me about his specific memories from Vietnam. He identified twelve memories, ranging in SUDS from 5 to 8. It was apparent that the successful processing we had done in the previous sessions had made him feel less vulnerable with his affect. We agree to begin the next session by targeting one of those memories with a SUDS of 7.

Session 5

Allen began the fifth session by saying he wanted to talk some more about his daughter and forego EMDR for this session. It is a difficult judgement for me to make. It is not easy to decide whether I think a client wants to talk in order to develop a more secure connection to me as his or her therapist, or whether the desire to talk is an attempt to avoid processing a disturbing target. Selecting a target in advance, as we had done, is often not a good idea because the client can generate a high degree of anxiety in anticipating the processing of that target in the coming session. In this session with Allen, I believed that his request was serving primarily a defensive role. We talked a little bit more about his daughter, and then I told him that I thought it important that we process his Vietnam experience, and that I thought doing this would influence his relationships with his wife and with his daughter.

Allen's war experiences were the Big T traumas to which Shapiro (1995, 2001, 2002) has referred. Most were very specific moments in time when Allen felt terror or horror. The earlier memories, even his sister's death, were target memories that were important for the loss they represented; they were, however, less powerful moments in time, less likely to be overwhelming. Allen's most disturbing war memory was of being caught in a crossfire in an open rice field with no way to call for air or artillery support. I wanted to ensure that he'd have a successful experience with our first attempt at desensitizing a portion of his war experience, so I selected a less disturbing target, the image of a huge bomb fragment flying through the air towards him. Although this fragment was flying towards Allen and could have potentially killed him, the negative cognition he offered was, "I'm inadequate." The key he identified to this experience was that he needed to choose whether to dive left or right, and that his life might depend upon making the right choice. The positive cognition (PC) was, "I can handle it," which I rephrased as, "I'm competent." The VOC on this cognition was 7 which indicated that the PC was not a good one. I decided to go on with this setup anyway, assuming that a better PC would come up during the processing. I think the problem with both cognitions was that they focused on competency rather than fear, the real emotional theme of this memory. He had suggested competency as the relevant theme because, as will become clear from the processing, he was wanting to avoid feeling the fear.

PM: When you think of that memory, what do you feel?

Allen: Fear. There is a recognition that I wasn't equipped to make such a decision, not analogous to moving out of the way of a wild baseball pitch, where if you guess wrong, you'd probably end up with a bump on your head or a bruise on your shoulder. In this situation, my life depended on the choice I made.

PM: How disturbing is it for you to recall now?

Allen: 5 or 6

PM: Where in your body do you feel the fear?

Allen: Well, right now I feel it mostly in my head. It's more intellectual. I'm actually feeling amazingly relaxed.

PM: When you think of the memory, how disturbing is it for you now on a scale of 0 to 10?

Allen: 3 or 4. I made the right decision; It didn't come near me. Maybe that's fate; maybe I couldn't control the response.

PM: Are you feeling comfortable now as you say that?

Allen: Very much so. That ratifies a lot of my beliefs.

PM: What are you feeling now?

Allen: Relief and relaxed that it's over; it was a short-lived terror.

PM: When you think of the memory, on a scale of 1 to 7 how true does that statement feel now, "It's over"?

Allen: It feels true. I feel more relief in recognizing that it is over or nearly over.

PM: I'm not sure what you mean by "nearly over." Are you referring to all these dangers you lived through?

Allen: Yes

PM: The shell fragments? [*Allen nods*] So on a scale of 1 to 7, it is nearly a 7.

Allen: Yes, 6 or 7.

PM: Is there still some fear?

Allen: Yes.

PM: Where are you feeling the fear now?

Allen: I'm really having an intellectual response.

When the affect connected to a client's memory is available, but the client is just not connecting to it, I want to find a way to help him access it. Allen was not actively choosing to connect to this memory on a predominantly intellectual level, and I needed to find a way to help him go more deeply. Although I did not expect to be successful, I decided to see if some alternating bilateral stimulation would help Allen to access this memory more fully.

Allen: ►◄►◄►◄ (30) In a sense, it's really no different than civilian life when you see a car coming towards you over the median. ►◄►◄►◄ (30) Life is full of choices, military or civilian. Sometimes we make the right choice and sometimes we make the wrong one.

PM: Think of the original image again, and tell me what you notice about it now.

Allen: It's still the same. It hasn't changed.

A memory cannot be desensitized or reprocessed until it is accessed. Again, I could see that Allen was not allowing himself to recall his actual experience. To help him to focus on his experience, I said in a challenging, almost disbelieving tone, "Are you sure you remember it?" Now, more than six years later, I still clearly remember his response to my challenge.

Allen: Oh yes, I can see the line of trees and the blue sky and the people around me. I remember it like it was yesterday. I always will.

Suddenly, he was volunteering details, indicating to me he was really accessing the memory. His eyes were moving spontaneously as he spoke, surveying the scene in his head. I seized the moment, and said, "Good, focus on that." I began another set of eye movements. I knew this set would be dramatically different than the previous ones. His pupils dilated as he vividly recalled the terror of the event. His processing of the terror lasted at most thirty seconds, but I believe those thirty seconds were a turning point in Allen's treatment. I think of that set as the thirty-second cure, *because, not only did his current target almost completely resolve in those thirty seconds, but all the processing he did thereafter took on a different quality. It's as though a light bulb had turned on in his head that said, "I have to remember it to get over it, and I can."*

Allen: No one was injured by the fragment; it flew over my head and fell behind me.

PM: You remembered the image and the fear that time.

Allen: Yes.

PM: Think of the original image. What's coming up now?

Allen: Well, you're not going to believe this, but I can still see that shell fragment, but now it looks like a big marshmallow. ►◄►◄►◄ This feels like it is a big breakthrough. ►◄►◄►◄ I see the fragment sailing gracefully over my head and cascading harmlessly onto the ground. ►◄►◄►◄ I don't see the fragment anymore; I see a bird flying instead of the fragment. I'm not sure if it was a dove of peace, but it was some sort of symbol of tranquility.

PM: Try to bring the original image back.

Allen: If I try, I can still see the fragment, but it's sailing harmlessly over my head, and the image is not as clear. ►◄►◄►◄ The screen in my head with the image went blank and I have a feeling of relief.

PM: How disturbing is the memory now on a scale of 0 to 10?

Allen: 1 at most.

If I believe that a client is capable of focusing fully on a disturbing memory, but is resisting, I might tell him Allen's story. I tell him that unless someone is willing to recall a memory, he cannot desensitize it. Once people have the experience of dipping into a fearful memory and seeing the memory fade into the distance, they gain confidence in the EMDR process and are far more receptive to recalling and processing other disturbing memories.

A typical difficulty, however, in treating more severe cases of posttraumatic stress disorder (PTSD) than Allen's is that the memory is overwhelming, and the client is unable to bring it to mind, even with the help of eye movements, without defending. In those cases it is necessary to help the client to titrate the memory by bringing it up in a partially dissociated form, so that recalling the memory is not overwhelming. One method suggested by Shapiro (1995), which I find effective, is to ask clients to imagine that they are viewing the traumatic event on a movie screen or a TV monitor that they can manipulate and control. If necessary, I suggest that they imagine adjusting the television so that it displays in black and white instead of color. Encouraging clients to review an image in this indirect way reduces the level of disturbance they experience. When these diluted images are substantially processed, clients can usually then go back and reprocess the images in undiluted form.

After evaluating the SUDS at 1, Allen reported the VOC as 6 at least. During several sets of installation, he made comments like, "I see the same setting, but the bird is turning and flying the opposite way," and "It's over, I survived, and probably learned a lot." He said, "I see myself as I see myself today. I can still see the image, but it's not the same. I'm not that frightened soldier. Now, I'm seeing myself in the image as I see myself today; I clearly survived." The VOC went up to 6 and a fraction; the SUDS stayed at 1. When asked why the disturbance was not down to a zero, he commented,

"It's more a theoretical thing. It just can't be zero. That would be too much."
When asked about the original image, he said, "Probably if I tried I could
remember it." When encouraged to try, however, he reported, "At least right
now, I can't bring it back the same way."

Session 6

We had decided in advance that we would treat Allen's worst Vietnam memory in this session, and I set aside an hour and a half for it. I began by
reviewing the processing from the previous session. The bomb fragment
image remained no longer disturbing.

Allen's worst war memory was of a fire fight in an open rice field that
began with the point man, a lieutenant whose job it was to call in air support, being killed by a sniper. There were Viet Cong in the trees on both
sides of the field, and Allen and his comrades were caught in a crossfire.

Allen: I can still see the tree line of the river, open furrows of dried up rice
paddies, helicopters overhead. I can see the lieutenant go down and other
people attempting to render aid. I can see the dike in front of me and there
is incoming fire.

PM: When you think of the memory, what negative thought comes to mind
that describes you.

Allen: I'm in danger, my life is in danger. Also there literally was a crossfire.
I remember thinking, "Which side of the dike do I get on?"

PM: So what does that say about you?

Allen: There's no good choices. Usually a barrier like that would be some
form of protection, but, in this case, because they were shooting at us from
both sides, which ever side of the dike I was on I would probably be exposed.

*I again decided not to belabor the cognitions in this target. I assumed they had to do with
not feeling safe, because feelings of vulnerability rather than helplessness characterized Allen's issues.*

PM: What are you feeling?

Allen: Uneasy, fear, grief or sadness about the lieutenant, uncertainty about
who we were up against—real very perceived danger because I could hear
the bullets going over my head—absence of command, which is typical.

PM: SUDS?

Allen: 6 or 7

PM: Where in your body are you feeling this?

Allen: In my gut—slight muscle tension. I know the outcome is not as terrifying as during the real time. . . . The focus now is on the fallen Lieutenant. . . .

This target had been rated at a SUDS of 8 two weeks before. I believe that the successful processing of the previous session had affected the other Vietnam memories, and brought this one down from 8 to "6 or 7." The processing on this target went very smoothly, with Allen able to access related affect. Later he recalled another man who went down that same day, a man who Allen knew by name. He marveled at how much greater an impact the death of this second man had because he knew the man's name. The final positive cognition for the session was "It's over and it was horrible" and "I benefitted as a person." He rated the VOC as a good solid 6 and the SUDS at 1 or 2. During installation he said, "I'm picturing a terrible scene without feeling anything disturbing." He rated the VOC now as 7. After the next installation set, he reported, "Just a little sadness that I had to carry this for thirty years without processing it." After the next set he responded, "Relaxation—that we have processed it and the result is clearly different than when we started," and then, "I think I just want to get on with things and see what resources exist with that unblocked right hemisphere that I've missed for so many years." The body scan was clear. "I feel very relaxed."

Session 7

The next session was Allen's seventh. He began with the comments that appear at the opening of this chapter. He was amazed at how deeply effected his life had been by his treatment, and especially the previous session. The SUDS from his problems relating to his daughter was 0. Of the twelve targets from Vietnam, all were now at a disturbance level of 1 or 2. Of those, the one that still seemed to carry the most disturbance, although the level was quite low, was of seeing bullets piercing the nearby bottom of a Huey helicopter that was carrying him out of a battle area. It processed easily, ending with a SUDS of 0.

Session 8

The following session was the eighth and last. Allen felt no need for more therapy. He said he was thoroughly pleased and excited about his new life, and assured me that if anything came up that needed processing he would call me. We ended the session after a half hour. As he left, he told me that if I ever needed a testimonial or someone to be interviewed by a reporter about the effectiveness of EMDR, he would be happy to do it. That was in 1997.

I contacted him for the first time since then in late 2002. Talking over telephone, I told him I was writing this chapter and asked him how he was doing. He said, "I'm doing fine. I don't know if it was the EMDR, maturity, the passage of time, or a combination of all of those factors that allowed me to be fine. I can hear the wash of helicopter chopper blades and I have no flashbacks—no reaction at all really. All of those issues are well behind me, now. I'm not just saying that—it's the whole truth and nothing but the truth. It's just great to have that behind me. I don't think I've ever been more effective or reliable or a better husband or father than I am now." I asked, "Then your relationship with your daughter has continued to improve?" He responded, "Yes, it has, in fact."

In thinking about Allen's treatment, I have at times thought about what happened to the memory of Allen's sister's death. Because we did not target it directly, which in hindsight seems to me an omission, I have wondered if it was nevertheless metabolized during the processing of Allen's relationship with his daughter. I asked him about it when we spoke over the telephone.

PM: I have one additional question that came up when I was reviewing my notes in order to write the chapter. You talked in the first session about your sister, and it was disturbing for you at that time to think about her death. I was not sure if that memory had been processed in the second or third session when we were focusing on your daughter. Do you have any recollection of that?

Allen: No, I don't recall it at all.

PM: Well, I guess another way to ask that question is to ask how it is for you now to think about the loss of your sister.

Allen: I haven't thought about her in years actually.

PM: Is it at all disturbing now for you to think about it?

Allen: No, it isn't.

For the therapist, EMDR is a forgiving process. Even if some promising opportunities are missed or the therapeutic choices made are not optimal, the treatment can be strikingly effective. In this case, Allen was able to rid himself of a variety of intrusive memories and flashbacks, to become more emotionally available for his wife and daughter, and to reawaken his own spontaneity and excitement about being alive. This eight-hour EMDR treatment, complete with its flaws, profoundly impacted his life.

References

Manfield, P. (1992). *Split self/split object: Understanding and treating borderline, narcissistic, and schizoid disorders*. Northvale, NJ: Jason Aronson Publishers.

Shapiro, F. (1995). *Eye movement desensitization and reprocessing: Basic principles, protocols, and procedures*. New York: Guilford Press.

Shapiro, F. (1989). Efficacy of the eye movement desensitization procedure in the treatment of traumatic memories. *Journal of Traumatic Stress, 2*, 199–223.

Shapiro, F. (2001). *Eye movement desensitization and reprocessing: Basic principles, protocols, and procedures. Second Edition*. New York: Guilford Press.

Shapiro, F. (Ed.). (2002). *EMDR as an integrative psychotherapy approach: Experts of diverse orientations explore the paradigm prism*. Washington, DC: American Psychological Association Press.

Watkins, J. (1971). The affect bridge: A hypnoanalytic technique. *International Journal of Clinical & Experimental Hypnosis, 19*(1), 21–27.

Young, J. E., Zangwill, W. M., & Behary, W. E., (2002). Combining EMDR and schema-focused therapy: The whole may be greater than the sum of the parts. In F. Shapiro (Ed.), *EMDR as an integrative psychotherapy approach: Experts of diverse orientations explore the paradigm prism* (pp. 181–208). Washington, DC: American Psychological Association Press.

8

HELPING THE HELPERS

A Firefighter with PTSD after
the World Trade Center Disaster

Gina Colelli

ON SEPTEMBER 11, 2001 there was a terrorist attack on the World Trade Center. Within minutes of the attack, hundreds of firefighters descended on the World Trade Center (WTC) in the hopes of rescuing people. Within an hour the WTC had crumbled, killing thousands of civilians and hundreds of firefighters, emergency medical personnel, and police officers. This case is about Mark, a twenty-year veteran of the New York City Fire Department. Mark is in a position of authority with hundreds of personnel under his jurisdiction. In the aftermath of the September 11th attack, he was responsible for overseeing his personnel at Ground Zero and making sure the operation was effective and safe. In addition, alongside his personnel, he searched and recovered human remains in the debris left after the WTC collapsed.

This case illustrates how the impact of a recent traumatic event can disrupt a client's defense mechanisms that were used to cope with a severe previous trauma. As is so often the case in EMDR processing, the processing of the recent event stimulated memories of the earlier event. During the history taking, Mark informed me of the death of his parents when he was a teenager; but he told me that it was not a significant problem for him. In hindsight, it is clear that I should have probed deeper into this assertion, rather than take it at face value. The original presenting symptoms of post-traumatic stress disorder (PTSD), resulting from the recovery work Mark

187

performed at the WTC, were significantly reduced in about three sessions, but could not be completely resolved until the earlier traumatic memory involving his parents' deaths had been processed.

Firefighters are accustomed to performing under extraordinary circumstances and stress levels. They view themselves as the rescuers, not the ones in need of being rescued. They get fulfillment from the dangers of the job, pushing themselves to the maximum of their limits. Firefighters have above-average job satisfaction and enjoy an incredible support system in the firehouse. They live together—making meals, eating together, sharing chores and sleeping quarters. They spend their free time together and share many family events. They have what is basically a home away from home. In many ways it is like a fraternity house. A common joke among firefighter-wives involves a brief dialogue between an adult and a child:

> Adult: What do you want to be when you grow up?
> Child: I want to be a firefighter.
> Adult: You can't do that if you grow up.

Mark's use of the defenses of compartmentalization and dissociation enabled him to cope with his childhood tragedy and develop a functional social identity. I speculate, however, that these defenses also contributed to a need for danger and excitement in his life. In one of his early sessions with me, Mark shared that he would miss the danger and excitement of the operation at the WTC, and feared what feelings may come up "now that there is nothing else to do but the usual."

Therapist's Background

When I first met Mark I did not have any experience with emergency personnel or *first responders*. I had nine years experience using EMDR, so I felt confident about my skills despite my lack of experience with this population. I allowed Mark to teach me what it was like to be a first responder and to enter the world of the people who have to perform in extraordinary circumstances. I received my Masters in social work in 1981 and have been in private practice since 1983. I was trained in psychodynamic psychotherapy and psychosynthesis. My experience is with addictions, eating disorders, and adults abused and neglected as children. I was (and still am) a resident of Manhattan when the attack on the WTC occurred. I had my own distress symptoms from being in New York, and suffered vicarious traumatization as a result of treating people who were directly affected by the disaster.

In the initial stages of treatment, the goal was to reprocess Mark's PTSD in five sessions or less. This goal was established by the EMDR Humanitarian Assistance Program's World Trade Center Disaster Relief Program, a volunteer program that I coordinated. The goal of a five session treatment assumed that there were no antecedent traumatic events feeding the current trauma, and was based on the research that had been done on EMDR and PTSD that has demonstrated that most single incident traumas can be resolved to an adaptive state of resolution in three sessions (Wilson, Becker & Tinker, 1995). Mark's PTSD symptoms were largely reprocessed in the first three sessions. However, a full resolution could not be accomplished until he had processed his grief and anger from the murder/suicide of his parents; the full treatment to date, has required sixteen sessions, and may involve more in the future.

Throughout the description of Mark's treatment I include my thoughts on the clinical dilemmas as they pertain to Mark and myself, as well as noting the many parallels between his experience at Ground Zero and his unresolved losses. I explain how the history of unresolved traumas enters into the reprocessing of a present day trauma. I also share my thought process on how I utilized his willingness to work on his experience at Ground Zero as a way to facilitate his ability to work on the earlier trauma.

First Session

Mark, a 50-year-old Caucasian man of medium height and build, looked considerably older than his stated age. His face was deeply etched with a furrowed brow and he looked every bit the part of a person who had seen a situation too unbearable to speak of. Mark was not part of the first wave of firefighters who responded to the attack on the WTC (commonly known as Ground Zero). He came to the site hoping to rescue victims. Along with the other members of the Fire Department he quickly realized the task would be recovery not rescue. On September 11, 2001, New York City lost 343 firefighters, the largest loss of personnel in the history of the Fire Department.

Upon starting his first session with me, approximately eight months after the WTC disaster, Mark stated that he came for EMDR therapy on the recommendation of a family member who had urged him months ago to get some support. He decided to come at this time because the recovery operation at the WTC would be wrapping up in a week. He thought that there would be a void and he would miss the "danger and excitement." Mark described himself as constantly feeling that there would be another attack on New York City. He also considered himself extremely irritable and "just not himself." He assumed that he would feel depressed and overwhelmed by grief for many years.

I evaluated Mark for PTSD based on the criteria listed in the *DSM IV-Revised* (American Psychiatric Association, 1994). Mark's symptoms were consistent with the diagnosis: intrusive thoughts, anxiety, hyper-vigilance, sleep disorder, and depression. Mark did not have any knowledge about the disorder so I spent some time explaining it to him. I provided Mark with a thorough explanation of EMDR and informed him of what he could expect in the treatment. He had done his own research on EMDR and felt confident that the method would be useful to him. I put aside two hours of time for Mark because I wanted to not only do a history but also provide treatment in the first session.

I evaluated Mark for his appropriateness for EMDR. He was in a stable marriage with two teenage children, had a circle of close friendships, and enjoyed many outside interests. He reported that he did not have a history of psychiatric hospitalizations or psychotropic medications. He didn't abuse alcohol or drugs. He reported that both his parents died when he was a teenager and that their deaths did not affect him. I did not ask how his parents died, which proved to be the clinical dilemma that affected the course of treatment as it had affected the course of his life.

Based on what he presented about himself he was appropriate for immediate EMDR. Mark stated that one of the major reasons he wanted to feel better was to be able to function on his job, "The way I used to before this all happened." He was highly motivated by his work, and reported having a high level of job satisfaction prior to the attack. He was concerned that his capacity for thought was diminished and that he was having trouble remembering how to perform routine tasks.

Over the course of the treatment Mark revealed many disturbing details of his experience at Ground Zero. He had not shared most of these experiences with anyone and it seemed apparent that letting him talk extensively during the desensitization phase provided him with a safe place to share and have his experiences validated. Mark and the other recovery workers did an extraordinary service for all the families and friends of the deceased. Everyone except those men who were retired would go to work and then after work put in a shift at Ground Zero or they would come in on their days off. They were willing to go to any length to find bodies and body parts. Mark felt that it was a "sacred trust" to try to recover bodies and body parts so that "the families have something to bury." He was distressed that the excavating machines sometimes dismembered the bodies and made it difficult to recover bodies intact.

The recovery workers found thousands of body parts and recovered them for DNA testing and ultimately to be returned to the families for burial. They excavated bodies that often fell apart in their hands even though they used the utmost care to remove them from the debris. Mark reported that his worst experience was having found a body that had melted; when they attempted to move it, the child's corpse became a gooey substance that dripped off a steel part of the building into his hands. During the course of our working together, Mark would often express concern about me hearing all of horrors that he had experienced. I would reassure him that although it was upsetting to hear what occurred, I was honored to be part of his recovery just as he was honored to have worked at Ground Zero. He was very grateful to have a place to work through his ordeal. In the initial sessions, hearing the description of the horrors experienced at Ground Zero created a stress response in me. I observed that my own proximity to the event and the very human reaction to hearing about the horror of looking for bodies and body parts at the site caused feelings of despair. Like Mark, I attempted to put my feelings aside so I could continue to be present.

Based on my experience talking to firefighters at firehouses and in training groups, I planned to use EMDR in the first session with Mark. Repeatedly they shared that the debriefing groups and individual counseling sessions did not eliminate their symptoms. The firefighters needed immediate relief; if they did not get some relief in the first session they would have the same reaction as they did to their other therapy experiences, which was not to return to treatment.

I employed the EMDR standard protocol with three modifications. The first modification was in establishing a safe place. As a matter of course, I would have a client create a place where they felt safe and install that resource. For two specific reasons, I changed how I created a safe place when working with Mark. After September 11 most people could not imagine a safe place because our concept of *being safe* had been so drastically shattered. Second, the idea of introducing imagined imagery seemed to pose the issue of whether or not any individual firefighter would find the concept too "way out."

Firefighters are very body-oriented, so I used a body exercise to create an internal safe place that has been described as successful with clients who are combat veterans or survivors of terrorist attack (Silver & Rogers, 2001). Focusing on creating a calming effect on the body circumvents the need to accept a cognitive definition of a safe place and teaches self-soothing. The exercise gives the client a sense of mastery and control because they learn that they can transform disturbing body sensations into a state of calmness.

GC: Mark, I would like you to locate a place in your body where you feel uncomfortable.

Mark: It is my shoulders.

GC: If it had a color, what color would that be? [*If he does not see a color I suggest another sensory awareness such as a shape, texture or weight*]

Mark: Dark gray I do a short set of eye movements to bring more focus to the sensation.

GC: Now I would like you to locate a place in your body where you feel comfortable.

Mark: In my thighs.

GC: If there was a color that went with that, what color would that be?

Mark: Yellow.

GC: I want you to just notice where you are feeling comfortable and the color that goes with that. I do not want you to try to change the feeling in any way. Just be aware of where you are feeling comfortable and the color that goes with that. [*One minute of eye movements.*] I would like for you to notice where you were feeling uncomfortable and tell me if it is the same or different.

Mark: It's slightly better.

GC: Okay, now notice where you were feeling comfortable and tell me if that is the same or different?

Mark: That is different. My legs feel more comfortable.

GC: Okay, once again I want you to notice where you are feeling comfortable.

After one minute or so of eye movements, I repeated the process of checking in both the uncomfortable and comfortable place, until Mark was feeling comfortable in most, if not all of his body and the uncomfortable part were diminished.

The second modification was in setting up a negative and positive cognition. Independently of each other, several EMDR-trained therapists have found that formulating a negative cognition with the firefighters involved with the WTC was frequently not successful. The response on the part of the firefighters was, "I didn't do anything wrong! They bombed the Towers!" One of the underlying issues for the firefighters was the sense of utter helplessness in a disaster of this magnitude. It would seem unlikely that they could imagine saying that they felt powerless or helpless when they are used to being the rescuers, not the people in need of being rescued. Firefighters are often not conscious of the amount of stress under which they operate. I found that the target material was easily activated, which diminished the need to have a firm negative and positive cognition. I suspected that a negative cognition would reveal itself during the reprocessing; in Mark's case, "I'm not safe" was a natural negative cognition. However, it would be ego dystonic for a firefighter to admit not feeling safe. Nevertheless, during the reprocessing when the ego defenses are relaxed, the dual attention makes it possible to recognize vulnerability.

The third modification—which I later abandoned in favor of more traditional eye movements for reasons that will be discussed later—was in the choice of the bilateral stimulation that was utilized in the treatment. Because the method is unusual and he was not accustomed to the therapeutic process, I wanted Mark to find using EMDR as seamless as possible. I have found that using a compact disk (CD) with a bilateral recording was sufficient when there is a high level of stress related to the trauma. I believe that then the anxiety level is so high that a more calming bilateral stimulation makes the anxiety manageable enough so the client can reprocess. I gave Mark a CD with a recording of ocean waves designed with bilateral stimulation. A CD is familiar and easy to use. And, in this case, a recording of waves was appropriate because water is a primary tool in a firefighter's job. Mark liked the CD and felt comfortable using it while we reprocessed his trauma.

When I asked Mark to identify the worst part of the experience at Ground Zero, he chose an image that people seemed commonly to choose—the towers imploding. This would be his target. (This image and the image of people falling from the towers were commonly held disturbing images.) When we set up the protocol I was unaware of the many distressing and stressful scenes to which Mark had been exposed during his tenure at the site; these were revealed during the desensitization phase. We started with the image of the towers imploding, his emotions (anger and anxiety) and his body sensations. The Subjective Units of Distress Scale (SUDS) was 9. Although he was not able to identify a negative cognition, I thought it best to start desensitization, because I believed that the innate healing mechanism activated by the bilateral alternating stimulation would bring his mind to where it needed to be in order to establish a state of adaptive resolution.

I kept the CD on continuous play during the session. This was based on my previous experience that continuous play neither made a difference in the quality of the reprocessing nor in being able to reduce the SUDS to zero when the stress level was extraordinary. Mark's first response was to exclaim that he could see the towers right in front of his face (not more than an inch away). After a short period of time I asked Mark to report what was happening. He reported that the towers had become distant and he was able to graphically describe different visual images that were occurring to him.

Mark: I am standing at the edge of the pit [*site where the towers stood*] watching the excavation machinery. They are picking up debris. The bucket is full of body parts and the machines have severed bodies. I can see body parts falling.

Mark was very upset and he reported how uncomfortable he was feeling, so I suggested that he be aware of his body sensations as a means to help him move through his intense feeling (abreaction). He was obsessing on the image, his face was flushed, and he was repeating that "Anything can happen at anytime." He said, "I don't know what to do. I just can't figure it out. Anything can happen anytime!" I wanted to ground Mark in the moment because of the intensity of his reaction and help him return to a state of dual attention so I reminded him, "Right now you and I are here safe." He responded, "That's it! I don't feel safe." Although there was a possibility of another attack on New York City, his perception that we were in imminent danger was irrational. The degree to which Mark felt unsafe was consistent with PTSD.

Second Session

In this session (one week after the first), Mark arrived looking haggard and reported that he had had two nightmares. When we checked in with the original memory he reported a SUDS of seven. This was higher than when we ended the last session.

I suspected that the higher SUDS were the result of incomplete processing and this was reflected in the nightmares he had had in the interim. He had dreamt that an excavating machine crushed him while he was working down at Ground Zero. There was a real danger because the excavating machines were working right along with the men digging for bodies. In the dream he had broken a leg and was trapped and couldn't move. In the second dream, he had a new BMW automobile but the transmission blew up. He stated that he felt trapped by his chronic symptoms and they interfered with his usual level of functioning.

I continued with the original target from the previous session: the towers imploding. Often, clinicians will become confused as to how to proceed when someone brings in material that is seemingly different from the original target but is just as compelling. More often than not, the material is another channel branching out from the original target and the client's recovery is best served by sticking with the original protocol until the SUDS is zero. If there is another target to reprocess that will become clear, and the therapist and client are then in a better position to reprocess the new target without the interference of the unfinished business of the original target.

Another common concern is when a client talks during the bilateral stimulation. Mark talked a lot during his reprocessing, and it was important to evaluate if the extensive verbalizations were a defense against the material or could be of assistance to his reprocessing. As noted above, I thought that it was necessary for him to relate his experiences and, because he was able to desensitize and reprocess the original image of the imploding towers to SUDS of zero, I was not concerned. As the treatment progressed it became clear that his verbalization did play a defensive role. At the end of the session, Mark had separated himself from the people he had grown fond of at the site, and he had found a way to memorialize the people who had perished. This allowed him to begin to move on.

Mark: It's ending. It's sad. It was exciting to be down there. It was rewarding and dangerous. I was in the zone. I won't see all the people I grew close to anymore. I hope I helped them. I immediately go to how can I make it better for Jack and Sally. [*Jack is another firefighter who lost a son and Sally is a volunteer who was with the firefighters every day.*] I have an umbilical cord attached to them. Jack is flipping over in his gear off a diving board [*Mark is an accomplished swimmer and diver*] and Sally is fading off into a dot.

GC: Bring up the original image and what do you get now?

Mark: I'm down at the edge of the pit standing over it. The corner of the pit is filling up with concrete in geometric patterns. I can turn around and face north, and I feel good. But I know we didn't get everyone. This wasn't an archeological dig like the one hundred year old cemetery that was found [*when the Federal Courthouse was excavated*]. Ground Zero should have been more like an archeological dig once all chance of survivors was written off. ►◄►◄►◄ I'm hearing that Bob Dylan song, "Twisted Leap of Faith"—the bones should be there. There should be one grave for everyone to go to. I see people standing in a single line, dropping a flower on the grave. Two Towers with a single grave in the center. I wouldn't go there. Yeah, I probably would stand there too. I didn't think the Vietnam Memorial would mean anything to me until I saw it. It affected everybody.

GC: Check the original image and what do you get now?

Mark: You know how you feel before you go on vacation? That's how I feel. My bags are packed and I'm ready to go on vacation. I'm never going to look back there ever again. I feel okay.

Mark reports a SUDS of zero and I installed his positive cognition of, "I'm okay." His Validity of Cognition (VOC) was six. His body scan was clear.

Months later, after considerably more treatment, Mark later wrote a letter giving a testimonial about this phase of his EMDR treatment. The following is a portion of that letter:

> After my second EMDR treatment in early May I went down to the World Trade Center to look for human remains on my day off from work. I had a renewed sense of energy and purpose. I felt better inside and was surprised when a few co-workers noticed a change in my appearance and outlook. I received comments such as, "You look good" and "Are you feeling better? You look relaxed," from friends at the site that knew of the stress I had been under. I was amazed, not only did I feel better inside but also people could see a physical change in me. I truly believe that the EMDR treatments helped relieve my PTSD symptoms, helped me to continue working efficiently at the World Trade Center and at the firehouse.

Third Session

During this session (two weeks after the second) I could see that Mark was moving on from his experience at Ground Zero and, as he suspected, deep feelings of grief came up. I sensed a disturbing depth to the quality of Mark's expression of grief. However, I was unclear if it was a result of the horrific experience he had gone through at Ground Zero or there was an earlier trauma foundation event. I didn't inquire about any earlier memories because my style is to follow clients in their process, because the information that is important usually comes out into the open during the reprocessing. If I sense that there is an antecedent event that is not emerging, and seems to be interfering with the processing of a present event, I explore this possibility with clients.

Mark reported, "Everyone is depressed. At a golf tournament, all the guys were talking about were dead people. My brain feels hung over. It's never going to end. Funerals are still going on. I'm being dragged down. I'm surrounded. I feel like I am dodging bricks." He discussed his concerns about the impact of the disaster on his personnel. He also reported that some of the members were drinking excessively and using illegal drugs. There were anecdotal reports of extramarital affairs. He was worried about their welfare and wasn't sure what he could do to help them.

Yet, Mark also stated that he was feeling more separated from his role at Ground Zero. He informed me that on Father's Day he received a phone call from another member (this is the term firefighters use for each other) at Ground Zero who reported that debris was being removed to a landfill without being checked for bodies. (Apparently, it turned out that the debris would be checked at the landfill for body parts.) The member wanted Mark to come to Ground Zero and stop the operation. Mark reported telling this member of the FDNY: "I'm done. There's nothing I can do about it anyway. The City makes the decision. They have to move on. I can understand that they need to rebuild. I can't do anything about it. I don't even want to."

Fourth Session

This pivotal session (five days after the third session) is when Mark revealed the murder/suicide of his parent's that had determined the course of his life. From my perspective, it was also a session that demonstrates strikingly how the EMDR method can accelerate conscious and unconscious memory accessing.

Mark arrived at the session saying that on his drive into New York City he decided this would be a good day for EMDR. He was looking dramatically better than when he first started therapy and he appeared and reported that he felt more relaxed. He updated me on the last five days: He attended a funeral of a fallen firefighter whose wife was pregnant at the time of his death; the baptism of the baby had taken place at the same time as the funeral.

Mark shared two events that had a significant impact on him. The first event occurred down at Ground Zero in the early spring before he had begun treatment, when it was reported to him that firefighters were drinking while on duty. The second event occurred the night before this fourth session when he arrived at the firehouse to find members drinking on duty.

During the first event, a fellow member down at the site reported to him that members who were on duty were drinking in local bars. He related, "There were fourteen teams down there with five guys on each team. Guys would drink on their breaks. Seven teams on, seven teams off. I found out that some guys were drinking on duty. I went ballistic. I strapped knives onto my belt and I went to every bar in the area. I walked in ranting and raving and threw them out of the bars. They would see me walk in and they would just get up and leave." When I asked what he was feeling he said, "betrayed." Subsequently the members who were on duty and drinking were disciplined and removed from the site. This was very important to Mark because he felt that they had disrespected the sanctity of the site and had neglected their responsibilities. The level of his anger, even though controlled, was extreme, and I wondered what in him was being triggered by their behavior. My speculation was heightened by the fact that he did what he did despite the fact that it was not his responsibility to police the members at the site.

I allowed him to continue with the following story. The evening prior to this session, Mark had arrived at the firehouse to find members drinking on the job. There were two lieutenants in the house and it would have been within their authority to order the men not to drink on the job, but they hadn't exercised that authority. He also chose not to intervene because he felt bad for the men because they had attended the same funeral. He over-identified with their depression and hopelessness. He added to his account: "Besides, I'm tired of being the bad guy." He was conflicted, feeling he was going against all his values because it was his responsibility to see that the members abide by the rules of the house. Early on he had the internal strength to do his duty on the job and at Ground Zero, but by this time he had attended over 100 funerals, he was burnt out, and he was in the midst of working on his PTSD with EMDR.

Mark went on to talk about how he couldn't bear to go to any more funerals because the despair overwhelmed him. We decided to do some EMDR on his feeling of despair.

We began with this image: There is a line of firefighters at a funeral, and he sees his own face drifting without a body. The worst part is that everyone is sad, and he feels dismal. Mark's negative cognition was, "I'm weak." His positive cognition was, "I'm better than that."

This was not a good positive cognition, but I did not address that because, as I was I setting up the protocol, I noticed that his eyes were moving back and forth. I asked him what was happening. He related the following: "I'm having a memory, but I'm not sure I should say anything because I don't want it to interfere with what we are doing now." I wondered if this was a reaction to the lack of history taking. My response was to suppose that it was precisely that. I told him that I trusted the mind to go where it needed to go in order to accomplish the healing process. I reminded him that in EMDR past memories and associated information could come up. He was clearly disturbed about telling me what was happening, so I encouraged him to share the information by taking a nondirective approach. I invited him to share his past memories with me because "chances are it will be helpful to your healing process."

He paused, and then said: "When I was 15 years old, my father strangled my mother and then committed suicide. It didn't seem to bother me. I still did sports and was good in school. I don't like to tell people because they will feel sorry for me and I really do have a good life".

I was taken aback, not only because of the content but also the matter-of-fact way that he presented this information. Obviously, his parents' death was a pivotal life experience. He reported the event, however, with as little affect as would be merited in response to a newspaper story recounting a story about someone else. During the intake interview, I had not questioned him when he said that his parents' death was not an issue. Had I done so, I could have anticipated more accurately the course of his treatment and planned accordingly.

I took a deep breath and slowly and audibly exhaled.

Mark continued giving background information about what had happened after his father strangled his mother. She had lived in a coma for exactly one month before her death. However, the last time he saw her conscious she was laying on a gurney, having great difficulty breathing. While his mother lay dying, his father was on a suicide watch in a psychiatric ward of a county hospital. When his father found out that she had died, his father managed to kill himself in the hospital. The last time Mark saw his father alive was when he was sitting in the back of the police cruiser before being taken to the police station. His father told him, "I strangled your Mother; I'm sorry."

I questioned Mark about what happened. Apparently, from what Mark could piece together, his father had had a psychotic break after suffering for some time from paranoid delusions. Mark described his earlier years as happy and as occurring within a loving family.

Mark told me, "I've been keeping that information separate because I didn't want it to interfere with what we are working on." This separation had a distinct parallel to his larger life. Given the urgency I had felt to begin the desensitization and reprocessing and provide Mark with some immediate relief in the first session, I had had to cut some corners. One of those "cuts" was to condense the process of orienting him regarding the EMDR process. (I think this is a good example of the need for adequate orientation.) He had managed to compartmentalize this experience and get on with his life in a reasonably well-adjusted manner, without the awareness of how this event shaped his life. That is, up until now.

Compartmentalization and dissociation are adaptive solutions that provide conditions for survival and continued functioning in overwhelming circumstances. They are defense mechanisms common in first responders. These defense mechanisms allow first responders to honor the commitment they have made to the public. We expect them to run into burning buildings and take other significant risks. If they didn't compartmentalize the events, they would become immobilized by the situations they encounter on a regular basis. Compartmentalization is usually learned during earlier life traumas and, if not, it is often acquired on the job. In the extreme, first responders they will suffer burn out and, if that is the case, they often have to transfer to a less active situation or a paperwork/desk job (Mitchell & Bray, 1990).

Normally, the EMDR protocol (Shapiro, 2001) would call for targeting the earlier of the two related memories. I'm not sure why I did not encourage him to focus on the earlier one; I think I was stunned by his revelation. I froze, unable to reformulate immediately the protocol in light of this dramatic new information.

Mark's target was a line of firefighters at a funeral he had attended. Using audio stimulation during the reprocessing Mark began to elaborate on the image.

Mark: I see my face. It is strange. It is moving in slow motion. It is moving side to side.

GC: What is happening in your body? [*I don't usually single out one of the components of the protocol except when I am working with people who are overly analytic or need some focus on their body so they don't physically cut themselves off.*]

Mark: There is tension in my chest. ►◄►◄►◄ I am alone. My jaw is tense.

GC: If your jaw could speak what would it say?

Mark: Help. That's strange! I don't know why I would say that. [*His breathing was heavy, he sighed and then reported that he was running, crying, trying to get away, turning and finding that there is no place to go. I imaged that this is what he felt after his father strangled his mother.*]

Mark: I tell myself to stay where I am and to be calm. I have to keep looking up. I'm looking for a place to go, a place of beauty and peacefulness. I need more beauty.

We were running out of time so I closed the session by asking Mark if he could find a place of peacefulness and beauty and go there. Mark's impulse to run from his emotions and to try to be calm is consistent with his usual coping mechanisms. When he hears himself say, "Help," he is surprised, because it is the exact opposite of how he is accustomed to coping with trauma.

I had particular concerns about Mark because I was leaving for three weeks and I worried what he may experience emotionally while I was away. I let him know that there was a psychotherapist covering my practice during this period if he wanted to have a session. I didn't imagine that Mark would go to someone else, but I wanted him to know that he could. Mark didn't choose to see anyone in my absence.

In retrospect, there are interventions I could have undertaken to increase Mark's sense of safety. I could have been more direct in linking his past with his present and I could have spent more time explaining what it meant that the memory of his parents came up and how we would work with it. A relaxation exercise before we closed the session and bringing him to a safe place could have stabilized his system. I think I might have also chosen to postpone the processing of this intense material until my return; I might have used this fourth session to find out more about his history and to explore more his safe places and other resources

Fifth Session

Predictably, when we met upon my return after about one month, Mark reported, "The past month has been the worst of my life." He had taken a vacation with his wife and her family, and during that time felt ignored and neglected. He was thinking about divorce because he felt that his wife was not caring or affectionate. I attempted to explore whether his reaction may be related to his revealing the murder/suicide of his parents. He avoided discussing this by saying he didn't know how talking about the past would help or what it had to do with his life now. Saying "What does the past have to do with the present" is a common avoidance response and is usually reflective of how highly charged the past event actually was. It was possible that his response was also indicative of the unprocessed affect that had been opened up in the previous session.

The depression that Mark was experiencing reflected the breakdown of his defensive compartmentalization. He could no longer avoid feelings of despair and anger, and they were interfering with his daily functioning. I speculated privately about the apparent parallel between his emotional withdrawal from his wife and his father's killing of his mother. In subsequent sessions, Mark revealed that he had spent his life trying to prove that he was a leader and not, like his father, a murderer.

Despite his depression Mark had stopped smoking the day before as a self-help measure. I interpreted this as his taking care of himself and being willing to take actions on his own behalf. This was a significant shift in his perspective from not caring about his job, decreasing his athletic activities, and saying he felt depressed. It was a life affirming action that was an indicator that he was feeling stronger despite how badly he had felt over the last month.

Mark had wanted to talk in this session and I followed his lead affirming his right to approach his treatment at his own pace.

Sixth Session

In this session (which occurred 17 days after the fifth session), Mark shared more details about the circumstances of the murder/suicide and how he coped during that period of his life. It seemed that his resistance was lessening as he revealed more, and he was markedly more comfortable telling me about the experience and sharing his anger.

Nevertheless, Mark wanted to target his feelings about Jack, another firefighter whose facial expression seemed to represent what Mark was feeling inside. I saw this target as a safe way for Mark to confront his feelings. He targeted Jack's face and the sad, determined, grim look he portrayed. During the reprocessing Mark related seeing himself sitting with his guts ripped out. I noted that this was probably how he felt about his parents' death. He was still very frightened of exploring this event. "I'm sort of peeking through Venetian blinds," Mark said. "I feel like I'm afraid to look outside. I mean I see light outside. I feel afraid to open the blinds and look outside. I don't know if I'm just afraid of my thoughts right now or what I think. I'm locked up inside someplace."

Mark related that he thought there were parallels between the way Jack felt and how he feels. I encouraged him to follow that direction. He reported, "Jack says, 'If I can live with it [grief] you can live with it.' I'm feeling very relaxed like my mind is being erased. It feels nice." Arriving at this point it seemed that he was ready to work on the death of his parents. At the end of the session, Mark said, "I have two sides. They are blending together. I can't be a 20-year-old hippie on a motorcycle anymore. I always tried to look at the sunny side of life. This is a big problem that I can't just

get away from. I'm trying to have good moments with all this other crap."
Mark was beginning to recognize his denial and avoidance. The session
ended with the target reported at SUDS zero. I installed the positive cognition, "I can handle this." He was not able to fully clear his body and that
was an indication that the memory of his parents' death was keeping him
from being clear of the somatic symptoms. Because we were at the end of
the session I closed with placing the body sensation in a container until we
would meet again and work on whatever was left over from the work we had
done.

Mark was working through his resistance to facing the pain and grief of
his parents by using his experience at Ground Zero.

Seventh Session

When we met again twelve days later, a week had past since the first anniversary of the WTC disaster and Mark had been feeling more productive.
He shared that he was afraid of dying on the job because the city government had not made any contingency plans in the event of another terrorist
attack. The government had consistently reported that New York City was
on high alert and he seemed to think that the issue was not *if* there might
be another attack but *when* there would be another attack. I didn't interpret
this as an irrational fear since the city would expect the fire department to
respond to any attack and, despite a year going by, there still had not been
any contingency plans or training in the department.

In this session Mark asked me if I thought that he should reprocess the
deaths of his parents. I suggested that he make the decision. Mark chose a
symbolic image to reprocess. His willingness to reprocess the tragedy was a
direct result of having reprocessed work around Jack especially when he
heard Jack say, "If I can deal with it [grief] so can you!"

I asked Mark for a picture that represented his parents' deaths. He picked
an image of leaves falling—the summer is over, and it is cold and bleak.
When I asked him for his negative cognition it was, "I'm fucked," and his
positive cognition was, "I'm competent." The cognitions did not match. The
negative cognition implied the issue of safety and the positive cognition
reflected the issue of responsibility. Normally, I would explore the difference
between the negative and positive cognitions in an attempt to clarify the
issue, but I didn't ask him more because he reported feeling cut off. I was
more concerned about his ability to work on this material and did not want
to direct him in a cognitive exercise that would take him farther away from

his emotions. This approach served him well because it is in this session that he did a considerable amount of processing around his parents' deaths.

Mark: I'm crying in my room, thinking what am I going to do? ►◄►◄►◄ Let's get going. I just thought I have to get it together. I'm not going to let anyone hurt me like this again. 10 minutes in my room then move on. I'm not going to cry. I'm not going to freak out. I'm going to get it together and do what I have to do. It's a very similar feeling to what happened down here [*Ground Zero*]. Put the clothes on, put the boots on, and do whatever has to be done. I saw my mother on the bed. They couldn't stop us from entering the house. I felt sorry for both of them. She was gurgling. Why do I feel guilty? He's the one that killed her. Maybe I feel bad because I don't have a father. I have a father but he killed my mother. I feel sad about my mother and I feel sorry about my father and sad too.

GC: Let yourself really experience it. [*I was trying to give Mark the message that his feelings were appropriate and he didn't need to hide them.*]

Mark: It's like a big blank. I tried to move ahead. [*I reminded Mark that he didn't need to "do anything" but just let things happen.*] Then I flashed on wakes and funerals. I pictured meat. My uncle was a butcher and he would bring us meat. I feel like its time to get things together. Put my life back in gear. Packing up boxes in the basement.

It sounded like Mark was comparing the recovery of body parts with meat and that he needed to get himself together, clean up, and move on.

It was time to end the session and the SUDS on the original target was 7. The relatively high SUDS rating was not a concern because I had anticipated that he would require several sessions to reprocess this highly charged material. I ended the session by bringing him to a nurturing place to help contain his affect and sooth his nervous system.

I was going away on business the following week and Mark was taking his children away the week after so his next appointment could not be scheduled for 2½ weeks.

Eight Session

In this session (which occurred 17 days after the seventh session) we didn't do any EMDR. I wanted to follow Mark's lead because the material was so difficult. Mark revealed more details about his job at Ground Zero and how it related to when he last saw his mother and father. I thought he sounded depressed and he replied that he had a train of baggage. I mentioned his parents, and he immediately reported having head pain and I asked what he thought he was carrying.

He related an experience at the WTC where they found a body that was difficult to retrieve intact. He felt as though he was caught in a time warp where things were repeating themselves, like the movie "Groundhog Day." The tragedy of the WTC triggered the same feelings he had when he saw his mother near death.

After lying in a coma for 30 days his mother died. A few days later, the county hospital called and told him that his father committed suicide. He said, "I got fucked then and we got fucked now." Mark was allowing his resentment to come up and I encouraged him to explore these feelings.

Ninth Session

In this session (which occurred 7 days later), Mark came to a resolution about his feelings of abandonment and shame after his parents' death. It was hard for him to believe that his mother had died and he was always worried people would think he was like his father.

In this section of the session, we checked in with the original image from session 7, and Mark saw the funeral home where his mother had been waked. He saw himself standing outside the funeral home and the leaves have not yet fallen from the trees.

Mark: I basically buried the whole episode. I hear the "Leave it to Beaver" music theme in the back of my head. ►◄►◄►◄ My parents have floated out of a genie bottle and they are saying, "You can't forget, you can't forget." No matter how I try to fill my head with good things that one bad thing keeps coming up. ►◄►◄►◄ Hearing about a parent being violent with a kid or somebody murdering someone it takes me back to the murder/suicide of my parents. ►◄►◄►◄ I've been trying to ignore these feelings for many years but now they come up almost every day.

GC: Let yourself really feel those emotions, imagine stepping into them. [*Because Mark tends to cut off his feelings I want him to know that he will feel better if he moves through the experiences rather than try to move around them.*]

At this juncture I introduced eye movements rather than the CD. I felt that Mark was not processing as well as in earlier sessions because he was feeling cut off from his experience.

I interpreted this as looping—i.e., when someone is stuck and the target isn't changing. I felt that introducing a different stimulation would facilitate his processing and it proved to be an effective intervention.

Mark: ►◄►◄►◄ I was always afraid that I'd be like my father. How could I prove to people that I could be a good leader, not a murderer's son or a murderer? How do I develop a persona that people can trust? Protector, counselor. How do you go from black to white? Bad to good. My parents screwed me. Their existence screwed them in the long run. I never wanted to be a fireman. Did I become one for people's approval? I was always encouraged to become a doctor, but I was messed up in college. I was lost.

He finishes the session with thinking about how his wife was a good choice as a life partner because she was family-oriented. I had encouraged Mark to speak with his wife about his disappointments in the marriage, and since then she had become more attentive, and he seemed more content. The SUDS is 3 and the image he saw was only half the funeral home.

Tenth Session

Mark knows that this month is the anniversary of his mother being strangled but he cannot remember the date of her or his father's death. He has been going through old boxes looking for the death certificate.

In this session (which occurred 7 days later), Mark finished reprocessing the memory of his mother's funeral and reached a SUDS zero on this target. Mark was able to process both the present and the past, and then integrate the two events. During the reprocessing, he envisioned his parents embracing him and saying, "You've got to remember the good times." He began to remember the positive things they did for him.

He appeared to have a profound shift in perspective when he reflected on the meaning of life. His images began to change and he started to envision the funeral home demolished and replaced with a new building. He also saw the WTC site being cleaned up. I used eye movements during this session since they worked well with him in the previous session.

Mark: I don't have to go to that place of grieving my parents' death any more. It's over and done with. ►◄►◄►◄ What came to me are the words, "You will understand." I'll understand what love is, what life is about, the meaning of it all. That's the reward. Love, life, death—that's what it is all about. The Jerry Garcia song, "The Wheel is Spinning" comes to mind. With the Trade Center. Life goes on. There was a lot of life even though there was all that death. People died but their spirits were still there. I guess not everyone understands this stuff. I had a grasp on it from my early days. It's not far out to me. It is what is.

GC: Go back to the original image. [*I have him return to target because it sounds like the SUDS has dropped considerably.*]

Mark: ►◄►◄►◄ There is an empty lot where the foundation was. The building is gone. I see the words, "We'll never forget. Brothers forever." It should be on a bumper sticker. I hear myself say, "Let's not forget ourselves. Take care of us." There are fires in buildings; they collapse. We could die. I see myself shoveling dirt on top—would like to fill up the hole at the trade center, grow something, life. There's a connection. There were never two lives, but always one. I'm just as much a murderer's son as I am a heroic fire fighter. ►◄►◄►◄ Driving to go fishing. There are good things to do. Accentuate the positive. If you expect sunshine. Look for the good. I'll always have a certain level of caution. When I heard the siren [*a fire engine had just driven by*] it sounds good to me. The original image is a stored image. I'm moving on. I'll never forget, but I'll always remember to rebuild.

The SUDS was zero.

Eleventh Session

Mark used this session (which occurred nine days later) to discuss a questionnaire that the Fire Department gave out on stress reactions to 9/11. Some of his symptoms remained and he interpreted that this was because he hadn't finished reprocessing his parents' death and that his symptoms didn't have do with Ground Zero.

Twelfth Session

On the anniversary of Mark's mother's death, he came into the session (which occurred seven days later) saying that he felt shame hanging over him. He talked about feeling embarrassed about feeling despair over both traumas. He connected that, both times, they were life-changing events, and he was forced to start his life over. During the session he realized that it was okay to honor the past and not be disabled by it. This marked a profound shift from his feelings of denial to accepting his vulnerability and anxiety.

I targeted his feelings of shame and despair by asking Mark what image represented those feelings. The image was climbing up a ladder from a hole in the ground. Mark had difficulty formulating a negative cognition; the best he could do was to ask why he hadn't climbed out of the hole. I didn't press him on this issue because he had been able to reprocess material in previous sessions without a negative cognition and he was activated by the strong feelings he was experiencing.

Mark went from feeling lost and confused to feeling he could handle whatever might come up in his life. This was reflected in the following process:

Mark: There's an open pit I can fall into. It's right over there. Watch out for that pit. You can't get out of it that fast. Now the pit is turning into a laundry bag. My mind just goes.

GC: That's okay just go with that. Let whatever happens happen. Don't censor it.

Mark: The bag has become almost a person. Ever see dirty coins from Jesus and Judas? Judas had a little bag. It ended up in my pocket. That's all my problems in that bag. Will they always be with me? It doesn't have to be that way. You can use it as a pillow, as I started feeling serious again. I was feeling lighter earlier. Okay I took this thing with me. You can always crawl back into your hole or you can just hang on to it. It will just be with you. Don't pull the bag back over your head. Don't go into the darkness. ►◄►◄►◄ The bag turned into a table. They were going to make the cloth into a handkerchief. You have to be brave and go on. I feel like it is in my hand, that I will always have it with me. It reminds me it was my bag of worries. It's in my wallet like a charge card. Filing it away. It's to certify that I had these problems.

GC: It's okay to heal. It's about moving through it. You can honor the memory of those who are dead with the good memories of when they were alive. You can have a good life. [*Mark's self identity as a murderer's son kept him connected to his parents through their tragic death. In the last EMDR session he could see his past with positive parental experiences. I wanted him to consider that he could hold on to them through the good memories and not feel guilty about having a good life.*]

Mark continued to move through the grief process and came to the conclusion that he can handle whatever comes up without running from his feelings.

Thirteenth Session

In this session (which occurred 13 days later), Mark resolved the grief and guilt he had about the fallen firefighters who were part of his life. Much as he did to resolve the grief and guilt he had around his parents' death, Mark resolved the death of his fellow firemen by remembering the good times. Equally important, Mark has his own rebirth and frees himself from unnecessary guilt and begins to embrace joy in his life. This rebirth gives him the fortitude to process more painful memories of the WTC disaster.

Mark arrived at the session saying that he felt terrific. He related seeing a motorcycle on the way to my office that had a license plate that read "Iamceo." He said that what popped into his mind when he saw it was, "Iamfree." He reported being at the collapse of a building that was "shades of the World Trade Center" and didn't experience any disturbance.

He reported a dream where dead bodies are falling out of the sky. We targeted the dream. I did not ask for a negative cognition.

Image: Bodies are falling, moving the way a helicopter does. The worst part is hearing the thud of the bodies hitting the ground. [*This image has been a common target for people. Many people reported that hearing the sound of the bodies was deeply disturbing.*] I am standing in the middle of a wreath of fallen bodies.
Emotions: Sad for the people.
SUDS: Six (6).
Body Sensations: Numb.

Mark: The memories of these guys will be here forever. Not just for me but for everybody. What they did and what they knew. They were there for us. They will be in my head. The spinning bodies are gone.
GC: Check the original image.
Mark: A token with the five guys on it. Another thing to put in the box of World Trade Center mementos. I packed up everything after the session 2 times ago. Packed it up really well in a strong sturdy box. The token goes in there too.
GC: What is the SUDS?
Mark: It's a 2.
GC: What makes it a two?

When I am told that an original image has a SUDS of two or three I want to get a sense of why so I ask the client to describe what makes the target the number it is. When a client tells me a one I ask what would it take to be zero. One is close enough to zero to usually have a very specific reason. It is usually about a future experience. For example, I don't know if seeing my sister will bother me until I see her. I simply tell the client to go with that and the SUDS usually will reach zero.

Mark: They were there. A sad feeling. I wish I could have fond memories of these guys all the time. But you can't. All those kids with out fathers. They are dead. It's a shame. There will always be a little bit of sadness. ►◄►◄►◄ I hear a voice, "These guys had a lot of fun and so should you." ►◄►◄►◄ The coin went swoosh. Whipped by me.

GC: What is the SUDS?

Mark: 0–1, It's not as real.

GC: What is the positive belief that you have about yourself now?

Mark: The guys are happy. They are playing trumpets. I'm a player too. It is okay to be happy and play. I'm okay. I install the positive cognition, "It is okay to be happy and play. I'm okay," and the body scan is clear.

Fourteenth Session

Two weeks later Mark arrived at his appointment saying that he has had intestinal problems for the last month, that he became "grossed out" at the smell of flowers at a wake, and that he was afraid that he could become like his father. It was the anniversary of his father's death, and he felt like he was having a relapse. I discussed common grief reactions to anniversaries and reassured him that what is happening was normal. We did not do any reprocessing during this session because he needed to understanding what was happening and talk about his internal experiences.

Fifteenth Session

When Mark arrived for his next session (which occurred seven days later) he appeared more animated and clearheaded. He reported feeling closer to his wife and more relaxed at home. He didn't recognize this "new person." Mark was having difficulty accepting these new feelings of relaxation so we targeted Mark accepting himself with his new, more laid back persona. I asked him to come up with an image of him relaxing and he shared the following:

Mark: It is almost too good to be true. Do I really get to be happy? Did it take this? Tragedy? I have never really felt relaxed. I always was doing things to relax, but I never felt relaxed. This almost seems too easy. I have more room inside myself. The top third of my brain opened up. My brain feels like it can breathe easier.

Mark made an appointment for three weeks later because he felt so much better. He was evaluating whether or not he was ready to terminate treatment. Christmas and New Years would occur during this period and we were both anxious to see how he would weather the holidays. Although last year was the first Christmas after the disaster at the WTC attack, everyone was still in shock and we anticipated that individually and as a community we would not feel the full impact until this year. I anticipated that the work Mark had done would hold and any issues that might occur would be minor compared to the issues that he had cleared. Mark felt very connected to me so I trusted that if he needed support he would call and make an earlier appointment.

Sixteenth Session

Mark arrived at his next session (which occurred nine days later) dressed in a black leather coat over a grey wool turtleneck and black slacks. He was planning on taking his wife and daughter to a very upscale restaurant for lunch. He was excited about it especially because his daughter liked to go to restaurants. He looked rested and relaxed. He said that he had taken to having naps in the afternoons on his days off and that it felt good to do that. He had taken the Fire Department test to see if he could be promoted to the next higher rank. He said he thought he would feel okay if he didn't get promoted but would be happy if he did. In the meantime, he had been waiting for a permanent assignment and did not get the firehouse he wanted because it was given to someone else. Despite his disappointment, Mark was pleased that he remained in the same district and advocated strongly for himself to the people in charge of making assignments. This was a significant change from earlier in treatment when he said he didn't care about the job or his career and didn't think that he would even bother taking the test or really care where he was stationed.

We reviewed the work we had done on Ground Zero and his parents' death. He said he felt sad, and he thought he would always be sad when he thought about it. He had just driven past Ground Zero on the way to his appointment with me and it felt like a cemetery to him.

He expressed his thoughts and feelings about being in treatment saying, "It's been a long time since I came here. You are a lifeline to me. If I were drowning in the ocean, you would throw a line and save me."

He spoke about what was happening at work and that Ground Zero still came up a lot, but he felt that the event would be with them "forever." He said he was trying to tell his kids a lot of things and emphasizing that they should remember what he was telling them. I asked him why he thought he was doing that and he said, "things happen." He recognized that his work was dangerous, and that there was always a possibility that he might die on the job. I commented that his daughter was the same age as he had been when his parents died and that maybe he was feeling this way because of that. He didn't know if that was why he felt the way he did.

I asked him to rate his parents' death on the SUDS scale and he said it was a two. He felt strongly that he didn't have anything to work on. He couldn't tell me why other than he wanted to "put it away." I pointed out that he had attempted to deal with their deaths in this way when they had first happened. He defended himself by saying that it would always be a part of his life and that he didn't want to always be "dwelling on it." He felt that he didn't want to work on it anymore and that he was fine the way things were now.

Mark had shown this type of resistance after he first revealed his parents' deaths and now, as then, I did not confront his defenses, hoping that by allowing him to manage his own process he would eventually choose to return to do some more work on this issue. Mark told me he wanted to continue treatment, but wanted a break of several weeks to see how he would handle himself. I supported Mark's decision to determine for himself how he wanted to do treatment, and told him I would welcome his return whenever he was ready. Rather than leave his next appointment time vague, he decided to schedule his next appointment. Based on the way he had managed his pacing in treatment to date, I expected him to utilize his future time with me to again take up the deaths of his parents and process them to a compete adaptive resolution.

Summary

The bulk of the original presenting symptoms of PTSD, caused by the recovery work Mark performed at the WTC, were reprocessed in about three sessions, despite there being antecedent material. The intense grief triggered in this processing lead to the revelation and exploration of the tragic death of Mark's parents, which he realized he had never worked through. Mark came full circle when he reprocessed his parent's murder/suicide along with the WTC disaster, resolving his deep sense of despair.

Mark reported feeling like a different person. He felt an unusual calm that, initially, he wondered might be depression. Having worked through most of the despair of his tragic losses, he found that he was no longer running away from his anxieties and was able to relax. His PTSD symptoms were eliminated and friends, colleagues, and family members commented on how much more relaxed he seemed. In a photography book about the WTC there are several pictures of him looking much older than he does now. He says that he feels he can now move forward and live his life with joy.

The emotions Mark was experiencing, although related to the events of 9/11, were fueled by his earlier harrowing experience of losing both parents to a murder/suicide. This case illustrates how a previous unresolved related tragedy can impact treatment of a recent traumatic event, and the importance for therapists of remaining alert to the possible presence of a successfully compartmentalized prior trauma. Even in the face of the obvious traumatic nature of a current event as overwhelming (for both subject and therapist) as the 9/11 attack, an earlier unresolved trauma can play a significant role in the present disturbance, and need to be addressed before the later trauma can be completely resolved.

References:

American Psychiatric Association. (1994). *Diagnostic and statistical manual of mental disorders, Fourth Edition.* Washington, DC: Author.

Shapiro, F. (2001). *Eye movement desensitization and reprocessing: Basic principles, protocols, and procedures. Second Edition.* New York: Guilford Press.

Silver, S. M., & Rogers, S. (2002). *Light in the heart of darkness: EMDR and the treatment of war and terrorism survivors.* New York: Norton.

Wilson, S. A., Becker, L. A., & Tinker, R. H. (1995). Eye movement desensitization and reprocessing (EMDR) treatment for psychologically traumatized individuals. *Journal of Consulting and Clinical Psychology, 63,* 928–937.

Wilson, S. A., Becker, L. A., & Tinker, R. H. (1997). Fifteen-month follow-up of eye movement desensitization and reprocessing (EMDR) treatment for PTSD and psychological trauma. *Journal of Consulting and Clinical Psychology, 65,* 1047–1056.

9

SNAKES IN THE GRASS: RAPID RESOLUTION OF A SIMPLE PHOBIA

Philip Manfield

KAY, AN INTELLIGENT, ENERGETIC WOMAN, a youthful fifty-four years of age, specifically requested EMDR when she called for her first appointment. She described her intense fear of snakes, for which she had been "successfully" treated twenty-nine years earlier at a university clinic using a graduated exposure method.

The impact of her phobia on her life was substantial. She reported being cautious whenever she would leave her house. She had all but given up hiking, something she loved, and had restricted the areas to which she was willing to travel. She was also a devoted windsurfer, but the task of getting her board through the grass to the water's edge, while being on the lookout for snakes, was daunting for her. She could not relax in her yard and was unable to go into the dog run beside her house since once spotting a snake moving across the gravel there.

I found Kay's keen ability to locate snakes amusing, as did she. She could go into her back yard with her husband and, if there was a snake in the yard, even fifty feet away, she would spot it. She would run back into the house, and it would take her husband minutes before he could see what she had been pointing at. The San Francisco Bay Area does not abound with snakes, but in the space of a year she had seen four in her back yard alone. When driving, she would constantly scan the shoulders of the roads for snakes. When she would point one out, people would accuse her of mistaking broken fan belts for snakes, but, as she put it, "I definitely knew the difference. There is no one in the state of California more proficient than I at telling a fan belt from a dead snake along the road."

She considered her graduated exposure treatment at the university clinic successful because, after three hour-long sessions, she was able to actually hold a snake in her hands. When describing it to me, she characterized this experience as one of the "high points" of her life. The treatment had begun with Kay viewing and becoming comfortable with a small caged boa constrictor across the room from her. In small, incremental steps, as she became comfortable with each new situation, she graduated to being able to sit near the cage, then sit near the uncaged snake, then touch it with one finger, and, finally, actually hold the snake. After a six-week delay requested by the clinic, she returned for her final test where she found crawling on the floor a four foot corn snake which she was asked to pick up. She succeeded in picking up the corn snake, which was heavier and longer than the boa. It was when the corn snake began to coil around her arm while she was holding it that she lost her composure and panicked. This treatment of her phobia was successful in reducing her immediate feelings of panic about snakes. Within several months of completing the treatment, however, her fear of snakes gradually returned, although never to the degree it had reached prior to treatment.

Favorable Indications During the First Session

Kay described her childhood home life as a happy one with happy children, an "Ozzie and Harriet" family. Some clients describe their childhoods in a similar way, but are actually doing so to avoid extremely painful memories; in Kay's case, however, her description of her happy childhood seemed congruent and believable. Her parents were not particularly anxious people. Her father had an apparently normal concern about snakes; he had told Kay that some snakes could be dangerous and offered other words of caution that would be appropriate for a four- or five-year-old child. Her mother had no fear of snakes; in fact, when she was in school, her mother had sometimes carried a snake in her pocket with which to scare the boys. Kay's fear of snakes did not appear to be part of an overall anxious personality. In fact, in her early twenties she had had a terrifying experience as a stewardess in which she could see the pilots and other stewardesses panicking, and she "knew we were going to die"; she had, nevertheless, continued to work as a stewardess afterwards with no residual disturbing feelings from that experience. This indicated a resilience that I would not expect from someone with an anxiety- or phobia-prone personality. She had no trouble describing a *safe place* memory: being in the kitchen of her childhood home talking and laughing with her mother after coming home from school. She also had no trouble identifying people whom she considered loving and supportive. Although not part of the standard EMDR protocol, I always ask about these *safe people;* the ease with which the client can identify them is a strong indicator of how well they will respond to EMDR and these safe people can be very useful if a cognitive interweave should become necessary. And, perhaps most important from an EMDR perspective, Kay could readily describe a specific relevant source event that met all my criteria for the likelihood of successful processing: her memory of the event was clear and detailed, including an associated image, body sensations, affect, and cognitions; the connection between the event and the symptom made psychological sense; and the event took place early in her childhood and appeared to be the first one associated with this symptom.

Normally, in the first session with an EMDR client, I take a thorough history, and do case formulation and safe place installation; I do not begin EMDR targeting and reprocessing the first time I meet with a client. With Kay, I made an exception; it appeared to me, from the brief history I had gathered and the ease with which she was able to identify safe places and loving people, that this phobia would process in a straight- forward manner using the source target Kay had identified, and that it was not related to broader or deeper issues that could complicate the processing.

Kay described the precipitating event as occurring when she was four years old. Her family was camping near Yosemite Park and a rattle snake had slithered through the camp site. When the snake's arrival was excitedly announced, Kay became frightened, and ran to the car for safety. Her grandmother followed her to the car to comfort her. While her grandfather and father pursued the snake, Kay and her grandmother talked about snakes. Kay remembered this experience as the first time in her life when she was really afraid. The most frightening part of the event, however, was a story her grandmother told her about snakes; her grandmother said that even after the snake had been killed and cut up and the parts thrown in a gully, they would continue to wriggle throughout the night. Kay imagined the possibility that the snake could find her while she was sleeping, and crawl on her even after it was dead, which was both disgusting and frightening. As an adult, Kay had thought about why her beloved grandmother would have told her this frightening story. She realized that this story was just one of many imaginative "fairy tales" her grandmother had told her, probably, to take her mind off sources of anxiety. For instance, Kay remembered one story her grandmother had told her to ease her fear of thunder, explaining that the sound was merely angels moving furniture in heaven.

Targeting the Precipitating Event

When this memory was targeted, Kay's heart rate became elevated, and her hands were clammy and shaking. Her disturbing image was that of the parts of the snake slithering in the gully. The negative cognition was, "I'm not safe." As a positive cognition, she proposed, "The world is a safe place." When this cognition was mentioned, I thought to myself, "It is really not entirely true that the world is safe," but in the context of snakes and the negative cognition, "I'm not safe," the proposed positive cognition made sense to me. The Validity of Cognition (VOC) was 5 and the primary feeling, fear. Her disturbance level (Subjective Units of Disturbance Scale [SUDS] was a 4 out of 10, and she reported feeling it in her torso; in addition, her hands were shaking and her legs were weak.

The EMDR *simple phobia* protocol calls for processing the first experience of the phobia, followed by the worst, the most recent, and, finally, an imagined future template in which the client can rehearse facing the once feared situation with equanimity. I often rely more on how a client appears to be responding physically than I do on her verbal report. In Kay's case, she rated her disturbance level at 4 but her elevated heart rate, clammy hands, weak legs and shaking indicated a considerably more intense response than I would expect with a SUDS of 4. In fact, given the other memories she had identified, none of which had been given a SUDS rating of over 6, I thought of this initial memory as both her first and worst snake experience.

The actual processing of the target was very rapid. The disturbance level spiked up from 4 and back down to zero in ten minutes. The associations she described were all related to the specific targeted memory. Ultimately, Kay realized that the parts wriggling in the gully did not represent a threat to her or anyone else. Because this target processed so easily and quickly, I felt comfortable using the last fifteen minutes of the session to address the most recent event involving a snake. There were actually two recent events: one involving a snake on the back deck of her home, and the other a snake in her home swimming pool. These both processed rapidly, and were completely processed by the end of the session.

At the end of the session, I suggested that the processing of her snake phobia was not yet complete so that it was likely that she would experience a fear of snakes in various situations during the week, and asked her to make notes about the circumstances in which this occurred. I explained that we could use this information to help us target the remaining components of her phobia. We discussed possible scenarios in which she might encounter a snake during the next week and how she would like to react. One scenario involved Kay walking in the gravel dog run by the side of her home and encountering a snake. Another involved walking out of the back door of her house onto the deck and seeing a snake.

In-vivo Experiences of Targets

Kay, like many clients who experience a rapid elimination of disturbing affect, remained skeptical about whether there would be an accompanying reduction in symptoms in the real world during the next week. Her phobia had been a constant feature in her life for more than half a century; she could not imagine that it could be eliminated in a few one-hour EMDR sessions, let alone in one session.

I, too, was a bit hesitant to accept her seeming transformation on face value. Although Kay's processing appeared to be genuine and effective, I was somewhat uncomfortable with it's rapidity, even for EMDR. I knew that her treatment twenty-nine years earlier had appeared to be completely successful until the corn snake had decided to become entangled with her. I have noticed on numerous occasions that clients sometimes desensitize a branch or component of a particular memory and are so relieved with the result that they tend to ignore a remaining aspect of the memory that may still be disturbing. This is often revealed during the body scan, but not always. My belief, in Kay's case, was that there was disturbing material remaining to be processed. Accordingly, I suggested that, before the next session, Kay go to the snake room of a local museum to have an in-vivo experience of the objects of her fear.

In my experience, in-vivo experiences can be extremely helpful in facilitating EMDR targeting. The key to using in-vivo experiences is to choose an experience that will produce a level of anxiety that helps the client to access the target more fully, but does not overwhelm the client to the point that he or she needs to defend against the affect associated with the target. Although in-vivo exposure is part of the standard EMDR protocol for *process phobias*, those phobias that require the participation of the phobic person in an activity connected to the fear, I have used it effectively in a variety of other situations, especially with clients who report a partial or total resolution of a significant target, but who do not appear to have completed the processing. For example, I have asked a client, who became anxious on hot days but was not anxious in my office, to call me on his cell-phone at an agreed upon time from California's central valley at mid-afternoon on a very hot day. Another client, an earthquake victim, could not sleep at night because every creak in his house would cause him to startle and jump out of bed; in my office, however, he felt fine because he did not feel exposed to any danger. I was able to stimulate the feelings related to the earthquake by having him close his eyes while an assistant walked around the room rattling the windows and doors or making sudden noises, the responses to which we desensitized.

Second Session

Kay arrived at my office for the second session feeling encouraged. Overall, she reported a significant reduction in her fear of seeing a snake. She reported having no apprehension at home, and found that she no longer visually scoured the parking lot at work for the possible presence of a snake before stepping out onto the pavement. Also, pictures of snakes on a survival program on TV had not induced anxiety in her.

She had been to the museum and found that she was able to stand in the doorway of the snake room and look from there at the snakes in their enclosures. At first she had glanced from the corner of her eye but eventually she had been able to look directly at a large one fifteen feet away, tap her thighs, and begin to relax. It was an "ugly white boa," which she reported finding far more menacing than the rattlers! To help give herself a sense of control, she gave it a name, "Harriet." When Harriet started moving, however, Kay became frightened and left the museum.

Because the experience with Harriet was so recent and immediately accessible for Kay, I suggested using this event as our first target for that session. Kay imagined Harriet crawling across her feet. Although she rated the SUD initially, as a "5 or 6," there were none of the accompanying physiological signs of fear that had accompanied the targeting of the precipitating event, confirming for me that, before processing, the precipitating event had actually been considerably higher in SUD than a 6. Again, the SUD level dropped to zero fairly rapidly once we began processing her experience with Harriet. I asked her to imagine going back to the museum and visiting the snake room again. As she did this she experienced a very small amount of anxiety, which disappeared quickly during processing. I asked Kay to imagine one of the situations she had identified at the end of the previous session, finding a snake on her deck. There was some disturbance associated with this imagined event, but it also processed quickly to a zero disturbance level.

The worst fear for Kay of a future snake encounter involved going out to the gravel dog run beside her house and finding a snake. During the past year, she had discovered snakes in the dog run on two occasions. The SUDS on this target was a 4, as she pictured the snake slithering across the walkway in the dog run. The first set of eye movements caused a drop in reported SUDS from 4 to 1. However, she was obviously still tense. "The dog run is empty. I can't see a snake." I asked what she noticed visually when she imagined encountering a snake in the dog run. She said that in her mental image, the snake was between her and the gate; she felt anxious and trapped. After several sets of eye movements, the disturbance had not diminished. I asked her what she thought was keeping this target from resolving, and she said that she felt trapped for good reason, because, confined by the fence of the dog run, she could not get away from the snake if it should decide to approach her. Her fear was not so much of being bitten as of the snake crawling across her feet.

My response to this comment was a brief discussion about what she knew about snakes. She knew that they would only attack her if they felt threatened and that they were generally frightened of people. I reminded her that the dog run was probably one of the safest places she could be, because the crunching of the gravel would announce her presence to any slithering creatures in the area; on noting her arrival, the snake would retreat. This thought was comforting to her, but she realized that the problem for her was that both she and the snake were trapped in this narrow dog run; even if the snake was frightened of her and wanted to slither away, it couldn't. I silently thought it interesting how distorted one's thinking can become when in a state of fear. I asked her if she had any idea how the snake had gotten into the dog run in the first place. She recalled a time when she had seen a snake in the corner of the dog run, and said it could have come in through the side fence from the neighbor's yard, but she had thought that it had probably come up the driveway and under the gate. Then she began to smile, and said, "I guess it could leave the same way it came in, couldn't it?" I nodded and initiated a short set of eye movements with that thought in mind.

She was still troubled, however, by the idea that she could not get past the snake to the gate, and she still felt anxious in her body, in her legs and upper torso. Her SUDS was back up to 4. I am usually reassured when client's disturbance levels drop and then go back up because it gives me confidence in the accuracy of their reporting; I am less concerned then about the possibility of clients telling me what they think I want to hear. I asked her to focus on the tension she was feeling in her body, and began another set of eye movements. During this set she seemed to become more anxious, and brought her knees up near her chest in what looked like a protective position. I suggested that she imagine her husband, in whom she had "total trust," removing all the snakes from the dog run. At the end of several more sets her disturbance level had again dropped to a 2. Then she realized that she did not need to reach the gate; she could use the side door of the garage to leave the dog run, and the snake would not be able to follow. This realization seemed to bring additional relief, and her SUDS dropped to 1, which she thought was a reasonable amount of disturbance for someone imagining encountering a snake. I installed the positive cognition that she could take care of herself.

After installation of the positive cognition and a clean body scan, there were a few minutes remaining to the session, possibly not enough to work on a full future template, but enough to supply her with an additional resource to help her imagine a successful encounter with a snake. Kay had adopted the names the university staff had assigned to the snakes at the clinic. Their name for the snake that she had been successfully able to hold was "Benjamin Boa." I suggested that she recall the sense of success and mastery that she had felt when she had held him. I reinforced this feeling with a short set of eye movements (14 passes), and she reported feeling pleased with herself. I asked her to locate these positive feelings in her body, and she indicated that she felt them in the center of her chest. I asked her to focus on that sensation and did another short set of eye movements. The experience reported by Leeds and Shapiro (2000), which is consistent with my own, is that longer sets of eye movements are more likely to bring up negative associations. As a result, when enhancing positive feelings, it appears to be advisable to keep the sets short. According to Leeds and Shapiro, some clients with poor affect tolerance can only handle sets of no more than eight passes before they begin to bring up negative associations. I asked Kay to imagine carrying Benjamin with her, as a shield against unfriendly snakes, and again reinforced this idea with a short set of eye movements. She reported that the idea of carrying Benjamin with her added to her sense of strength and security, and in fact she was able to imagine walking around her backyard without being fearful. We agreed that she would return to the museum snake room during the week and check her progress.

Third Session

Kay was exuberant when she returned for the third session:

> Well, I wouldn't have believed it if you'd told me two weeks ago this could happen. Over the weekend my husband and I went windsurfing and I didn't worry about snakes at all. I just carried my gear through the grass to the water, and it didn't bother me. Of course I looked at the grass to see if there was anything there before I walked on it. Who wouldn't? But, I was not upset. For so long, I've been terrorized by the idea of seeing one there. My husband was amazed. Then, on Wednesday I went to the Lindsay Museum. I was dreading it, and forced myself to go, but it was okay. I could go into the snake room and stand two feet away from the snakes and just watch them, and I felt fine. They actually seemed interesting.

Kay had brought with her to the session a typed list of eighteen "Remaining Snake Images," each rated in disturbance from zero to ten. There were three sixes, two fives and the rest were threes and fours. One of the threes on her list was a memory of when she was at camp. One of the boys at the camp had caught a snake and had it coiled in his hand; he was waving it at the girls. Another time, which she rated a SUD of six, a boy threw a snake in the air over Kay's head and, in her terror, some blood vessels in her eyes had burst. Ironically, one of the most disturbing of her eighteen remaining memories was her experience with "Bobby Corn snake," the snake that had begun to wrap around her wrist at the clinic.

We agreed to target her experience with Bobby, my reasoning being that it was one of her three worst remaining memories, and I thought the unpleasant residual feelings from her experience with Bobby vitiated what was otherwise a very powerful memory of mastery for her, one that was directly associated with her symptom. My hope was that by desensitizing the experience with Bobby Corn snake, we could make that memory of mastery more accessible to her.

The target moment was when Bobby began to coil around her arm. Her negative cognition was "I can't handle this." and the positive, "I can handle this; this is no big deal." In hindsight, these were not the best of cognitions because they didn't reference her perception of herself in the present, but only her experience in the past. Better negative cognitions might have been, "I'm helpless," "I'm weak," or "I can't take care of myself." A better positive cognition would have been, "I can take care of myself." These would be about her and less oriented around the specific experience with Bobby in the past. Her VOC on "I can handle this; this is no big deal" was 2. The disturbance level she reported on the memory was 5, but again, judging from the amount of anxiety she displayed when she recalled the event, I believe her disturbance level was higher than that.

PM: What feelings come up when you think of that memory?

Kay: Great anxiety. I feel like I'm not in my body. The physical thing is disappearing. I feel the terror in my torso; there is a little tightening in my chest. ►◄►◄►◄ (25) Bobby went away pretty quickly. This is the fastest an image has left me.

PM: What about the physical sensations you were describing in your chest?

Kay: I can still feel it physically.

This was the first time Kay reported not being in her body as she recalled a snake memory. This memory was apparently strong enough to bring up a disposition towards dissociation and avoidance. Although I welcomed the feelings of relief that she repeatedly experienced, I responded to each by calling her attention to something that I thought might help her be back in touch with the dysphoric affect that she was tending to avoid.

Kay: ►◄►◄►◄ (25) I feel calmer.

PM: Do you remember how he felt on your wrist?

Kay: Yes. I can feel myself tightening up again now.

PM: Think of that. ►◄►◄►◄ (25) much better.

PM: How disturbing is the memory now?

Kay: It's not. I can't bring it up now.

PM: How true does the statement feel now on a gut level, "I can handle this. This is no big deal?"

Kay: It's a 6.

PM: What keeps it from being a seven?

Kay: I could hold a snake, but I don't want to. ►◄►◄►◄ I don't really care. I would rather not ever have to hold another snake again. ►◄►◄►◄ I'm so happy that I can look at the movement.

PM: When you held Bobby and he started coiling around your arm, did you feel betrayed?

I was not satisfied that this memory was fully desensitized. Kay was saying that it was not disturbing, and yet she was also saying she did not want to hold a snake again, indicating that some disturbing thought was coming up for her; I had no need for her to offer to hold a snake in order for me to consider her fully cured, but she was spontaneously thinking about how disagreeable that idea was for her. When processing does not appear to be moving, and it is apparent to me that clients are feeling something that they are not aware of or are not reporting, I sometimes ask them specifically about the feeling. These are not deep penetrating questions. If I see moisture in their eyes, for instance, I might ask them if they are aware of it and, if so, what that moisture might be saying. Kay had mentioned, when she first described her experience at the university clinic, that the therapists and staff had promised her that Bobby would not be active, so I felt confident in asking if she might be feeling some sense of betrayal.

Kay: Oh yeah! They swore up and down how docile he was, and, once I got up my nerve to pick him up, right away he starts wrapping around my arm. ▶◀▶◀▶◀ The word that kept coming to my mind was *trust*. I didn't have that there. ▶◀▶◀▶◀ I suppose that goes back to my grandmother. I trusted her and she told me that horrible story, and she scared me. ▶◀▶◀▶◀ There are a lot of memories, like the church camp, where I didn't have control over other people. The kid that threw one over my head. Some really interesting thoughts. ▶◀▶◀▶◀ I'm working on, "Don't come near me." ▶◀▶◀▶◀ Yeah, that's the real incident, the snake coiled in the boy's hand at the church camp. I do believe my mother intervened. ▶◀▶◀▶◀ (40) I don't see the kid with the snake; I just see my mom. ▶◀▶◀▶◀ More peaceful.

PM: When you think of the memory, how disturbing is it for you now?

Kay: It's a 0 or 1. I feel okay with it.

I wanted to check if this memory of the Bobby Corn snake incident was really handled.

PM: If they asked you to come back to the university clinic tomorrow for a follow-up to their study, how would that be for you?

Kay: I wouldn't do it.

PM: Think about that. ▶◀▶◀▶◀

Kay: I just got rid of all those people at that clinic. The memory bank is erased. It feels fine.

PM: What about feeling betrayed?

Kay: I'm okay with it now.

I installed the thought, "I can handle this; this is no big deal," and asked her to scan her body for uncomfortable sensations; she said there were none. With the remaining time we decided to process her memory of seeing a snake at a local reservoir, one of the other events on her list that was still fairly disturbing. It was one of the more recent events, but not the most recent. Because targets seemed to process so rapidly for her, I thought there would be enough time in the session to process this memory. I asked her to describe it. "I was coming back in from windsurfing and it crawled across the path. I just froze. My husband had to come and get me. I couldn't move." We were nearing the end of the third session. Kay had reported strong successes in processing her phobia, and yet it seemed to me that the memory she was about to process did not seem so different from memories she had already processed. There appeared to me to be no danger of losing this target by interrupting her as she focused on it, so I decided, before she became more deeply involved in the target, to suggest that she look at the possibility of a secondary gain from her phobia.

PM: It just occurred to me that you've gotten a lot of help from people around this problem, your friends, your niece, your husband. I imagine that if you didn't have this problem any more, there would be some loss for you; you wouldn't need people to help you. You'd lose that caring interaction.

Kay: That's an interesting thought. ►◄►◄►◄ (25) That is perfectly okay with me, perfectly okay. I want to be rid of this fear. Should I go back to the reservoir memory?

PM: Yes, please.

Kay: I remember seeing it crawl across the path. I felt terrorized.

Her negative cognition was, "I can't handle this." The positive cognition was, "This is really no big deal; I can handle it." The feeling associated with the memory, in addition to the terror, was surprise, a "startle factor." She reported thinking the snake was going to crawl on her. The SUDS level was 5 or 6.

PM: Where are you feeling that in your body?

Kay: My legs and upper torso. ►◄►◄►◄ I can see the grass path and a very, very faint image of the snake. It's not moving. ►◄►◄►◄ (30) I'm even having a hard time picturing the path. ►◄►◄►◄ (30) I've spent the last 15 years of my life on the shore there watching the grass and worrying about what's in it, and right now I'm having trouble picturing the grass. My body is calming down.

She reported that her disturbance level was down to zero, her VOC at 6. After a brief installation set, her VOC was up to 7. After another short set, she reported having a hard time bringing up the image. She said that she no longer felt reticent to walk in grass or on trails in the local parks; she thought she could hike now. I pointed out that her fear had not really been of the poisonousness of snakes, but of them being long and slithery. I suggested that when she saw a snake in the future it would no longer be a major event for her; she could just look at the snake and say "So what?" She liked this idea.

Kay: For years I have wanted to walk with my husband to the top of the park ridge to view the fireworks on July 4. This year I'm going to do it.

PM: Imagine yourself doing it.

Kay: Okay. ►◄►◄►◄ (14) So what?

This idea was a useful one for Kay. When I contacted her in late 2002 and mentioned that there was a notation about "So what?" in my notes that I did not understand, she responded, "I do think we did a session on 'So What' and that still sticks with me when I am in a place I perceive to be 'snaky.'"

Fourth Session

At the beginning of the session Kay related to me:

Kay: I cleaned out the dog run with comfort and no fear this week. I took a walk around the reservoir with a friend and wasn't nervous, and even walked up to the ridge trail, which is a super big deal for me. I would have never done that in a million years. My husband told me last night that he no longer considers me phobic. I thought about the incidents on the list, and I can't bring up any of them now with clarity. None of them are disturbing at all.

PM: What about the memory of your experience with Bobby Corn snake?

Kay: That has definitely diminished. I really have no disturbing feeling about it now. I think of it as positive. I don't think of it as disturbing.

PM: How do you think it will be for you when you encounter a snake in the future?

Kay: I don't like snakes, but I'm more normal about it now. When I walk the dog, I'm not walking him in the street anymore. I used to have to walk down the middle of the street to keep away from the grass. Now, I walk on the sidewalk. I don't have that unreasoning terror. I can't bring up that feeling in my body anymore. I'm at peace. I've carried that around for 49 years; it's been a part of every day. What stuck with me from last week was you saying, "If you see a snake, so what?" That's kind of a new philosophy for my life. I thought, "Kay, you'll deal with it." I'm normal now. I'm sure I can easily go to the museum. I'm going to go soon.

Twenty five minutes had passed in this session, and Kay was happy with the results she had achieved and saw no need for further treatment. I suggested that we terminate the session and consider it a half session, and she paid for it accordingly.

Before writing this chapter, I contacted Kay to see how well the results of her EMDR treatment had held during the two and a quarter years since I had last seen her. She told me that she had been doing very well. She described an incident in which she'd found a dead snake in her back yard and had watched without anxiety as her husband had scooped it up with a stick and thrown it away. Then she called me back the next day to tell me that a testimony to the effectiveness of the treatment was that she had actually forgotten to mention to me her most significant encounter with a live snake since the treatment:

> A year or so after completing my EMDR therapy, I still *thought* myself to be quite frightened of snakes, but certainly no longer phobic. My husband, mother, dog and I were playing in a mountain stream and I spied a water snake along the shore (of course it would be me that sees it and no one else!) and immediately jumped out of the water and ran off a bit as I normally would do in this type of situation. However, to my surprise, I noticed that there was no bodily reaction of sweating, rapid breathing, weak knees or panic. So, for the very first time in my life, in an uncontrolled environment (in the wild), I decided that I could return to the shore and look at the snake, which I did and watched it swim away. It was just like the very active water snake at the museum that I had forced myself to watch so I would get used to the movement of a snake. The *reality* was that I was not afraid watching the snake. There is still in me a discrepancy between what I think I will feel when I see a snake and what I actually feel when I do. I cannot express the elation at being able to get myself to go to the shore to look at that snake, something utterly impossible before EMDR. "So What!"

Kay's treatment illustrates the complexity and subtlety of treating simple phobias. Kay's phobia involved snakes, but more particularly the movement of snakes. This particular sensitivity is consistent with the precipitating event in which she was frightened by being told that the parts of the snake would continue to wriggle through the night after the snake was long dead. Even during that initial event, however, she was not afraid of being bitten; she was afraid the snake would slither over her feet. During exposure therapy, Kay was able to hold a four foot corn snake in her hands, but when it began to move and coil around her arm she became overwhelmingly afraid; the movement of the snake triggered her strongest fear reaction. Since her treatment with EMDR, snakes have ceased to be a significant issue in her life. For years she would spot every dead snake she passed lying by the side of the road; now, she explains that she doesn't see them because she is no longer interested in looking for them.

References

Leeds, A. M., & Shapiro, F. (2000). EMDR and resource installation: Principles and proce-
dures for enhancing current functioning in a resolving traumatic experiences. In J. Carlson & L. Sperry (Eds.), *Brief therapy strategies with individuals and couples* (pp. 469– 534). Phoenix, AZ: Zeig/Tucker.

PART II

TREATING ADULTS WITH HISTORIES OF CHRONIC CHILDHOOD TRAUMA OR ABUSE

10

HEALING HIDDEN PAIN

Resolving the Effects of Childhood Abuse and Neglect

Silke Vogelmann-Sine

I RECEIVED MY GRADUATE TRAINING in clinical psychology at the University of Hawaii, with Leonard Ullmann, one of the pioneers of behavior therapy (Ullmann & Krasner, 1965, 1975), as my advisor. The clinical training took place within the framework of the scientist-practitioner model, with a strong emphasis on research and evaluating treatment outcomes. As students, we were required to conduct careful functional analyses in order to understand contingencies maintaining problem behaviors: What behaviors were maintained by positive reinforcement, what behaviors by negative reinforcement? We were trained to implement cognitive-behavioral interventions in order to change attitudes, thoughts, or overt behaviors. Our "bag of tricks" included designing behavioral programs to alter contingencies to produce more desirable behaviors, assertion training, in vivo desensitization, and cognitive restructuring. During various internships/trainings, I was also exposed to humanistic and psychodynamic approaches, including training in Nicholas Cummings's approach, brief intermittent psychotherapy throughout the life cycle.

I would like to express my deep gratitude to my husband Larry F. Sine, Ph.D., for his valuable suggestions and comments regarding this chapter. My appreciation also goes to Lori Yim, my secretary, for her exceptionally good typing skills and her patience in making revisions.

Prior to my training in EMDR, I had become dissatisfied with the progress I made with clients who had been sexually molested as children. I felt that available treatments, though helpful, did not adequately relieve their deep emotional suffering and pain. These emotional wounds were too overwhelming for some clients to learn the necessary survival skills, such as leaving a partner who battered them. After being trained in EMDR in 1991, I began to use the method systematically with a few suitable and motivated clients and saw results that were previously unimaginable: After using EMDR, these clients no longer suffered unbearable shame or deep-seated rage and finally experienced an internal peace they had never known. Furthermore, I observed the spontaneous emergence of new behaviors and beliefs that these clients had been unable to learn previously. They were able to recognize signs of an abusive relationship and then to leave. EMDR seemed to have permitted them to shift to a new internal state of being. They began to feel worthy.

These outcomes convinced me that, in motivated clients, EMDR had the power to access and reprocess early traumatic experiences that had not been resolved by other methods. Some of my long-term clients improved and terminated therapy. When they returned during a crisis, I found that the pain that had been resolved with EMDR had not come back. It seemed that EMDR caused a physiological shift to occur such that the behaviors and negative beliefs driven by unresolved trauma no longer dominated the lives of these clients (Shapiro, 1995).

My husband is also a clinical psychologist who trained in EMDR at the same time I did. We began to wrestle with the issue of how to integrate EMDR into our clinical practices as part of a comprehensive therapeutic treatment program. The answer for us was to reconceptualize psychopathology from a trauma-based perspective (e.g., Briere, 1989; Linehan, 1993; Miller-Perrin & Wurtele, 1990; van der Kolk, McFarlane, Weisaeth, 1996) and think of therapy as a process of assessing and overcoming the short- and long-term limitations suffered as a result of growing up in invalidating environments (Linehan, 1993) and experiencing ongoing childhood trauma. If we want to help a client, we need to understand how unresolved traumatic experiences from the past manifest in the present and what interventions are necessary, including EMDR, to restore healthy functioning. Inner child healing has become an important metaphor in accomplishing this task. Clients are generally able to understand how they learned to protect themselves from their inner vulnerabilities and, in the process, became alienated from their real feelings and their hurt inner child. They can recognize that the needs of this child have not been adequately met in the past and that it becomes the role of the adult self to connect with, nurture, protect, and guide the child (e.g., Bradshaw, 1990).

When EMDR is incorporated into a treatment plan, the treatment outcome is primarily determined by clients' willingness and ability to trust their therapists and face the painful feelings that are limiting their functioning. Each treatment plan has to be carefully designed in order to assist individuals to overcome behavioral adaptations based on trauma and assist them to function more adequately in the present. I have found it most effective to educate clients about their trauma history and the adaptations they have made and enlist them as active participants in the healing process. A collaborative relationship is necessary in order to determine whether clients are willing and able to take the risks necessary to face painful emotions and experiences in order to overcome barriers in their lives. The therapeutic journey discussed in this chapter is inspiring because it illustrates the complexity of such a healing process. Susan's story demonstrates that EMDR is a tool that can help clients go back in time and develop those parts of their personalities that could not emerge because of an invalidating environment.

Client's Background and Initial Treatment

Susan was referred for therapy by her vocational rehabilitation counselor, who knew about EMDR. The counselor reported that Susan had been out of work for 11 months after filing a workers' compensation stress claim, and had continued to feel depressed and function poorly. Susan wanted a female therapist because she had been unable to make progress during eight months of traditional therapy with her previous male therapist.

The first session was spent gathering background information. Susan indicated that she had been unable to continue working at her last job because of being traumatized by the lack of support and criticism she received. She described the organization for which she had worked as "highly dysfunctional," adding that she felt "victimized and battered." She could not make progress in therapy because she thought that her therapist "did not want to hear her out." She believed she "did not have permission to bring up real issues but had to show him she made progress so he would feel good about the work he did with her" (and, presumably, like her). Looking back, she realized that she took care of him rather than herself. When he recommended that she was ready to go back to work, she had to acknowledge the truth and tell him she was not functioning well and definitely not ready to return to work. Susan felt completely unsafe. She worried that people at work would "dump their anger" on her and that she would attract abusive people and be incapable of protecting herself.

She could name only a few places where she felt safe: a karate self-defense class, Codependents Anonymous (CODA) and Adult Children of Alcoholics (ACA) groups, and some classes at the local college. Otherwise, she was "hiding out" at home. She emphatically stated that she was not work-ready, needed to learn to protect herself better, and felt confused and unable to "sort things out." She recognized that her problems at work were "somehow" related to the problems she'd had when growing up at home. She thought her supervisors had a "skewed reality" that caused her to doubt herself. She was told that she was the problem. Susan thought that her supervisors expected to be pacified and that she should do what they wanted and not complain, no matter the cost to her personal and professional integrity.

Susan exhibited vegetative signs of depression: too much sleep or none at all, weight gain, and extreme lack of energy. She also complained about feeling sad. She had been on Zoloft (100 mg daily) for three weeks when she started therapy with me. She had taken Prozac for two and a half years and had stopped taking it about five months before seeing me because she disliked being "controlled" by medication. However, her symptoms had become too troublesome, and she had resumed taking medication.

Susan had a longstanding history of depression with episodes of major depression. She'd had suicidal ideation at age 16 and became suicidal again while grieving about her emotionally unavailable family in therapy prior to coming to Hawaii. She realized then that she had grown up in a family where both parents were heavy drinkers, possibly alcoholics. She began to get a glimpse of the types of dysfunctions that occur in alcoholic families. (Sadly, her parents continue to be in denial about their alcoholism.) Susan was the second oldest of five children and the only girl. She once was touched inappropriately by her older brother. Fortunately, she fought back and avoided a more serious violation. Her needs were not important and her feelings did not count. She had an undetected visual impairment until she was in the ninth grade. Furthermore, she was on Librium from age four until age 12 or 13 for petit mal seizures. Susan had not known what these pills were for, but she did notice that she felt better when she forgot to take them. When she finally stopped taking them without advising her family or doctor, she felt "liberated."

She had a college degree and subsequently attended seminary, hoping to become a religious counselor; however, she did not complete her education in the seminary. She lost her motivation when told by students and teachers

that her calling was considered "second class" because she was more interested in counseling than in the "business" of the ministry. She also stopped
because she was disillusioned at being "hit upon" by married men at the
seminary. Susan acknowledged a lifelong history of "stuffing" her feelings
because it was unacceptable to show weakness.

Susan filed a workers' compensation stress claim nine months after starting a new job in Hawaii, claiming that she was being scapegoated in her
position. She began feeling victimized three months into her job (and went
into therapy about that time), when an employee complained about her and
her supervisors blamed her for the problem without properly investigating
the situation. At her six-month performance evaluation, there were still no
problems noted by her supervisors, but Susan felt she was "out of sync" with
the members of her department. She was told that she should move her
clients quickly through the social service system, whereas she felt that clients
were being moved so quickly that important needs were being overlooked
and that she should be more thorough with her cases to avoid crises. Believing her integrity was being compromised and recognizing her views were
not being validated, she began to suffer from nausea and headaches, often
having to go home ill. She kept a journal about the situations at work causing her distress and her attempts to resolve her difficulties. After terminating
work, her symptoms decreased significantly, and she no longer suffered from
nausea and vomiting.

Independent medical evaluations by psychiatrists hired by the insurance
company noted that Susan's perception about the job situation was not
shared by her supervisors, who cited a myriad of performance problems (i.e.,
they claimed that she tended to blame others for her problems and frequently would use illness as a reason for going home early).

Thus there were three different views: (1) Susan's statement that she was
overly stressed, not given clear directions in the midst of a chaotic work
situation jeopardizing the well-being of her clients, and that her supervisors
were covering up the reality of the situation; (2) the physicians' diagnosis of
her as suffering from a major depression; (3) her supervisors' statements that
she was a "marginal worker." The basis for the work injury—rumors of her
wanting to transfer out of the department, which Susan denied being true
at the time—was symbolic of her feeling of not being understood in her
department. A number of problems seemed to be operating: inconsistent
supervision, not being told exactly what to do, and philosophical differences
involving what she felt her job entailed versus what her supervisors said
should be done.

The reports questioned the extent to which pre-existing personality characteristics interfered in the resolution of Susan's depressive episode. Her history of somatic complaints suggested chronic anxiety and dysphoric symptoms. Her motivation to seek the help of a new therapist was also questioned. Within one week of being told that she should return to work, she requested a new therapist. Was this an indication of malingering?

The IME suggested that to avoid long-term disability, Susan should receive "aggressive" vocational rehabilitation. She should be required to have a short-term trial of volunteer work with a subsequent transfer to another agency. After two and a half months of treatment with the new therapist, she should return to work.

What Was the Real Story?

Susan's situation began making sense when viewed from a trauma-based perspective. To avoid rejection at home, she had learned to survive by pleasing her family and doing everything as perfectly as possible. This survival pattern had generalized, leading to lifelong, compulsive people-pleasing and perfectionism designed to avoid painful rejection and criticism. In fact, she was phobic about being criticized. Her pain about her childhood was largely dissociated. When she tried to do her best in her new job, only to have her competence questioned by people she considered to be "burned out" and dysfunctional, her pattern of compulsive people-pleasing and perfectionism began to fail her. This was like being thrown back into her family of origin without any way to protect herself (which Susan accurately described at intake). Previously dissociated feelings and perceptions locked in from her past were activated and began to overwhelm her (Braun, 1988a, 1988b). She began feeling like an abused child in an invalidating environment (Linehan, 1993): No one supported her, no one cared for her, and she was all alone. These perceptions were linked to unbearable painful affect dissociated and locked into her body (so-called somatoform presentations) in the form of agitation, anxiety, and depression. Nausea and vomiting were also part of this symptom picture. Traditional therapy was not working for Susan, and she continued to feel unsafe with her previous therapist because he was a man—and, therefore, could not be trusted. The fact that the symptoms improved once she left work was also understandable. She was no longer confronted with supervisors who acted just like her parents; thus, the dissociated feelings and self-perceptions were less activated, and her normal defenses protected her once again.

The childhood abuse Susan reported was primarily emotional in nature. She exhibited typical symptoms experienced by these victims, such as a heightened ability to avoid, deny, and repress; chronic perceptions of danger; other-directedness; being out of touch with many aspects of reality; low self-esteem; phobic behaviors; a profound lack of inner worth (e.g., Briere, 1989; Linehan, 1993; Miller-Perrin & Wurtele, 1990; van der Kolk et al., 1996). She could only perceive that authority figures at work were wrong and that they did not accept her. She was unable to grasp that her behaviors may have contributed to some of the difficulties.

An analysis of her deficits included both skill as well as motivational/ emotional ones. Skill deficits included the following areas: perceiving situations from other people's point of view, setting appropriate boundaries, being assertive rather than aggressive, solving interpersonal situations effectively, and tolerating painful emotional states. Emotional deficits included fluctuations between being overwhelmed by usually dissociated affect and feeling numb. She had longstanding habits of avoiding uncomfortable situations; for example, not dating for one and a half years, procrastinating with difficult and unpleasant tasks, and sleeping, spending, and eating excessively to avoid unpleasant feelings.

Initially, the insurance company was only willing to pay for short-term treatment. With the consistent use of EMDR, an adherence to designated timeliness, and Susan's remarkable progress, however, the insurance company cooperated by paying for a total of 48 sessions (50 minutes each) over a period of 15 months, which included six months of therapy after Susan was placed into a new job. Susan subsequently continued therapy for 13 months, using her own insurance to pay for an additional 22 sessions. At the completion of therapy, the claims adjuster wrote me a letter indicating that Susan has made an appropriate adjustment to her job. He also wrote: "Please accept our sincere appreciation for your professional services which facilitated Susan's remarkable recovery." Susan's recovery is a tribute to her willingness to be healed and the power of EMDR to heal. Without EMDR, such progress would not have been possible.

I helped Susan understand that she exhibited pathological people-pleasing behavior and perfectionism because of unresolved issues from childhood and that she was unable to set healthy boundaries in social situations. She had learned perfectionism and people-pleasing to survive at home as a child, and these survival strategies had become part of her personality, designed to keep her from feeling overwhelming hidden inner pain. These compulsive behaviors contributed to procrastination: Her work had to be perfect, so she would put off attempting to attain her unrealistic goals as long as possible.

She needed to rely on supervisors to validate her work and required excessive reassurance because she was not able to validate herself. She had great difficulties taking criticism. I told her that recovery would involve taking risks by learning to decrease her people-pleasing and perfectionistic behaviors and beginning to face her underlying pain. She needed to learn how to cope appropriately, even when criticized.

Susan had a difficult time breaking through her denial and often felt I was somewhat unsympathetic to her situation. She initially believed she was blameless and that her supervisors were "evil." This issue had to be addressed repeatedly throughout treatment, and she needed reassurance that I had to take a tough-love approach in order to assist her in moving beyond her victim role to achieving mastery over these situations.

Establishing an Explicit Treatment Contract

I talked about how EMDR could assist her in resolving painful issues from the past. I made her aware that her feelings about the past were not consciously available, and that she could not improve as long as she stayed away from difficult job situations and played it safe. We made a contract that she would place herself in a volunteer work position, which would allow her to experience difficult social situations and thereby counteract her avoidance. Subsequently, overwhelming affect and difficulties experienced in these situations would be targeted with EMDR and reprocessed. By targeting current issues as they arose, or family-of-origin issues when accessible, she would gradually be able to resolve more and more of the traumatic material and be less bothered by it.

The treatment contract involved volunteer work initially for 20 hours and then full-time. Subsequently, she would be placed in a full-time job. Treatment would help her learn how to maintain adequate boundaries and learn the skills to cope with a variety of difficult social situations. She agreed to continue her involvement with Adult Children of Alcoholics, Co-dependents Anonymous, and the self-defense class. She also was asked to establish a support network of safe people she could call whenever she felt overwhelmed. I reassured Susan that I would respect her needs and go no faster than she felt comfortable. Susan made the agreement to be honest with me and tell me when she would notice "people-pleasing" during therapy to avoid another treatment failure. She acknowledged that being honest with me would help her become more honest with other people.

Alteration of the Standard EMDR Protocol

I viewed Susan's psychological condition as a depressive disorder and a personality disorder with obsessive-compulsive, avoidant, and dependent features. I ruled out a dissociative disorder. Her personality disorder implied the presence of longstanding behavioral survival patterns that were developed to cope with the abuse experienced as a child. A critical treatment component involved experiencing real-life situations, new ways to cope, and using EMDR whenever Susan experienced overwhelming and painful feelings. This served to decondition the effects of present stimuli that had become dysfunctional triggers.

The goal was to resolve as much of the underlying material as was available and enable Susan to gradually become more functional in the present. Negative affect and beliefs about herself were to become less valid and positive beliefs more valid. Over time, I expected that Susan would become capable of reprocessing early memories, leading to deep inner healing.

Susan's therapy to ameliorate the effects of ongoing childhood trauma may be described using the metaphor of an onion. EMDR sessions take away one layer of the onion at a time, allowing certain feelings and perceptions to emerge. Often this requires a restabilization phase. The client needs to learn to manage a new level of adaptation that frequently requires new skills. New EMDR targets are chosen based on situations eliciting overwhelming affect, which are seen as restimulation experiences tying into earlier traumatic memories. As increasingly more layers of the onion are peeled away, the client becomes capable of coping adoptively with new situations, fully facing and processing painful childhood experiences, and grieving for early losses. It seems that a self-healing mechanism is indeed accessed with EMDR (as described by Shapiro, 1995). If all appropriate cautions are in place (Shapiro, 1995), only as much material is accessed as the client is capable of handling at a given time. The therapist's job, therefore, is to pace the process carefully so that the client can function appropriately at each new level of adaptation and to respect the client's inability or unwillingness to go further at any given point.

It is important to note that EMDR treatment occurred within 50-minute psychotherapy sessions, with 25 to 40 minutes actually being EMDR. Furthermore, using this approach, single EMDR sessions frequently do not resolve a target (achieving a SUDS level of 0 and a VOC of 7). Painful material is accessed gradually, and clients resolve only as much material as they can at any given time. Similar targets are reprocessed repeatedly, and underlying family issues are processed more completely over time. This approach implies that positive beliefs are integrated and generalized gradually. Clinicians can expect that, for a period of time, clients are simultaneously believing and not believing positive beliefs reflecting self-worth. Frequently a VOC of 1 occurs, especially initially, indicating that the client is incapable of believing a chosen positive cognition. This is not seen as a barrier to implementing EMDR as long as the client begins to take small steps towards improved self-acceptance by consistently installing positive beliefs appropriate to the situation (e.g., "I am making progress," "I have the courage to face my past," "I do the best I can").

EMDR Readiness

Before implementing EMDR, the readiness of the client to face painful feelings needs to be carefully evaluated. Susan understood that, in order to recover, she would have to face painful feelings from her childhood. She also knew that she might feel worse before she would feel better. Susan was an ideal EMDR candidate, for she was highly motivated to use the technique to improve. She had tried traditional therapy several times and was frustrated and discouraged with the lack of results. She believed EMDR was her last hope. She decided to do whatever it took to resolve her inner pain in order to heal and get better. It is important to recognize that such determination to improve is frequently not present in clients, who then resist the EMDR process, especially when painful feelings emerge and they temporarily feel worse.

Susan had worked on herself for quite some time and had excellent self-soothing skills. At the same time, her longstanding history of avoiding overwhelming feelings caused her to be scared of beginning the EMDR process. Nevertheless, Susan was ready for EMDR because she had good ego strength, intelligence, a strong spiritual faith, and social support through her recovery groups.

The goal of the first EMDR session (her second therapy session) was to decrease her fear about the EMDR procedure and facing her feelings. The target was "I am scared to do EMDR and face feelings." The negative cognition was "I can't stand feeling pain" (Subjective Units of Distress Scale [SUDS] at 7); her positive cognition was "I'm OK with my feelings and being conscious of them" (Validity of Cognition Scale [VOC] at 4). She said she "felt these feelings in her head." EMDR was administered using the EyeScan 2000, an instrument with a moving light that Susan followed. The first set of eye movements was given.

SV: What is coming up?

Susan: I got anxious with side-to-side movements. The pressure in my head is less ►◄►◄►◄.

SV: What do you get now?

Susan: EMDR reminds me of the EEG I took when I was a child.

SV: When you think of doing EMDR and face your feeling, how much distress is coming up now?

Susan: It's a 5 [*down from* 7].

SV: What does the number 5 mean?

Susan: I feel that there is a wall or guard.

SV: [*At that point, I introduced a cognitive interweave.*] Is it OK to get to know the wall or guard? [*I felt that Susan was close to accessing material that had been dissociated and that she was experiencing the dissociative barrier as a wall or guard. The cognitive interweave was designed to help her approach and integrate this experience.*] ►◄►◄►◄

SV: What do you get now?

Susan: The flashing light reminds me of the EEG and its flashing lights. It also reminds me of puberty. I had bad cramps and stayed in bed. Mom panicked and thought I had appendicitis. She took me to the hospital for observation, but no one visited me. I felt abandoned. I'm not important. I feel I'm being punished for being sick and putting my parents through it. I feel guilty. ►◄►◄►◄

SV: What do you get now?

Susan: At first, I got nothing. I felt pressured to have to come up with something. Then I remembered that at the same age, I had a molestation experience with my older brother. He wanted to see what my breasts looked like. I refused, and he tried to grab me, and I fell back, onto the bed. When I did, I giggled [*in what she knew now was in fear and hysteria*], and he left saying, "Don't tell anyone because you liked it, you laughed and enjoyed it." I also took a swing at him when he tried to grab me later on the stairs. ►◄►◄►◄

SV: What's coming up now?

Susan: At about the same age, I remember three different situations with Dad. He made comments about my first bra; it made my breasts look pointy and unnatural. My cousin came to visit and Dad criticized me for not shaving under my arms. No one taught me that underarm hair might be inappropriate at this time in my life. Dad wrestled with me, and I told him to stop, and then he was never affectionate with me. I feel very sad about the lack of affection from him. ►◄►◄►◄ [*Tears welled up in her eyes, and she wept quietly during this entire set.*]

Since the session had come to an end, I asked Susan how scared she was to do EMDR and face her feelings. Her SUDS by then had decreased from 7 to 3 and her VOC score of being OK with her feelings and becoming conscious of them had moved up from 4 to 5.5. The session was closed by placing the feelings into an imaginary filing cabinet and going to her special calming place, which was a park with Greek pillars and a gazebo. She said she felt about 13 years old. I was pleased with this result because Susan had connected with feelings dissociated in childhood, possibly at age 13. This session had provided her with the opportunity to access, integrate, and understand these experiences. Susan was prepared to be uncomfortable after the EMDR session and knew she could call me if she needed support.

At the next session (her third), Susan realized she had become "codependent" at the previous session and worried about not doing things right and what I would think. She also said she began feeling an increase in anxiety since the EMDR session and realized that "people are not safe." She was still very worried and kept her guard up. She acknowledged that the EMDR procedure was very illuminating, but she was scared that feelings and memories might come up and she would need to cope with such unpleasant experiences by herself. She also felt body memories and tension in her head. She realized that her family was emotionally abusive and neglectful and that she had coped by running away to avoid them. Unfortunately, she still remained vulnerable. She said that when she was small and had stood up to her family, she was medicated with Librium for being "too emotional." Her feelings were never validated—worse still, they were seen as an illness. It is no wonder that she became terrified of her feelings. Her mother never hugged her, and she did not get a sense of acceptance. Susan was very surprised that these insights came up spontaneously. She said she now feels as if she is 15 years old, and at times, three years old. It was as if frozen feelings had thawed. She acknowledged that she continues to have a pattern of isolation and not asking for help. She felt afraid to "bother" others. She said that she had one friend who was a role model, and she could use her as a mother figure because she was nurturing. Since she had not made the effort to get a sponsor, she was reminded to do so. Susan needed to learn that people would be there for her.

Susan required considerable reassurance and restabilization to feel safe after the first EMDR session. The next three sessions were spent stabilizing her by providing emotional support. She reported that when she began experiencing feelings of anxiety, she found herself rocking and wringing her hands like a small child to soothe herself. She also coped with such feelings by excessive spending and eating. In addition, she started worrying about men making inappropriate advances. She needed reassurance that I would respect her pace and not create unreasonable pressure to have her return to work before she was ready to do so. On the other hand, I also made her aware that the insurance company required an adherence to a certain schedule, requiring her to do volunteer work and then return to a full-time position. A delicate balance had to be achieved between reasonable external pressure and honoring Susan's need for time. Since Susan had excellent skills in meditation and affect containment, she only needed reminders to use these tools to help her cope with unpleasant feelings. Since she had been so isolated, she was asked to get a sponsor with whom she could talk on a daily basis and discuss her feelings.

At her sixth therapy session Susan was willing to have her second EMDR session. As the pressure mounted for Susan to start volunteer work, she wanted to process her last job situation, which had caused her to file a workers' compensation claim. She hoped EMDR would reduce her anxiety. The target was "I am at the mercy of these bullies." Her negative cognitions were "I am a bad person, limited and incompetent" (SUDS at 8). Her desired cognitions were "It was a learning experience. It is over. I am able to stand up for myself" (VOC at 2). She located the discomfort in her stomach, chest, and throat. As soon as she started her first set of eye movements, she began to sob deeply. After the second set, which consisted of continued sobbing, she reported that the pain had decreased from 8 to 3, and that she felt it in her throat. After the third set, she reported that all the physical pain was gone. She thought that a little residue was left because her muscles were aching and she felt a void. She said that it may have to do with the fact that she has trouble expressing herself and that's why she had pain in her throat. After the fourth set, she recognized that she believed she would be beaten down if she confronted others and thus chose to avoid confrontations as much as possible.

As a cognitive interweave I suggested that she think about the possibility of standing up for herself now; however, she was not ready to accept this idea. Susan insisted that assertion does not work because "there are vicious people who beat you down" and only useless "verbal sparring" occurs. At the end of this session, her SUDS level had decreased from 8 to 0 and her VOC score had increased from 2 to 3. The session was closed by placing the remaining negative feelings into a gift package. Susan chose the metaphor of a gift package because she felt that obstacles and challenges are gifts from the universe that would be transmuted into positive learning experiences. She had begun to trust the EMDR healing process. She spontaneously installed a new cognition that expressed hopefulness about her progress and the improvement she was making with EMDR. The second EMDR session revealed how much progress Susan had made. She had no trouble getting in touch with feelings and allowing herself to cry; she was beginning to face her fears of rejection.

The following session, her seventh, was spent with her vocational rehabilitation counselor setting a timeline for starting volunteer work. Although Susan was scared, she agreed to contact a number of agencies to explore options. In the next session she told me how difficult it was for her to call people a second time after she had not reached them the first time. She felt paralyzed, anticipating massive rejection. She noticed a similar feeling of anticipating rejection when she did needlework, which greatly surprised her.

This pattern of increasing awareness exquisitely illustrates the process of trauma recovery using EMDR. Susan realized that her fear of rejection when doing needlework was clearly connected to past issues. Targeting this current situation provided an opportunity to continue processing her oversensitivity to rejection, which had caused such difficulties at work. The target was "I am stitching and counting, and I'm not allowed to make mistakes." Her negative cognitions were "I am imperfect. I am not good enough" (SUDS at 5). The positive cognitions were "This is a learning process. I can make mistakes. It's OK to go back and redo steps" (VOC at 3.5). She felt the feeling primarily in her stomach but said it extended "all over" her body. She was asked to think about her needlework and focus on the pain in her body. Immediately, Susan connected to a past memory when she was going to do some painting for a Christmas project. There was no time to do it, but she completed a similar alternative project. She bought all the necessary items but believed her family had no appreciation of the work she had done or that it would have taken time to learn the skill to complete the original project.

During the next set of eye movements, she sobbed silently, her whole body shaking. Afterwards, she said initially it felt unsafe to cry and have feelings, but then she allowed herself to express sadness. She cried without making a sound because she "was never allowed to bother others." After the third set, another memory came up about her and her father. He was "perfectionistic" and expected her to win the girls' competitive championship in skeet shooting while she was only a beginner, without any help from him. Although Susan performed well, she was not good enough for her parents and was left feeling hurt and rejected. She then became immersed in a massive abreaction, "sinking into a deep well of pain" that had been repressed but was now able to surface, releasing some of this pain.

After the fourth set, Susan said that she'd always felt good about her work, but when things "went wrong" at her last job, it proved to everyone that her family—and especially Dad—were right: "I am a failure." The remaining four sets helped her recognize the presence of ingrained beliefs, such as no matter what she does, she will not be good enough; and she can't win because she cannot do things perfectly. She believed that placing her name on something meant it had to be perfect, otherwise she wouldn't even try. She worried that if she did not monitor herself, inevitably someone would judge her negatively and ask her why she had not done a better job. Rejection and shunning threatened her constantly.

Considerable time was spent on installing new beliefs she desperately wanted to feel, such as, "These situations are in the past"; "It is OK to be human and make mistakes"; and "I do not need to take on other people's feelings." She repeated these statements several times until they felt more believable. At the end of the EMDR session, her SUDS level had decreased from 5 to 0 and her VOC had shifted from 3.5 to 6. She said that though the positive beliefs did not feel completely true, "strong seeds had been planted."

The ninth session was primarily spent working through issues of needing to be perfect. Susan chose writing reports for the courts as a target. She pinpointed the following negative beliefs: "I need to get it right the first time because failures are not acceptable," and "I am not good enough" (SUDS at 8). When thinking about this situation, her desired cognitions were "I am allowed to make mistakes," "I'm able to set boundaries," "I'm OK as a person" (VOC at 1). She said she experienced the feeling in her stomach and face. She cried throughout the entire EMDR session, consisting of seven sets of eye movements, during which she processed her perception of having been victimized at her last job. She identified what she believed to be the elements of this victimization: She'd thought that she was doing a good job, but her supervisors did not give her a chance; they piled "more and more" work on her but would not give her guidance or support; they wanted her to fail; more and more conditions were added on, causing her to fail. "No matter how good I am, I'm doomed to fail." The seeds of positive beliefs had taken hold, and she spontaneously shifted to, "God loves and accepts me." She felt peaceful when she thought of God's love. At the end of the session, her SUDS had decreased from 8 to 3 and her VOC had increased from 1 to 4.

Susan completed an EMDR session in the morning, returning to my office in crisis in the early evening. She had gone to her karate class and was told to use force on her karate teacher. She felt petrified that he would hurt her if she used force. It suddenly dawned on her that she had no rights whatsoever. In the session she verbalized the beliefs that had burst into her awareness: "It is not OK to use force to get my needs met, and it is not OK to be weak because I will be destroyed." She "fell apart" after the karate session and could not stop crying. She wanted to use EMDR to process the target: "My karate instructor is not a safe person." The negative cognition was "I'm in danger" (SUDS at 10); her desired cognition was "I am safe" (VOC at 1). She cried throughout the four sets of eye movements, saying that asserting herself would place her in danger. She installed, "I can begin reclaiming my power." At the end of the session, her VOC had increased from 1 to 5 and her SUDS had decreased from 10 to 2.

Following this session Susan felt an inner strength she had not known before. Unexpectedly, her family contacted her to let her know that her father had died. Susan did not want to attend the funeral. Her feelings were strong and clear, but she was not sure whether she had the right to follow these feelings. She contacted me to talk about it. After our conversation, she was more aware that she did not feel safe seeing her family and that she needed to protect herself. She decided not to go to the funeral.

At the next session Susan reported that she had discontinued taking her medication after the third EMDR session. She wanted to experience her feelings and process them with EMDR. She did not want to be "numbed out" anymore. She was pleased with her decision not to attend the funeral but she continued to feel "damned if you do, damned if you don't."

Since Susan needed to prepare herself for the challenges she would face at her volunteer job, a few therapy sessions were spent discussing situations that had been problematic at her last job, with time spent teaching her skills to cope in more appropriate ways. She was reminded to notify the workplace when she was sick or would be late or unable to come in. I suggested that she do her best to avoid absences and go to bed at a reasonable time. She was prepared to deal with negative and critical people and assert herself appropriately without coming across aggressively. Role-playing was used to practice these skills. She agreed to enforce a time-out period on herself when feeling upset in order to determine what had caused her to feel hurt and what she could do about it. She began to realize how important it was to identify her feelings and use them as cues for problem-solving. To raise her level of social awareness, we discussed how different actions might be perceived by others. Nevertheless, she continued to feel afraid at the prospect of volunteering and worried about being "battered," even though she felt more prepared to deal with difficult situations.

Three months after starting therapy (a total of ten sessions, five of which were EMDR-focused), she was able to begin a volunteer job for 20 hours a week. Susan took on this challenge with trepidation. However, as she gained trust in her ability to cope, she was able to focus less on others and more on herself, decreasing the traumatic adaptation of other-directedness. She learned how uncomfortable she felt with people if she did not know whether or not they liked her. She needed to know in advance that they would accept her in order to feel safe, though she recognized that this was unrealistic. Susan acknowledged that in the past, she had dichotomized the world into good and bad. She was terrified of bad people but always had "white knights" to back her up (e.g., the ombudsman, the complaints office). Now Susan believed that she had to "fight her own battles" and assume responsibility for creating safety by setting clearer boundaries.

EMDR was used whenever Susan reported feeling overwhelmed with painful emotions between sessions and wanted to work through these feelings. The chosen EMDR targets were based on Susan's observations of herself at her volunteer job and in other situations. Observing herself made Susan acutely aware of her deep inner wounds from childhood. She increasingly recognized that she was extraordinarily sensitive to criticism and rejection. She scanned facial expressions to determine whether she was in danger. When someone appeared emotionally distant, she believed she had done something wrong. She addressed this hypersensitivity with EMDR at the fourteenth treatment session (her sixth EMDR session). During this session, she processed the target "I feel physically attacked when other people make demands and put me on the spot." "I am not safe" was her negative cognition (SUDS level was 8), and "I set limits," her positive cognition (VOC was 2).

Susan cried throughout the entire EMDR session and was able to process underlying family-of-origin issues, including that when she was "put on the spot," it was unacceptable to say no. She was not allowed to ask for space, and her mother frequently suggested that she was doing something wrong or was guilty. She always had to second-guess her mother as to what she wanted her to do. She was never good enough, never OK. Even if someone liked her, she felt she would be rejected as soon as the person "saw who she really was." Positive installations consisted of recognizing that these situations are in the past and the people she encounters now are different from her mother. She could see that now she had the right to give herself space. She could tell others what she needed. She no longer had to comply with requests automatically. After Susan discussed with me what she needed, considerable time was spent installing templates for future actions. She pictured responding to requests by saying that she needed time to think and would get back to them, check her calendar, or get more information before she could give an answer. These new skills created a sense of hope, relief, and safety. At the end of this session her SUDS level decreased from 8 to 2 and her VOC increased from 2 to 4. She felt she still needed practice in order to feel more confident in herself.

As Susan began to reprocess the painful memories from her childhood, she discovered how profound her pain and her sense of not belonging were. At the 18th session, five months after starting therapy, she targeted "I don't have a place in the universe unless I am perfect." Her negative cognition was "I am unlovable, unacceptable, unworthy" (SUDS at 9); her positive cognition was "I am like everyone else—allowed to learn and make mistakes" (VOC at 1). The sessions consisted of very long sets, throughout which she exhibited uncontrollable sadness.

Susan: ►◄►◄►◄ (103) They [her family] hated me. I had to figure out what to do that they wouldn't reject me. They called me fat and ugly. Crying didn't help, and I had to keep all my tears in. ►◄►◄►◄ (128) They were so mean. I could not get away from them. I could only walk on eggshells. I felt so powerless and useless. I once hit my brother because he was mean. ►◄►◄►◄ (86)

Susan said that everyone was mean and no one ever complimented her. They could not say anything nice. In the ninth grade the teacher told her parents she needed glasses, but the parents did not listen to her, again denying Susan's reality. A geography teacher finally helped her get glasses. She recognized that some people had demonstrated that they cared for her at least a little bit. However, whenever someone was supportive, her mother would discount them. Installations consisted of her deserving a place in the universe. She pictured herself sitting on God's lap. The session was closed by placing the residual negative feelings in the gift box; her SUDS level had decreased from 9 to 4 and her VOC had increased from 1 to 3.5. It was remarkable that at the sixth EMDR session, after a lifetime of suppressing her feelings, she was able to access such deeply felt pain.

At the twentieth session Susan asked to use EMDR to process her feelings about her last supervisor. This unresolved issue continued to bother her a great deal and caused her to feel overwhelming anxiety about attending the volunteer job on a full-time basis. Her target was "My supervisor destroyed my reputation when I did not do what she wanted me to do." Her negative cognition was "I am stupid and worthless" (SUDS at 8); her desired cognition was "She has her own issues and is separate from me" (VOC at 1). Susan cried throughout the entire EMDR session, processing her anger and frustration. She felt the supervisor had placed her in an impossible bind. She was asked to give up the priorities she thought were important and, therefore, the job became impossible for her. Susan could not understand why the supervisor would not talk to her and work things out. She spontaneously came up with positive belief: "I can only do my best; I accept my limits." At the end of the session her SUDS level had decreased from 8 to 0 and her VOC had risen from 1 to 7. She had progressed to believing that these statements were completely true. After this session she felt safe volunteering full-time. She had achieved these goals after five and a half months of treatment and eight EMDR sessions.

As Susan progressed, working successfully on her volunteer job for 40 hours a week, she had to face the issue of obtaining employment. This situation was very scary for her. Periodically, she expressed her anger at me because she thought I was blaming her for what had happened at her last job and that I did not recognize how destructive and dysfunctional the situation had been. She believed I blamed her for her behavior and for growing up in a dysfunctional family. Actually, her fear was beginning to overwhelm her. She needed repeated reassurance that I did not blame her and would support her in facing difficult situations at her new job. I reassured her she was not alone. With the mounting pressure to return to work, she began reexperiencing the abuse suffered at her last job and was eager to continue reprocessing issues on a deeper level than she had processed earlier. She began using EMDR at almost every session prior to returning to fulltime work. She did not feel safe returning to work unless these targets were neutralized. Targets processed (sessions 22 to 24) included feeling like a member of a bomb squad at her last job but not supplied with the appropriate tools to diffuse the explosives; her pattern of not confronting problems and feelings, fearing anger or criticism in response; and setting safe boundaries.

During session 25, Susan recognized that she had begun to shut down because very uncomfortable feelings were coming up for her. She targeted "crying was not OK at home" and now gave herself permission to be sad and cry. She cried throughout the session and expressed some fear that people would get mad at her for crying. Now she had a crying pillow at home and felt she deserved to buy the best teddy bear she could get to soothe herself. Susan became ready to do inner child work (Bradshaw, 1990) when she realized that she had been injured badly during her childhood and that she could not rely on others to heal this part of herself. She was the only one capable of nurturing and healing the wounded inner child, a very difficult task for her. Through role-playing, Susan learned that understanding and acknowledging feelings was a critical step in this process. Shutting down meant ignoring her innermost feelings and constituted a repetition of the emotionally abusive message she experienced at home: *Your feelings don't count.* She had a difficult time connecting and talking with her inner child but was willing to work on it, knowing it would take time to learn this skill after a lifetime of ignoring and suppressing feelings. Soothing her inner child paid off for her. Her feelings became stronger, and she was learning to label them. She also began to recognize when her feelings were appropriate to situations encountered in her life. She started to trust some of her feelings. Nevertheless, she still believed Mom would have loved her if she had been different as a child, and she still blamed herself for the abuse.

At the twenty-seventh session Susan was able to process a deeply in-grained belief that she is bad, has bad qualities, and does not deserve any-thing (SUDS at 10). She cried throughout the session and was able to reduce the distress level to a 5. Susan said that her mother was so afraid of spoiling her (because she was the only girl) that she never hugged or cuddled her. Her parents did not protect her from her brothers, who destroyed her dolls. She cried when her youngest brother was born because, since he was yet another boy, she remained without allies. She felt deep compassion and caring for her inner child and reassured her that she is fine the way she is and that mistakes are acceptable.

At the twenty-eighth session Susan processed the target "I can never let my guard down because people will hurt me." Again she sobbed throughout the session as she processed not being comfortable with who she is and the fear that whatever she has will be taken away. Any accomplishments are "flukes"; eventually, someone will discover she is incompetent and she will get fired. Her parents had not expected her to succeed, certainly had not expected her to earn a college degree. They expected her to go to a trade school this, even though her pediatrician had told her parents *when she was four years old* that she was "college material." They simply did not believe it. Her mother especially had very low expectations after Susan was diagnosed with petit mal epilepsy. Susan hoped that other people would treat her more kindly and was very disappointed when this did not happen. She realized that she had never learned to protect herself. She had been waiting for Prince Charming to protect her because she did not know how to protect herself. Spontaneously, during an EMDR set she recognized that her parents were limited in their ability to love and care because they themselves had not been nurtured. How could they give something they'd never received? Her parents would never dream of going to therapy. It was shameful to take such action. What would people think? She installed healing imagery by visualizing people who were emotionally supportive and caring of her. She nurtured and reassured her inner child: "We are fine the way we are; we don't need to be fixed; we don't need to be perfect; we are allowed to make mistakes; we just need to be who we are." I felt gratified by the progress Susan had made. She had laid a foundation of positive beliefs for herself and she was now capable of building on the strength of these new beliefs.

Session 29 consisted of processing negative cognitions that it was not acceptable for Susan to care for herself, that anything she would choose would be of no value, and that whatever she does is wrong. During this session she reprocessed her despair and confusion that, even if she is assertive, people would continue to be mean and judgmental, and men would continue to make inappropriate advances. During a later set of eye movements she began to realize that, though being assertive is an important survival skill, it is no guarantee that the other person will treat one well. She recognized that she needs to protect herself by setting limits and boundaries with negative people and interacting with them only minimally. We spent time on this issue, discussing at length how to handle a variety of situations by choosing appropriate responses. She became clearer about what it meant to set boundaries.

Susan started her new job after the twenty-ninth therapy session and her fifteenth EMDR session. She had recovered sufficiently to be work-ready after eight months of treatment. Susan had turned a corner. Now she no longer jumped to the conclusion that everything was her fault, and when faced with rejection, criticism, or indifference, she felt hurt for a relatively short time. She began using her feelings to cue herself when she needed to solve a problem. Her success at her volunteer job had prepared her and given her confidence. When she left her volunteer position, the staff was sad to see her leave and thanked her for the contribution she had made. Susan gave everyone a hug and felt she had bonded with the staff. She was relieved; she had succeeded. She had reached a milestone in her trauma recovery.

Susan beamed when she came to one of her sessions. An aunt had called her and blasted her on the phone for not attending her father's funeral. She felt shame and guilt only for about five minutes and was able to terminate the conversation. She was delighted not to need her aunt's approval. She also recognized at that moment how she had been living in a "state of shock," denying the reality of her family situation, and that she had been a "gaping inner wound" all of her life.

Initially, Susan was overwhelmed by anxiety and fear at her new job. She recognized that this anxiety was part of learning what others expected her to do and getting to know the personalities of supervisors and co-workers in a new setting. She had made a good choice. The work assignments were clearer and much more manageable than at her last job. However, Susan faced a major challenge when one of her co-workers accused her of being too firm with her clients. Although Susan felt anger and fear, she was able to meet with her supervisor and the co-worker and present herself very professionally. Afterwards her supervisor commended her for her behavior. She also learned that she needed to limit interactions with this co-worker to minimize conflict. She chose to be polite but distant. Susan was pleased. After protecting herself and implementing these strategies, she no longer had problems.

The insurance company authorized weekly sessions for two months after Susan started the job and sessions every two weeks for another four months in order to help her feel comfortable adjusting to the work situation. During this period she attended a total of 19 additional therapy sessions and used EMDR during 12 of them (see Table 10.1 for the EMDR targets chosen). After this, Susan continued to see me for another year, using her own insurance. During this time she sought the assistance of a naturopathic physician to improve her physical health. In addition, she began to address her fears about men. Initially, Susan felt she would "lose her identity" if she became involved with anyone. Gradually, as underlying issues were resolved, she became more comfortable dating and more adept at setting appropriate boundaries. She became increasingly aware of any internal or external cues alerting her to uncaring behavior, and she had no difficulties leaving unsuitable relationships. Susan terminated therapy soon after she joined one of the spiritual centers in Hawaii and committed herself to develop her spirituality. At her last session she installed positive beliefs, such as accepting abundance into her life and feeling safe with people.

Interestingly, as Susan began feeling safe to date, she lost weight almost effortlessly, about 50 pounds over a six-month period. Maybe now she could afford to look attractive because she was capable of maintaining her own identity with men. How did EMDR assist Susan in recovering from childhood trauma? Susan recovered from being in a state of shock and denial. She had described herself as a "gaping inner wound." EMDR permitted her to access dissociated feelings and memories from her past. It was a gradual process, requiring many EMDR sessions. Over time, Susan reprocessed the pain experienced in her childhood and was freed to perceive the world from an adult point of view. Her trauma recovery was startling: She was much more in touch with her feelings, the world had become a safer place, and she had acquired self-worth. She was now capable of setting boundaries with people to protect herself. The effects of developmental arrests no longer

TABLE 10.1
Overview of EMDR Targets and Significant Accomplishments
During Therapy Lasting 28 Months

11 MONTHS OUT OF WORK

Session 2	I'm scared to do EMDR and face feelings.
Session 6	I'm at the mercy of these bullies.
Session 8	I'm stitching and counting, and I'm not allowed to make mistakes.

DISCONTINUED ZOLOFT

Session 9a	[Writing reports for the courts]
Session 9b	[Crisis] My karate instructor is not a safe person.

STARTED VOLUNTEER JOB 20 HOURS A WEEK

Session 14	I feel physically attacked when other people make demands and put me on the spot.
Session 18	I don't have a place in the universe unless I am perfect.
Session 20	My supervisor [at last job] destroyed my reputation when I did not do what she wanted me to do.

STARTED VOLUNTEER JOB 40 HOURS A WEEK

Session 22	I'm a member of a bomb squad and need to diffuse bombs, but supervisor does not give me the tools.
Session 23	I avoid confronting problems and feelings because I will be yelled at and criticized.
Session 24	Setting boundaries is not safe.
Session 25	Crying was not OK at home.
Session 27	I am bad; I have bad qualities; I don't deserve anything.
Session 28	I can never let my guard down because people will hurt me.
Session 29	It's not OK to care for myself; whatever I choose does not have any value; whatever I do is wrong.

STARTED FULL-TIME JOB

Session 31	I'm not able to be aware of myself and my feelings.
Session 32	Oh, my God, they will catch me doing something wrong.
Session 33	I am disappointed in myself.
Session 35	I have to be perfect to deserve love and acceptance.
Session 36	I cannot move ahead unless I am perfect.
Session 38	If I ask, I get slapped on the head.
Session 40	Someone will attack me, and I won't be able to protect myself.
Session 43	Life is unjust, and I will be judged harshly no matter what I do at work.
Session 44	I have to work all the time; any mistake I make is looked at negatively, and the positive is ignored.
Session 45	My feelings are being discounted.
Session 46	[Feeling overwhelming sadness; has been unable to control crying in her car.]
Session 48	I need to stuff myself with food.
Session 50	I have to be perfect.
Session 52	My job is to fix the family so that they will like me.

TABLE 10.1
(continued)

STARTED FULL-TIME JOB

Session 54	He [a boyfriend] is unwilling to work on himself.
Session 56	A client yells and blames me.
Session 59	Mom told me she felt used and had taken the hope chest under false pretenses [five years ago].
Session 64	He [her boyfriend] is not able to express his feelings to me and give me reassurance.
Session 67	People stand there and laugh while throwing stones.
Session 70	If I accept the positive, I will be knocked off my place.

dominated her life. She had laid a solid foundation for herself. A comprehensive treatment program had been necessary, requiring her to face disturbing and painful situations (in vivo desensitization) so that she could practice new skills and learn that she could protect herself. Susan was transformed because she had the courage to face her pain and work through it.

References

Bradshaw, J. (1990). *Homecoming: Reclaiming and championing your inner child.* New York: Bantam Books.

Braun, B. G. (1988a). The BASK (behavior, affect, sensation, knowledge) model of dissociation. *Dissociation, 1*(1), 4–23.

Braun, B. G. (1988b). The BASK model of dissociation: Clinical applications. *Dissociation, 1*(2), 16–23.

Briere, J. (1989). *Therapy for adults molested as children: Beyond survival.* New York: Springer.

Linehan, M.M. (1993). *Cognitive-behavioral treatment of borderline personality disorder.* New York: Guilford Press.

Miller-Perrin, C. L., & Wurtele, S. K. (1990). Reactions to childhood sexual abuse: Implications for posttraumatic stress disorder. In C. L. Meek (Ed.), *Posttraumatic stress disorder: Assessment, differential diagnosis, and forensic evaluation* (pp. 91–135). Sarasota, FL: Professional Resource Exchange.

Shapiro, F. (1995). *Eye movement desensitization and reprocessing: Basic principles, protocols, and procedures.* New York: Guilford Press.

Ullmann, L. P., & Krasner, L. A. (1965). *Case studies in behavior modification.* New York: Holt, Rinehart and Winston.

Ullmann, L. P., & Krasner, L. A. (1975). *A psychological approach to abnormal behavior.* Englewood Cliffs, NJ: Prentice-Hall.

van der Kolk, B. A., McFarlane, A. C., & Weisaeth, L. (Eds.) (1996). *Traumatic stress: The effects of overwhelming experience on mind, body, and society.* New York: Guilford Press.

11

"AM I REAL?"

Mobilizing Inner Strength
to Develop a Mature Identity

Joan Lovett

CHRIS INTRODUCED HERSELF as a high-achieving adult child of an alcoholic family. Despite her notable success as a business executive, she suffered from low self-esteem that affected her relationships and prevented enjoyment in her life. At age 44, she was going through her third divorce and was plagued by extreme panic attacks when she was alone, particularly at night. She found herself wanting to get a terminal illness so that she could die courageously. Beliefs that she was not good enough to live and that she didn't deserve to be happy circulated in her mind and sometimes kept her in bed all day with a cover pulled over her head. During our first meeting, Chris discussed her desire to get over some of her fears and to deal with feelings of inadequacy that had inundated her since her third husband's departure.

Chris had been in therapy for four years and had recently begun taking Prozac (20 mg daily). She felt that therapy and medication kept her out of a suicidal depression, but she was still motivated to feel "not at such a loss." A colleague suggested that she try EMDR. Chris discussed her interest in EMDR with her therapist, who recommended me. Chris wanted to continue her current therapy, alternating with EMDR sessions.

I would like to express my deep gratitude to Adrianne Casadaban, Sandy Dibbell-Hope, Robbie Dunton, Robert Gilden, Karen Harber, Phyllis Klaus, Philip Manfield, Vivian Mazur, Zoe Newman, Thelma Peck, Francine Shapiro, and Landry Wildwind, whose ideas have enriched my own and have contributed to this chapter.

My training prior to EMDR was in behavioral pediatrics. I was trained in EMDR in 1992 and found it useful for helping children resolve their traumas, enhancing the learning of self-soothing skills, and "reparenting" children who had been neglected and abused. Chris's "inner child" had been wounded by years of criticism and neglect and my work with children was well suited for her.

Chris's history emerged slowly over the entire treatment process, which consisted of 18, 90-minute sessions at weekly intervals (for one month), then every other week (for five months), then monthly (for two months), extending over a total period of eight months. The first session was devoted to taking an inventory of Chris's complaints and symptoms and an initial history. After that, every session included about half an hour of conversation, during which Chris identified issues she wanted to address, and about an hour of EMDR-facilitated therapy targeting beliefs, memories, and symptoms that disturbed Chris.

Chris's memories of her childhood were punctuated by pictures of her drunken father raging at his young children, shouting obscenities, and chasing them with a butcher knife. In anticipation of these rages, her mother would hide in the attic with her children. One time, having watched as her father stormed up the stairs to the attic, Chris kicked him and he fell back down the stairs. She felt terrible about hurting her father but simultaneously elated that she had protected her siblings and mother from his wrath. She remembered the day her inebriated father fell asleep while driving, and 10-year-old Chris and her 13-year-old sister managed to steer the car from impending death. Desperate rage later impelled 14-year-old Chris to break all the furniture in her house and to hold a knife to her father's neck. ("It was either attack him or commit suicide," she explained.)

Chris's mother tried to prepare her for life by reminding her that "You have to be tough in this world because things will only get worse." Chris recalled an incident in which she tried to get her mother's attention after cutting her foot on a piece of glass. Chris's mother, waiting in line for food stamps, angrily told her bleeding five-year-old daughter to find her way home and take care of herself. Chris sadly recalled that her foot hurt for years following the injury. Chris's mother maintained that if you showed weakness in any way, you were crazy and should be locked up—a dictum that left Chris believing that she would go crazy if she expressed her true feelings.

As a young child Chris developed a ritual that she used to cope with her "white empty feeling," which was how she described her profound despair. (I thought that the "white empty feeling," represented her experience of chronic, early childhood deprivation.) To comfort herself when she felt this desperate, lonely neediness that continued to haunt her even as an adult, young Chris would intone, "You are really here. You are really in this house. These are really your parents. This is really your city. This is really your universe." This gave her the feeling of being *insignificant*, which was comforting to her but also profoundly scary. The intensely anxious feeling reminded her that she was truly alive. Chris lamented that she couldn't change the reality of her childhood, but remembered attempts to take control of her environment in various ways, such as reciting her validation mantra, changing her sheets, and scrubbing her bathtub.

The memory that best represented Chris's adolescence was a visual image of herself huddled in a closet. At school, an environment inhabited by rough gangs, she wished she could be invisible. Her high school years were dominated by the wish that she were dead. She courted suicide on these occasions, by attempting to drown herself, by cutting her wrists, and by overdosing on drugs. She felt utterly lonely and lost. Remarkably, one of Chris's high school teachers recognized her potential and encouraged her in school.

Chris was the first person in her family to graduate from high school. Although she went on to graduate from a top-ranking university and business school, no family member ever sent her a graduation card or acknowledged her accomplishments. Thanks were not forthcoming when Chris bought a house for her wheelchair-bound mother and her drug-addicted sister, when she took over the parenting of her sister's child who had been removed from her custody because of abuse and neglect, or when she provided financial support for family members.

Chris came to therapy with a modest hope, initially vague, that she could be "more together" and could begin to take care of herself as well as she took care of others. She believed, "If your parents mess you up, shame on them. If you mess yourself up, shame on you." Currently, Chris held a position as a business executive, where she was rewarded for taking care of people and taking care of business. She helped support her two biological children, her nephew, a foster child, a grandchild, and several siblings, as well as her mother.

Chris saw herself floundering in the wake of three failed marriages which had been based on her willingness to ignore her own needs while taking care of men: an immigrant who needed food and shelter, a student who needed financial assistance through law school, and a man with a "terminal" illness requiring devoted care, who surprised everyone by recovering and then leaving Chris. She frequently attended meetings for Adult Children of

Alcoholics (ACA), where she recognized that every participant was looking for a parent. At meetings, she practiced resisting the urge to take care of everyone. Chris had made one effort to enjoy herself since her husband was no longer with her—she had begun to dance again.

I hoped that Chris could begin to give herself the loving attention she was capable of giving others. I imagined that it must feel dangerous for Chris to acknowledge her own needs. As a child she had been required to hide her vulnerabilities in a household where feelings were equated with weakness and insanity, where needs were met with rage, and where taking responsibility meant taking blame. I suspected that outmoded double-binding beliefs still trapped Chris, so that it felt dangerous for her to acknowledge her needs—yet it was becoming unbearably costly for her to continue to suppress them and deny her own value.

A Complex Case

I regarded Chris's case as *complex* for several reasons. Unlike straightforward cases in which EMDR can be used to target a particular trauma, phobia, belief, or feeling, this case involved a childhood of chronic neglect and abuse and a lifetime of relationships based on abdication of self. The client had never had an experience of healthy intimacy, so we could not use a pretraumatic state as a template for her desired sense of well-being. Even Chris's goal to feel "not at a loss" was vague, and she could not imagine it when we began working together. In addition to reprocessing childhood traumas, I decided to use EMDR to enhance Chris's learning of self-soothing skills, to facilitate the acquisition of developmentally appropriate beliefs, and to accelerate her learning of new social skills. Desensitizing and reprocessing experiences of childhood neglect are not enough to give the individual an experience of being nurtured. The supportive and caring attitude of the clinician can be augmented by EMDR-enhanced experiences of nurturing.

Much of my work with EMDR has involved children. There are many traumas that children can reprocess only with the aid of creative educational interweaves. When an adult client has not had the opportunity to internalize nurturing and compassionate parenting, the clinician must guide the therapeutic work by providing emotional as well as educational support. My work with Chris focused on developing her capacity to validate and nurture her own tender vulnerabilities. At the same time, I insisted that she examine what she had already successfully learned in order to begin to view herself as capable and deserving.

This case was almost as challenging as working with a child who is still living in a family where she is repeatedly denigrated. Chris was entrenched in a situation with a vindictive husband, out-of-control teenage children, and a financially and emotionally dependent clan. Her system of beliefs assuring "safety" required that she nullify herself. The complexity of this case will become more apparent as EMDR is used to target "representative" childhood memories, which contain a myriad of contradictory and self-destructive beliefs.

The Safe Place

I decided to spend an entire session working with Chris to develop a "safe place." This technique is useful for helping the client experience the positive power of her imagination and sense feelings of safety, relaxation, and comfort in her body. It can provide respite between sessions, if turbulent thoughts or feelings follow. It can also serve as a *place* from which a client can view a memory that is too frightening to enter, or a *place* to which to escape if an abreaction occurs. Chris frequently used the experience of her safe place to activate positive feelings between sessions, as well as after we had finished our work together.

Chris imagined her safe place to be a tropical island where the ocean is clear, the sand warm, and the air warm. She saw herself there with someone, family or friends, in a culture where fun, eating, sex, music, and dance were part of life, and in an environment where she could be close to nature. The island would be populated by wild horses that she could ride. (A childhood memory surfaced of getting a pair of cowboy boots—the only present she had ever received that she had actually wanted. She had frequently worn those boots to play in the concrete area near her apartment, where she had pranced in the crushed glass, pretending she was a horse, wild and free.) She wanted to feel "gorgeous, free, and sensual."

Imagining the feelings she might have if she felt safe, Chris identified feelings of being fully present, living in the moment, noticing everything, and of tranquillity. She commented, "The island feels risky in a good way. I can take normal risks comfortably." She imagined running free on the beach and being able to relate to people comfortably. EMDR enhanced these feelings, and Chris was pleased with her introduction to this new approach.

Next, we made an abstraction of "the good feeling." I find that, for some clients, the "abstraction" of the feelings associated with the safe place can serve as an easily accessible model for relaxation. Chris described the color, shape, texture, size, and smell of the good feeling. We used eye movements to strengthen and ground the good feeling associated with the small, warm, sandy, orange circle that smelled like the ocean and fried fish. I encouraged Chris to practice both intensifying and reducing the vividness of the image and its accompanying feeling so that she could gain control over it. Chris imagined herself in her safe place and felt that with the good feeling she could relate to people honestly and in a relaxed way. I encouraged Chris to practice getting in touch with her safe-place feelings between sessions, especially if she needed to soothe herself when she had upsetting memories.

In assessing Chris's first experience with eye movement, I was encouraged that she was able to visualize a safe place and experience the physical sensations of relaxation and safety in her body, that she had such a rich imagination, that she was highly motivated towards personal growth, and that she liked her EMDR experience. Her childhood had certainly been stressful, but she had had some positive experiences and astounding successes in the work arena. Fortunately, she had not been physically or sexually abused, although she had witnessed the abuse of siblings and other children in her home. I was cautiously optimistic that EMDR could help Chris eventually achieve her goal of being "not at such a loss."

I was concerned about whether Chris would be able to tolerate reprocessing traumatic memories without plunging into a suicidal depression, especially since she was in the midst of a divorce with a vindictive husband and attempting to cope with acting-out teenage children. I planned to communicate with Chris's therapist, anticipated using EMDR to offer support rather than reprocessing until her situation stabilized, and prepared to continue using EMDR to reinforce the safe place and any signs of strength. I was concerned about the severity of dissociation represented by the "white empty feeling of despair" and resolved to wait until I knew Chris better before addressing any traumatic memories.

When Chris returned in a week, she reported that when she had left my office she had bought herself the computer she had been wanting for a long time. She claimed that she had gotten along amazingly well over the weekend without her husband and had visualized her safe place "a lot." Finally, she had given a work-related presentation that was well received. Although Chris had not begun reprocessing any troublesome memories, her initial improvement may have resulted from enhancing her sense of self through the safe-place visualizations.

Chris claimed that she had always had "ups and downs" and that the experience of feeling consistently good made her feel guilty. She stated, "I don't deserve to feel good." I asked what she would like to believe about herself, setting up the EMDR framework for cognitive reprocessing. "I do deserve to feel good," she replied. Chris revealed that her long-held belief that "I don't have value" was recently "proved" by the fact that she was the only family member not invited to her uncle's wedding. Furthermore, she was afraid that "I cannot defend myself." In relation to her family, Chris stated that she'd like to believe herself to be "as generous as I can be. I'm valuable to my family. I'm fine regardless of how they feel about me." Later, we reprocessed her self-depreciating beliefs.

Chris asserted that she would like to explore more of those areas that "are giving me what I need, like 'I feel centered. I feel right. I can validate myself.'" I encouraged Chris to develop the image of herself as already holding those positive beliefs. I intended to use EMDR to enhance the positive cognitions about herself that already felt true. She remembered her work-related presentation when she and a colleague had stood in front of 75 people, supporting each other, sharing, answering questions, sensitive to the needs of the audience, but at the same time able to stay on track with the message Chris wanted to deliver. I employed eye movement to strengthen Chris's feeling of being "all right."

Using EMDR for Bridging

I decided to use a method I call *bridging* to begin to connect Chris's work successes with feelings of positive self-esteem. Drawing on her healthy self-esteem and the learning processes that led to her successful career, I planned to assist Chris in developing the possibility that she could bridge the gap between her work life and her personal life. For example, I knew Chris needed to work on boundaries issues in her personal life. Her report of her workshop indicated to me that she was quite capable of taking care of herself while respecting other's needs and demands. I explained that we could apply that sense of power and experience of appropriate boundaries to her intimate relationships.

Recalling her position of power during her presentation felt good to Chris, she enthusiastically generated a list of beliefs she had about herself in relation to work. These positive cognitions were: "I'm worthwhile. I have something to offer. I'm respectable. I'm an adult. I have valuable experiences to share. I can set appropriate boundaries. I'm confident that I can do this." For Chris, these positive cognitions felt completely true when applied to work but barely true at all when she thought about her personal life.

We used eye movement to reinforce the "wonderful" feeling associated with having healthy power. Chris remembered people handing her their business cards and realized that she could be sensitive to them but limit how much they occupied her time or space. She stated, "I told myself I can do these things in all my relationships with folks. I can say 'It's time to stop now.' I don't have to continue answering their questions when the conference is over and it's time for me to go for dinner. I can meet their needs and still not deny my own needs."

We used EMDR to accentuate Chris's other work successes. For example, she remembered going to lunch and choosing to sit next to the board president, who said she would recommend that Chris get a raise. Three additional job offers were made to her after that presentation. The following is a transcript of the remainder of the session.

JL: Do you deserve to be valued?

Chris: ►◄►◄►◄ Absolutely. ►◄►◄►◄ I have valuable experiences to share.

JL: Where do you feel that in your body?

Chris: In my hands. ►◄►◄►◄ Folks give sincere thanks. I know I have a unique combination of business skills and political vision. I'm appreciated for my unique combination of skills, and I'm trustworthy.

JL: Where do you feel that in your body?

Chris: In my stomach. ►◄►◄►◄ I know I'm reliable. I know I'm trustworthy. I do my best.

JL: What were your professional and personal goals in the workshop?

Chris: Professionally, to share my knowledge and promote my organization. For myself, personally, for experience and for marketing myself. ►◄►◄►◄ I can take responsibility for my own accomplishments. ►◄►◄►◄ I made those things happen. I always thought that it was luck . . . but I did it. ►◄►◄►◄ There was some luck, but mostly I did it. ►◄►◄►◄ Very powerful—I did the work. ►◄►◄►◄ I feel like a man. ►◄►◄►◄ I can continue to do it. ►◄►◄►◄ I'm walking straight and tall. This kind of power gives me a sense of security. ►◄►◄►◄

JL: What kind of power is it safe for you to have? [*I asked this question to promote the bridging of her professional power in her personal life.*]

Chris: All the power that has to do with work. I'm capable of not misusing it. ►◄►◄►◄ I'm capable of using power for my benefit and for other people's benefit. ►◄►◄►◄

JL: How can you use your power in your personal life?

Chris: I'm not feeling as intimidated by my son. ▶◀▶◀▶◀ I can learn to use my power for my child's benefit. ▶◀▶◀▶◀ I can learn to effectively and lovingly use my power for my child's benefit. ▶◀▶◀▶◀

While Chris was enumerating the positive aspects of her power, I sensed that these positive associations were only a part of Chris's perceptions of power. At that point I invited her to draw a picture of her power, so that we could have a visual image of it. I hoped that drawing an image of her power would help Chris see it as a commodity she could mold, rather than a ubiquitous force that threatened to destroy her. Chris decided to imagine an image that would represent the power *she desired.* She drew a picture of a pyramid with herself (represented as a stick figure) standing in the middle of it, with "bad power" beneath her. She moved her eyes back and forth as she looked at her drawing. (I anticipated that we would need to reprocess her memories associated with "bad power" during a future session.)

Chris: [*Concluding the eye movements*] I don't have to be manipulative. ▶◀▶◀▶◀ I can meet my healthy needs. ▶◀▶◀▶◀ I can meet my healthy needs.

The Critic and the Personal Power Goddess

Chris returned for her fourth session saying that she wanted to learn to use her power to "make good personal choices." She acknowledged that she had an "inner critic" who always tried to make her avoid the "desperate lonely neediness" at all costs. This critic advised Chris to ignore her own needs and do whatever others wanted so that she would never be left alone. We discussed how the critic had helped Chris as a child so that she wouldn't be attacked or abandoned. I noted that now that Chris was an adult, the critic only made her miserable by immobilizing her with destructive criticism. I playfully introduced the possibility that the critic was an employee whom Chris could choose to fire or retrain. I find that humor can help to loosen rigid concepts. Chris enjoyed the idea of her critic as an employee and decided that she wanted her to become her protectress. She bestowed a new title on her once-vigilant critic—"The Personal Power Goddess"—who would function as a guardian angel, staying in touch with what Chris really needs and wants, while taking others into consideration.

Popky (1996) begins his addiction protocol by having the client visualize what her life will be like when healthy motives, rather than unhealthy forces, are guiding her. The function of this technique is to assure the client that she can survive and thrive without the influence of this familiar but destructive force. Chris did eye movements as she imagined how her life could be if she were guided by her Personal Power Goddess. When she was able to visualize how her relationships would look if she were guided by her Personal Power Goddess, it was easier for her to let go of old beliefs that had given inappropriate power to her critic.

Umbrella and Transitional Cognitions

During the next sessions Chris wanted to focus on achieving the belief "I am significant." I asked if there were an image or memory that was representative of her belief "I am insignificant." The primary image that came to mind was that of her childhood loneliness ritual. Although EMDR initially reduced her anxiety when she viewed the loneliness image, her VOC remained low when she thought about her significance in relation to her personal life. When she returned for subsequent sessions, her anxiety about the loneliness image had bounced back up. At first it was puzzling to me that targeting the loneliness image and aiming for the positive cognition "I am significant" was unsuccessful. Examining this "failure" led to my realization that Chris would feel truly significant and safe in her personal life only when she also felt lovable, respectable, and worthy.

As her therapy progressed, a variety of positive cognitions emerged in relation to her marriage, her parents, her children, her friends, and herself. All of these cognitions were contained in the statement "I am significant," which we designated as the *umbrella cognition*. The memory of the loneliness ritual represented her negative cognition "I am insignificant." The desired positive cognition "I am significant" could only feel true to Chris once she had integrated the following *sub-cognitions* that spanned five categories of her life:

- *Marriage:* I am good enough. I deserve to be happy. I deserve to be appreciated and appropriately rewarded for my contributions. I deserve emotional support. I deserve kindness.
- *Parents:* I have value. I have a positive presence in the world. I'm valuable to my family. I can validate myself. I'm fine regardless of how they feel about me. I'm as generous as I can be. I deserve respect for who I am regardless of anyone else's point of view. I am a lovable kid. I deserve to be treated well. I can value my own womanliness.

- *Children:* I deserve to be treated respectfully by my children. I can maintain a respectful attitude towards my children.
- *Friends:* I can be responsible to myself and aware of the needs of others at the same time. I can choose to be around people who respect me.
- *Self:* I am lovable even in my needy, vulnerable state. I can learn how to get in touch with what I want and need. I'm entitled to ask for what I need and want. I deserve to have my healthy needs met. It is safe for me to show who I really am. I can be who I am and ask for what I need in a relationship. I can learn to use my power effectively and lovingly to make good personal choices for my benefit and for other people's benefit.

Looking back at Chris's eight-month process, it is apparent to me that EMDR helped her to clear her anxiety around each of these issues. Subsequently, her anxiety around the core issue represented by the loneliness image began to diminish. After she had integrated each of the desired subcognitions, she was able to view the image of her childhood loneliness ritual calmly and to believe fully, "I am significant."

Throughout Chris's therapy, many transitional cognitions evolved that served her until she began to change the reality of her current situation. For example, her desired cognition that "I am responsible to myself and aware of the needs of others at the same time" did not match her experience with friends. She needed time to practice making decisions that took her own needs into account.

Instead, *transitional cognitions* that felt true and achievable were composed. These usually began with "I'm . . . beginning to . . . learning to . . . practicing . . . working on . . . ." For example, she found it helpful to propose, *"I'm practicing* being responsible to myself and aware of the needs of others at the same time." These transitional cognitions felt congruent with her inner state and afforded her a sense of satisfaction as she worked toward her desired positive cognitions.

The Loneliness Image: Heart of the Tangled Beliefs

Chris ruminated over her childhood ritual of reciting "I am insignificant. I am real." Chris explained that she repeated these phrases like a mantra, as a way of comforting herself. The tangle became apparent: The dissociated "white empty feeling" of being only a tiny shell of a body, linked with the physical sensation of terror, became her evidence that she was truly alive. This realization was simultaneously a comfort and a horror.

The emptiness image, her anxiety, and her entire sense of self were all tied in with the belief that the only thing valuable about her was her ability to take care of others. In childhood, she'd had to take care of her parents. As an adult, she felt obliged to take care of men with whom she had intimate relationships. For Chris, taking care of someone meant vacating her own being.

Even as an adult, feelings of dissociation and extreme anxiety were entangled with the notion of being alive. Whenever Chris felt present and alive, she panicked, feeling she was threatening her survival by acknowledging her perceptions. Paradoxically, only by feeling anxious could she feel safe. As Chris put it, "I was scaring myself into responsibility." Unfortunately, for Chris "responsibility" had the dual meanings of staying alive by taking care of others and taking the blame for whatever went wrong in anyone's life. Chris explained, "I gave up what I wanted in order to survive. I survived by not asking for anything because wanting or needing anything meant that I was crazy and should be locked up. I felt my only choice in life was either having feelings and being locked up or being 'strong' and not having any feelings."

It seems to me that posttraumatic thoughts are sorted into only one of two categories: *true/false, safe/unsafe.* This type of dichotomous thinking would be beneficial in a life-and-death situation where considering the ramifications of a particular decision might waste precious life-saving moments better used for escape. In a true emergency, there is no time for examining gradations of meaning. Just as a human is either alive or dead, posttraumatic thoughts are labeled with absolutes. Posttraumatic Chris felt as if she either could live by suppressing her feelings or die by expressing them.

The Long Road Back from Dissociation

Five sessions into Chris's therapy, after we had established a good working relationship and we both felt confident that she could handle some additional turmoil in her life, we decided to target the "white empty feeling" and the "I am insignificant" ritual with EMDR. I intended to proceed cautiously in this complex case involving some degree of dissociation, although I felt confident that Chris was on the mild end of the dissociative spectrum and that I was prepared to handle her reactions. I hoped that EMDR would help untangle Chris's beliefs that the physical sensations of anxiety meant life and that insignificance meant safety.

Chris focused on the image of the ritual, her negative cognition "I am insignificant," and the "white empty feeling, " and began to move her eyes. Soon she experienced intense panic: Her pounding heart and the feeling of being "really alone" confirmed for her that she was "real." Despite several sets of EMDR, she repeatedly experienced terror as she viewed her childhood recitation. The following is a segment of that session, beginning with my intervention to end her abreaction. It occurred to me that we needed to address Chris's erroneous belief that only anxiety signified that she was alive.

JL: What, besides the anxiety, reassures you that you are really alive?

Chris: ►◄►◄►◄ I bleed. I cry. I feel lonely. ►◄►◄►◄ It's causing me anxiety, but I like it.

JL: How could the anxiety be comforting?

Chris: ►◄►◄►◄ It made me be responsible. Feeling real meant I had to do the responsible thing and take care of others. It meant, *This is not play.* I was scaring myself into being responsible.

JL: Is there anything besides anxiety that makes you feel responsible towards others?

Chris: ►◄►◄►◄ The payoff for being responsible was that I got taken care of. I took pretty good care of myself. There was food in the house, and Mom was there.

JL: Anxiety and responsibility towards others seemed to keep you safe when you were a child. What are your alternatives now?

At this point Chris became very sad as she thought about how inadequate her mother was. She recalled the incident of her mother neglecting to care for her when she cut her foot on glass and needed stitches. We used EMDR to reprocess that memory, but Chris continued to feel intense sadness. Then she thought about her father and traumatic events in his life that had caused his drinking to escalate. Reexperiencing the intense sadness about her parents' lives and their inadequacies, Chris noted that she felt separate from her body. I believed that she was dissociating from the painful memories stored in her body.

JL: Would you like to come back into your body?

Chris: I kind of like the feeling of being separate. I don't want to give it up because what's left is the chaos and stupidity and adults who don't act like adults. . . . I survived. I saved money. I worked.

JL: Think about that.

Chris: ►◄►◄►◄ I feel sad. Their own sadness was so heavy.

JL: Their own sadness wasn't your responsibility and wasn't about you.

Chris: ▶◀▶◀▶◀ Sometimes I take their sadness on. Sometimes I deliberately fight it. My father never got to live his life. I use that feeling to go after what I want. ▶◀▶◀▶◀ I have the feeling of turning their negative energy into my positive energy. [*She indicates that she feels this transformation going on in her head.*] ▶◀▶◀▶◀ I hate injustice. I don't like to be dependent, and all that's a reaction to them. I got an education. Mother never understood it—she didn't even send a card to acknowledge my college graduation. Father doesn't even know who his children married!

JL: Looking back at the original incident we started with today, how upsetting does it look?

So many memories about Chris's parents had surfaced that I wanted to be sure that the processing was still related to the original target. I was concerned that Chris not get flooded by anxiety arising from issues that were not necessary to process at this time. I decided to redirect Chris to the image of her childhood ritual and her experience of the "white empty feeling."

Chris: I feel about half as anxious as I did when we started. I feel vaguely disconnected, but less than before. My parents exhausted me. I always did that ritual before I went to bed. I thought, "Take control here, Chris." I saw a lot of stupid adults. The guy downstairs beat his wife, I saw children abused, my sister got molested when she was five. Another sister got hit by a car and our parents didn't do anything—that sister is now a drug addict. My parents' attitude was "Oh, well, get over it." No one was valued.

JL: Can you imagine valuing yourself as a child? [*I wanted to mobilize Chris's adult resources to repair the deficits left by her childhood experience of not being valued.*]

Chris: ▶◀▶◀▶◀ I bought myself my first coat by saving the money myself.

JL: Can you imagine being the parent you needed as a child? ▶◀▶◀▶◀ [*Chris nods.*]

I encouraged Chris to practice parenting herself, to give herself the tenderness and understanding that she had needed as a child but had not received. If a client is unable to do this for herself, I step in as her surrogate parent, offering kindness, patience, soothing, and appreciation, so that she has the experience of being accepted, even with all of her needy, whimpering, vulnerable feelings.

Chris: She just needs someone to be with her.

JL: Can you imagine giving her all the care you needed and deserved?

Chris: ▶◀▶◀▶◀ [*nodding*] I stayed sensitive.

Chris said this lovingly and appreciatively. I viewed this statement as an indication that she was beginning to accept, even cherish, her vulnerable feelings, because before this moment, Chris had viewed her sensitivity as a weakness.

JL: Would you like to thank yourself for that?

Chris: ►◄►◄►◄ [*nodding*] I want to thank myself for graduating from college. ►◄►◄►◄ I wake up every morning and thank myself. ►◄►◄►◄ I learned from reading. ►◄►◄►◄ I want to thank myself for learning. ►◄►◄►◄

Closing an Incomplete Session

By the end of this session the original scene still elicited anxiety, but about half as much as when we started. The desired cognition "I am a significant person" felt "more than half true." I was concerned about Chris having to go for two weeks between sessions after this incomplete one. I asked if she could imagine putting all of the experiences away until she returned to my office. I then asked if she had an image to remind her that she had survived, and that she could work on these old memories, in her own way, at the appropriate time, when we were together again. Chris remembered herself as a young girl, wearing the cowgirl boots she had wanted and gotten, prancing in the vacant lot on the crushed glass and reveling in her own spirit, feeling wild and free. We used EMDR to reinforce the image and her life-affirming feeling. I reminded Chris to call me if she wanted to see me sooner than our next scheduled appointment.

Beginning Integration of Her Tough Exterior
and Her Vulnerable Interior

In the next visit, her sixth session, Chris chose to focus on her belief that she was unlovable. I asked her if she had an early memory that represented this belief. She remembered attending one dance in junior high and then never going to another. The dance wasn't fun for her, and she had felt awkward and ugly. When Chris shared those feelings with her mother, her mother had screamed, "Life is tougher than one stupid dance!"

We reprocessed that anxiety-provoking memory and, again, Chris found it useful to imagine that she was the adult responding to the sensitive adolescent. "I'd get her a haircut and buy her some new clothes," Chris offered.

Then she felt overwhelmed with sadness when she remembered that, as a child and adolescent, she had never gotten any encouragement or positive attention for her feelings. Sometimes she felt, "Life is not worth it because I can't even make these folks [referring to her parents as well as her current and former husbands] love me." We used EMDR to target the sadness. For best results, it is important to fully reprocess the feelings (and their location in the body) as well as the memory.

Chris realized that she usually acted as if she wasn't bothered by anything, because she didn't want to risk having her feelings rejected. She claimed that she was always shocked when people, even her own daughter and husband, accused her of not needing them. The following is an excerpt of a session in which Chris began the process of integrating her "tough" exterior with her "vulnerable" internal part. I simply asked Chris to move her eyes while she paid attention to the two parts of herself that she had been describing.

Chris: I'm shocked people don't get it when I'm miserable. ►◄►◄►◄ It's like there are two people. The person people respond to—they think I'm strong. But there's a part of me that doesn't feel strong at all. [*Chris looked at me questioningly.*]

JL: Would you like for the strong part to talk with the part that doesn't feel that way? [*I thought that Chris's strong part could teach the part of her that didn't feel strong. Chris nods.*]

Chris: ►◄►◄►◄ Both parts are part of who I am. I need to believe it.

JL: Where do you feel it coming together?

Chris: ►◄►◄►◄ I have a fear of acknowledging the vulnerable part because I'm afraid people will respond the way my mother did. I wonder what it would feel like to be with myself in that place and not to be uncomfortable. ►◄►◄►◄ It's hard.

JL: Can you be there for just one minute? [*I wondered if Chris needed to test whether she could trust me to accept her while she felt vulnerable.*]

Chris: ►◄►◄►◄ I get to be just the way I am. [*smiles*] ►◄►◄►◄ The not having to do any activity. Just being. ►◄►◄►◄ Say—this is it—to be, and not to have to judge or get cranked into activity ►◄►◄►◄ It would be nice not to have judging voices.

JL: Does your strength come from you or from the judging voices?

Chris: ►◄►◄►◄ No, there isn't any value to the voices. ►◄►◄►◄

Chris laughed as she recalled a nun telling her that God loved her more than he loved the Catholic kids. She then remembered her oldest child saying "I love you" to her, just the day before. Looking back on the original incident of the junior high dance, Chris felt relaxed and comfortable. As we linked the original image of the dance, the feeling, and the cognition "I am lovable" with EMDR, Chris said, "I feel like a really lovable kid. It's nice to get a balance from hearing that I'm lovable inside myself and from people who know me." Chris felt "good" and "protective" of her vulnerable, sensitive kid-self.

The Current Reality

After eight EMDR sessions that ended positively, Chris had achieved some clear gains: deeper understanding, increasing confidence, clearer sense of self, and fewer panic attacks. However, she continued to experience marked shifts in mood, usually mirroring another person's emotional volatility. When her mother had a heart attack and lamented that life didn't feel worth living, Chris abruptly panicked and was flooded by suicidal feelings. When she began to spend time with a man who liked her, she felt giddily happy. When her children expressed dismay about her bringing a new person into their lives, however, her mood plummeted downward. When the husband she was divorcing moved in with another woman and sued Chris, she felt despondent about her own life and considered moving away. When he later talked about them getting back together, she felt dismayed at the possibility of "losing" herself again.

When I asked Chris what she needed to help her feel more certain that she would not "lose herself" again, she answered that she had to finalize her divorce and begin to demand respectful behavior from her teenage children. We came up with the idea of a *Campaign for Respect* that involved laying out guidelines for clear and respectful communication with her husband regarding co-parenting concerns and with her children for polite behavior. Chris, eager to have her own children feel free to express their feelings, had allowed them to become verbally abusive to her. We discussed how children can learn to express their feelings and be respectful at the same time. I conferred with Chris's regular therapist, and she agreed to assist Chris in implementing her Campaign for Respect.

Chris also began to spend time working alone in her garden. Her reward was a yard of beautiful flowers and an increasing sense of "grounding" in her body. We used EMDR to enhance these rewards.

JL: Where in your body do you experience the feeling of being in the garden?
Chris: ►◄►◄► In my shoulders . . . I feel so peaceful.

JL: Stay with that.

Chris: ►◄►◄►◄ I'm thinking about how well I take care of plants. It doesn't take a lot to make a lot of beauty. ►◄►◄►◄ I should treat myself the way I take care of my plants.

JL: Where in your body do you feel that?

Chris: ►◄►◄►◄ In my chest. ►◄►◄►◄ One can do that for oneself.

JL: Stay with that.

Chris: ►◄►◄►◄ I feel it in my abdomen. ►◄►◄►◄ It's a nice image. ►◄►◄►◄ Taking care of yourself is giving other folks something, too. Now I know what it feels like when the somatic part and the psychic part are in the same vessel.

Reprocessing Childhood Traumas

Chris gradually negotiated the seemingly treacherous and perplexing puzzles of her childhood with characteristic courage. She diligently reprocessed childhood memories as they came to her in dreams, thoughts, and feelings. As she remembered a day in 11th grade when she'd walked the halls alone and felt that she didn't fit in, she became extremely anxious. The beliefs she still held about herself were "I'm not good enough. I don't fit in. I'm invisible. I don't exist." Her desired cognitions were "I am good enough. I can take care of myself in that situation. I'm significant." She reexperienced the empty, lonely, floating feeling of not being connected and processed enormous anger and profound sadness, finally beginning to feel compassion for herself. Again, Chris thanked herself for surviving.

Beginning in this session, Chris also painstakingly worked through several memories of her father yelling at her when she was a young child, stimulating the now-familiar cognitions "I am insignificant. I'm invisible. I don't exist." This time the desired positive cognitions were "I have value. I have a positive presence in the world. I am learning to be around people who value me." Yet again Chris experienced "all that loneliness; no way out," and the terrible despair of not wanting to live. She felt responsible for her younger brothers and sisters. She took on the burden of everyone's pain. In our sessions, as Chris voiced her anger, she gradually stepped into the present.

Chris: ►◄►◄►◄ [*She clutches her throat as she envisions talking to her father.*] Start acting like an adult. ►◄►◄►◄ Take a look. See your children ►◄►◄►◄

JL: What comes up for you now as you look back at the original incident?

Chris: I wish I weren't there. I want to be here now. ►◄►◄►◄ I love my bed. I'm very safe there. ►◄►◄►◄ I thank myself for surviving.

JL: Going back to the original incident, how upsetting does it look now?

Chris: About half as upsetting as when we started, but I still feel sad and angry in my gut. ►◄►◄►◄ I feel angry in my heart and in my eyes. It's similar to the anger I felt in my second and third marriages.

JL: What does the angry, sad, hurt part of you need?

Chris: ►◄►◄►◄ All levels of appreciation. ►◄►◄►◄ I can be more open and recognize the feelings of being valued and appreciated. ►◄►◄►◄ I like that. I want that.

JL: Do you want to promise yourself that it's your intention to notice when you are valued? [*It seemed to me that Chris needed experience judging when people really valued her, as opposed to only needing her and being willing to use her.*]

Chris: ►◄►◄►◄ [*nodding*] I don't feel as needy. I feel like, "Yes! I can do this." ►◄►◄►◄ There are opportunities available to me. I can recognize, go for, and feel those valued feelings. ►◄►◄►◄ I can even feel my value as a woman. ►◄►◄►◄

JL: How does the original incident look now?

Chris: I still feel sadness in my stomach. ►◄►◄►◄ I missed an opportunity when I was little. I can try to learn now. ►◄►◄►◄ A little voice just said, "Now you can do it as an adult." ►◄►◄►◄ It's only a little upsetting looking back at it now. ►◄►◄►◄ I had a very nice image of being like a ghost and walking right through my dad, out the door, and into the present. ►◄►◄►◄ It feels too good to stop. ►◄►◄►◄ I have a positive presence in the world. ►◄►◄►◄ I am learning to be around people who value me. ►◄►◄►◄ Feels good.

Here: Reunited

Several more intense sessions of EMDR applied to memories of childhood scenes with Chris's parents yielded definite progress. She extended the Campaign for Respect to include a campaign for self-respect. Finally, Chris made this proclamation:

Chris: The desperation is not there any more. I don't feel I'm trying to fill a bottomless pit. The lid is on the pit and now I can really appreciate the good feelings I deserve. Boundaries are a lot clearer. I accept myself more. I feel good that this is who I am. I've accomplished a lot. . . . I feel incredibly fortunate. I really value who I am and what I have. I am exactly where I want to be, except I'd prefer to be in an intimate relationship. It feels like I can finally make decisions. I really feel I have personal power. There's an acuity thing. Things are sharper. Even driving to work—I can *really feel* the steering wheel. When I walk down the street, I can *really feel* the sidewalk under my feet. It feels very good. It feels like an exciting journey. So much has changed.

I understood these experiences as indications that Chris was no longer dissociated. Chris said that she felt ready to decrease the frequency of her visits to once a month. I agreed that it made sense for her to stabilize and enjoy her newly achieved feeling of being "whole and present" before she continued reprocessing childhood memories. I also wanted to support her judgment about what she needed for herself. When she returned, she wanted to use EMDR to work on more memories of her dad. Excerpts from that session follow.

Chris: I have a memory of my dad, sober, sitting in front of the TV, with his dinner on the stool in front of him, and the paper and books around him. I was eight or nine years old. His attitude was, "It's none of your business. Go away." It made me think "I have no value. I can't be heard." He shut me out. I want to believe that I do have value. Picturing it makes me feel loneliness, depression, and sadness.

JL: Where do you feel those feelings in your body?

Chris: In my eyes. ►◄►◄►◄ I feel inadequate as a parent. ►◄►◄►◄ I feel an overwhelming sense of not being able to meet somebody's needs. ►◄►◄►◄ I have a hard time looking at it—I want to change the scene— I don't want it to be that way. ►◄►◄►◄ I have that caged animal feeling. I can't get what I want.

JL: Whose responsibility was it? [*I introduced a cognitive interweave because I sensed that the process was beginning to loop and that Chris needed some grounding.*]

Chris: My dad's. I feel it in my eyes. ►◄►◄►◄ I don't mind the sadness. It's the other stuff, like "I'm not good enough." ►◄►◄►◄ It's very sad because his children are a lot like him, and he could have shared a lot of good things. I did enjoy the things he enjoyed. ►◄►◄►◄ We had some similar interests. I feel the loneliness in my stomach. ►◄►◄►◄ As a teen, there were no adults there for me. ►◄►◄►◄ There were five kids in my family and every weekend we had to leave home because he was drunk. ►◄►◄►◄ I got a good thing out of that—I don't do that with people. I appreciate my ability to empathize and reach out. ►◄►◄►◄ I don't want to lose empathy. I do want to lose being depressed and blaming.

JL: How would an adult make a child feel accepted and, at the same time, not too responsible?

Chris: ►◄►◄►◄ You could talk with them. You could let them know that what you're struggling with has nothing to do with them.

JL: Would you like to imagine yourself as a child and giving yourself what you need?

Chris: I would invite the child in. ►◄►◄►◄ I can see myself with my dad. He is inviting me in and talking about my day and giving me the choice of staying with him while he reads.

JL: Think about having choices. [*I employed the cognitive interweave to bring Chris back to the present.*]

Chris: ►◄►◄►◄ [*smiles*] When I was a teenager, I used to pack up my things and pretend I had places to go. Mom called it crazy.

JL: You were practicing! You knew that you would have choices eventually. Do you have choices now?

Chris: ►◄►◄►◄ Yes. I don't even have to get involved. ►◄►◄►◄ I can remember doing things with him when I was younger, more playful kinds of things. ►◄►◄►◄ [*smiles*] I still feel sad. It's been a confusion. I've struggled for a long time to say what I feel without getting depressed. If I don't say what I feel, it's not healthy and I get depressed. If I say what I feel, I get it reflected back and get depressed. It would be ideal to be able to say it and not have all the other stuff. ►◄►◄►◄ I want to experience that feeling—of not feeling my body is full of open pores.

JL: Your skin is a good analogy for your personal boundary. Skin is a perfect covering for your body because it is selectively permeable; it keeps out what's harmful but keeps in essential body fluids. Would you like to think about your skin protecting you by being selective? Think about how that protection and regulation go on naturally and automatically.

Chris: ►◄►◄►◄ [*She nods.*] That will be nice to practice. ►◄►◄►◄ There is just some sadness left, no anxiety. I can picture my dad a little better, and it is sad. ►◄►◄►◄ I can practice and learn! ►◄►◄►◄ It feels true that I do have value. ►◄►◄►◄ I can learn and practice. ►◄►◄►◄ I can have fun and make appropriate choices automatically. It's an intrinsic value that doesn't have to do with my ability to get my parents to be different. That feels life-affirming. I feel it in my stomach. ►◄►◄►◄ It's good. One feels compassion for them. ►◄►◄►◄ I'm going to forgive myself. ►◄►◄►◄ It's OK for me to be learning this.

The cognitive interweaves I used in this session—"Whose responsibility was it?" "How would an adult make a child feel accepted?" "Think about having choices"—were all intended to assist Chris in adopting an adult perspective as she viewed her relationship with her father. Following this session, Chris called her father for the first time in years and they talked about her teenage child. Chris was amazed that she didn't feel anxious about making the call and even more amazed that her father listened to her. She planned to visit him later that week. I thought that the visit would help Chris appreciate the reality of how different her adult position was from the old, dependent, fearful position of childhood.

A Stronger Sense of Self

Chris now found herself frequently having a strong desire to be by herself. She began to treasure moments alone. She exclaimed that she was really enjoying herself. She recognized that she was accepting memories as part of her life and was still able to live in the present. Finally, a month later, Chris wanted to confront a memory of her father when he was drunk.

Chris recalled that as a preteen and adolescent, she had dealt with her father's drunkenness either by becoming totally enraged or running away from it.

Chris: As an adult you have many more options. The ultimate one is removing yourself. As an adult you can say, "You need help" or "This is what you can do" or "This is what I can do." As a kid you can't do that. It always comes back to, "Where are you going to live? Where are you going to go?"

Chris targeted the image of her father at the bottom of the stairs screaming obscenities at his children, as Chris and her siblings struggled to barricade themselves from him. Chris was quickly inundated with feelings of total despair and depression, which she located in her eyes. Her negative cognitions were: "I deserve to be treated that way," "I'm powerless and I can't stop it," "I'm despicable as a woman." Her desired cognitions were: "I deserve to be treated well," "I want to give it back to him," "The problem doesn't belong to us," "I have the power to choose who I'm going to spend time with," "I can value my own womanliness."

Chris: ►◄►◄►◄ I feel terribly upset and angry. ►◄►◄►◄ I wonder what it would have been like to have a loving father. ►◄►◄►◄ What a loss. He didn't have a clue. ►◄►◄►◄ I wanted male affection. I had it more when I was younger. I remember going over to a friend's house, and her father saw me and said, "Give my buddy Chris some ice cream." He knew we couldn't afford it at my house. They even took me on vacation with them. ►◄►◄►◄ I had some male teachers who gave me appropriate attention. ►◄►◄►◄ I used to pray for my father to stop being an alcoholic, but I gave up. Then I began to pray, "At least get me through this." I had to give up something of myself to get that strength.

JL: What do you have to give up?

Chris: The right to want my feelings. I gave up what I wanted in order to survive. ►◄►◄►◄ I look back at the scene and I wish it had been different. It happened. It's part of who I am. I would have wanted it differently, but it wasn't. I want something now. ►◄►◄►◄ I feel like, for the first time, I'm saying what my mother didn't say: "You were appropriate." ►◄►◄►◄ This is too good! I want someone to listen, talk, ask about school, be interested.

JL: Was that appropriate? Healthy?

Chris: Yes.

JL: What was crazy here? [*This cognitive interweave was intended to help Chris validate her own feelings.*]

Chris: ►◄►◄►◄ Not getting those needs met! ►◄►◄►◄ I don't get upset looking at the original incident. It's sad that I wanted those things and didn't get them then, but because I thought I had survived by not wanting them, I never got them from any male.

JL: Give yourself some compassion. It is sad . . . and you did survive . . . .

Chris: ►◄►◄►◄ It feels completely true that I deserve to be treated well. I deserve to treat myself well. ►◄►◄►◄ I'm practicing using my power to choose with whom I'm going to spend my time. ►◄►◄►◄ I'm practicing *choosing*. ►◄►◄►◄ I'm learning to feel comfortable with my power to choose. ►◄►◄►◄ I'm learning to value my own womanliness. ►◄►◄►◄

In her next to last session Chris targeted memories of her pregnancies, and used EMDR to confirm her feelings that she does deserve to be loved and cared for when she's in need, and she does deserve to have people help her. In her final session with me that year, Chris summed up her current experience: "Looking back at the picture of being in bed and doing the loneliness ritual, it doesn't make the white hole it used to make. Last night I was lonely, but it seemed appropriate. I could bring up the picture of the ritual but not create the sensation of it. I am significant. I can really feel things now. I have a much more realistic view of what's important. I still feel like I'm integrating all this. When I don't do it right, I'm forgiving to myself and say, 'Next time, I can try again!'"

Follow-Up

Ten months later Chris returned for two sessions, saying she wanted to work a little more on personal relationships. (She had been taking only 10 mg of Prozac every other day and felt ready to stop.) She had written a letter to a suitor, telling him clearly that she was only interested in a friendship. She loved being alone and treasured her time by herself. Recently she had met Tom, whom she found very attractive. This new boyfriend was very intense and demanding of Chris's time. Chris added, "I'm content and happy with who I am and what I am. He adds excitement." Although Chris felt lovable, she was concerned that feeling loving might mean that she had to give up her wonderful new sense of self.

Chris: I want my separate life, but I also want to do new and exciting things with Tom. I want to understand what my needs are. I want to decide what is best for myself in my own time and my own way. I want to be very clear. I want to be able to say, "This is what I'm willing to do for the relationship." . . . [*reaffirming*] Having myself is more important to me than anything. I'm not willing to give up what I've gained in terms of loving myself, being clear, and responding to my own needs. I want to maintain a sense of loving myself.

Chris explained her current dilemma. She felt old childhood issues triggered by having a man want her in his life.

Chris: It feels like I have a choice of being like Mom or like Dad. It feels like Dad satisfied all his own needs. He bought alcohol for himself, instead of using money for his own children. Mom played the withholding, suffering martyr. Loving her meant feeling sorry, obligated, and guilty. If you meet your own needs in a love relationship, that means you're selfish—like Dad. If you sacrifice yourself in an intimate relationship, that means you're a martyr—like Mom. [*balancing the picture*] Dad was self-educated. He loved learning. Mom was a people person. She loved taking care of babies and tending the garden.

Chris decided to use EMDR to focus on her parents. I suggested that she move her eyes back and forth as if looking from one parent to the other. I thought that this technique might help Chris to view her parents as separate from herself and to sort out which of her parents' characteristics she would like to retain and which ones she would leave with them.

Chris: My parents do what they loved. ►◄►◄►◄ It's sad they couldn't do what they loved. ►◄►◄►◄ [*Although these statements may seem contradictory, I think Chris was presenting two perspectives on her parents' lives, confirming that her parents made their own choices, and perhaps implying that she was free to make choices in her own life.*] I'm grateful for my life. ►◄►◄►◄ I've been lucky. ►◄►◄►◄ I can see them both now. I can feel and be there, but I don't have to react. I can see what's theirs, what's mine. ►◄►◄►◄ I feel empowered.

This was the end of our work together. Chris was pleased that she felt so much clearer about what really belonged to her and what didn't. She had realized for the first time, "I don't only exist because I'm a mother, or because I'm in or out of a relationship, or because I do well at my job." She affirmed that her feelings now came from inside herself and didn't come from external sources. She clearly felt "real," and she felt strong. She was getting ready to practice being her real self and being involved in an intimate relationship at the same time.

Summary

Chris was a 44-year-old woman who had extremely low self-esteem, depression, panic attacks, and symptoms of dissociation when she began EMDR-facilitated therapy. Eye movement was used initially to reinforce healthy beliefs, physical sensations, and feelings related to experiences of safety, competence, well-being, and success based on prior learning. EMDR was then employed to target painful memories of childhood scenes with her parents, as well as erroneous beliefs and feelings of intense anxiety. Although none of the memories targeted occurred before age five, the "white empty feeling" that was targeted seemed to represent the earlier deprivation. The desired positive cognition "I am significant" became the "umbrella cognition" containing various *sub-cognitions* (such as "I am lovable," "I deserve respect," and "I can take care of my needs").

As Chris reprocessed traumatic childhood memories with EMDR, more and more of these sub-cognitions were integrated. Progress was not linear, but reprocessing the client's issues as she presented them gradually led to a width:1102px; height:1615px

more stable, flexible, and resilient sense of self. Eventually, the negative self-assessments dissipated. After 18 sessions Chris felt strong and confident, fully present, and eager to be involved in intimate relationships that were based on mutual respect.

Follow-up two years after beginning therapy confirmed the effectiveness of Chris's work. She continued to feel confident and healthy, had established a satisfying, intimate relationship, and had received two raises at work, which she attributed to her increased ability to be fully present when she related to colleagues and clients.

References

Popky, A. (1996, July). *Addiction protocol*. Paper presented at Annual EMDRIA Conference, Denver, CO.

12

TREATING A HIGHLY DEFENDED CLIENT
Reworking Traditional Approaches

David C. Manfield

IN 1991 I RECEIVED some promotional literature for the first EMDR training in my community of Portland, Oregon. It included a letter from a local
psychologist touting the effectiveness of EMDR and a copy of Francine
Shapiro's early study (Shapiro, 1989) describing eye movement desensitization [EMD] a revolutionary new technique involving eye movements for
treating trauma. My background was eclectic and I am always interested in
effective ways to treat trauma, so I was intrigued. I wondered, however, why
a training was necessary to learn to wave one's finger in front of a client,
particularly as it appeared to me that the procedure was clearly described in
Shapiro's study. I proceeded on my own, experimenting with several of
my clients who were willing to try something new, albeit experimental, that
might work for them. The results were mixed but encouraging enough that
I decided shortly thereafter to take the training.

I found out that there was a little more to EMDR than I had realized.
Since then I have successfully used EMDR with a variety of clients and
looked for new ways to integrate the procedure into my clinical work. For
example, I have found that highly defended clients (always a challenging
client population for me to work with) can benefit from EMDR. William
was one such client for whom the use of EMDR posed several problems.
Presenting multiple defenses and substantial initial resistance to EMDR, I
believe his treatment illustrates common pitfalls and offers strategies for
using this special technique with difficult clients.

Client's Presenting Problem and Case Formulation

On initial presentation William described lifelong and severe inhibitions that included a problem urinating in public bathrooms (paruresis). In addition, he complained about profound social alienation and low self-worth, expressing deeply cynical views about humankind and his capacity to relate to others. He described his problems in the first session as follows:

> For about as long as I can remember, I've believed that something is wrong with me. In fact, probably more than one thing is wrong with me. I have this fear in the bathroom that makes it impossible for me to use a urinal if someone is in the vicinity, sometimes even if they're just outside. If they're in the room with me, I think they're watching. I somehow think they have some power over me, that they could hurt me or punish me, and it frightens me.
>
> In general, people frighten me a lot. I'd rather be alone. I just don't think people are a very compassionate bunch. What would my friends think of me if they knew that I have this problem? I wonder if they'd still like me. I doubt that I could feel like anyone's equal if this problem were on the table. Frankly, I think people are basically cruel. That's why my social life is so limited. I've only got a few friends, none of them very close.
>
> I don't think people understand me. This problem sets me apart. I'm different. I admit I'm sensitive about it, and quite honestly, I'm probably a little too thin-skinned. But, truthfully, I think people would ostracize me if they knew, like the Beta monkey in those studies of dominance. The weakest gets the scraps. Actually, people seem to ostracize me anyway. I think they can sense my lack of confidence, my discomfort, and they instinctively reject me.
>
> There are other things, too. I'm not very happy, and I rarely really enjoy myself. When I watch other people, I can't help comparing myself with them—how much happier and contented they seem to be with their lives. They have families to go home to, and loving partners with whom to share their lives. I basically have my work, and that's about it.

Ostensibly, William had initiated therapy to solve his "bathroom problem." However, the possibility of a future without relationships loomed just as large. In spite of his extreme loneliness, he could not establish meaningful contact with others. William traveled often, but almost always alone. Occasionally, he'd hike with one or two individuals he'd met on his travels, but these relationships never seemed to develop. William viewed this as evidence that he was inherently unattractive and uninteresting to others, though the isolation was more likely the result of fear of criticism and attack and the shame and anger that permeated his object relations.

Highly analytical, with a profound need to externalize his problems, William had developed elaborate defensive explanations for his isolation. He had rationalized his fears in the context of his social phobia. He believed he could not risk socializing with others for fear he might need to use a rest room and, failing success, embarrass himself horribly. This problem became the focal point of his existence, making it impossible for him to manage a friendship without potential alienation and perpetuating his sense of being different, foolish, and at risk for ridicule and annihilation. At 40 years of age, William had had no sexual intimacy, though he longed for it.

William believed that his parents must have shamed him during toilet training and therefore concluded that his condition was programmed too early in life to be treatable. In general, he viewed his parents as shaming and intrusive. Moralistic, punitive, and self-righteous, they used intimidation and neglect as key methods of control. William was not allowed to complain; to do so risked his father's wrath. Appearance was everything. Apart from his grades in school, in which he was expected to excel, William was essentially ignored. Meals were provided, but William was otherwise on his own, left to figure life out by himself. Assertiveness was quashed, expression of emotion punished. William's anger, in particular, was considered unacceptable. He learned to live his emotional life internally, viewing relationships as threatening to his very existence.

William's identification with his problem helped him rationalize his social inhibitions and protected him from internalized and denied terror and rage from his early upbringing. His social phobia allowed him to externalize his problem; "the sphincter simply won't relax." Surely, he believed, he would have many friends and lovers were it not for this problem. This client's self-image required the maintenance of this symptom to defend against the revelation that without it, he must confront the terror of intimacy and the potential criticism this might entail.

William had adopted a submissive/subordinate role in his relationships to ensure his safety and minimize the possibility of attack. He poignantly described himself:

> You know, I'm smaller than most, and just once, I'd like to turn the table on those who ridiculed me for it. Kick some dirt in their faces. Teach them what it's like to feel inferior. It's an unfair universe, and just once I'd like to be on top. There was a time when I tried to act tough, be the intimidator, push people out of my way. I was looking for respect, but it

just made people angry. I've given up on that one. But I guess I'm different from the subordinate monkeys; I may be jealous of the leaders, I understand they can hurt me, but I don't respect them.

William finds himself enslaved by his relationships and only rarely allows himself to fantasize being the dominant and physical intimidator. This uncomfortable dynamic gets played out frequently in the work place when he is faced with colleagues' demands he considers unfair and demeaning. Yet he puts in extra hours in the attempt to please others to win their favor, not just avoid their wrath. The subtext, however, is that William becomes angry when people treat him as a subordinate. Some of this anger leaks, and he is greatly embarrassed by it. EMDR has been useful in helping William target those moments when demands are made on him, and he has been able to establish alternative responses that "get rid of those laws altogether" and promote his sense of self as reasonably strong, entitled, and assertive.

Preparation: Safe Place

Ordinarily, developing the safe place is a fairly brief and useful intervention for closing down the unfinished treatment hour or when the client is overwhelmed with the material that is emerging. As Andrew Leeds has suggested in personal conversation, the safe place is also a wonderful diagnostic tool. Lower functioning clients will sometimes have difficulty imagining a psychologically safe place, and considerable time and attention may be required to establish it. William, for example, is caught in the never-ending cycle of seeking intimacy, then withdrawing from it out of fear for his safety. He initially imagined himself on an isolated mountainside, away from the dangers of relatedness, but after a moment, found the isolation intolerable. The best he could muster was a marginal image of relatedness; he, on the mountainside, a few people on the horizon, sufficiently distant to provide safety from attack while avoiding absolute and desperate isolation. This unusual safe place illustrated his core relationship issue, which would play itself out in the therapeutic relationship in the form of approach and avoidance.

Phase One: Initial Protocol and Treatment Failure

William had attempted therapy for his social phobia on two prior occasions without successful outcome. One of these terms of treatment was with an

EMDR clinician who used several behavioral approaches as well as the EMDR, including hypnosis, in vivo desensitization, and systematic desensitization (Wolpe, 1958), with no significant improvement noted.

After William established the safe place, my initial intervention targeted the presenting symptom directly. I asked William to focus on the moment of greatest anxiety when, standing before the urinal, he experiences an acute self-consciousness, a keen awareness of anyone present or approaching, and the ever-present fear of humiliation, should he fail to urinate appropriately. In this case, as is typical in a public bathroom, William's negative cognition was "I am in danger." Though he seemed to gain insight occasionally and sometimes associated to earlier childhood experiences, no substantive symptomatic change occurred.

Since targeting the symptom seemed to have no obvious benefit, I elected to target events from the past that seemed to have some bearing on the problem. We conducted an extensive clinical history, as William recalled his earliest memories of feeling self-conscious in bathrooms. He recalled avoiding school clubs and activities as a teenager and suspected that his current bathroom concerns were probably related to this. Generally the memories were speculative and emotionally remote. Processing these "memories" with EMDR was generally unproductive.

I then revisited systematic desensitization, with a twist. Because systematic desensitization is commonly employed (see Zgourides, 1987) for this particular problem, and because William had no apparent success with this procedure, I attempted a variation, using EMDR as part of the desensitization process. I asked William to identify a hierarchy of increasingly threatening situations, where it would become progressively less likely that he would be able to urinate. The hierarchy of fears began with urinating at home alone, later included using the bathroom with a good friend in the apartment, and, in the most extreme example, urinating at an open urinal in a crowded sports arena bathroom. As prescribed by Wolpe's original protocol (Wolpe, 1958), the client pairs the least anxiety-inducing image with deeper relaxation, until the relaxation can be sustained without anxiety. I asked William to identify the negative beliefs that he typically associated with the fear, and I initiated eye movement. Unfortunately, as elegant and promising as this approach appeared to be, the outcome was the same: William was unable to eliminate the anxiety completely for even the most non-threatening of imagined situations.

The problem was further exacerbated by William's need for control. He frequently interrupted the process just as we were to begin the eye-movement procedure. He would often initiate the treatment hour with some new concept he'd picked up on the Internet or read in a book. For a while he was convinced that he had a rare genetic anomaly, then later certain that his issues were those of codependency. He insisted that I read the materials he'd uncovered and discuss them at length. As a result we rarely had enough time remaining in our sessions to initiate EMDR. Although desperate for connection but terrified by it, he continually modulated his cooperation and participation by explanations, elaborations, and tangents to establish himself as neither too close nor too distant from me.

Phase Two: Establishing the Alliance

The failure of the desensitization approach highlights what I see as a key concern when working with the highly defended individual: The client must cooperate and take initiative in treatment; an adequate treatment alliance must be established. I suspect that the protocol I had developed would have been effective in most cases of paruresis. But EMDR is no different from any other modality, in that a therapeutic alliance is necessary and may take weeks, if not months, to establish.

After eight sessions of weekly treatment, though familiarity and some trust had been established, William continued to obstruct EMDR by intellectualizing and elaborating endlessly. Drawing attention to the pattern, I wondered aloud to what extent fear might be playing a part in this. This simple interpretation seemed to make an impression. In the weeks that followed, William made a concerted effort to initiate EMDR earlier in the hour. After three months of therapy, a meaningful therapeutic alliance had been established, characterized by cognitive and emotional continuity across sessions, with EMDR as the focal modality.

Phase Three: Isolating the Core Targets
and Points of Intervention

As I noted earlier, identifying appropriate targets for EMDR was somewhat difficult. William had no specific memories associated with bathroom trauma and did not respond to behavioral targets associated with the symptom in any significant way.

In contrast, focusing on characterological issues provided a structure for identifying meaningful targets and consistent interventions that, over time, seemed to deepen the work and address issues that appeared at least indirectly relevant to his presenting problem. From an object relations perspective, William's primary issues seemed to be narcissistic with schizoid elements, manifested by extreme caution about, if not outright fear of, relationship, exquisite sensitivity to criticism, and pervasive control of affect. Understanding the characterological issues helped in identifying the key cognitive issues and recurring mini-traumas William seemed to struggle with daily. For example, I targeted all issues pertaining to relationship and the negative beliefs and affects associated with them. I targeted his narcissistic fear of criticism, low self-worth, shame, as well the schizoid fears of isolation and loss of control. The negative beliefs seeming to reverberate through the work included "I am out of control," "I am worthless and defective," and "I am in danger/will be destroyed."

Characterological issues also helped inform the timing of EMDR interventions. The schizoid dimension was played out by William's need for contact and meaningful relationship, counterbalanced by the fear of being attacked or ignored. Consequently, there was a fairly active pattern of approach and withdrawal within and outside the therapy. Once identified, these shifts allowed us to confront the withdrawal and the underlying material that might have evoked it. In addition, I watched for fleeting moments of affect. An expression of feeling, closeness, or spontaneity was typically followed by dysphoric affect, a pattern initially discussed in the EMDR context by Philip Manfield (1995). Though William could barely sustain the emotion long enough to target it, these flashes of affect were often productive points for EMDR intervention.

William would often complete a set of eye movements that appeared to move him emotionally, only to disavow or deny its significance during the feedback. Sometimes the affect would appear dysphoric, but the feedback following the eye movement would be tangential or analytical. At such times it was critical to pick up the affective thread in any way possible, if only to return to the original target. In the following excerpt, the client describes the fear he experiences with the hiring of a new coworker.

William: It feels like fear, it feels like it's uncomfortable. It's unsettling. It's like, sometimes I fear that I'm going to meet people and they won't like me. I mean, there's a fear in there somewhere.

DM: Do you have a particular scenario that you can use to focus on when you feel particularly afraid?

William: Well, there was this occasion when my coworkers invited George out for lunch. There was the instant thought that they may or may not invite me along, and I felt paralyzed in fear.

DM: Fine. What's the negative belief you presently hold about yourself that you associate with that image?

William: I don't know, it's too obscure. There's like a panic.

While, in general, it's worthwhile to take as much time as necessary to identify the appropriate negative belief, this may not always be practical. I have been willing to trade an accurate negative cognition for affective continuity and a deepening of experience. As William was rarely so concrete about a fearful event, I felt it critical to follow the affective thread and risk proposing the negative cognition myself.

DM: I'm going to guess that the negative belief is "I'm in danger." [*William gave a nod of agreement, but his need to please left me unsure of this response.*] And the positive cognition you'd like to replace it with?

William: "I am safe."

Eliciting the positive cognition "I am safe" provided some reassurance that the negative cognition was reasonably accurate. However, sensing that William had already begun to distance himself emotionally from the memory, I elected to skip the VOC. What followed confirmed my suspicion.

DM: You stated that you felt a panic. Just how disturbing is that memory and those emotions for you right now, from 0 to 10, where 0 is neutral?

William: It's not disturbing now. [*William is withdrawing from the exposure and reestablishing a safe zone with me. Understanding this, I reintroduce the target and once again ask for a level of disturbance.*]

DM: Now, simply focus on the moment when you felt panicked and picture it as best as you are able.

William: Actually, I would say that it is a 6 or a 7. I mean, I was disturbed at myself, my panic, my reaction, and I immediately caught it and said, "OK," you know . . . .

Once again, I needed to intervene because William was about to tell me a story and intellectualize. Prompt intervention was necessary to keep William within the experience. Historically, and perhaps paradoxically, as his affective experience has deepened, William has needed less redirection. The intrinsic reward of deepening his awareness and establishing meaningful relationship has been sufficient to ward off, if only briefly, his fear of being hurt.

DM: Just recall the memory, the feeling of panic, and the thought "I'm in danger." [*When the client indicates he "has it," I initiate eye movement.*]

William: ►◄►◄►◄ I was concentrating on telling myself that I wasn't angry. ►◄►◄►◄ All of a sudden I got the feeling that someone was making me do something. I felt angry at George, then I started feeling kind of angry at you.

William's transference issues with my directive manner are consistent with the larger issues that he is addressing at work. William works overtime to ward off attack but sacrifices his need for nurturing and relationship to achieve that degree of safety. He is deeply resentful of this sacrifice. My directiveness may have exacerbated his fears of domination/annihilation. If I overstep and encourage EMDR at a time when he is not inclined to take those risks, I become a threat, and he is likely to react in anger.

DM: Good. Just notice that.

William: ►◄►◄►◄ I'm losing control. ►◄►◄►◄ It is real interesting because as I think about this, it goes way, way back to when I was a kid, to when my parents would want me to go to the country club on Sunday night. I wouldn't go. They liked to go there and eat dinner with the whole family, and I didn't want to go, and the reason I didn't want to go is—I don't know—I didn't think anybody loved me. It was my way of getting attention, to throw a tantrum. My parents didn't hold me, didn't touch me, didn't tell me anything about myself. I resented not getting enough love, and I wanted to somehow get them in the position where they would prove to me that they loved me by telling me how much I meant to them and how much they wanted me to come along. [*William is wet-eyed and obviously deep in his experience.*]

I noted earlier that it is often pragmatic to suggest a negative cognition to get the process moving. Oftentimes the cognition is not the best—i.e., proves not to fit—as the client moves towards the most pressing issue spontaneously with the eye movement. In this case, the original cognition does not fit; William moved from what was presumed to be the issue of danger to the issue of control. Out of this work, he began to realize that his fairly chronic need to manage the session was born out of the blocking belief that if he relinquishes control, he may vanish or cease to exist in the interpersonal world. The positive cognition proved to be "I am safely in control."

Negative beliefs associated with control, danger, and self-worth reverberated throughout the work. The prior examples are illustrative of the core negative beliefs "I need control to survive" and "I am in danger." In addition, William struggled with basic issues of self-worth. All three themes were reexamined repeatedly throughout the therapy.

The transcript also shows William's rapid withdrawal from exposure and the need for my directiveness to help him focus on the affective thread and work through what appears to be a more meaningful piece for him. The directiveness is tolerated by this client, despite his fear of domination, because of a basic trust and shared understanding about my intentions. His willingness to disclose his anger at me both validates his trust and allows him to (sometimes) follow my direction. Asserting his anger counterbalances his fear of domination. The regularity with which I intervene to refocus him on the affective thread may provide a containment function that serves to deepen his trust in the relationship.

Phase Four: Addressing Defenses

Dissociation

William had occasion to doze off, abruptly, almost without warning, always following moments of particular vulnerability. (This has happened with other clients as well.) In one example, William had been imagining himself as a four-year-old and was recalling the utter despair and resignation associated with longing for contact with his preoccupied and absent parents. The image was generated in the context of a reparenting protocol discussed later in this chapter. In the context of this image, William held the negative cognition that "Those who don't respond to me don't care about me, and I am unlovable." During the eye movements, I suggested to William that he imagine his adult self providing the love he'd missed for the four-year-old within. His eyes moistened, and he seemed quite moved. Moments later, his eyelids began to droop, and it was all he could do to stay awake. Having ruled out narcolepsy and having encountered this with him before, I initiated a variation on hand-tapping. I asked William to slap my hands alternately, and this had the salutary effect of keeping him awake and moving him successfully through the process.

Projection/Paranoia

When William is in a bathroom, he is primarily concerned with who else is present. When no one is present, he can stand up and relieve himself in the urinal, but the closer to him anyone is, the more difficult that becomes. He states that he is acutely aware of the noise he makes when he urinates and is self-conscious when the stream of urine is weak and inconsistent. He believes that others in the room are keenly aware of this failing and are privately ridiculing him for his inadequacy. Typically in such situations, he will sit down on the toilet seat and urinate quietly. Generally he has success in that fashion:

> When I'm in a stall, it feels like there are a dozen people in there with me. And if I fail, even if my stream is weak, they're ready to pounce. It's almost as if the walls of the stall are glass. Transparent. I'm sure people are taking pleasure in my misery. Even though my head knows this is all nonsense, it feels that way to me. I've tried to relax, I've tried to convince myself that I'm safe. Self-hypnosis. You name it. They are always waiting for me to fail.

Initially, William was reluctant to even consider the possibility that others weren't observing him and privately amused with his failure. To address the paranoid projection, William had to clearly distinguish the rational from the irrational, let the "cognitive part of the brain" go for a minute and "lean into" the irrational belief that appeared to drive his fear. In the bathroom example above, William was acutely aware of others in the bathroom and projected this awareness as scrutiny by others. Targeting himself in a bathroom stall, William's negative and irrational cognition was "I am exposed and in danger." EMDR allowed him to establish the positive cognition "I am relatively safe and unobtrusive" with greater conviction than he'd initially felt it, though further work is still required in this area.

Phase Five: Addressing Blocking Beliefs and Core Self-Representations

Roughly four months into the therapy, William had become substantially more comfortable with affective exposure and was taking considerable initiative in the sessions. However, all efforts to address the bathroom symptom directly were continually derailed by blocking beliefs associated with low self-worth, lack of entitlement, and defectiveness. These beliefs invariably provoked a pressured monologue to convince me of his utter helplessness. Beliefs such as "I am too unimportant" or "too defective" emerged consistently in the work, often when Subjective Units of Distress Scale (SUDS) were somewhat lower and the work seemed to be approaching integration. These came up so consistently, I deemed it necessary to focus on them exclusively.

I am in the process of developing a protocol for personality-disordered clients, which has proved especially effective for addressing the issues of low self-worth and poor boundary setting that emerged in William's therapy. It is, in effect, a reparenting protocol in which the client's adaptive self is used as parent. The reparenting protocol begins by asking the client to draw upon any prior experience of infants he has known and identify an image of himself as a newborn, including the positive and negative cognitions associated with that image. I have yet to work with a client, regardless of level of functioning, whose cognitions of self were anything but innocent and lovable as a neonate. These cognitions are subsequently reinforced with the eye movement. Much as one might use videotape imagery of a discrete trauma, I ask the client to view himself at one year of age and then two. At each stage, we discuss the developmental processes at that age, how he might have looked, and how his family was likely to have responded to him. As experiences and memories emerge that challenge the client's sense of self or well-being, the standard EMDR protocol is employed. Cognitive interweave using the client's adult resources is employed to reparent the injured "child." The process continues chronologically through the elementary years and into adulthood. The entire protocol can take weeks, if not months, to complete.

William maintained a positive self-image through twelve months of age. But the cognitions began to reflect his negative view of himself and his environment as he imagined himself older. William viewed himself as the defenseless, chronic object of scrutiny with a nearly phobic fear of confrontation and the annihilation that might result. His self-image was weak, vulnerable, unlovable, and socially inadequate. He imagined his parents to be uninterested and impatient with him as he began to explore the world a bit. Since his parents viewed him as a burden, he adopted this view as his own. He believed that he was "bad" and "self-centered." During the prior session, the client had established the positive cognition "I am lovable" for his vision of himself at age one. Following is an excerpt detailing the erosion of the cognition.

DM: Now imagine yourself at 18 months. Picture the activities you were likely to be involved in. Perhaps you had begun to run from your mother. Notice if you're talking. What else are you aware of at this age?

William: I was probably starting to get into trouble. I'm sure my mother was annoyed with me plenty. She had to follow me around, baby-proof the place, clean up after me. I probably cried a lot. I think I was kind of difficult.

DM: Does your perception of yourself at that time cause you any discomfort now?

William: Well, I don't know about discomfort, but I kind of feel bad for my mother. I gather I was a bit of a handful, pretty self-centered.

DM: Can you picture how that might have looked when you were "a bit of a handful"?

William: Yeah, I see myself crying at the lunch table.

DM: And what words would you attach to this picture that might be true about you, even now, deep down inside?

William: I suppose that I'm a bad child and a burden to my mother.

DM: So your present belief is that you're bad and a burden.

This set-up for EMDR was remarkably simple and straightforward, quite different from earlier attempts. Evidently, the remote and perhaps hypothetical nature of this protocol for early childhood made the process less threatening; consequently, William was significantly less distancing in his responses. Once the basic set-up was complete, desensitization began. Cognitive interweave became necessary after several sets of saccades with little change. William persisted as follows:

William: I was just a difficult kid. I see myself throwing my dish off the table and really pissing her off. I must have been a terror.

DM: Last week you established that at age one, your adult view of yourself is as innocent and appropriately dependent. Isn't that right? [*William nods.*] Just notice that.

William: I see that now. I was just being a kid; It wasn't my job! [*quite excited now*] That was her job to take care of my needs.

Ultimately, William succeeded in establishing the positive cognition "I am OK. It wasn't my job." The cognitive interweave links into the prior week's work, as well as his adult perspective on childhood and childrearing. The protocol helped William differentiate from his parents by establishing clearer boundaries and honing an appropriate sense of responsibility for who he was as a young child. The reparenting protocol appears to have had a synergistic effect on William, as he has since been more adept at distinguishing his irrational projections, owning his anger, and placing appropriate responsibility on others.

Phase Six: Exercising Improved Boundaries

Improved boundaries have given William a sense of empowerment and enhanced self-worth. Because of his childhood history, William experienced little or no sense of boundary protection or insulation from the demands and needs of others. As an adult he continued to feel exposed and vulnerable at all times and consequently projected his power and autonomy onto others, especially in the workplace, where he felt competent but overwhelmed. As a consultant to several members of the sales staff of an engineering firm, he was routinely asked to provide support, at times being scheduled for meetings and presentations without advance information. He found it difficult, if not impossible, to resist this encroachment on his time, and as a result he often worked well into the night to do his best. Privately, he deeply resented his co-workers for denying him a social life, for assuming that "since I have no family, it's no skin off my back." After roughly six months of weekly therapy, William began to recognize his anger and the irrationality of his enslavement to his coworkers. As the fear of annihilation began to ebb, he was able to accurately assess the risks of speaking up and asserting himself.

At this point William began to realize the pervasiveness and insidiousness of his rage. This development set the stage for a critical breakthrough in his primary phobia as William began to own his projections of anger onto all those folks whom he assumed scorned him in the bathroom for his "obvious defect." He ended a recent EMDR session laughing at the silliness of it, concluding that "these people don't know me and are obviously not angry at me.

After roughly eight months of weekly EMDR treatment, William has made considerable progress, becoming less self-critical, less intimidated by others, and generally optimistic about his future. He finds his bathroom experiences to be less trying, sometimes thankfully uneventful, often "frustrating." I hope to return to the EMDR systematic desensitization procedure shortly. With his strengthened sense of self, I believe many self-statements that formerly blocked successful processing will cease to be a problem. As a result, I am hopeful that revisiting this procedure a second time will produce solid behavioral change.

Conclusion

Several key points emerge for consideration when treating the highly defended client with EMDR, in particular clients whose primary defenses are distancing ones. The first is to carefully gauge the client's level of functioning, the depth of therapeutic alliance, and the client's perceived sense of safety. These factors determine the appropriateness of EMDR, and presuming that, the style and directiveness of the clinician.

Secondly, the use of EMDR with highly defended clients may require a directiveness that exceeds the basic protocol designed by Shapiro (1995). Once the therapeutic alliance has been established, the clinician must balance, while being sensitive to, the client's need for control over the therapeutic process, hopefully avoiding unproductive periods of defensive distancing. This balance and sensitivity, inherent in all effective treatments and psychotherapies, is particularly important when the modality is as potent and emotionally evocative as EMDR can be. The case of William illustrates the risks in a directive approach, such as initiating EMDR too early, promoting a withdrawing or angry transference, or choosing the wrong cognitions. Knowing your client well and securing an effective working alliance is crucial to success.

Using EMDR with the well-defended client is a creative endeavor. The cognitive interweave becomes an elaborate and central feature of the work, drawing on the clinician's full breadth of training and clinical experience. EMDR can serve as a viable and valuable treatment modality for the highly defended client when teamed with an understanding of the client's characterological issues and the skilled and thoughtful application of such innovations as the reparenting protocol and the enhanced systematic desensitization.

References

Manfield, P. (1995). *EMDR with narcissistic clients*. Paper presented at the EMDR International Conference, Los Angeles.

Shapiro, F. (1989). Eye movement desensitization: A new treatment for post-traumatic stress disorder. *Journal of Behavior Therapy and Experimental Psychiatry, 20*, 211–217.

Shapiro, F. (1995). *Eye movement, desensitization, and reprocessing: Basic principles, protocols, and procedures*. New York: Guilford Press.

Wolpe, J. (1958). *Psychotherapy by reciprocal inhibition*. Stanford, CA: Stanford University Press.

Zgourides, G. (1987). Paruresis: Overview and implications for treatment. *Psychological Reports, 60*, 1171–1176.

13

"IT WAS A GOLDEN TIME . . ."
Treating Narcissistic Vulnerability

Jim Knipe

BY EARLY 1994, EMDR had transformed my practice as a psychologist in many ways, but one way stood out: The proportion of individuals in my caseload with more severe and complex emotional difficulties had increased. What seemed to have happened was that, with the addition of EMDR, the clients with relatively uncomplicated posttraumatic stress disorder (PTSD) or other anxiety disorders (about 50%) were rapidly completing therapy, changing the diagnostic mix within my practice. In comparing notes with other EMDR therapists, I found they were observing the same shift in their practices. The basic method worked very quickly with consciously experienced, clearly identifiable traumatic memories. For those clients who have built up formidable psychological defenses in their lives—ways to protect themselves against the pain of disturbing memories—the process of change tended to be relatively slower (though still more rapid than had occurred without EMDR). This chapter focuses on EMDR-enhanced therapeutic protocols to treat individuals whose painful life experience is separated from consciousness by complex defensive structures, particularly those associated with narcissistic and avoidance defenses.

My previous work as a therapist had been guided by object relations theory, the posttraumatic stress disorder model for understanding recurring disturbing emotions, Mary and Bob Goulding's conceptualization of inner child work as "redecision therapy" (Goulding & Goulding, 1979), and Milton Erickson's utilization of so-called client resistance to facilitate, not impede, the therapy process (Erickson & Rossi, 1979).

On an evening in October of 1992, I was feeling mostly elated but also a little depressed. I had just completed the first day of the EMDR level I training, and it was apparent, from the taped therapy sessions I had watched and from the brief supervised practice where fellow trainees and myself had traded roles of therapist and client, that this method worked with amazing rapidity. It was thrilling to contemplate how the field of therapy could be transformed, and many clients could benefit, but I was also feeling bewildered and threatened that many of my cherished assumptions about how people change and grow were now shown to be incorrect or at least outmoded, not to mention the fear that my 23 years of experience as a psychologist had suddenly become obsolete. What I see now is that all information and experience that was useful in guiding therapy before EMDR remains important in focusing the power of the EMDR method. To borrow a metaphor from the EMDR training, the invention of power tools doesn't mean that carpentry skills are no longer necessary.

I finished the levels I and II EMDR training in 1992 and became an EMDR Facilitator in 1994. I was involved as a therapist in Wilson's experiment (Wilson, Becker, & Tinker, 1995), a well-designed study that showed the efficacy of the method in resolving disturbing memories. I was also privileged to be involved in the pro bono EMDR trainings in Oklahoma City following the bombing in 1995.

The methods described in this chapter are based on the observation that EMDR is useful in facilitating the processing of negative affective information as well as positive information that is associated with negative material. Typically, positive experiences in normal living, such as good times with friends, warm romantic moments, successes, and achievements, are mentally processed in the days following the event. After a while, the pleasant event is incorporated into the person's sense of self. For example, a lottery winner might initially say, with intense positive affect, "I don't believe it!" A few days later, presumably after thinking again and again of the good news, the winner might say, with somewhat less intense affect, that the news was "finally starting to sink in." We all enjoy processing life's positive experiences in this way, when we can.

In many of the clients I have worked with, the healing power of EMDR is prevented or impaired by *unresolved positive feelings* that block the client's full awareness of the negative experience associated with trauma. This can occur when the overall complex of posttraumatic images, self-defeating cognitions, unpleasant feelings and sensations (what Francine Shapiro calls the unprocessed *memory network*) contains embedded strong positive affect that is highly valued by the client. In the case of a person with narcissistic defenses, the positive material may block awareness of negative memories, especially if the positive experience occurred in the larger context of trauma and neglect. In such instances the positive part of the experience is idealized through selective memory and strengthened in intensity, because it serves as a defense against the core PTSD. The negative part of the memory is partially or wholly dissociated and is thus less accessible to processing.

Under certain circumstances I have found it useful to target positive affect in order to facilitate EMDR—the target being either the positive affect that serves as a defense against the client's negative memory, or the positive feeling of relief that occurs when a client is able to avoid negative affect mentally or behaviorally. In other words, for many clients, the defense they present in therapy can often provide the best point of access for the use of EMDR in resolving their problem. For example, a woman in her late forties was attempting to resolve her feelings of being angry, embarrassed, and frustrated when a friend had given her feedback that she was "too sensitive to criticism." With eye movements, she quickly got to many *feeder* memories of times when her mother had been very faultfinding and, in response, she had tried to be "perfect" and thus not vulnerable to being hurt. As we continued EMDR, focusing on one of the memories of being criticized, the feelings of fear and worthlessness continued to loop through several sets of eye movements, and so I asked, as an interweave, "Were there times when your mother thought you were perfect?" She said, "Oh, yes! It feels really good to think about those times." I asked her to hold in mind a representative example of these positive times, together with the feeling of being, in her words, "lovable and perfect." After one set of eye movements, she said, "I don't need to feel lovable that way anymore." She then was able to resolve the particular memory of her mother's criticism and the upsetting comment from her friend within the session. A positive memory, and an associated self-image, had remained overly valued and idealized because it had served as a defense against the pain of negative memories. Using eye movements, the client was able to see this connection and bring both memories to resolution.

The above example describes an individual with relatively high tolerance for information that is potentially threatening to the self-image. Thus she would be at the more benign end of a spectrum, which is defined, on the one end, by an integrated sense of self in which self-esteem is based on a realistic assessment of one's positive qualities and, on the other end, by the clinical picture of narcissistic personality disorder. This spectrum extends through gradations of increasing assumptions of entitlement and superiority, increasing loyalty to an idealized false self, and decreasing awareness of the needs and feelings of others Johnson, 1987; Kohut, 1971; Masterson, 1981).

Couples Therapy

Glenn was towards the narcissistic end of this spectrum. My intent in presenting his case is to illustrate how EMDR can be used to target and reprocess material other than negative affect. Usually, even in such cases, the standard EMDR procedure is the approach of choice and is likely to be used successfully. What I will highlight here are the times when non-standard EMDR procedures were used to get past an impediment to processing. In particular, during one session a Level of Urge to Avoid (LOUA) measure was used; in a later session, a longstanding obstacle to treatment was partially resolved by targeting the Level of Positive Affect (LOPA) associated with the individual's sense of entitlement and "specialness."

Nearly always, the mask the narcissist presents to the world, with or without awareness, serves as a cover for vulnerability, shame, and a sense of extreme disorganization or fragmentation. These feelings, in turn, can be assumed to originate in early trauma or neglect. As Johnson (1987) has pointed out, use of the term *narcissism* is unfortunate, because it connotes shameless self-congratulation that often is in great contrast to the basic feelings revealed by clients in therapy. In writing case studies, protection of the vulnerability of the client is always a concern, but this is especially true for clients who courageously enter therapy for treatment of this human problem. For these reasons, identifying client information is substantially disguised.

Glenn first called me requesting an appointment, not for himself but for Pauline, his partner for the previous eight years. Both were professionals in their late fifties. They had something like a permanent relationship, although one with built-in emotional distance. Each of them maintained a separate residence, and their frequency of contact—several times a week was generally suitable to both of them. He was calling me on this day because of a repeated conflict they had been having that he thought was her fault, and he said she had agreed to enter into individual therapy to correct this problem. When I told him my policy that clients call for their own appointments, he seemed to think that that was an odd rule, but said he would tell her.

Pauline called for her own appointment, came in for a total of nine sessions, and did some excellent work, primarily through assertion rehearsal and EMDR. As a result she was able to understand and partially resolve a longstanding codependent sense of guilty responsibility for the feelings of others.

About a month following termination of this work, she called requesting an appointment for the two of them. As sometimes happens in couples, the positive changes that had occurred in Pauline had altered the *ecology* of their relationship. An issue in her therapy had been how to express her own feelings clearly and appropriately when he was being controlling (e.g., telling her that a particular outfit she was wearing didn't look good and that she should change it) or putting her down (e.g., suggesting she was childish and unsophisticated for wanting to go see a particular movie). She was now feeling much more confident and was also able to communicate more clearly, with the result that she was finally holding her own. Glenn grudgingly admitted, when he thought about it, that Pauline's newfound power was a good thing for her, but he would nevertheless become angry and blaming whenever arguments occurred.

When the three of us met, Glenn made the statement that he was not comfortable talking with a therapist. He said, "I've always thought that people should handle their own problems and not have to depend on somebody else to tell them what to do." When he said this Pauline winced, but he did not seem to be aware of the judgmental implication of his remark. As we sorted out this misunderstanding about therapy, it became clear that what was more troubling to him was the requirement of self-disclosure and the insecurity of being in a situation where he felt insufficient control. In spite of his nervousness and reluctance, however, Glenn was able to talk about the specific relationship concerns that they had been having recently. He acknowledged that, with Pauline being clearer in her communication, there were advantages to both of them knowing each other's needs and working out disagreements. We met for three additional couples sessions. It was helpful for them to have a "referee," and they were able to come to agreement in several areas of previous contention. One problem, though, resisted resolution. Two months earlier Glenn had had an angry confrontation with one of Pauline's male coworkers, a person whom Pauline had to work with closely on a daily basis. Glenn was very angry with Pauline for not backing him up in this incident, and he would frequently quiz her about her work-related contacts with this man. Glenn implied that there was something improper about Pauline's behavior, but when specifically questioned, he stated that he had no concerns about her having an affair; he was simply angry at her for not lining up on his side. He said, unapologetically, "I know it's not completely reasonable, but I just feel that she should back me up."

It was clear from the tremor in his voice that he was feeling even more anger than he wanted to show.

I asked him if his anger at that moment was any kind of problem to him, and he replied, "My anger is always a problem, according to Pauline! She has been trying to get me to go to therapy for a long time, but I know two or three guys at work who have been in therapy for years, and I can't see that it's done them any good. To tell you the truth, that's why I didn't want to come here in the first place. I don't have a high opinion of therapists." Although there was an antagonistic tone to these remarks, it was a positive development for Glenn to voice his reasons for staying distant from the therapy process; now, with some of his reasons revealed, they could be addressed.

This type of challenge often arises in the therapy of individuals with narcissistic traits, and I suspected that an opportunity would be missed if I did not respond to him with confidence while also avoiding countertransferential defensiveness. I replied, "I try to keep therapy short-term whenever possible. How about coming in for three individual sessions to focus on whatever is uncomfortable for you about your anger? I won't give you a money-back guarantee, but I bet you'll know by then if therapy can be useful to you."

Individual Treatment

Glenn had seen the success of Pauline's EMDR work and, after three sessions of very active couples work, he felt more comfortable with me. He agreed to come in by himself for "Just this one thing"—i.e., his intense and uncomfortable anger towards Pauline's coworker. When we began this individual session, he once again expressed reservations about therapy, and EMDR in particular: "Even if this method can take away my anger, I'm not sure I want that to happen. I have certain standards of acceptable behavior. If I'm not angry, what's to prevent other people from acting in ways that are unacceptable?" I responded by saying, "It seems there are two separate issues here. One is your ability to respond to other people the way you choose, even get angry with them if that is what you decide. Therapy will in no way take away from your ability to do this. What could change is something else—your discomfort and frustration in these situations. That's something that only hurts you." With this distinction in mind, he was willing to proceed.

When we did the EMDR set-up, Glenn was able to think of a number of negative cognitions about the man and Pauline, but he had difficulty identifying one that was self-referencing. What he finally arrived at was "I can't let go of it," with a positive cognition of "I am able to see this situation in perspective." This positive cognition had a Validity of Cognition Scale (VOC) of 6, even though he was easily able to acknowledge that the memory was giving him much more upset feelings than he wished. Ordinarily, I would ask further questions to resolve this discrepancy, but in his case, I let it stand, assuming that the rating of 6 represented his idealized wish. The positive cognition had been identified, which was sufficient for the purposes of beginning the EMDR processing. His Subjective Units of Distress Scale (SUDS) on the emotions of *anger* and *frustration* was a 6.

If a client identifies anger as his primary emotion, I will often ask for a negative cognition about the other person before asking for a self-referencing negative cognition. The purpose of this additional step is to allow the client to express his grievance against the other person. It is often important that this grievance be "heard" before the client will have full access to a self-referencing negative cognition. Also, the word *anger* can actually have some very different meanings, and sometimes it is useful to clarify which meaning the client intends. Anger can be an empowering emotion, but when a client names anger as his problem emotion, it is often a cover or defense against a more core feeling, such as helplessness, fear, or worthlessness. It is often helpful to clients to suggest a qualifying adjective: for example, "Is what you feel a kind of helpless anger?"

Glenn's case also illustrates a connection between anger and narcissistic defenses. For most people the emotion of anger tends to elicit traits of entitlement and self-centeredness, empathy is lessened. As a group, narcissistic individuals tend to become angry more easily as a way to enforce compliance with their idealized pictures of how others must be and how they wish to be perceived by others. In addition, other people are frequently misperceived as angry and attacking when they are not in resonance with the narcissistic person's preferred self-image.

Often the individual has very little insight into how his anger functions to protect the idealized image, which in turn protects against feelings of shame and fragmentation. For these reasons, in this session I did not confront Glenn regarding his distorted view of this situation with Pauline's coworker. Instead I focused on empathizing with his unpleasant feelings, particularly the hurt and fear that lay beneath the angry surface. His main negative cognition about Pauline was that "She should know what I need. I shouldn't have to tell her." This issue, which had been prominent in their previous conflicts, had been partially resolved when Glenn had come to acknowledge that it was unfair to expect her to be a mind reader and "just know" that he, for example, wanted to be left alone to read the paper, wanted her to initiate sex on a given night, and so on. The resolutions reached in previous sessions remained in place but had not generalized to many situations that had not been discussed. His desire for Pauline to discern and meet his needs was now resurfacing especially strongly in response to this incident.

Following the assessment of target, we began desensitization with eye movements. Very quickly, the "anger and frustration" associated with the co-worker's face were considerably diminished. I asked him to bring up the target picture once again.

Glenn: I don't feel angry at him anymore. He's not really important in all this. It's Pauline I'm angry at. ►◄►◄►◄ I just wish Pauline would be able to tune in to what I need. ►◄►◄►◄ I know what I need from her, and I can see sometimes she's trying, but somehow it always falls short. ►◄►◄►◄ For some reason, I'm thinking about my mom. She died when I was14. ►◄►◄►◄ I didn't cry that day—the day she died.

At that point his voice faltered with emotion. After another set of eye movements, he said, apparently in reference to his emerging feelings, "Sorry." Without directly reassuring him but speaking in an accepting voice, I said, "Stay with that," and started another set of eye movements. (Sometimes, the transference issues that come up during EMDR can simply be processed without discussion.)

Glenn: I know it's probably OK with you that I get upset, but it's not OK with me. ►◄►◄►◄ But, anyway, I get frustrated sometimes with Pauline.

I couldn't tell if the emotion he had been feeling had been processed or had just been put out of mind. When we went back to his initial target, the SUDS had dropped down to 2, and though not a complete EMDR session (which would be a SUDS of 1 or 0), Glenn was very pleased with the result. Since we were nearly out of time, I asked him what he had learned in this session, as a way to facilitate closure. He said, "I'm still thinking about this picture of my mother that came into my mind. My mom was always there for me. Pauline never comes through like that, but somehow I don't feel so angry at her right now." After we had finished the standard first-session EMDR debriefing and he was getting up to go, he said, "I haven't thought about my mother in a long time. She was a remarkable woman."

Over the next five months my contacts with Glenn followed an erratic course. During the month following the above session we met three times and focused on his anger regarding Pauline's frequent phone contacts with her adult son. In these sessions, Glenn talked at length about the deficiencies of this young man. He was able to acknowledge at one point that he experienced relief when he vented in this way. In addition, we used EMDR in one session. Glenn had a general dislike for Pauline's son, attributed a number of negative qualities to him, and regarded the frequent phone calls as "intrusive." The result of EMDR with this issue was similar to the result with Pauline's coworker; the disturbing picture and body sensations became less intense with sets of eye movements and the SUDS level dropped from 6–8 to 2–3. In these instances it was my impression that the remaining unprocessed information was not something he wished to address. His understanding of the therapy contract was that he was coming in to diffuse his frustration and to receive understanding and support, not engage in self-exploration. Following these sessions, he chose not to set up an additional appointment, saying, "I'm going to be out of town a lot, so I'll get back to you."

After a break of about a month he called saying that he thought Pauline was in need of more therapy, since she had been "impossible" during their vacation. We followed a similar sequence as before, with Pauline calling for her own appointment, and then, in three EMDR sessions, bolstering her communication skills and self-esteem by targeting conflicts they'd had. This, in turn, was followed by a couples session, which was followed by Glenn being willing to come in individually to target the same conflict issues from his perspective.

Following two partially successful EMDR sessions, he said he would like to "stop for a while." He expressed satisfaction with how the therapy process had gone and said that he and Pauline were getting along much better. With a trace of an ironic smile, he attributed this improvement primarily to ways that Pauline had "gotten down to business" and worked on her problems.

Both Pauline and Glenn had benefited from therapy, but it was clear that the work was not yet finished. I received a phone call from Glenn about six months later. He started this conversation complaining about Pauline, stating that he wanted her to re-enter therapy, but then caught himself and said, "Maybe it's my problem, too." I offered to set up another time, either with him or with both of them, and he said he would think about it, but he did not call back. It seemed the brief work we had done had marginally increased his ability to see himself more realistically, with both positive and negative qualities, but this shift in his sense of self was not sufficient for him to re-enter therapy. Then, eight months later, he called requesting an individual appointment. His voice conveyed considerable emotion over the phone. When he came in for a session two days later, he was uncharacteristically agitated and rambling, more upset than in any of our previous contacts. He said, "My father had a heart attack two months ago and insisted on going back home—the home he has always lived in—five weeks ago. I asked him to say with me, but we both knew that wouldn't work. I've been calling him every night, trying to be responsible, though sometimes I dread every second of it. Pauline and I can't talk about it. She thinks I should be more supportive. But I've never been very good at being patient. Sometimes I just wish I could make it all go away."

Glenn and his father had never been close and their conflicts had been especially intense during the years following the death of Glenn's mother. His father was described as hypercritical, angry, and controlling. Following the heart attack, Glenn and his father would frequently have intense arguments centering around his father's not taking his medicine, not getting out to see his friends, not eating correctly, etc. Over the next several months Glenn and I had sessions on a weekly basis, and he used the therapy time to ventilate about difficult situations that had occurred with his father, with Pauline, and occasionally at work. Often, he seemed apprehensive that I would react judgmentally, and he appeared relieved when I was able to mirror his experience accurately and uncritically. I did not confront his guardedness but, instead, attempted to respond in a way that disconfirmed his threatened feeling—i.e., by expressing acceptance, support, and acknowledgment of how painful these conflicts were to him. We used EMDR to relieve what Glenn called *stress*: specifically, a combined feeling of helpless anger and emptiness that often occurred when he was unable to control the behavior of others. These sessions greatly relieved this stress, and as we continued, through repeated examples, he was able to see that his need to control was actually an attempt to soothe his own discomfort. With this understanding, there was an increased willingness and ability on his part to relinquish some control and disclose more personal information. As he risked himself in this way, our initially shaky therapeutic alliance became stronger. He was developing more trust that I truly accepted his ways of experiencing people and events.

One day, four months after re-entering therapy, he arrived at our weekly session with a stony, impassive expression that seemed to indicate intense anger. As he sat down, he silently handed me a copy of a memorandum from his supervisor at work, informing him that he had been passed over for a promotion within the company. He had received the memo in a meeting an hour earlier. He was angry about being "humiliated." In several places in the memo, he felt he had been "damned with faint praise." He said, in a rambling outpouring of words, "I feel chopped off at the knees. If I could get another job, I'd quit today. This can't be happening!" From his previous work he had some awareness that the anger he felt was not the empowering kind, but was his way of dealing with intense emotional pain. He said, "There must be some of my stuff in this. Could we use EMDR? I'd like to try it, to see if it can help me get rid of this feeling."

I thought it might, but I was concerned about him having an incorrect idea of what might occur if we used EMDR. I said, "If we use eye movements, it will be like inviting all these feelings to come forward. The advantage to that would be that you could understand this situation better. But EMDR won't *cover* up the feelings." He said, "I'm angry right now, but I know I'm scared, too. There is something here for me to figure out. I want to go forward, not backward." The sessions of the previous four months had given him some momentum he was more aware of the potential benefits of allowing himself to be vulnerable and explore the origins of his feelings. My sense of things in this session was that EMDR might indeed assist him in gaining perspective on the situation, and so we proceeded.

Early in Glenn's therapy I had tape-recorded a guided imagery relaxation induction, which he had used at home to develop an ability to self-soothe. We took a few minutes to go through some relaxing imagery, and he became somewhat more relaxed. When we returned to talking about the memo, though, his disturbed feelings quickly returned. The most charged negative visual image for him was the sight of the words on the paper. This image was so upsetting that it was difficult for him to even formulate a negative cognition, but then the thought, "I'm no good," came to mind. He was in a state of considerable anguish, feeling like a failure, so I decided not to risk further performance anxiety by asking for a positive cognition. Instead I suggested one: "I'm OK and I can cope with this." He replied, with a trace of humor, "On a scale of 1 to 7, that's a 0-minus!"

When I asked him to identify the emotions he was having, he said, "Well, I'm as angry as I've ever been, but even more, I feel terrified! It is very hard for me to think about what happened today. I'm fighting the urge to change the subject. To tell you the truth, I want to walk out that door!" He was expressing an impulse, not a real wish to end the session. As we continued to talk, I reassured him that he could respect his own feelings, his own pace, and not deal with this issue today if he didn't want to. This comment seemed to increase his fear, frustration, and irritation with himself. During the year and a half since our first contact, he had come to have more trust in therapy, and he now regarded EMDR as a useful tool. Nevertheless, his self-protective patterns of avoidance persisted, especially in the aftermath of his severe disappointment at work. It was becoming more and more apparent that he was experiencing extreme ambivalence: all of his *intention* was focused on working through this issue; all of his energy was aimed at escaping it.

The impasse of these conflicted feelings was becoming increasingly uncomfortable for him. It was clear that he regarded his avoidance impulse as a problem.

So, with about 45 minutes left, I said, "You wish this had never happened this morning, and your not wanting to talk about it or think about it is understandable, given the painful feelings you're having. On the other hand, you know that we could use the remaining time of this session working on the issue of what happened at work today. So, given all this, how much do you not want to think about it? How much, in your gut feeling, would you rather talk about something else, 0–10?" He said, "It's a 9, maybe more," and he located the sensations of this 9 in his chest and feet. Then I asked, "Can you just think about that 9? Just be aware how much you would rather talk about something else, and follow my fingers?" He nodded and we did one set of eye movements.

JK: What are you aware of now?

Glenn: I just can't believe I didn't get that job. ►◄►◄►◄ I don't know what I'm feeling. I'm feeling everything at once. I want to go hide somewhere. I'm so mad I can't stand it. ►◄►◄►◄ I was just so sure I would get it. ►◄►◄►◄ It's going to be very hard to face everybody. There are people who will be happy I didn't get it. What can I do now? ►◄►◄►◄ I guess I can get through it. ►◄►◄►◄ That feels a little better.

JK: Glenn, when you realize that we could spend the remaining 35 minutes of this session continuing to talk about what happened at your office today, how much, 0–10, right now, do you not want to?

Glenn: It feels better now, a 6 or a 7, but I still don't want to think about it.

JK: Tell me about that 6 or 7.

Glenn: I know I'll survive. It's not life and death. But it feels like it is. ►◄►◄►◄ When I'm in that building, I am *this person*, a person who is always in charge, and I know what I'm doing. When I say something, people listen. I have a certain status and respect. If I don't get this job, it will all come crashing down. ►◄►◄►◄ It's about a 4 now. It's not pleasant, but I can think about it.

JK: What is the unpleasant emotion that you feel?

Glenn: I don't know . . . out of control, I guess, and bad, like I've done something wrong, like I'm really in trouble.

JK: Can you stay with that?

Glenn: Yes. ►◄►◄►◄ It makes me feel like I'm just an ordinary person, second-rate; I'm just a nobody. I still feel really bad, like I am bad. ►◄►◄►◄ It just makes me feel ordinary and bad. That's all I can say.

We tried changing direction of eye movements, and other interventions, but he seemed to be deeply stuck in a loop of thinking. As an interweave, I asked, "Is there any difference between being ordinary and being bad?"

Glenn: Well, no, for me it doesn't feel like it. I don't want to be ordinary. ►◄►◄►◄ All my life, I've pushed myself to be the best. ►◄►◄►◄ If I can't be at the top, it feels like a long way down. ►◄►◄►◄ I remember when I was in sixth grade, I brought home a bad report card. My father and mother had an awful fight. ►◄►◄►◄ He was yelling at me, she told him to stop, that he was being cruel, and he hit her. She was crying, but he kept on, yelling, "If you keep spoiling him, he won't ever amount to anything!" I think that's when I ran to my room. I hated him that day! ►◄►◄►◄ [*with tears in his eyes*] My grades were always good after that. I couldn't let him be right. ►◄►◄►◄ That was a long time ago, but it doesn't seem like it.

As we continued, Glenn's discomfort with this old memory diminished, and he was able to see that, as he put it, "This person I am at work, that idea of myself started around that time." When the session was almost over, and we went back to the original picture of the memo, he was feeling much less discomfort, much more in control. At this point, his SUDS score was a 3, and the emotion was now "still pissed, but mainly sadness." I asked him what he had learned in this session, and he said, "I set a high standard for myself, higher than most people would have. I've liked it that way. I see now that when I've wanted to be at the top, there has been a lot of anger in that, proving that my mother was right, my father was wrong. It makes a lot of sense that I've made that so important."

This method of targeting avoidance defenses is adapted from Popky's (1994) EMDR protocol for addictive disorders. The method he has developed is complex, but one of several innovative aspects is the use of the 0–10 scale to measure Level of Urge (LOU) for the addictive substance in situations that trigger the urge to use. Since addiction can be thought of as substance-induced avoidance of feeling, I have tried adapting the LOU to avoidance itself, as in the above example. This adaptation is a method that is appropriate only in situations of intense ambivalence: when a client has already experienced the healing power of EMDR, wishes to work with a highly charged issue, but is prevented from doing so by quasi-automatic avoidance defenses. It is an alternative to techniques that foster an experiential distancing from an emotionally charged target (e.g., "Make it a small black and white picture," "Put up a screen of bulletproof glass," "See it in the distance, 100 yards away") and can be used when these techniques have been shown to be ineffective, or, as in Glenn's case, when the client's focus is on escaping from or avoiding a disturbing target. It is important that the client be fully aware that this procedure is, in fact, a way to initiate processing, albeit through a "back door." Using this method, any traumatic information that comes up can be metabolized in a way that is more comfortable and somehow "softened," since the client is able to keep his avoidance defense as he does the work. It is typical that as the Level of Urge to Avoid (which I abbreviate as LOUA) drops to around 4, the client will be able to shift to a direct awareness of the target, including being able to identify associated emotions and SUDS (which still may be as high as 10).

I have found this approach to be useful whenever a client is aware that his avoidance pattern is interfering with reaching his desired treatment goals. Defensive avoidance is part of the clinical picture for many different types of emotional problems, and thus the use of this LOUA method extends beyond individuals with narcissistic traits. The specific way of targeting avoidance may vary according to the particular needs of the person. For example, when standard EMDR processing is blocked, the therapist might ask, "When you think of being there [in a threatening and vague memory situation], how much do you not want to know what happens next, 0–10?" or "When you think about [some feared upcoming and unavoidable event], how much, 0–10, do you want to get it over with?" Frequently a client will experience numbing of sensation when attempting to bring up a highly charged image. This numbness, which is a mild form of dissociative avoidance, will often lift if targeted like any other body sensation. Sometimes, though, this is also ineffective. If the client can sense the presence of the traumatic anxiety or helplessness "under" the numbing, it can be helpful to ask, "How much do you want to get away from the anxiety by being numb, 0–10?" Strong dissociative barriers (e.g., numbness without any conscious anxiety, or the amnesiac barriers between alters in dissociative identity disorder [DID]) are strong for a reason within the ecology of the personality system, and this method would usually be unwise for those clients.

For Glenn, this approach was very useful. He came back for his next session five days later, and we retargeted the incident with his report card and the fight between his parents. He still felt some sadness associated with this memory ("about a 4"). As we continued the processing, he realized that this incident had been a turning point in his early life

> I used to tell everybody that I came from a good, normal family. When I got to be an adult, I came to see that my father was a bully, but now I un-

derstand how that affected me. I can remember being in sixth grade and never knowing when my father would criticize me, tell me I'm not acting right. One day he would ignore me, the next day he'd go on and on about what a disappointment I was. I could never say anything back. My brother, who is four years older than me, would join in and take his side. By the time I was in seventh grade, I'd figured out that if I could do everything just right, they would mostly leave me alone. My father would still pick on me sometimes, but I got good at not letting it in. He couldn't hurt me so much if I did everything right. I've spent my whole life trying to be that seventh-grader, so I wouldn't have to be the sixth-grader.

These two sessions were very important in setting the stage for further work. During the next four months, my support and mirroring continued to be very important in maintaining our therapeutic alliance. With increased trust in me, he was now able to target additional disturbing memories with EMDR, and he became more aware of the many ways he had tried to live his life as "the seventh-grader." His efforts had been motivated not only by the need to protect himself from his father's unpredictable rage, but also by his wish to please his mother, whom he deeply respected. He stated:

> Everybody liked my mother, but she and I had a special relationship. She used to call me "Flash," like in the Flash Gordon comics, because I could always take charge, always think my way out of any situation. And she would support anything I wanted to do. She was never critical.

Little by little, Glenn became aware of how he had come to identify strongly with an image of himself as "special" and "always in control." This image was strongly supported by his mother and provided a buffer against the helplessness and humiliation that accompanied the negative treatment by his father. With EMDR, we targeted several memories from early childhood with various themes: powerlessness, when he was beaten up by his brother; abandonment and "badness," when criticized by his father; or loneliness, during the many times he heard his parents bitterly arguing. The overall result of these sessions was that he was able to glimpse, for the first time, the truth of the positive cognition "I am a lovable and worthy person." As he continued to resolve more of the core trauma, he was able to see his defense against that trauma more objectively. He was coming to have increasing clarity about how his "special" image, which originally was a solution to a problem, was now contributing to hurts and stresses in his present life.

This image, which at times had seemed more important to him than his own basic needs, could generally be described as that of a person who (1) is more attractive, lovable, and worthy than other people and therefore more deserving of special status and attention; (2) always "acts right" and is therefore justified in becoming angry if his behavior is criticized by others; (3) is entitled to give other people extensive direction regarding "right" behavior, including getting angry at them if they don't act correctly. It was initially disturbing but ultimately helpful for him to realize that his own critical and controlling behaviors were modeled after his father.

As Glenn made these connections between childhood events and present-day feelings, he was able to see that his investment in this image created a lot of work for him. For one thing, it was often difficult to behave in ways consistent with the image, and, in addition, he had to get other people to respond to him in a way that validated his idealized picture. Sometimes these efforts made him vulnerable to frustration and counterattack from others, since they would often not agree that he was entitled to this controlling and special role.

This entitled concept of himself had perhaps contributed to his setback at work, although generally it had worked fairly well for him in his professional responsibilities, many of which involved managing and directing the activities of other people. But in his relationships with friends, Pauline, and his father, his need to be "this special person" was the source of considerable difficulty and stress. A helpful metaphor for him was that of a statue on a wobbly pedestal, vulnerable to being bumped over. Over many months, with EMDR and discussion, therapy moved ahead in a back-and-forth process. As trauma-based material was resolved, he had less need for defense. As this occurred a shift became possible away from his identification with his "special" image and towards an acceptance of his real self became possible, including increased compassion and sadness for the hardships he had suffered as a child. This altered perspective towards his childhood in turn allowed the emergence and resolution of more traumatic material. Little by little, he was healing the split within his sense of himself. He was coming to see that his idealized self-concept, which he once would have defended with life-and-death desperation, was not serving him well. In addition, he was discovering the increased comfort of accepting his real feelings.

One day he came into his session with a concise and insightful report

I've been thinking about what we've been talking about, how part of my problem is always wanting to be special and in control. Even though I understand it better, I still get restless and irritated if Pauline and I are out with friends, and she is listening to someone else instead of me. I'm noticing how I feel, but that doesn't *change* how I feel. I still get mad at her.

A particularly disturbing incident was very clear in his mind, and so we proceeded with the standard EMDR set-up. We focused on the most disturbing moment—when Pauline was enjoying talking and laughing (though, he said, not flirting) with a male friend of theirs. Glenn recognized that, even though he was feeling anger, Pauline had not been inappropriate in her behavior. His anger was familiar to him but also troubling in light of his new insights. As had been typical before, he had trouble thinking of a negative cognition, and could only come up with "I must be doing something wrong," and, after further discussion, a more troubling negative cognition, "There is something wrong with me." The positive cognition was "I know I'm OK," with a VOC of 5. His SUDS on "frustrated anger and helplessness" was a 6, with tension in the face and chest. After the first few sets of eye movements, he said, exasperated, "I can see that all of this frustration is because I just want to be special. What's wrong with that? Don't we all want to be special?" I said, "Stay with that," and initiated another set of eye movements. Then he said, with an angry tone, "I'm just feeling worse! This isn't helping today." He appeared to be feeling very distressed and on the verge of becoming angry at either me or himself. His specialness defense had become weakened, and he was feeling frightened and vulnerable without it.

I said to him, "We all want to be special in the sense of having uniqueness and value, but it seems that what you're wanting there in the restaurant is to be special, to be acknowledged as special, in the way we have discussed in recent weeks." He nodded. I went on, "Think of this. When was it, in your life, that that feeling of being special, really being special, was truly fulfilled, was complete? Can you think of a time that you felt that way, either in the recent past or long ago, when you were a kid?" He said, "It's hard to think of anytime in the last few years. I used to feel that way when I was growing up, I guess, at times with my mother." I said, "Can you think of a particularly positive time with your mother, when you felt that way, perhaps more than any other time?" Glenn's eyes started to fill with tears. He hesitated and then said, "Right before she died. We all knew she didn't have long. My brother was in a bad accident—he'd been drinking. I could tell she was so hurt and disappointed. My father tried to defend him. Mom started to get angry back, but then she stopped herself." He paused. "I remember, she turned to me and said, 'You're so responsible, Glenn. Thank God, you're so responsible!'"

I asked him what emotions went with this memory and he said, "A warm feeling, feeling good about myself," which he felt "all over, especially in my chest." On a 0–10 scale, he said the intensity of this positive feeling was a 10.

I asked him to hold in mind the visual image of his mother, hearing her words, feeling the good feeling, thinking of the pleasant sensations, and we did an additional set of eye movements. He then said, "It feels so intense to remember that. I haven't thought about that in years, but that's the feeling I always had with her." I said, "Stay with that," and initiated another set of eye movements. He said, "My brother and I were always fighting; he and my father always against me. And after she died, it got so much worse." An outpouring of tears came with this realization. As we continued sets of eye movements, Glenn's perspective on this memory began to shift.

Glenn: I'm wondering why I was so pleased on a night when my brother was hurt. I'm seeing now that maybe I was self-centered. ►◄►◄►◄ I enjoyed being in the center. Mom made me feel like I belonged there.

JK: When you think of it now, do you feel that same kind of positive feeling?

Glenn: Yes and no. It feels like whenever I was with Mom, especially during the years before she died, was a golden time. But it feels different now when I think of it.

JK: Notice that difference, the difference between how it feels now and when we started talking about it today.

Glenn: ►◄►◄►◄ I feel more "grown up" when I think of it now, like I see myself as a boy needing that special attention from her, but the feelings themselves are not so intense right now.

JK: Is this related to what you wanted in the restaurant?

Glenn: Yes, I can see that it is the same feeling.

When I asked Glenn to bring up the image from the restaurant again, he said his anger was gone and his frustration was "about a half!" of a SUDS point. He gave a VOC of 7 to the cognition of "I know I'm OK," and went on to say that he felt more "normal" seeing the origins of his compulsive needs for specialness, attention, and control.

In subsequent sessions Glenn came to see more clearly how his attempts to emotionally recreate the "golden time" with his mother had been disruptive to his adult relationships. Several more times, it was useful for him to focus on positive memories. For example, one session began with the satisfaction and sense of safety from criticism he felt when he would do yard work "perfectly," and another focused on a time when he received an award in school that his older brother had previously not received. In each instance, he was able to see that his positive feelings had comforted him by taking his mind away from disturbing aspects of his life at the time. But the positive feelings had also misled him in a way that created difficulties in his perception of himself and in his interactions with others.

At the end of one of these sessions, he said, "I learned to shut my father out, and my brother, too. I built a wall that protected me. Now I see why I always want to talk more than listen. It is as though my circle of awareness only included myself and the attention of others towards me—but left out what they were thinking and feeling, as if that weren't important. Lately, I've been trying to include what others feel within that circle, and things go better. Sometimes it even feels better." He reported that Pauline, his friends, and people at work were all commenting on the positive changes they saw in him, saying that he seemed "lighter." He reported being less bothered by the behaviors of his father that had previously irritated him. At his last therapy session, he said, "I see now that Mom had a picture of me, of how I was, and she loved her picture of me. I did too, but that picture left a lot of me out."

Discussion

Glenn's case illustrates several aspects of this particular variation on the standard application of EMDR protocols. The duration of therapy was nearly three years, with irregular and intermittent sessions, not the three-session resolution sometimes seen with simple PTSD. The focus of treatment was an identity structure, not the relatively isolated damage caused by a specific event. Also, more than half of these sessions resembled traditional therapy, with discussion, relationship-building through positive regard and accurate, empathetic mirroring of Glenn's unpleasant affect, and towards the end of treatment, supportive confrontation of defenses. Traditional therapy methods, combined with EMDR, facilitated a processing of trauma (i.e., an increased integration of traumatic events into his sense of self) and a consequent diminished need for defense. As Glenn's defenses of avoidance, entitlement, and specialness became less necessary, a shift occurred in his self-definition. Without the prior shifts in his understanding of himself, the intervention of targeting his positively valenced memories would almost certainly have been unsuccessful. This sequence of events often occurs in a time frame of years, not months.

The importance of this time frame and therapy sequence was made plain to me in an unfortunate way with another client, a man I had been seeing in weekly sessions for nearly one year, who had not yet made a sufficient shift away from identifying with his entitled self-concept. When we targeted a memory of entitlement, he became alarmed and then self-protective in a way that was a setback (though temporary) to his therapy. This illustrates the point that, with this method, much caution and clinical sensitivity are necessary. Glenn possessed a partially individuated sense of self and thus would best be described as suffering from a trait disorder rather than a full personality disorder. In psychodynamic language, Glenn presented a narcissistic defense covering a basic neurotic structure. Though this method worked well for him, there probably is a point on the spectrum of narcissism past which this method should not be used, or should only be used very judiciously, due to the risk of removing defenses too rapidly. Minimum prerequisites would be a strong therapeutic alliance and a clear, empathetic understanding of the client's needs and feelings.

This approach to the treatment of narcissism is guided by the methods of Masterson (1981) and Johnson (1987) and generally follows the structure of what they describe as an effective therapy process. Confrontations with the client are minimized so as to avoid the misperception of attack; empathetic understanding of the self-soothing function of symptoms is emphasized and often interpreted to the client. The conceptualization of these authors—that narcissism originates in a developmental arrest—is generally consistent with the present view, which sees this disorder as originating in response to early trauma, either of commission or omission. Both approaches conceptualize narcissism as stemming from nostalgia for an earlier time of life: in Masterson's view, always the second year of life; in the view presented here, more possible variation in onset. An important difference, though, between these object-relations approaches and the method described in this chapter is that transference phenomena are not seen here as the sole means of therapeutic progress. Interpretation of events in the client-therapist relationship remains crucially important as a way of assisting the client in identifying self-defeating defenses and strengthening a realistic sense of self. The addition of EMDR, though, whether focused on negative or positive material, seems to enhance and accelerate the therapy process in that it provides a way to more rapidly remove the distorting influence of unresolved trauma.

An object-relations therapist might observe that this EMDR approach undermines the utilization of transference phenomena, since the intrinsic structure of EMDR violates therapeutic neutrality. It is proposed here, though, that this difficulty is minimized as long as the therapist is able to remain neutral regarding client goals and is able to respond in an objective and detached way to client behavior. If neutrality, in this sense, is preserved, it is still very possible to use the therapeutic relationship as a "blank screen" upon which the client's projections can be visible to both client and therapist.

I would like to emphasize that, usually in cases like Glenn's, nearly all of the EMDR follows the standard procedure taught in the levels I and II trainings. It is only when this standard procedure is repeatedly blocked that the LOUA and LOPA approaches are used. Glenn's case is also meant to show another typical occurrence: that generalization effects do not seem to occur nearly as readily with avoidance or positive affect targets, even when a particular memory is completely processed. When this approach is used, it is often necessary to go back to several different target events with similar themes, spending time on each one, in order for a significant shift in the person's present-day functioning to occur. In these cases, the installation of the positive cognition does not seem to take place so completely throughout the memory network. Thus variations of the initial problem, with lessening intensity, may recur unpredictably, making it unclear when therapy has truly been completed. Sometimes follow-up sessions are necessary for an extended period of time after the main work of therapy has been done.

An additional point is that an investment in an entitled sense of self can take many forms, and the entitlement can occur in an isolated and circumscribed way in an individual with an otherwise mature and realistic self-concept. Sometimes an investment in entitlement will emerge within an information channel during standard EMDR, and will block processing. If the positive feelings can be identified and targeted, the distortion in expectations can often be rapidly understood and processed. This type of intervention can function as an interweave, allowing standard desensitization to continue.

Unwanted Positive Affect

Some clients arrive at therapy with a presenting problem that includes positive affect that is not welcome or desirable. For example, a woman in her early forties was repeatedly frustrated with herself for spending time, against her "better judgment," with a man who only wanted sex, no commitment. Weeks would go by without contact, and she would decide to no longer see him; but then her resolve would "melt" the moment he called. She said, "My feeling of attraction is all out of proportion, especially considering how he always ends up treating me. I just wish I didn't feel so good when he acts so loving."

We targeted "feeling lovable and feeling loved," which she associated with hearing his voice on the phone. Within a minute or two of eye movements, a memory emerged of feeling abandoned and displaced around the time of her parents' divorce, when she was four. During these times, mirroring and loving attention from either parent were rare and precious. She was able to resolve this old issue during three EMDR sessions. When we went back to the present-day image of the phone call, she smiled and said, "It doesn't make sense that he makes me lovable just by calling me!" Subsequently, she reported that her anger and desperation had dissipated, and she was even able to continue spending time with this man, but on terms that were now mutually agreeable.

Feeling Positive about a Negative Self-Concept

Another type of situation is one in which a client has a positive feeling about a very negative identity. These situations sometimes occur when a person grows up in a chaotic home environment, internalizes the chaos as shame, and accepts the shame identity because it helps him avoid a sense of fragmentation. The negative identity is positive because it helps him know who he is in the world.

For example, a male client in his early thirties who had previously done some very productive EMDR work, began a session saying, "I really don't want to be here today." He was experiencing new and unexpected situational stresses at work and, in addition, had just had a very upsetting argument with the woman he was seeing. Since he had previously experienced therapeutic gains, he was confused and frustrated by his apathy in the present session. I asked him to hold in his mind the thought "I don't want to be here" and notice what he was feeling in his body. He reported tension in his chest and abdomen, which persisted without change with continued sets of eye movements.

My past experience with him suggested the presence of an unconscious blocking belief, and so I asked him if he felt any emotional impact in response to the statement "I'm lazy and unmotivated." He immediately related to this statement and rapidly elaborated: "I'm worthless, I'm fat, I'm ugly, I'm a thief, I'm an abuser, I'm a drunk, I'm a manipulator." None of these statements accurately described him in his present life but did reflect the "bad" role he had had in his family growing up—a role that had distracted his parents from their own shortcomings and that he had acted out well into adulthood. I asked him what feeling went with these thoughts about himself, and he said, "Comfort." There was, of course, a bit of sarcasm in this remark, but he was basically being truthful. As a child the criticism he received from his parents when he was bad was preferable to the general oblivion of "nonexistence" that occurred at most other times. Holding in mind the statements about himself, his score on "comfort" was a 9, with many pictures from his childhood flowing in and out of his awareness. The theme of these pictures was one of him repeatedly being in trouble. We targeted the most representative of these pictures, and the number on "comfort" quickly dropped to 0. As this occurred, intense feelings of rage and helplessness emerged. From our previous therapy sessions we had both known that these emotions were part of his make-up, though they had not been so accessible. Now he began to understand how his childhood experiences had negatively impacted his identity, and he was able to considerably relieve chronic feelings of depression he had had throughout his life.

Limitations of Anecdotal Information

These non-standard methods have frequently been useful in assisting clients in breaking through the defenses that stand in the way of their reaching their desired therapy goals. But sometimes these methods have not been useful, for reasons that were unclear. We are in the early stages of a long process of learning how to use EMDR, and perhaps other methods of accelerated information processing, to resolve human emotional problems. In trying out any new method of treatment, it is important to realize that we are in a process we hope will be helpful to the client, self-correcting as we go, and to inform the client of the experimental nature of what we are doing.

The scientific method can be a great help in sorting out effective from ineffective procedures, and it can be especially helpful for problems with measurable dependent variables, such as the symptoms of uncomplicated PTSD. But for more pervasive issues of personality structure, the course of therapy is much longer and the measurement of results more difficult. It has been said, "There is no such thing as 'anecdotal evidence.' There are anecdotes, and there is evidence." By this standard, nothing in this chapter constitutes evidence. We need to put our therapy processes to the test to see if they lead to the desired outcomes. But, to quote a colleague who works with criminal offenders, "We really can't know if our therapy works until ten years from now." Our clients come into therapy entrusting us to help them achieve certain ultimate outcomes. What this chapter describes are procedures that appear to bring about shifts in client functioning that we anticipate, and we hope, are related to those outcomes.

References

Erickson, M. H., & Rossi, E. (1979). *Hypnotherapy: An exploratory casebook*. New York: Irvington.

Goulding, R., & Goulding, M. (1979). *Changing lives through redecision therapy*. New York: Brunner/Mazel.

Johnson, S. M. (1987). *Humanizing the narcissistic style*. New York: Norton.

Knipe, J. (1995). Targeting defensive avoidance and dissociated numbing. *EMDR Network Newsletter, 2*, 6–7.

Kohut, H. (1971). *The analysis of the self: A systematic approach to the psychoanalytic treatment of narcissistic personality disorder*. New York: International Universities Press.

Masterson, J. E. (1981). *The narcissistic and borderline disorders*. New York: Brunner/Mazel.

Popky, A. J. (1994). *Smoking protocol*. Paper presented at the EMDR Annual Conference, Sunnyvale, CA.

Wilson, S. A., Becker, L. A., & Tinker, R. H. (1995). Eye movement desensitization and reprocessing (EMDR) treatment for psychologically traumatized individuals. *Journal of Consulting and Clinical Psychology, 63*, 928–937.

14

LIFTING THE BURDEN OF SHAME

Using EMDR Resource Installation to Resolve a Therapeutic Impasse

Andrew M. Leeds

MEREDITH WAS IN HER EARLY TWENTIES when she first came to see me. She was a slender woman with pale skin and sorrowful eyes. During her initial sessions, she emphasized concerns with depression, social isolation, and a sense of hopelessness about her life. As I worked with her over time, I found that the clinical tools available to me were inadequate in helping Meredith fully resolve her depression. Eventually I developed a new clinical tool, which turned out to be the missing piece I needed to help her move through her impasse.

Therapist's Background

My initial training in the 1970s exposed me to a range of process-oriented somatic psychotherapies, including work with breathing, Gestalt therapy, guided visualization, family systems, and Vipassana (insight) meditation. These methods shared an emphasis on the benefits of attending to feeling, self-awareness, observational skills, and mindfulness. I encountered the limits of these approaches when I worked in a specialized substance abuse treatment program and later sought additional training in cognitive and behavioral methods and Ericksonian hypnosis. In the 1980s I studied self-psychology and the transferential processes involved in developing the self system.

When I began using EMDR in 1991, I was initially quite uncomfortable with the structured elements in its protocols, which grated against my early humanistic training. But the results of applying EMDR were often so remarkable that I persisted in using it. What I observed happening in my clients during successful EMDR reprocessing was astonishing to me then, and has continued to impress me.

Client's History and Background

Meredith's life and personal history were full of suffering. When she was ten, she was diagnosed with a degenerative, autoimmune disorder known as systemic lupus erythematosus. As a result of her illness she had lost muscular tissue in her legs and arms, had chronic, painful inflammations in the joints of her hips, wrists, and ankles, and suffered from bouts of fatigue that at times left her unable to cope with even modest tasks. She told me that she was struggling with massive self-loathing and was trying to free herself of a religious addiction into which she had fled to escape the emotional pain of her childhood. In addition, she complained of severe anxiety in groups, made worse by her belief that she was fat. She remained preoccupied with thinking she was fat even when her weight dropped to 89 pounds.

Meredith had been in psychotherapy with me for six years when I sat down to write this chapter. I took my first training in EMDR after I had been seeing Meredith for six months, but I did not consider offering it to her for a long time because her case was complex and did not appear to fit within the standard posttraumatic stress disorder (PTSD) protocols. In addition to enduring the continuing assault on her body image and physical capabilities by the slow progression of her disease, she was a survivor of significant childhood neglect and abuse. This type of background often leaves a person with incomplete adaptive resources and necessitates an extended client preparation phase before offering standard EMDR treatment.

Meredith told me that both her mother and father were verbally abusive. Although her mother sometimes called her names, Meredith said that her mother's emotional neglect and lack of empathic interest were much greater sources of shame than her verbal abuse. She remembered her father as an authoritarian whose constant verbal abuse was a form of "mental rape" from which there was no escape and which left her feeling powerless.

Meredith had an older sister who was her mother's favorite and "could do no wrong." Mom always took her sister's side in any disagreement. When

Meredith was about four, her parents adopted a male cousin who became the son her father had always wanted. This cousin had been neglected and abused by his alcoholic mother during the first four years of his life, until her death in an auto accident. Her cousin's father was a traveling salesman who did not want to change his career or lifestyle to become a single parent and so asked Meredith's parents to raise his son. Meredith's adopted brother, who was quite close to her in age, demeaned her throughout her childhood. From ages 10 to 15, he constantly threatened and beat her. There was no escape from his blows or his cruel words, and she found no protection from her mother or father.

Her grandmother was her mother's main source of emotional support until she died when Meredith was two. Her mother then joined a fundamentalist church. When Meredith was six her parents divorced and there was a messy custody battle in which her mother initially prevailed. Then followed years in which she could find no sanctuary from her brother's abuse. She said that the divorce signified the start of a hopeless future.

In the years after the divorce, Meredith also became involved in her mother's fundamentalist religion. Through the church Meredith sought a supportive community that would provide some relief from her despair and hopelessness. By the time she was in high school she had many friends, including boyfriends, and was often able to avoid the hazards and emotional emptiness of her home life through her busy social calendar.

After high school she decided to attend a nearby fundamentalist college, where she became increasingly socially isolated and developed an "addiction to the church." She played the fervent role expected of her in the church and appeared to be genuine in her faith.

At college she studied special education. She was befriended by her academic advisor, Brother Stephen Milford, who became a positive father figure for her, reaching out to her and offering her some of the spiritual and emotional counsel she needed. However, in spite of Brother Stephen's counsel and supportive presence, Meredith gradually realized she was not finding an end to her emotional pain in the church. She moved off campus into the community where I practice and where she thought she might continue her education at a local state-supported public college.

She had worked for a year, part-time, at a specialized preschool program for disadvantaged children, but she could not work on a regular basis because of her illness, which was held partially in check by strong drugs that she knew could damage her liver and kidneys and which she believed she could not take for the rest of her life.

Progress and Frustration in Treatment

I had been seeing Meredith for nearly two years before I offered her any EMDR reprocessing. Her therapy had been progressing quite slowly, but positively. She had entered treatment with the stated goal of accepting herself as she was, but she still had periodic episodes of intense feelings of shame. At these times Meredith would stop talking and lower her reddening face into her hands. Silent tears would run slowly over her inflamed fingers and down her wrists. I had learned that I would only prolong the painful silences if I tried to offer reassurance or ask about what she was thinking or feeling at those times.

In spite of these frustrating and painful episodes, I was encouraged by changes Meredith had made during the first two years of therapy. She had returned to college, where she was making excellent progress towards completing her undergraduate degree in an innovative program that included a peer learning community. She was slowly exploring relationships with men. Her initial experiments were with men who were several years older than she and unavailable for a committed relationship. Her deeper emotional needs for genuine intimacy and attachment remained unfulfilled in these relationships. However, these men did provide a source of affirmation of her attractiveness and sexuality. With each succeeding relationship, she demanded more emotional availability.

Her studies in feminism, psychology, and educational theory offered her ideas and a community that helped her develop new, more mature perspectives from which she could view the damaging failures of caregiving she had experienced as a child.

Several close relationships she developed with women in her learning community helped her form new foundations for self-esteem. Two of these relationships were with women who had similar backgrounds of childhood abuse and emotional isolation. These relationships evolved into strong emotional attachments, providing twinship transferences that helped her affirm her strength in having endured a common legacy. The deep and intense intimacy they shared was affirming for her in ways that she had never before experienced.

As Meredith walked once more down the hallway toward my office, I tried not to let my head shake with concern and frustration. She lived with the daily pain of inflamed joints and the threat of further wasting of her body tissue. After seeing Meredith for two years, I knew that, given what she had endured, she had accomplished significant changes in our work together. Yet she still carried a deep burden of shame that surrounded her core sense of self. Although less frequent, there were still many awkward moments of prolonged silence when words failed her and the room seemed to fill with shame as she lowered her face to her hands. Quiet sobs shook her shoulders and left me contemplating my own sense of inadequacy, for I still had not found a way to help her dissolve this painful legacy of her past. I believed that therapy should offer Meredith more than adaptation to a less defended sense of self while leaving in place a core of shame and self-denigration. There had to be a way to help her reach a new sense of self that dissolved that core of shame. Based on positive outcomes with other clients, I believed that EMDR reprocessing could play a part in her treatment, but I was not sure how to incorporate it into our work. None of the protocols I had learned in the basic and intermediate EMDR trainings (in 1991) offered a set of strategies to address the therapeutic challenges I faced with Meredith.

The Standard PTSD Protocol and Model

The first standardized EMDR protocol, which was extensively researched (Shapiro, 1996), is applicable for the treatment of adult-onset PTSD. The theoretical model for explaining EMDR's treatment effects (Shapiro, 1995) proposes that trauma overwhelms the adaptive capacities of the person and causes an imbalance in areas of the brain that normally help us adapt to emotionally distressing life experiences. As a result of this imbalance, the brain cannot resolve the traumatic disturbance. The traumatic memory remains in an active (unresolved) form in short-term sensory memory (also referred to as nondeclarative memory). The unresolved traumatic memory gives rise to intrusive sensory images and body sensations and inhibits the development of a full narrative perspective on the experience (van der Kolk, 1996). The trauma remains a "here-and-now" experience for the person rather than becoming an old memory. The standard EMDR protocol presupposes that the person possesses a preponderance of healthy understandings and adaptive emotional resources acquired before the trauma. The client must possess a reasonable capacity for self-soothing and emotional regulation that may have been overwhelmed by the trauma but which must have developed to an adequate extent prior to the trauma.

In the standard PTSD protocol EMDR theory proposes that the eye movements (or other alternating stimulation), together with the other procedural elements in EMDR reprocessing, restore neural balance and the memory networks that contain the traumatic memory to link up with larger reservoirs of adaptive understandings. Under these conditions the emotionally traumatic experiences are rapidly reprocessed by the brain's intrinsic capacity for emotional learning.

In cases where the trauma is more pervasive or began at an earlier age, not only psychological functioning but also neurological development and structure are affected. Van der Kolk (1996) cites three studies describing decreased hippocampal volume in persons with PTSD, including veterans and adults who were severely abused as children. From the perspective of the EMDR model, when trauma is more pervasive, begins in childhood, or is compounded by limited healthy coping models, adaptive adult resources may be less developed or available. (For an overview of the effects of traumatic stress on children and adolescents, see Pynoos, Steinberg, & Goenjian, 1996.)

During EMDR reprocessing, these clients may show greater tendency to emotional flooding brought on by spreading activation from one specific memory to many associated memories linked by high levels of disturbance. Adaptive resources or perspectives may be less readily available to the client when the traumatic material is stimulated. In such cases the EMDR clinician can offer the more active version of EMDR, referred to as the "cognitive interweave," which was described in chapter 1. During EMDR reprocessing, the clinician deliberately stimulates existing adaptive resources that may be in a different memory network or offers new information that is not available in the traumatic memory network.

Early in my involvement with EMDR, a number of EMDR clinicians had discussed with me the perplexing problem of what to do in cases where there are insufficient pre-existing adaptive memory networks on which to draw for a cognitive interweave. Such clients lack the coping skills for self-soothing and emotional containment. In these cases, we found that the cognitive interweave is not sufficient to stimulate a resumption of adaptive information processing. During reprocessing, many of these clients become flooded by effectively laden material, remaining at a high level of emotional distress without achieving a positive therapeutic outcome.

It became clear that some clients could not be treated with the prototypical PTSD three-phase protocol of first addressing the past trauma, then the current stimuli, and finally the future template. The question that emerged from these discussions was, "Is there any way to use EMDR when the adaptive resources of the client are inadequate even for cognitive interweave to help?" Generally, the only choice seemed to be to use established cognitive, behavioral, and dynamic approaches to help the client gain sufficient adaptive resources until standard EMDR protocols might become appropriate.

Treatment with Meredith

For all these reasons it was nearly two years after my initial training in EMDR before I offered any EMDR reprocessing to Meredith. At that point, after using EMDR successfully with a number of other clients, I had established a baseline of typical responses to the reprocessing. The PTSD and phobia protocols had proven extremely helpful to survivors of auto accidents, airplane crashes, domestic abuse, physical or sexual abuse in childhood, and prolonged grief reactions, and even to adolescents dealing with adjustment problems.

Meredith had seen the certificates gradually appearing on my office wall indicating my training in EMDR and later showing my status as a facilitator with the EMDR Institute. We had spoken about EMDR on occasion, and she said that she was interested in discovering whether it could be helpful in her therapy. Because my thinking about EMDR was still organized around the PTSD protocol, I directed Meredith to look for a specific memory as the target for our initial EMDR work.

Although Meredith had been verbally abused by her father and physically and verbally abused by her brother, the initial focus for reprocessing that emerged had more to do with generalized beliefs of "I don't fit in" and "I'm not seen because my point of view is not accepted." These beliefs were being stimulated in her peer learning community at college. At those times she became so flooded with emotion that she was unable to fully participate in the group activities.

When I asked her what early memory was linked to these beliefs, she described telling her mother and sister of her youthful aspiration to become an attorney. She remembered that they responded by laughing at her. Her Subjective Units of Distress Scale (SUDS) level on this memory was between 8 and 9. It was especially painful to her that her mother had not been able to see her potential and offer support and encouragement. When asked to state a preferred belief about these memories, she said, "I'd rather believe 'It was her problem that she couldn't see me' and that 'I'm accepted for who I am'."

In this same context, she remembered being told as a young girl by her sister that she was so emotional that if anyone yelled at her, she would just cry. She also had an image of jumping up and down in frustrated anger when her mother refused to protect her from abusive behavior by her brother. These images from the past helped define the issues with which she struggled.

In therapy, she continued to have almost no capacity for emotional containment. When feelings of shame, sadness, distress, or anger were stimulated, she displayed emotional fragmentation and was unable to verbalize what she was feeling, the current stimuli to which she was responding, or her associated thoughts or memories. Instead she hid her face in her hands and wept silent tears. These moments of inarticulate and helpless emotional flooding seemed to reflect an internalized schema based on her mother's early modeling of weakness in the face of her brother's abusive behavior as well as her mother's inability to offer her daughter any real recognition or soothing. Later I learned that during these episodes of emotional flooding, cruel voices in the form of demeaning thoughts assaulted Meredith from within. I suspected that these voices were introjections of her brother's (and father's) verbal abuse and that her silent crying represented both a defensive behavior learned in childhood to endure incidents of verbal abuse as well as an inability to access any inner resources for self-soothing. Even after she had calmed down, Meredith would remain unable to describe the demeaning and critical words of these inner voices or when she had first heard them. Similar episodes occurred outside the consulting office in her peer learning community, where she would also become helplessly flooded with emotion and be unable to speak or interact.

Incomplete Treatment: Emotional Flooding and a Failed Early Installation

In spite of the general sense of safety she felt in our well-developed therapeutic alliance of two years, Meredith responded to our initial attempt at reprocessing with the same kind of "meltdown" as she experienced in her school setting. We targeted the memory of her mother's and sister's laughter at her aspiration to become an attorney. She was able to progress partially through the material. She reported the SUDS as coming down to a 2.5, but during the desensitization phase, I believed she was holding back her actual feelings. I silently wondered if, in order to please me, she was pushing herself to attempt the reprocessing before she really felt ready.

With the desensitization incomplete, I wanted to see if we could end the reprocessing on a more positive note. Sometimes it is possible to close an incomplete EMDR session with an installation begun while the SUDS is higher than 0 or 1. Sometimes a modified positive cognition can be elicited that represents what the client has learned or gained from the reprocessing so far, such as "I'm learning I can heal the pain of the past." When this is done appropriately, it can help clients establish and maintain a positive framework between sessions for understanding the residual disturbance and unresolved issues of the memory. They can affirm what has been gained even as they sense that there is still more to do.

With some clients, however, even such a modified positive statement can stimulate more disturbance due to its emotional and cognitive dissonance with the unresolved memory network. Early installations at a SUDS rating above a stable and ecological 0 or 1 can also be interpreted by clients as a demand by the clinician to "feel better" or "get over it." Clients can imagine they are being pressured to simulate well-being. Thus an "early installation" needs to be done with sensitive clinical judgment and an absence of "demand characteristics." That is, it must be offered with neutrality regarding the outcome and with an alternate strategy in reserve for closing the incomplete session if the early installation is not successful.

With Meredith none of the usual methods for closure and containment were helpful for residual disturbance. Structured relaxation and guided imagery safe-place exercises had not helped her achieve calm in the past when feelings of shame were activated. Cognitive interventions had been mildly helpful in previous sessions, but only after Meredith had silently and slowly brought her level of disturbance down to a more moderate level on her own. Since the SUDS level had fallen during the desensitization phase from an 8 or 9 pretreatment to about 2.5, I thought that an early installation might stimulate an enhanced adaptive perspective on the residual material.

I asked Meredith to focus on what was left of the disturbing memory and to hold her positive statements in mind at the same time: "It was her problem that she couldn't see me" and "I'm accepted for who I am." However, after adding eye movements in the early installation, the VOC did not rise. Instead, Meredith began to cry and we had to close the session as incomplete. In retrospect, it is clear that I should have helped Meredith modify the original positive cognition to something that might have been more helpful, such as "I'm learning to accept myself for who I am." In this case, her increased emotional distress also helped me realize that EMDR installation is not equivalent to a cognitive-behavioral intervention.

Because none of the usual strategies for closing an incomplete session had ever worked during these "meltdowns," I was forced to sit silently as Meredith slowly found her own way back to a state of calm. Before she left the office, we spoke about the treatment session, and I helped her note her accomplishment of staying with this difficult material more than she ever had before.

One week later the SUDS level on that memory had risen to a 6.5, which I took as reflecting both the incomplete processing of the memory and a lot of associated disturbing material that had prevented the acceptance of the installation of her preferred belief. She then told me that she didn't want to reveal her deeper feelings in therapy. She thought that showing her feelings made her too raw, too vulnerable, and she was too concerned about what I thought to be able to be spontaneous and allow her feelings to show. We explored these thoughts and feelings, and I offered her validation for these concerns and encouraged her to find her own pace and her own path toward healing.

The following week Meredith surprised me by saying that she wanted to do more reprocessing on the same childhood memory of being ridiculed by her mother and sister for her ambition to become a lawyer. Since she felt inclined to continue and had asked for more EMDR, I agreed to proceed. Her preliminary negative cognitions were: "I'm little," "You can do whatever you want to me," "I'm out of control," and "You're trying to hurt me." We finally settled on "I can't protect myself." Her preferred self-statement was "I can protect myself." Her pretreatment VOC was 3; her initial emotion was anger with a SUDS of 5.

We then did a series of eye-movement sets. With the second set she reported, "I feel a lot of heat in my chest." She looked very uncomfortable, with a mixture of intense emotions on her face that seemed to combine anger, pain, shame, and determination. There were few obvious signs of relief as we continued to reprocess her distress. At several points I felt quite uncomfortable with the reprocessing work.

I generally cope with my clients' distress during reprocessing with a sense of calm, empathetic acceptance because it normally seems to be clearly leading to therapeutic gains. I could not tell if this was so for Meredith at that point. Something about the reprocessing was restimulating intense feelings of shame from her childhood. The identified target was a memory of not getting the kind of recognition and support she needed from her mother and sister. Yet she seemed to be reexperiencing the intense feelings of shame that characterized the intrusive shaming with her brother and father.

Her father had repeatedly told her, "Don't think you can ever do anything without me knowing it. I'll always find out." She believed that her inner life was never private, that her thoughts did not belong to herself but to her father and brother. With hindsight I now believe that Meredith's distress in response to the identified target of her mother and sister was being fed by these stronger feelings of shame associated with her father and brother. As a child, she had seen her mother and sister as her only hope for affirmation and a sense of her own identity. The memory represented another reminder that this hope was not to be realized. Because the level of her distress was not attenuating, I saw myself as pushing Meredith deeper into feelings of shame.

Countertransference and Demand Characteristics

I finally decided I needed to prompt her in some way that it was OK not to continue and yet also offer her more support. I responded to these counter-transference feelings by saying, "I feel like I'm doing something to you," referring to the EMDR. She confirmed my concerns that she felt pressured to do EMDR, saying, "If I don't do EMDR, my process is slow and boring." Yet she was determined to press ahead and did not want to stop.

As we continued further eye-movement sets, some slight shifts appeared to be taking place in her facial expression. Then she said, "I think I'm inade-quate if I'm scared." After another set: "I think I fool myself about my ability to process." After about eight sets her reported SUDS decreased to a 2. She said she felt less uncomfortable and slightly numb. I again decided to pro-ceed with an installation in spite of the SUDS being only down to 2. I sus-pected that the SUDS would not go to 0 or 1 in that session, and I wanted to see if it were possible to move toward a positive resolution.

After working for a few more sets on the installation of her positive cogni-tion ("I can protect myself"), she stated her Validity of Cognition Scale (VOC) was a 4. As in the previous session, the VOC had not risen as much as is typical, signaling incomplete processing. I again chose not to attempt the body scan, since the reprocessing was clearly incomplete. After the in-stallation we brought the session to a close with the usual debriefing. She seemed OK and appreciative of the work we had done.

I, on the other hand, was left with strangely mixed feelings and with self-critical thoughts. It was apparent that the approach I was taking in offering EMDR focused on this early material was not entirely suited to her needs. I was also left with lingering feelings of somehow having played both the part of a perpetrator as well as that of healer in these EMDR sessions.

At that point my initial hesitation in offering EMDR seemed justified, and I felt embarrassed by my decision to offer reprocessing focused on this early memory. In spite of these feelings, I continued to sense that there was an important role for EMDR with Meredith. I decided not to push ahead with more EMDR until I had come up with an entirely new approach that would respect Meredith's expressed discomfort with displaying emotional responses and, at the same time, help her to tolerate the emotions she had learned to consider so unacceptable. Meredith also seemed to share my mixed feelings about this work; she did not ask for more EMDR for quite some time, and I did not press the matter. Other present life issues were coming to the foreground, including struggles in her current relationship. For some months these took our attention away from further reprocessing of early memories.

Meredith had been in some relationships with emotionally unavailable men, with whom she had played a role of victim to the men's emotional wounds and their lack of emotional support. One theme that emerged in her therapy was that of power versus powerlessness. Meredith said, "I can get some power back by exaggerating my powerlessness." I reflected on our EMDR sessions and asked myself if I had failed to offer Meredith what she needed in a way that paralleled her mother's failure to respond empathically. Had she unconsciously exaggerated her powerlessness in the EMDR session as part of this pattern?

She told me how, when she was a child, her brother would escalate his physical abuse if she fought back at all. She eventually came to believe she was best able to "get to" him if she exaggerated her helplessness. He looked down on her for this (as she did on herself). It didn't necessarily lead him to soften his attacks, but at the time it was her only way to irritate him and thus get back at him.

Searching for a New Approach to Overcome Shame

Our therapeutic alliance remained strong throughout this phase of our work. Even when progress was quite slow, there was never a question of Meredith wanting to leave treatment. Following the incomplete EMDR reprocessing, with any other client I might have offered psychoeducation about the nature of emotions to help her develop a framework for being less judgmental about whatever feelings might emerge. I had already discussed emotions and affect theory (Nathanson, 1992) with Meredith, and she had also read some books on shame and was familiar with models for nonjudgmental understanding of her emotional responses. However, the appropriate information and understanding Meredith had about her feelings were in a form that did not help her tolerate those feelings. I needed to help her build bridges in her experience so that she could move beyond a merely conceptual understanding to develop her capacity to accept her feelings as an experienced reality.

Some of this integration had already been taking place through our therapeutic relationship. I continued to offer a nonjudgmental acceptance, interest, and empathic attunement to her emotions. Yet for a long time, in the back of my thoughts was a continuing hint of another approach that could supplement the general benefits of the transferential learning occurring in our therapeutic relationship and in her friendships. I sensed there was a way to use EMDR to help lessen the excess of shame that so often flooded her and to accelerate the integration of her own capacities for self-soothing, self-reflective empathy, and self-support.

We did some further EMDR on current sources of stress on a few occasions after about three years of treatment. At one point Meredith felt blocked in working on a paper for a college course and was getting quite angry with herself. We used EMDR on this blockage, and this led to more work with anger at not having been acknowledged and supported by her mother. The level of disturbance reduced somewhat. She chose to install the positive cognition, "I'm moving on." In such EMDR sessions, I continued to silently note that Meredith was still not ready to directly address some of the early memories of abuse from her brother and father.

This pattern of EMDR targeting was not typical of my work with other clients who had early childhood memories of abuse by male family members. Only gradually did I begin to understand that Meredith's perceived failures of her mother to provide affection, empathy, and support had rendered her unable to tolerate affect in relationship to others. Her parents' inability to form secure childhood attachments with Meredith left her with a legacy of pervasive shame that arose whenever her interpersonal relations stimulated distress, sadness, or anger. She seemed to expect that all of her emotional responses to others would only lead to further failures of empathy.

During these many long months I slowly came to realize I was often paying too much attention to treating the traumatic effects of violence and verbal abuse and not enough to issues of failures in attachment and emotional development as a result of inadequate early emotional attunement. I had first learned about the dangers of focusing excessively on an early history of violence and verbal abuse in 1986, when working with my first case of what was then called multiple personality disorder. Yet what I had learned to apply to working with dissociative disorders I still had not fully integrated into my understanding in formulating treatment approaches outside the dissociative spectrum.

My synthesis of what I call "EMDR resource installation" took place in late 1994. It wasn't until 1995 that I read an earlier seminal article by Barach (1991), which further helped reorient my clinical approach to focus assessment and treatment first on issues of inadequate early attachment and the development of the self system before addressing the trauma of violence and verbal abuse.

About three and a half years into treatment, Meredith brought in a former boyfriend for a few conjoint sessions. Months after their breakup, he had begun objecting to her new relationship and wanted her back. During their relationship, he had been helpful in many practical ways and had been a stimulating intellectual companion, but his capacity for empathy was quite limited and he had a tendency to be controlling in an overbearing way. During these conjoint sessions, he asked her to reduce his emotional pain about her new relationship by limiting her activities and avoiding certain places where they had spent time together—or, better still, work to renew their relationship. Meredith was able to hold her ground and to set reasonable limits on how much she was willing to accommodate his requests. She was able to assert her right to participate with her new boyfriend in important activities in her community rather than give in to his demands that she take some responsibility for his pain.

A few weeks after bringing that relationship to a final closure, Meredith told me she wanted to use EMDR to address another area of concern. With much hesitation and obvious embarrassment, she gradually disclosed she had some memories that had long been a source of great distress to her. She did not tell me about these memories in that session or in the next. Instead we explored the distorted beliefs she held about the meaning of these experiences and what it might mean for her to tell me about them.

I found it noteworthy that Meredith was apparently still not ready to directly address the earlier painful memories of her father's verbal abuse or her brother's verbal and physical abuse. Nor did she offer to address the early memories of her mother's emotional neglect. Those memories seemed to me to be the sources of her distorted beliefs about her worth. Instead, she wanted to reprocess these later experiences, which for her symbolized irrefutable evidence that she was an intrinsically worthless and hopeless individual for whom there was no possibility of redemption.

In our previous reprocessing work the source of Meredith's distress had been others' behavior towards her. Like most survivors of childhood abuse and neglect, she had formed the irrational belief that these things happened to her because she was a "bad," "unlovable" person. She could at least see intellectually that this belief was wrong and was the result of her limited perspective on life when she was a child.

On the other hand, the undisclosed memories involved situations in which she had initiated activity that she had quickly realized violated her norms of acceptable behavior. Because these memories involved voluntary behavior, she believed they demonstrated she had no hope of redemption. Her distorted beliefs about the meaning of these memories were fixed and pathognomonic, quite out of proportion to what she had actually done.

It took several sessions for her to tell me about these experiences that had taken place when she was preadolescent, a time of great stress and turmoil in her life. Over the next few sessions we discussed her experiences and I gave her some corrective information, emphasizing that her feelings of remorse showed her deeply moral character. I pointed out that, in contrast to her sense of shame, those who feel no remorse, take no responsibility, and maintain denial for inappropriate behavior are the real villains.

After acknowledging these ideas, she said that knowing these things didn't affect her deep shame and didn't alter her belief that she was an "evil" person. She then asked to do some EMDR reprocessing on the memories with the hope that she could lessen the intense feelings of shame and worthlessness. With serious but silent misgivings, I agreed to proceed with EMDR.

She selected one of the memories and found a specific "picture" that represented the event. I asked what words went with the picture that described her negative belief about herself. She said, "I don't deserve to be loved" and "I can never be forgiven." When asked what she would rather believe, she said, "I was hurting. Even in that moment I deserved to be loved. Those actions do not mean I'm permanently wrong. I can forgive myself." We settled on the positive cognitions "I deserved to be loved" and "I can forgive myself." The VOC on these preferred beliefs before treatment was 2. When she focused on the negative statements and the memory, she felt self-hatred, anger, and shame with a level of disturbance (SUDS) of 4. Based on what happened during that session and her lifelong inability to let anyone know what she'd done, I would interpret the relatively low pretreatment SUDS of 4 as indicating some repression of affect rather than only mild disturbance.

We did 14 sets of eye movements in the first session focused on this memory. The level of distress rose and remained high. I changed the direction of the eye movements; I used cognitive interweaves; I reminded her of the corrective information I had given her about her behavior. With each set of eye movements her level of distress remained high. She was choking and coughing, crying and rubbing her eyes. Her throat hurt and felt raw. I asked if someone else had done this, would she say that they could never be forgiven? She could not even reply. Finally, she said, "It wasn't someone else, it was me who did this, and so I never deserve to be loved."

With no evidence of a shift towards a resolution after 30 minutes of intense reprocessing, I brought the session to a close, using a combination of the safe-place exercise and the image of a container. She visualized putting her memories and feelings in a strong container until we could work with them further. We talked until she felt able to leave the office. I arranged to see her in two days for a follow-up visit.

The follow-up session opened with her explaining how she was unable to feel any compassion for herself. She thought she ought to be punished for what she had done. She talked about her involvement in the fundamentalist religion and having to confess her sins and participate in various sacred church rituals, none of which had lessened her shame or relieved her of guilt. She reiterated: "I'm fucked up. I can never be forgiven."

She then described a memory that had resurfaced the previous day from when she turned five years old. Her father was repairing the family car, and she asked, "Daddy, when is Aunt sending me my party dress?" However, with the common mild speech impediment of a five-year-old, it sounded as if she had said "potty dress." Her father immediately ridiculed her for this pronunciation problem. She recalled the intense humiliation she felt when he made fun of her speech. Her feelings of excitement changed abruptly to feelings of humiliation and rage. She got hold of her brother's slingshot to try to hurt her father, but she was unable to do so, and then he ridiculed her for that failure.

She asked to do some more EMDR focused on the memory of her father ridiculing her and the words she wished she could have said to him. Because this memory had emerged following the previous treatment session, I accepted it as the next aspect of the material to be addressed. We did about nine sets of eye movements, some of which were quite long. Two sets were over 250 repetitions. She struggled to give herself permission to express her anger at her father for his humiliation of her. She heard a voice inside her crying out, "Where were they?" Where were her parents when she needed to feel loved and worthy? "There's nothing I can do."

She told me she was connecting with places of feeling in herself she had not felt since she was a young child. It wasn't safe to feel. No one was there for her. There was a tremendous sense of isolation and the complete absence of compassion from the outside. Finally, in response to my asking, "What does the compassionate part of yourself say now?" she found a voice that could say, "I'm sorry that no one was there for you then. I'm here for you now." We layered in that voice with two long final sets of eye movements of 200 and 100. At the end of that session she said, "I can breathe. My chest feels more open."

The following week she described having felt "lots of grief and pain" since the previous session. She had shared much of this pain with her boyfriend Todd. Instead of the more remote calm offered to her in the previous relationship, he had cried with her and met her in her distress. She appreciated and felt reassured by his emotional support and the greater warmth in their relationship. Yet he had also spoken about some of his concerns that the progression of her disease might lead to further disabilities. She had felt the urge to apologize to him for having the degenerative illness that created so many limitations in her life and now in his, too.

She shared with me her fear that her physical condition was evidence that she should not be in a loving relationship with Todd. She talked about the ways in which living alone for years had protected her from her fears of being controlled or abandoned by others. Her appreciation of the depth of compassion Todd was able to offer her was leading her to consider the possibility of living with him in the future, and this was raising anxieties she had not had to face before. We spoke briefly about both these emotional issues and some practical questions I had about how living together would affect the stability of her situation. When I asked a follow-up question about the memories we had reprocessed in the previous two sessions, she reported that these were not quite as disturbing. The new voice of compassion that had emerged at the very end of the previous session had helped her feel slightly more reassured, and she expressed the hope that we could find ways to increase this compassionate perspective and go further in the work of addressing these disturbing memories.

Two days later we met again. In this session I found the answers to the question of how to adapt EMDR to meet Meredith's needs. The session opened on a challenging note in which Meredith expressed some transference feelings of disappointment about the questions I had raised about her preliminary thoughts of living with Todd.

I listened to these feelings with interest and acceptance. Yet, strangely, while listening to her speak and considering how I had dealt with her in that session, I was thinking about the seed of compassion that had emerged at the end of the previous session. I suddenly saw another direction in which we could proceed. I would focus first on strengthening her for the work that lay ahead. I asked if she wanted to deal with her disappointment in my response to her in the last session, or if she wanted to focus on developing a more compassionate acceptance of herself. She chose to focus on developing self-acceptance.

I asked her to find an internal image that would represent a greater self-acceptance. She described a dream image from the previous week of a large "being in the sand" who represented courage and the capacity to act. In her dream she knew that with his help, she could do anything that was required of her. I asked her to hold the image of the sand creature in mind and to notice where she felt a resonance with this image in her body. She reported a feeling of openness in her throat. I asked her to hold both the image of the sand being and the feeling of openness in her throat in her awareness at the same time, and we then did a series of eye movements.

With the first set of eye movements her throat continued to open, and she felt a sense of greater strength. With the second set she reported a sense of readiness for conflict, a tight readiness with trembling and anger. With the third set, she reported the emergence of a fighting spirit: "I could finally fight back against my brother with a sense of righteous indignation." With the fourth set, she reported, "It's safe for me to be angry now. I have the right to be angry." With the fifth set, she said, "I feel more expansive all over."

This first resource appeared to be well developed. I asked her to find another image that would represent another attribute she would need to address the disturbing memories. After a few moments of quiet reflection, she said she had the image of a wise woman who represented maternal energy and compassion. Again I asked her to note where in her body she felt a resonance with the image, and she reported a soothing feeling in her lower chest. I asked her to hold both the image of the wise woman and the feeling in her lower chest in awareness. We did another series of eye movements to strengthen this image.

The feeling in her lower chest got stronger during the first set. Then with further sets, she mysteriously reported being aware of a singular sense of time, "like the ticking of a clock in how my body is being." With the next set, she said, "I think she's here for dignity and self-respect." The image changed. An older black woman appeared, sitting on the porch, rocking. She's seen everything in life and she says, 'Baby, don't let him treat you that way.'" After the next set, Meredith said, "She holds space for me even when I want to regress, and she holds my own sense of trust." With yet another set, she said, "I just keep hearing, 'Trust what comes up, and trust.'"

During this installation, I did not interrupt Meredith to ask for clarification about her mysterious comments on her sense of time. Had I asked her to explain this, she might have lost contact with the emerging emotional qualities or blocked her deepening sense of trusting "what comes up." This willingness to attend to the emotional undercurrents of the treatment process, rather than being overly focused on the literal verbalizations of the client, is needed for positive outcomes in EMDR-based treatment.

We then moved on to a third resource. She remembered the image of Brother Stephen Milford, her professor and academic advisor at the fundamentalist college, who had helped her "come out." She told me that "He had cried with me, he had shown me real empathy." She felt a resonance of this image of her professor in her solar plexus. The positive words that emerged spontaneously with this image were "I'm strong enough to hold my anger." I asked her to hold the image, the location of the feeling, and the positive words, and we added the eye movement.

After the first set of eye movements she said, "He was also the first person to let me know that I'm OK." After the next set she said, "I feel it in my solar plexus, the place where I'm most vulnerable and that's closest to my core." After the next set, "I feel energized again . . . and I feel a connection with what is in my throat." I asked her to hold the connection between her throat and her solar plexus and continue the eye movement. After the next set she said, "Being able to be angry is a part of being OK."

I then asked her to identify another resource to help her face her troubling memories. An image of a lion came up. She said this was a male image of fierceness. I asked her to link this image with a feeling in her body and added the eye movement.

After the first set of eye movements she said, "The lion also sleeps. It's the importance of slowing down . . . of being centered and calm in one's power . . . and the power that comes from being able to move quickly from one [calm] to the other [fierce]." With the next set of eye movements she said, "It's like I realized that sleeping is part of the fierceness. If you can't sleep, you can't be fierce. When you sleep a lot, the fierceness can be a shorter period of time." I asked her to identify positive words that went with her understanding of this image, and she said: "It's safe to let go. I'm naturally powerful." We continued the eye movements, and then she reported: "Towards the end of that set of eye movements, I had a sense of being physically strong and muscular, and that's part of the commanding presence. I have a sense of how very grounded they [lions] are in the way they walk, with intense dignity."

Meredith then began to wonder aloud how we would use these images when we continued work on the disturbing memories. Before answering her question, I asked her to hold each of the images within her at the same time and to notice the places in her body where she felt the resonance with each. From my notes I repeated the positive phrases out loud that went with each image. I asked her to focus on the sand-being and repeated her words, "I have the right to fight back. I have the right to be angry"; then with the wise woman of color, "I trust what comes up. I trust myself. I respect myself"; with Brother Milford, "I'm OK in my core. Allowing anger is part of being OK"; and with the lion, "I am naturally powerful. It's safe to let go." Then we did two more sets of eye movements to strengthen all the images, feelings, and words at the same time. At that point I answered her question by explaining that before focusing on a disturbing target in future sessions, I would ask her to bring forward some of her "allies" (her word for these resources) to support her in addressing the target; then we would strengthen her contact with the allies by adding eye movements before reprocessing the target.

The following week, when Meredith entered my office, she looked and moved so differently I was astonished. The intense grief and distress of the previous weeks were gone. Instead she moved down my hallway with a smooth gait and an erect posture that conveyed dignity and poise. Meredith reported being freer of pain than she could remember in many years. Her face glowed with life. I tried to act as though this were a perfectly naturally occurrence, but it was a much more positive response than I had expected.

We continued the work begun the previous week and found other images of positive resources. We installed two or three more of these images in that follow-up session. The next session reviewed the changes that Meredith felt were taking place as a result of these resource installations. She felt much stronger, confident and more vital. We explored the implications of this for her identity and her present relationship for another session or two, before we returned to the preadolescent experiences which had been so emotionally charged for her. We were then able to successfully reprocess these memories to completion in two consecutive sessions.

Integrating the Use of Imaginal Resources in PTSD Protocols

I opened each of those sessions by asking Meredith to bring forward as many of the positive images as she wanted present before addressing each of the troubling memories, one at a time. She brought forward each of the images of her allies in turn, together with its associated physical location and positive words. Each was strengthened with two or three sets of eye movements. With those resources stimulated and active in her awareness, we targeted the memory that previously had been impossible to resolve. It now moved through a more typical EMDR treatment response, going from a VOC of 3 on "I can forgive myself" and "I deserve to be loved" and a SUDS of 6, to a VOC of 5 and a SUDS of 3 in one session. I noted how, with less repressed affect and more adaptive defenses available, the preliminary SUDS had risen from the pretreatment rating of 4 noted earlier. In the next treatment session the SUDS fell further to a 2, and the VOC rose on both cognitions to a 6.

During the reprocessing of these memories, when Meredith occasionally reached places where her facial expression, breathing, or verbalizations suggested her distress level was high and not changing, I drew on one or another of the allies as I would normally have used a cognitive interweave. Instead of asking a question to stimulate the adult perspective, I just asked Meredith to be aware of the place in her body where she felt the sand-being (or the wise old woman or the lion) and the image of that ally along with whatever she had reported after a set of eye movements.

Scientific Foundations For the Use of Imaginal Resources

I have tried to convey some of the flavor of my struggle to find a treatment approach that would meet Meredith's needs. The solution in her case may be obvious in hindsight, although clinicians often find themselves in similar struggles without a research validated method to guide them through a particular client's treatment. While there is as yet no specific outcome research on the use of this type imaginal resource together with eye movements, I believe there is some scientific research that indirectly supports the use of a strategy based on imaginal resources.

In van der Kolk's seminal article, "The Body Keeps the Score: Memory and the Evolving Psychobiology of Posttraumatic Stress" (1994), he described research that shows how traumatic memories are differentially stored in the right hemisphere in the form of vivid, disturbing sensory images and physical sensations with powerful linkages to emotional memories in the amygdala (see also van der Kolk, McFarlane, & Weisaeth, 1996). When these traumatic memories are activated, left-hemisphere-mediated speech capacity (narrative) is dramatically inhibited. I believe this research provides neuropsychological reasons why linguistically-based cognitive strategies for resolving traumatic memories can fail when the traumas are early and chronic. Like art therapy, resource installation provides a bridging strategy to utilize the less inhibited capacity of the right hemisphere to access alternate positive images and sensory memories even when left-hemispheric narrative resources remain relatively unavailable.

With Meredith, what had seemed an insurmountable impasse using a standard PTSD protocol had become amenable to significant resolution when addressed with a non-standard protocol. The key to this approach was to install multiple positive resources without deliberately activating the distressing emotions and associations of a specific disturbing memory or current stimuli. I have coined the phrase *EMDR resource installation* to describe this protocol. I have since used this approach with other challenging clients who have childhood histories of significant failures of attachment with their primary caregivers. In these cases, their histories and current functioning led me to conclude that their capacity for self-soothing and affect modulation was not yet developed to the point where they could tolerate directly targeting distressing memories using the standard EMDR protocol.

Sources for Principles Used in Resource Installation

I was greatly helped in my understanding of Meredith's shame by Nathanson's book *Shame and Pride* (1992). Nathanson described the roles that shame and the memory of shame play in clients with failures in childhood attachment. Through rereading and thinking about his ideas and interpretations of Silvan S. Tomkins's theories (1962a, 1962b), I began to realize how Meredith's chronic childhood experiences of shame led to deficits in her psychosocial development and to a fixation on more primitive psychological defenses. It seemed to me that as long as Meredith's defenses remained organized around unresolved memories of shame, shame would be a burden she could never lay to rest. Nathanson helped me understand how her emotional and psychosocial development had become frozen at the developmental stages in which the burden of shame was imposed. To achieve a therapeutic resolution, I slowly realized I had to find ways to help her lift that burden to find a new understanding and acceptance of her emotional responses to life.

Meredith's confidence in the safety and empathic attunement of our therapeutic alliance and the working through of transferential responses offered important vehicles for her healing. However, to help her move through the impasse in her treatment, I had to shift my attention away from thinking only in terms of the therapeutic alliance and resolving past traumas. I needed to deepen my understanding of how her capacity for self-soothing and cohesion had been distorted by chronic childhood failures of empathic attunement and inadequate caregiving. I also had to find a way to adapt my treatment approach to identify and enhance the resources Meredith needed to develop: courage, safety, adult perspective, and compassion for self.

In the moment of shifting my strategy from past trauma to strengthening present resources, I was focused solely on finding another direction that would be more promising. In hindsight, it is clear this prototype resource installation strategy emerged from several specific strands, including being done by others in the EMDR Institute, my own early training and experiences, and Meredith's own unique capacities. One early influence was the "adoption" model presented by Wildwind (1992), who articulated the idea of using the "installation" phase of EMDR without targeting a disturbing memory as a way of helping chronically depressed clients to incorporate positive "parental" resources, thereby filling in gaps from attachment failures in their past. Another influence was an increasing emphasis on using the "safe place" exercise in standard EMDR PTSD protocols (Shapiro, 1995) with the option of adding eye movements in the absence of a traumatic memory to enhance client stability.

I also drew on work I had done in guided imagery in Santa Cruz in 1976 and 1977 with Harris Clemes, who taught me that clients have inner resources that will emerge spontaneously if we establish safety and convey a relaxed inner focus together with a non-demanding but positive expectancy. I know that I was influenced by the principle of utilization and other seminal ideas in the work of Milton Erickson (1980; Erickson, Rossi, & Rossi, 1976; Haley, 1985), and hypnosis training with Paul Carter and Stephen Gilligan. Carl Jung's theories about archetypes clearly influenced some of my thinking about resources (Jung, 1966; Jung, von Franz, Henderson, Jacobi, & Jaffe, 1964). In addition, the theories of self psychology (Kohut, 1977; Wolf, 1988) and object relations (Greenberg & Mitchell, 1983) played a part in conceptualizing the value of self objects and transitional objects as resources in developing the self system of the client.

All these influences led to my decision to "do something else" when the standard EMDR PTSD protocol and cognitive interweaves failed to lead to a positive treatment outcome for Meredith.

Follow-Up on Meredith and Cautionary Concerns

Meredith remains in treatment. Over the three years since the phase of treatment described above, her gains have held. The new sense of self that consolidated during the resource installation phase of our work led to a number of positive outcomes for Meredith: She soon took a stronger leadership role in her learning community; she became a teaching assistant and showed significant resilience in dealing with the challenging interpersonal stresses of that position; she completed her undergraduate education and went on to earn a master's degree.

Meredith and I returned to work on disturbing childhood memories on several occasions. Prior to reprocessing each of these memories, I would ask Meredith which of her resources she wanted to bring forward. We would then do one or two sets of eye movements on the selected resources. With the addition of these brief initial preparatory steps, the disturbing memories responded well to conventional EMDR reprocessing.

Current treatment issues with Meredith focus on managing her chronic disease. We have developed a modified EMDR protocol based on the protocol for somatic disorders (Shapiro, 1995), intended to help her stabilize her illness into remission with less dependence on damaging medications. She has a conscious, committed relationship with Todd that has continued to deepen.

Positive clinical outcomes in my practice and informal reports from other clinicians who have used variations on resource installation strategies offer preliminary support for the hypothesis that methodologies similar to the basic EMDR procedures can be successfully organized into alternative protocols. Until there is more controlled research to guide us in structuring our work with clients who have histories of inadequate attachment and chronic shame, I invite other clinicians to consider resource installation protocols as potentially useful in enhancing the integration of developmentally appropriate emotional resources and more mature defenses for affect modulation and self-soothing in clients who would otherwise be overwhelmed in the face of traumatic memories.

On the other hand, I believe it is important to make clear that this single case description of an application of EMDR resource installation does not provide a simple template for all other clinical situations where the client's defenses have become frozen around memories of shame from a childhood filled with abuse and neglect. Meredith's capacity to readily generate healing images of her "allies" was the result of a great deal of committed self work over a period of several years that included long-term individual psychotherapy, group imagery processes, art therapy, extensive reading in feminist psychology, and participation in a healing community. Being able to draw on these rich experiential resources made the development and use of resource installation much simpler with Meredith than it might have been with many other clients.

Other clients may need much more structured development of specific resources. They may not have, or may not be able to access, appropriate models of resources that need to be developed and installed. They may need to have missing information and healthy models developed through reading, structured group activities, and other psychoeducational interventions. Clinicians need to carefully consider how and when to integrate resource installation procedures into the overall treatment plan. For example, clinicians treating clients with dissociative disorders need to give extra attention to the appropriateness of the resource installation procedure for all elements of the client's self system.

I am currently working on articulating a more comprehensive and systematized approach to assessing the need for, and ways to use, resource installation and other resource development strategies. I believe such strategies can be integrated into the treatment of many clients with chronic maladaptive problems. The principles proposed in this chapter cut across a number of *Diagnostic and Statistical Manual* (DSM) Axis I and II diagnostic categories because they are based on eliciting the resources needed for self-soothing, self-sustaining, and self-affirmation. The central theme of this project is deepening our understanding of how to lift the burden of chronic childhood shame, which is the legacy of failures of childhood attachment. The aim of this project is to articulate specific strategies to catalyze our clients' development of a resilient and richly textured self system.

References

Barach, M. M. (1991). Multiple personality disorder as an attachment disorder. *Dissociation, 4*, 117–123.

Erickson, M. E. (1980). *The collected papers of Milton H. Erickson on hypnosis* (4 vols.) Edited by E. Rossi. New York: Irvington.

Erickson, M. E., Rossi, E. L., & Rossi, S. I. (1976). *Hypnotic realities: The induction of clinical hypnosis and forms of indirect suggestion.* New York: Irvington Publishers.

Greenberg, J. R., & Mitchell, S. A. (1983). *Object relations in psychoanalytic theory.* Cambridge, MA: Harvard University Press.

Haley, J. (1985). *Conversations with Milton H. Erickson, M.D.* (3 vols.). New York: Norton

Jung, C. G. (1966). *Two essays on analytical psychology. Vol. 7. The collected works of C. G. Jung.* Princeton, NJ: Princeton University Press.

Jung, C. G., von Franz, M. L., Henderson, J. L., Jacobi, J., & Jaffe, A. (1964). *Man and his symbols.* Garden City, NY. Doubleday.

Kohut, H. (1977). *The restoration of the self.* New York: International Universities Press.

Nathanson, D. L. (1992). *Shame and pride: Affect, sex, and the birth of the self.* New York: Norton.

Pynoos, R. S., Steinberg, A. M., & Goenjian, A. (1996). Traumatic stress in childhood and adolescence: Recent developments and current controversies. In B. A. van der Kolk, A. C. McFarlane, & L. Weisaeth (Eds.), *Traumatic stress: The effects of overwhelming experience on mind, body, and society.* New York: Guilford Press.

Shapiro, F. (1995). *Eye movement desensitization and reprocessing: Basic principles, protocols, and procedures*. New York: Guilford Press.

Shapiro, F. (1996). Eye movement desensitization and reprocessing (EMDR): Evaluation of controlled PTSD research. *Journal of Behavior Therapy and Experimental Psychiatry*, 27, 209–218.

Tomkins, S. S. (1962a). *Affect imagery consciousness: The negative affects* (Vol. 2). New York: Springer Publishing Company.

Tomkins, S. S. (1962b). *Affect imagery consciousness: The positive affects* (Vol. 1). New York: Springer Publishing Company.

van der Kolk, B. A. (1994). The body keeps the score: Memory and the evolving psychobiology of posttraumatic stress. *Harvard Review of Psychiatry*, 1(5), 253–265.

van der Kolk, B. A. (1996). Trauma and memory. In B. A. van der Kolk, A. C. McFarlane, & L. Weisaeth (Eds.). *Traumatic stress: The effects of overwhelming experience on mind, body, and society*. New York: Guilford Press.

van der Kolk, B. A., McFarlane, A. C., & Weisaeth, L. (1996). *Traumatic stress: The effects of overwhelming experience on mind, body, and society*. New York: Guilford Press.

Wildwind, L. (1992, April). *Working with depression*. Paper presented at the Advanced Clinical Applications of EMDR Conference, Sunnyvale, CA.

Wolf, E. (1988). *Treating the self-elements of clinical self psychology*. New York: Guilford Press.

INDEX